# GOING COASTAL NEW YORK CITY

*Going Coastal*

# New York City

**URBAN WATERFRONT GUIDE**

Third Edition

Barbara La Rocco

GOING COASTAL, INC.

New York

2025

Copyright © 2009 Going Coastal, Inc.

Photographs © Photographers as indicated

All rights reserved
ISBN 978-0-9729803-2-6 (paperback)

Maps © Zhennya Slootskin, Graphics & Data, Inc.
Going Coastal ™ is a registered trademark of Going Coastal, Inc.

---

Library of Congress Control Number: 2025912126

All rights reserved. No part of this publication may be reproduced, stored in a retrieval system, or transmitted in any form or by any means—electronic, mechanical, photocopy, recording, or any other—except for brief quotations in printed reviews, without the prior permission of the publisher.

Printed in the United States of America
Third edition

# The Author

Barbara La Rocco is president and founder of Going Coastal, Inc., an EPA Environmental Quality Award-winning nonprofit formed to connect people to coastal resources and promote the responsible use and public enjoyment of the waterfront environment. Born on the Throgs Neck coast of the Bronx, Barbara developed a passion for the coastal environment while attending the University of Central Florida where she organized cleanup campaigns for the degraded Weekiva Springs, which received the Disney Community Service, Keep America Beautiful, and Pitch-In Awards. As director of Trash & Litter Control for Beaufort County, Barbara initiated the Adopt-a-Highway program in the coastal community of Hilton Head, SC. She is the author of *The Mafia Cookbook: Recipes from Gangland Kitchens* and the new edition of the WPA's seminal work *A Maritime History of New York*.

# Going Coastal, Inc.

Going Coastal, Inc. is a nonprofit formed to connect people with urban coastal resources, encourage a sense of community and common history and motivate active conservation. Through the efforts of our volunteers and information initiatives, we encourage adults and children to appreciate, enjoy, and preserve the coastal environment. We accomplish our mission by publishing books and information initiatives and through community outreach and educational programs.

With awareness, we open many doors. Our programs are designed to inspire action. The waters surrounding New York City contribute to our happiness and standard of living. Going Coastal, Inc. is dedicated to helping people find their way to the water and in the process make new friends for coastal conservation. Our organization is at the service of all with similar aims.

"Plan an urban cruise where the Half Moon once lingered among the canoes of the Lenape and Mohican. Sail and gunkole in the urban archipelago, instead of just rushing through it. Cruise the Upper Bay and linger in the shallows around the Statue of Liberty and Ellis Islands, away from the commercial shipping. Let the tides sweep your vessel through the Hellgate and along the urban gorge between Roosevelt Island and Manhattan's towers. In the Lower Bay, below the Narrows and the arching Verrazanno, drop a hook at Great Kills on Staten Island, or Jamaica Bay, or Sandy Hook. In every direction your gaze will be rewarded by the sights of a thriving port, abundant bird life, and unexpectedly tranquil harbors."

    William Kornblum, author of *At Sea in the City*

# Discovery

When one hundred years had elapsed after Hudson's discovery of the river, the people of New York did not hold any celebration. But when the second century had rolled by, the anniversary of the discovery was deemed worthy of celebration. Dignitaries from around the globe feasted on Hudson River oysters and duck. The toast by Simon Clinton, the surveyor general and brother of Mayor DeWitt Clinton, proposed: "May our successors, a century hence, celebrate the same great event, which we this day celebrate."

The next anniversary was a double one, the explorer would divide his honors with artist-inventor, Robert Fulton, for the first use of steam in navigation. One hundred years later, the tercentennial "Hudson-Fulton Celebration" of 1909 occurred. The celebration was a memorable one - one hundred and sixty miles long. Many thousands participated in it, and millions witnessed it from the banks of the historic stream. This excerpt from Frederick W. Seward's *Reminiscences of a War-Time Statesman and Diplomat,* published in 1916, describes how New Yorkers commemorated Henry Hudson's chance discovery.

In 1909, the Dutch government sent over a replica of the *Half Moon*, which collided with the Staten Island made replica of the *Clermont* at opening festivities in a crowded New York Harbor. The Wright Brothers' performed exhibition flights taking off from the parade ground on Governors Island flying over Grant's Tomb.

Going Coastal dedicates this book to the courageous captain and the majestic river on their 400th Anniversary, and invites all who journey here to take a voyage of discovery around the coast and on the waters of New York City, a metropolis made of islands and inlets.

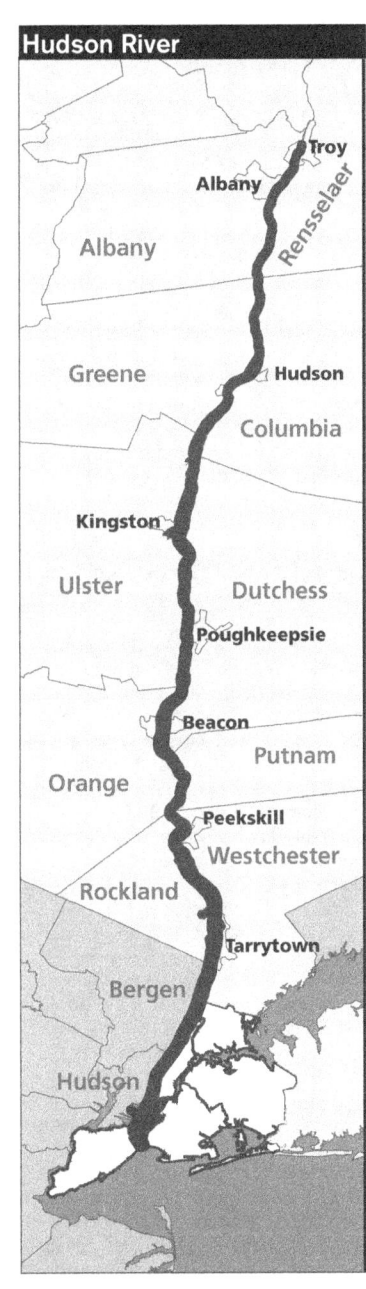

# Henry Hudson

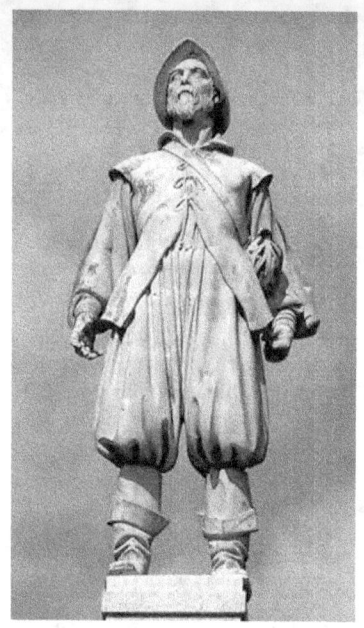

Henry Hudson was the first European navigator to explore the river that now bears his name from its mouth at the southern end of Manhattan Island to the head of navigation 150 miles to the north above the present location of the City of Albany. Hudson was not the first European to see the river. Giovanni da Verazzano, an Italian employed by the King of France, had explored the large bay it empties into in 1524, and had noted the river's existence. That same year Estevan Gomez, a Portuguese navigator sailing for Spain, also explored the bay and saw the mouth of the river. Both Verazzano and Gomez were looking for a strait that would take them to the Pacific Ocean and China, and both decided the broad river extending into the interior of the continent was not that strait.

Nothing is known of Hudson's early life. We do know that by 1607 he was married, living in the city of London, and had three sons. In September 1608 his son Oliver's wife provided him with a granddaughter named Alice. We also know that in the years 1607 and 1608 Hudson had completed two voyages of exploration in the employ of the Muscovy Company of London. All four of Henry Hudson's known voyages had the same objective, finding a new route to China. Portugal had developed the route to India around the Cape of Good Hope. Spain had discovered the Straits of Magellan. England, France and the Netherlands all hoped to find another route to Asia in the northern hemisphere.

Some leading scholars believed the far northern latitudes' exposure to months of "midnight sun" meant the sea would be free of ice around the North Pole. Hudson's voyage of 1607 was based on this theory. He sailed due north hoping to break through into this open sea and sail across it to Asia. Inevitably, he encountered ice he could not penetrate and had to turn back, having probably gotten closer to the North Pole than any predecessor. On his voyage of 1608 he sailed north again, but further to the east to an area north of Russia. The results were the same. He had not achieved his purpose, but he had expanded knowledge of the Arctic. One of Hudson's contemporaries was the English adventurer John Smith. Smith was now involved in the establishment of the first permanent British settlement in North America at Jamestown, Virginia. Indians had told Smith of a great river to the north which provided a route to a western sea. This information was passed along to Hudson who became determined to explore this river when the opportunity presented itself. Hudson asked the Muscovy Company for support for a third voyage but was turned down.

At this point he was approached by a representative of Dutch interests. He proceeded to Amsterdam around the fall of 1608 expecting to be employed by the East India Company, but its directors were not ready to make the decision. They finally signed a contract on January 8, 1609 after hearing Hudson had been talking to representatives of other potential patrons, including the King of France.

The East India Company provided Hudson with a ship, the *Half Moon*, financing for its crew and provisions, and pledged the additional sum of 800 guilders upon completion of the voyage. His instructions were to seek a northeast passage to China in the region of Novaya Zembla, north of Russia. Hudson kept a journal of the 1609 voyage, but only an excerpt survives. The journal kept by Robert Juet, who had also been on the 1608 voyage, does survive.

Hudson initially sailed northward along the coast of Norway in compliance with his instructions. In mid May they were in the region of the North Cape. The weather was stormy and very cold and the mixed Dutch and English crew refused to go any further. A storm drove the ship to the westward and Hudson decided to change course and head for North America. They visited the Faroe Islands and eventually arrived on what is now the coast of Maine. Hudson sailed south to the Chesapeake Bay, but made no attempt to contact the English in Jamestown. He then sailed north along the coast to Sandy Hook and entered the lower bay.

It was now the beginning of September. On the 4th a landing by ship's boat was made on the Long Island shore and the first indians were encountered. There would be numerous meetings with the native people over the next three weeks, many very friendly encounters but a few violent. When Hudson sent a boat through the Narrows on September 6th it was attacked and John Colman the seaman in charge, a veteran of the 1607 voyage, was killed by an arrow through the neck. The *Half Moon* entered the upper Bay on September 11th. The following day they anchored within the river somewhere off the west side of Manhattan Island. They continued northward anchoring most nights in different locations until the 19th. Hudson was now in the vicinity of the present city of Albany. It was clear the river was not a strait leading to Asia. The sea to the west John Smith had heard of was actually the Great Lakes which the indians were able to reach by portaging their small craft. Until the 23rd Hudson conducted further explorations of the river using the ship's boat, probably as far as the present city of Waterford. Then he began the voyage home.

With food running short the *Half Moon* first called at Dartmouth, England on November 7th. The English were unhappy with Hudson's sailing for the Dutch and he and the ship were temporarily detained there. He was able to send his logs and journals on to Amsterdam as required by his contract and the ship was eventually released. The Dutch East India Company took immediate note of the abundance of furs in the newly explored region and began planning voyages there to trade with the indians. Hudson was hired by a group of British merchant venturers to make another search for a route to Asia. In 1610 he sailed the ship *Discovery* westward, calling at Iceland and Greenland, and entering the Davis Strait north of Labrador. He explored the full length of the strait and then the eastern shore of the large bay now named for him, wintering over at its southern end. The next summer the crew mutinied, took over the ship, and cast Hudson adrift with several others in an open boat.

*By Norman Brouwer, maritime historian and author of International Register of Historic Ships*

# NYC Maritime Timeline

|  |  |
|---|---|
| 1524 | Italian explorer Giovanni Da Verrazano discovers New York Harbor. |
| 1525 | Black Portuguese navigator Estéban Gomez charts Lower Hudson River. |
| 1609 | Henry Hudson arrives on the Half Moon and explores the Hudson River. |
| 1611 | Adrian Block establishes trading posts on the Battery. |
| 1624 | The first settlers arrive in New Amsterdam from Netherlands. |
| 1626 | Dutch Gov. Peter Minuet purportedly pays $24 for Manhattan. |
| 1640 | Ferry service begins between Manhattan & Fulton Street, Brooklyn. |
| 1647 | The first pier is constructed on the East River at Pearl and Broad Street. |
| 1664 | British take control of the city without firing a shot, rename it New York. |
| 1676 | "Great Dock," built at Whitehall, is the city's main anchorage until 1750. |
| 1686 | City government begins to landfill Lower Manhattan shoreline. |
| 1693 | First bridge, Kings Bridge is built between Manhattan and The Bronx. |
| 1695 | Colonial Governor hires Capt. William Kidd to help stop piracy |
| 1774 | New York Harbor holds its own "Tea Party." |
| 1776 | The Battle of Long Island. |
| 1784 | *Empress of China* inaugurates America's trade with China. |
| 1800 | The federal government takes control of Governors Island. |
| 1801 | New York (Brooklyn) Navy Yard opens on Wallabout Bay. |
| 1807 | Fulton's steamship *Clermont* makes its voyage up the Hudson River. |
| 1811 | Vanderbilt starts ferry service between Manhattan and Staten Island. |
| 1817 | Packet ship *James Monroe* inaugurates first scheduled sailings to Liverpool. |
| 1822 | Fulton Fish Market opens on the East River. |
| 1824 | The country's first dry dock is built on the East River at E 10 Street. |
| 1825 | Erie Canal opens linking New York Harbor to the hinterlands in the west. |
| 1830 | New York becomes America's leading port. |
| 1840 | The tugboat, *John Fuller* becomes the first fireboat in NY Harbor. |
| 1844 | The New York Yacht Club is founded aboard a sailboat in NY Harbor. |
| 1845 | The first extreme Clipper, the *Rainbow*, is built at Smith & Dimon Shipyard. |
| 1846 | Hudson River Railroad is built along the westside riverbanks. |
| 1850 | Salt marshes that stretch from the Brooklyn Bridge to Bay Ridge are drained. |
| 1851 | Hell Gate's rocks are blasted improving passage to Long Island Sound. |
| 1851 | *America* wins England 100 Pound Guinea Cup, renamed America's Cup. |
| 1853 | There are 55 piers on the Hudson River and 57 piers on the East River. |
| 1855 | Castle Clinton is joined to the Battery by landfill. |
| 1862 | The ironclad USS Monitor is launched at Greenpoint, Brooklyn. |
| 1862 | City Island's first commercial shipyard opens. |
| 1864 | Erie Basin opens in Red Hook, Brooklyn. |
| 1869 | First person buried in Potter's Field, Hart Island, a 24 year-old woman. |
| 1870 | Floating pools offer free summer recreation in the rivers around Manhattan. |
| 1870 | Port industry shifts from the East River to the Hudson River & Brooklyn piers. |
| 1873 | The first Floating Hospital, *Emma Abbott* is launched by the NY Times. |
| 1880 | Coney Island's Iron Pier is built for steamship traffic from Manhattan. |

|  |  |
|---|---|
| 1882 | South Street is the country's first block to receive electricity. |
| 1883 | Brooklyn Bridge opens. |
| 1885 | Pier A is constructed at the Battery. |
| 1886 | The Statue of Liberty is dedicated on Bedloe Island. |
| 1888 | Pelham Bay Park opens. |
| 1890 | City's first sewage treatment plant opens on Coney I |
| 1892 | Ellis Island welcomes its first immigrant, 15 year old Annie Moore of Ireland. |
| 1893 | World's fastest yacht, *Feissen* is built on City Island by A.B. Wood. |
| 1894 | Riverside Park is built along the edge of the Hudson River. |
| 1895 | The Harlem River Ship Canal opens. |
| 1897 | Harbo & Samuelson set rowing record across Atlantic from Battery Park. |
| 1898 | The five boroughs are consolidated into Greater New York City. |
| 1903 | Williamsburg Bridge opens. Coney Island Polar Bear Club is founded. |
| 1907 | Chelsea Piers open to accommodate large ocean liners. |
| 1909 | Opening of the Manhattan and Queensboro bridges. |
| 1912 | NYC is world's largest port, a position it holds for the next 50 years. |
| 1914 | The dredging of Ambrose Channel is completed. |
| 1916 | Oyster beds in city waters are closed due to typhoid fever outbreak. |
| 1917 | Croton Aqueduct begins delivering drinking water from the Catskills. |
| 1921 | Port Authority is established. |
| 1927 | The Holland Tunnel opens. Cyclone Rollercoaster opens at Coney Island. |
| 1930 | Statue of Liberty opens to the public. |
| 1931 | George Washington Bridge opens. Floyd Bennett Field is first city airport. |
| 1934 | East River Drive (FDR Drive) is completed along the East River. |
| 1936 | Triborough Bridge opens. |
| 1938 | Belt Parkway is constructed on the Brooklyn-Queens waterfront. |
| 1940 | New York Yacht Club admits women to membership. |
| 1951 | The United Nations builds their headquarters on the East River. |
| 1954 | Ellis Island immigration depot closes. Jamaica Bay wildlife refuge opens. |
| 1956 | World's first container ship sails from Port of NY for Houston, TX. |
| 1957 | New York Aquarium opens on Coney Island. |
| 1964 | Verrazano-Narrows Bridge opens. Steeplechase Park closes on Coney Island. |
| 1966 | Brooklyn Navy Yard closes. |
| 1970 | Port shipping moves from Manhattan's westside to Elizabeth, NJ |
| 1972 | Clean Water Act passes. Gateway National Recreation Area is created. |
| 1972 | South Street Seaport restoration begins. |
| 1973 | World Trade Center Twin Towers are completed. |
| 1979 | Empire-Fulton Ferry State Park opens on the Brooklyn waterfront. |
| 1983 | Battery Park City esplanade opens on fill from WTC excavation. |
| 1991 | Hudson River Park construction begins. |
| 1995 | USCG leaves Governors Island. Chelsea Piers Sports Complex opens. |
| 1999 | Gowanus Canal flushing tunnel is repaired after 60 years. |
| 2003 | Governors Island is sold by the federal government to New York State for $1. |
| 2009 | Henry Hudson Quadricentennial Celebration |

# Table of Contents

| | |
|---|---|
| The Author | v |
| Discovery | vii |
| NYC Maritime Timeline | x |

## Go Coastal

### Getting to the Coast — 2

### Manhattan — 3
| | |
|---|---|
| Harbor Islands | 11 |
| The Battery | 12 |
| Hudson River | 15 |
| Battery Park City | 16 |
| Hudson River Park | 18 |
| Riverside | 25 |
| Upper Manhattan | 29 |
| Harlem River | 32 |
| Hell Gate | 36 |
| East River | 37 |
| Turtle Bay | 38 |
| Roosevelt Island | 40 |
| Stuyvesant Cove | 43 |
| Seaport District | 45 |
| Stone Street District | 48 |

### The Bronx — 50
| | |
|---|---|
| Hudson River | 51 |
| Harlem River | 53 |
| Bronx Kill | 55 |
| East River | 56 |
| Bay of Brothers | 57 |
| Bronx River | 57 |
| Westchester Creek | 61 |
| Long Island Sound | 63 |
| Eastchester Bay | 63 |
| Hutchinson River | 66 |
| City Island | 67 |
| The Pelham Islands | 68 |

### Brooklyn — 70
| | |
|---|---|
| East River | 71 |
| Newtown Creek | 72 |
| Bushwick Creek Inlet | 73 |
| Wallabout Bay | 74 |
| Fulton Landing | 76 |
| Upper New York Bay | 78 |

| | |
|---|---|
| Buttermilk Channel | 79 |
| Erie Basin | 80 |
| Gowanus Canal | 82 |
| Gowanus Bay | 83 |
| The Narrows | 84 |
| Lower New York Bay | 87 |
| Gravesend Bay | 88 |
| Coney Island Creek | 88 |
| Atlantic Ocean | 90 |
| Sheepshead Bay | 94 |
| Jamaica Bay | 95 |
| Shell Bank Creek | 96 |
| Gerritsen Creek | 97 |
| Dead Horse Bay | 98 |
| Mill Basin/East Mill Basin | 99 |
| Paerdegat Basin | 100 |
| The Creeks | 101 |

## Queens  103
| | |
|---|---|
| Jamaica Bay | 104 |
| Grassy Bay | 105 |
| Rockaway Peninsula | 108 |
| Grass Hassock Channel | 109 |
| Beach Channel | 110 |
| Rockaway Inlet | 111 |
| Atlantic Ocean | 114 |
| Rockaway Beach | 114 |
| East Rockaway Inlet | 115 |
| Long Island Sound | 116 |
| Little Neck Bay | 116 |
| Upper East River | 120 |
| Flushing Bay | 121 |
| Flushing Creek | 122 |
| Bowery Bay | 124 |
| East River | 125 |
| Anable Basin | 128 |
| Newtown Creek | 129 |

## Staten Island  131
| | |
|---|---|
| Upper New York Bay | 132 |
| The Narrows | 134 |
| Lower New York Bay | 136 |
| Great Kills Harbor | 139 |
| Raritan Bay | 140 |
| Fresh Kills Creek | 148 |
| Richmond Creek | 151 |
| Arthur Kill Tributaries | 152 |
| Kill van Kull | 153 |

# Get Wet

| | |
|---|---|
| Annual Events | 158 |
| Aquatic Life | 161 |
| Beaches | 167 |
| Birding | 172 |
| Boatbuilding | 177 |
| Boating | 180 |
| Bridges | 186 |
| Cruiseliners | 192 |
| Dining with a View | 196 |
| Excursion Boats | 204 |
| Fishing | 208 |
| Harbor Forts | 221 |
| Historic Ships | 226 |
| Lighthouses | 233 |
| Maritime Museums | 239 |
| Paddling | 245 |
| Rowing | 254 |
| Sailing | 257 |
| Scuba Diving | 262 |
| Surfing | 268 |
| Swimming | 272 |
| Water Resources | 275 |
| Photo Credits | 279 |

## United States

95,000 miles of coastline

The U.S. Economic Zone extends 200 miles seaward from the coast

Half of the population lives within 50 miles of a coast

## New York State

3,200 miles of coastline

70% of the state's population lives within coastal counties

41% of the state shoreline is publicly owned

## New York City

534.5 miles of shoreline

146 miles of navigable waters

40% of the city shoreline is publicly owned

# Getting to the Coast

## Subways

The 656-mile subway system is the fastest and cheapest way to get to most waterfronts in the five boroughs. City buses are more time consuming, but reach more shore locations than subway lines. Subways and buses run 24 hours a day. Fares are paid by MetroCard. Buses also accept exact change, not dollars. Transfers from subway to bus or to a different subway line within two hours are free.

The subway closest to the water is the Rockaway IND line, traveling over Jamaica Bay. Originally built in the late 1800s, the elevated line carrying the A trains to Far Rockaway opened in 1956. When the train travels across Jamaica Bay you have a close up view of the houses on stilts and the bay's endangered wetlands. The line diverges into two spurs at Broad Channel, one journeying west to Rockaway Park station at 116 Street and the other east to Far Rockaway. Coney Island's Stillwell Avenue Station is the end of the line for Brooklyn beachgoers. A glass wall "My Coney Island Baby" created by Robert Wilson shows iconic images of the famed amusement district.

A trip on the subway can also be an exploration of New York's maritime heritage and coastal surroundings. Stations feature nautical artwork that ranges from plaques of ships at Columbus Circle and tiles of fish at Delancey to Houston Street with Deborah Brown's mosaic scenes of whales, sea turtles and manatees, and the abstract *Mermade/Dionysus and the Pirates* on the platform at Brighton Beach. *Stream* winds along the passageway of Long Island City Court Square Station. South Ferry Station has Doug & Mike Starn's mosaic map of old New York overlaying a graphic of Manhattan, showing the historic water lines. A fitting way into South Street Seaport is past the maritime murals of the historic seaport decorating passageways at the Fulton Street, Broadway Nassau Station. The six 1913 terra cotta murals, created by Fred Dana Marsh, were originally wall

panels in the Marine Grill in the former McAlpin Hotel at Herald Square, installed here in 2000. Sheepshead Bay Station features a giant replica of a vintage postcard highlighting views from the fishing village's past.

Transit maps are available at all visitor centers, subway ticket booths and online mta.info/nyct/maps/submap.htm or by calling MTA customer service at 718-330-3322.

## Greenways

Over 100,000 cyclists ride in New York City each day. About 4,000 people commute by bike over bridges into Manhattan and an estimated 1,000 cross the Brooklyn Bridge alone. Ocean Parkway is the country's oldest greenway. Opened in 1895, the roadside path for walkers and cyclists connects Prospect Park to the beaches of Coney Island. It is a National Scenic Landmark designed by Frederick Law Olmsted. In the 1930s, Robert Moses incorporated greenways and esplanades in the construction of waterfront parks such as Riverside Park and East River Park. Bicycle and pedestrian paths were an integral part of the city's circumferential roadway system. Many are still in use or undergoing rehabilitation.

In recent years, New York City has completed 400 miles of a planned 900 miles of on-street and off street bike lanes. The NYC Greenway will be a 350 mile network of exclusive pathways hugging the city's shore and connecting the boroughs. So far, about 190 miles of greenway are in place including a 32 mile route that circumscribes Manhattan Island. It is part of the Hudson River Greenway (hudsongreenway.state.ny.us) along the entire length of the River that will eventually link to a potential East Coast Greenway, running along the Atlantic Coast from Maine to Florida.

The NYC Cycling Map covers greenways and bike lanes in all five boroughs. Maps are available at bike shops or online at http://www.nyc.gov/html/dot/html/bicyclists/bikemaps.shtml. Other great online resources about city cycling are Bike New York (bikenewyork.org) and Transportation Alternatives (transalt.org).

**Rules of the Road:** Bicycles are not permitted on sidewalks unless bicycle wheels are less than 26 inches in diameter and the rider is 12 years or younger, or if signs allow. They are also prohibited on expressways, drives, highways, interstate routes, bridges and thruways unless authorized by signs.

### Bikes on Transit

• Subways: Bicycles are permitted on subways at all times, though it is recommended to avoid rush hour. Swipe your MetroCard, turn the turnstile and enter through the service gate. 718-330-3322 mta.info/bike
• Metro North/LIRR: Lifetime Bike $5 one-time fee. Obtain permits at Grand Central or Penn Stations, apply online or call MTA Customer Service 212- 672-1290. mta.info
• Staten Island SIRT: Bicycles are allowed outside of commuter hours.
• Buses: QBx1 Whitestone Bridge bus has bike racks, load at Queens: Whitestone Expwy. Service Rd. at 20 Ave. & Bronx: Hutchinson River Expwy Service Rd. at Lafayette Ave.

### Bike Rentals

**Bike and Roll** Pier 84, Hudson River Park Hours: 9 AM-7 PM Price: $30-$99/day, $8-$15/hour 212-260-0400 bikeandroll.com

### Bicycle Parking

There are bicycle racks available near many subway and rail stations. Do not chain your bike to subway railing; as it will be confiscated. Bicycle parking racks are placed for free at any business or property upon request. 212-442-7687 nyc.gov/html/dot

## Blueways

New York City has the largest number of ferry riders in the country. Ferries and water taxis offer a unique way to travel and sightsee in the Big Apple. You can take a ferry to a ball game or beach or visit attractions like Ellis Island and Governors Island. More than 130,000 people take a ferry to work each weekday.

The Staten Island Ferry, the first publicly owned mass transit system in the U.S., transports 20 million passengers annually and is the city's most popular tourist attraction, traveling past the Statue of Liberty and Robbins Reef Lighthouse every half hour. Four ferries make the 5.2 mile, 25-minute voyage 104 times a day carrying 60,000 passengers a day between Staten Island and Lower Manhattan. Rides are free. Another 20,000 people use private ferry transportation to Manhattan each day. Cross-Hudson service was rejuvenated in 1986 by New York Waterway's Arthur E. Imperatore, at one time the largest privately owned commuter ferry operator in the country. Water taxis resembling yellow checkerboard cabs loop around Manhattan, Brooklyn and Queens.

The Port Authority of New York-New Jersey serves as a ferry transportation clearinghouse for the metropolitan area. Commuter ferries operate about every 15 minutes during rush hours, Monday through Friday from 6:30am to 10am and 4pm to 7pm. Off peak and weekend schedules vary. All boats and terminals are handicap accessible. Children's fares generally cost about half the adult ticket price on most ferry boats.

**Governors Island** Access is seasonal by ferry only. Boats depart from the Battery Maritime Building, Slip 7, just northeast of the Staten Island Ferry Terminal and from Brooklyn's Fulton Ferry Landing. 212-825-3045 govisland.com

**Liberty State Park Water Taxi** The water taxi operates between Liberty Landing Marina, Bayonne, NJ and the World Financial Center. Bicycles are permitted at no extra charge and pets are allowed. 201-432-6321 libertylandingmarina.com

**New York Water Taxi** A fleet of low emission, low wake vessels and commuter ferries. No fee for

bicycles, which are fixed to racks on the outside deck; only room for about three bikes per boat. No pets allowed, except for assisted life dogs and seeing eye dogs. 212-742-1969 nywatertaxi.com

**New York Waterway** The operator offers free shuttle buses to and from midtown and downtown, which run express from the W 39 St. Terminal. Just flag down a bus or board at Waterway bus stops. Bicycles $1. Dogs in carriers are allowed. 800-533-3779 nywaterway.com

**Seastreak** One of Europe's largest ferry companies operates high speed catamarans from NJ's Atlantic Highlands to Pier 11/Wall St. and E 35 St. There is a $3 charge for bicycles. Dogs must be on a leash and stay on the outside portion of the ferry. 800-262-8743 seastreak.com

**Staten Island Ferry** No vehicles are allowed on the city operated ferry at this time. Bikes are allowed at no charge, cyclists should board on the lower level. Pets in carriers only. 718-815-2508 nyc.gov

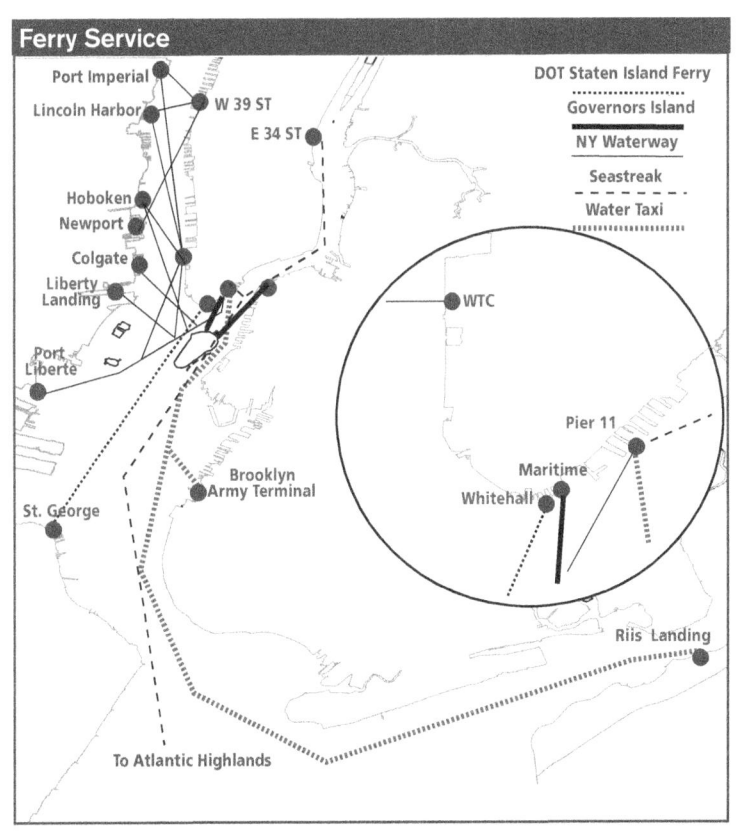

# FERRY ROUTES

| LANDINGS | FEES | ROUTES |
|---|---|---|
| **Governors Island Ferry** | | |
| Battery Maritime Bldg. Fulton Ferry Landing | Free | Governors Island National Monument Governors Island, Pier 101 |
| **Liberty Landing Water Taxi** | | |
| World Financial Center. | Vary | Liberty Landing, Liberty State Park; Jersey City |
| **Staten Island Ferry (NYC Dept. of Transportation)** | | |
| Whitehall Terminal | Free | St. George Terminal, Staten Island |
| **New York Waterway** | | |
| Midtown West Pier 79, W 39 St. | Vary | NJ: Belford/Harbor Way; Edgewater Ferry Landing; Hoboken 14 St.; Lincoln Harbor/Weehawken; Newport; Paulus Hook; Port Imperial/Weehawken |
| World Financial Ctr. Battery Park City | Vary | NJ: Belford/Harbor Way; Paulus Hook, Hoboken 14 St.; Hoboken NJ Transit; Harborside, Port Imperial |
| Pier 11, Wall Street | Vary | NJ: Belford/Harbor Way; Liberty Harbor; Paulus Hook; Port Imperial/Weehawken; Port Liberte |
| **New York Water Taxi** | | |
| Pier 11, Wall Street | Vary | Ikea (FREE); E 34 St; Schaefer Landing; Hunters Point; Fulton Ferry Landing; Red Hook/Fairway; Brooklyn Army Terminal; Riss Landing |
| Hudson River Stops | Vary | Battery Park; WFC; Pier 45; Pier 66.; Pier 84 |
| East River Routes | Vary | Wall St./Pier 11; South St. Seaport; E 34 St; Fulton Ferry; Shaeffer Landing; Hunters Pt. |
| **Seastreak Ferry** | | |
| Pier 11, Wall St. & E 34 St. | Vary | NJ: Atlantic Highlands, Highlands; Sandy Hook |

Routes and fees are subject to change. Contact ferry operators directly or check online at panynj.gov or nyc.gov/html/dot

Go Coastal

7 Getting to the Coast

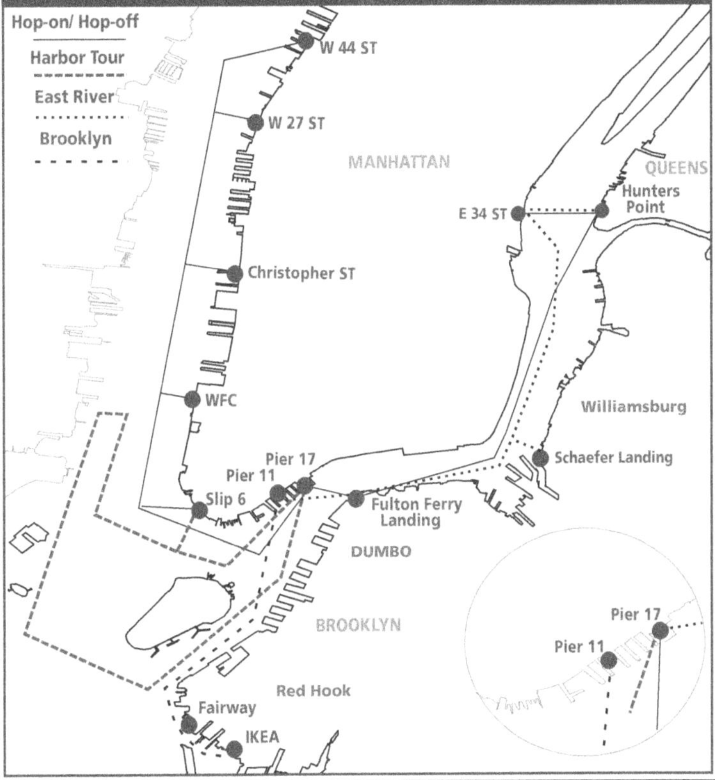

# New York Harbor

New York Harbor is one of the world's best natural harbors and the city's chief asset. It is surrounded by the most populated coastal region in the United States and the largest city in the world by land area. An arm of the Atlantic Ocean, the threshold of the harbor is marked on the north by Rockaway Point, Long Island, and on the south by Sandy Hook, New Jersey. The greatest natural depth, at the Narrows, is less than 30 feet. There are 240 miles of federal channel in the harbor, where main channels run 45 feet deep and are being dredged to 50 feet to accommodate larger ships. Historically the busiest harbor in the world, New York's waters are used for moving people, freight, rail cars, waste, and for recreation and commercial fishing. The harbor, divided at the Narrows into Lower New York Bay and Upper New York Bay, is encircled by Manhattan, Staten Island, Brooklyn and northern New Jersey. The large Lower Bay features beaches, parkland, and natural areas interspersed among residential communities. It takes in the Hudson, Harlem, East, Hackensack, Passaic and Raritan rivers; Jamaica, Gravesend, Flushing, Newark, and Raritan bays; Newtown Creek, the Gowanus Canal, Erie Basin, Arthur Kill, and the Kill Van Kull.

New York Harbor is located at the apex of the New York Bight, a natural indent in the coast extending from Montauk, Long Island, to the New Jersey shore, which forms a right angle at the mouth of the Hudson River. The harbor is tidal with a range of five to six feet and a current of one to two knots at ebb tide. It is an estuary, where salt water from the ocean mixes with fresh water from the Hudson River within sheltered bays. The estuary extends up the Hudson River to the Piermont Marsh near the Tappan Zee Bridge, covering 770 miles of shore, 534.5 miles within city limits. Its brackish waters are an extremely productive ecosystem home to all kinds of animals, birds, plants, and aquatic life. Only about 25% of the city's original wetlands survive. These are environmentally vital for wildlife habitat and economically valuable because they absorb storm water, trap pollutants, and buffer the city from flooding and storms.

New York Bight

# Manhattan

New York is a port city that has prospered from its enormous natural harbor for more than 400 years. Manhattan has 28.5 miles of water frontage bound by Upper New York Bay and the Hudson, Harlem and East rivers. New waterfront parks and public spaces have at last opened much of its bulkheaded shore.

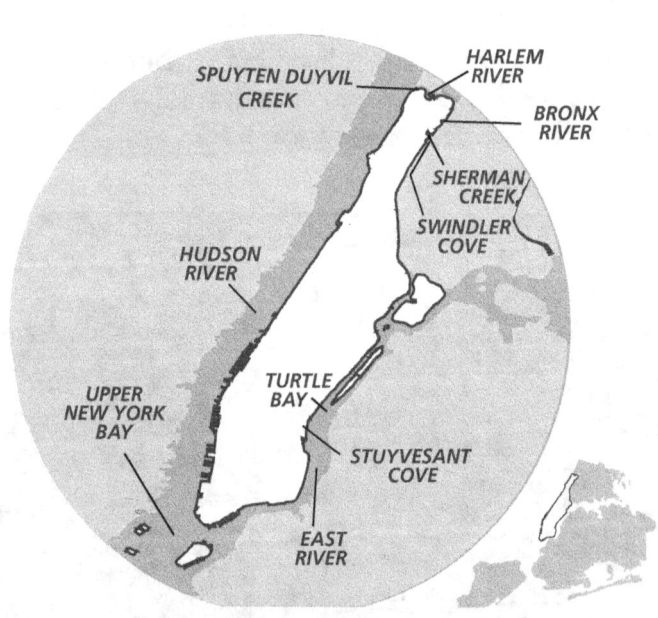

# Harbor Islands

**Liberty Island** 12 acres. Liberty Enlightening the World was a gift of friendship from the people of France designed by sculptor Frederic Bartholdi, who modeled her after his mother. The 305 foot tall Statue was erected in 1886 atop star-shaped Fort Wood, which was built for harbor defense in the War of 1812 and sits in New Jersey waters. The torch is a functioning lighthouse. Visitors enter the base of the Statue, stairs lead to a promenade which once served as a gun platform. At the statue's feet there is a balcony for 360° harbor views or climb 168 stairs to the head of Lady Liberty, 260 feet above sea level, for a bird's eye view of New York Harbor. The waters surrounding Liberty Island are a restricted security zone. No docking of private vessels. 212-363-3200 nps.gov/stli

**Ellis Island** 28 acres. The island was for a time called Gibbet Island after the gallows device used to hang pirates there. From 1892 to 1954, Ellis Island was the main immigration station in the country, receiving more than 12 million steerage and third class steamship passengers. Over 40% of Americans, roughly 100 million people, trace their ancestry through Ellis Island. After it closed, the federal government tried to

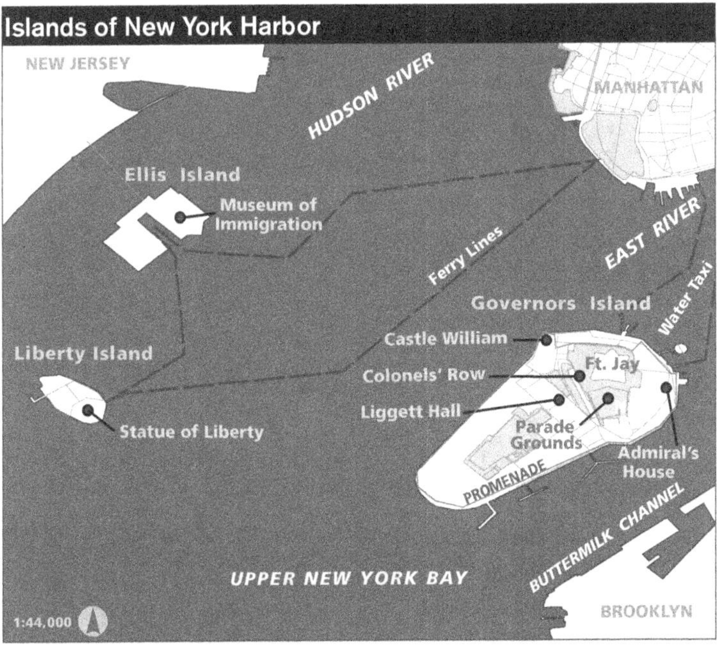

## Islands of New York Harbor

*Map showing: NEW JERSEY, HUDSON RIVER, MANHATTAN, Ellis Island with Museum of Immigration, Ferry Lines, EAST RIVER, Water Taxi, Governors Island with Castle William, Colonels' Row, Liggett Hall, Ft. Jay, Parade Grounds, PROMENADE, Admiral's House, Liberty Island with Statue of Liberty, UPPER NEW YORK BAY, BUTTERMILK CHANNEL, BROOKLYN. Scale 1:44,000*

sell the island, but it remained derelict for thirty years. Finally rehabilitated, it opened in 1990 as the Museum of Immigration. No docking of private vessels. 212-363-3206 nps.gov/elis

Statue of Liberty Ferry: Statue Cruises provides the only access to Liberty and Ellis Islands, departing from Battery Park and Liberty Landing (NJ) daily, every 30 minutes. A fee is paid for the ferry only; admission to the islands is free. Visitors pass through security screening before boarding tour boats. A Monument Access Pass, valid only for specified tours, is recommended. 877-523-9849 statuecruises.com

**Governors Island** 172 acres. Just 800 yards off the tip of the Manhattan, Governors Island has been in military use since 1755, serving as an Army base, prison camp, and U.S. Coast Guard headquarters. The island was known as "Nooten Eylandt" (Nut Island) to the Dutch because of its abundance of hickory, oak, and chestnut trees. It hosted the historic 1988 summit between President Ronald Reagan and Soviet Premier Mikhail Gorbachev that led to the destruction of the Berlin Wall. The Coast Guard left the island in 1996, and in 2003, the federal government returned the island to New York State for the token sum of one dollar.

The 1812-era fortifications Castle William and Fort Jay, the Parade Grounds, Colonels' Row, the Victorian and Romanesque Revival architecture of Nolan Park, and the western esplanade make up the Governors Island National Monument, 22 acres managed by the National Park Service. Development of the island is administered by the Governors Island Preservation and Education Corporation (GIPEC). Access is seasonal and ferries depart from the Battery Maritime Building. On the island, there are many free programs and even group kayak trips offered by Downtown Boathouse. New York Water Taxi's new beach picnic area opens in 2009, even as the future of this magnificent place remains uncertain. Private vessels are not permitted. Kayak landing by permit only. GIPEC: 212-440-2202 govisland.com; NPS: 212-825-3045 nps.gov/gois

Governors Island Ferry: The island and scheduled free ferry function seasonally from the Battery Maritime Building. Also, by ferry from Fulton Ferry Landing to Pier 101 on the eastside of the island.

## The Battery

The Hudson River and the East River converge at the southern tip of Manhattan, where they drain into Upper New York Bay. The area is named after a row of canons now mounted northeast of the old Customs House at Bowling Green, the city's first park. During the Revolutionary War a lead monument to King George III in the park was pulled down and melted for bullets. This land was settled by Native Americans over 10,000 years ago. The old Algonquin trading route called the Wiechquaekeck Trail, now called Broadway, begins at The Battery, cuts across Manhattan, and ends near Albany. In 1625, the New Amsterdam settlement was established here by the Dutch West India Company.

People have been tampering with the Battery since the Dutch colony took root. Most of the Battery was at first underwater until landfill doubled its size, moving inland the circular battery Castle Clinton, originally built on a reef 200 feet from shore. The Brooklyn-Battery Tunnel was built under the park in the early 1940s. In recent years, the rebuilding of the South Ferry subway terminal exposed segments of wall from an 18th century battery and artifacts, such as giant oyster shells and a 1744 coin. Timbers and seawall of the old Whitehall Slip, built in 1730 and filled in by the 1850s, were unearthed.

# The Battery

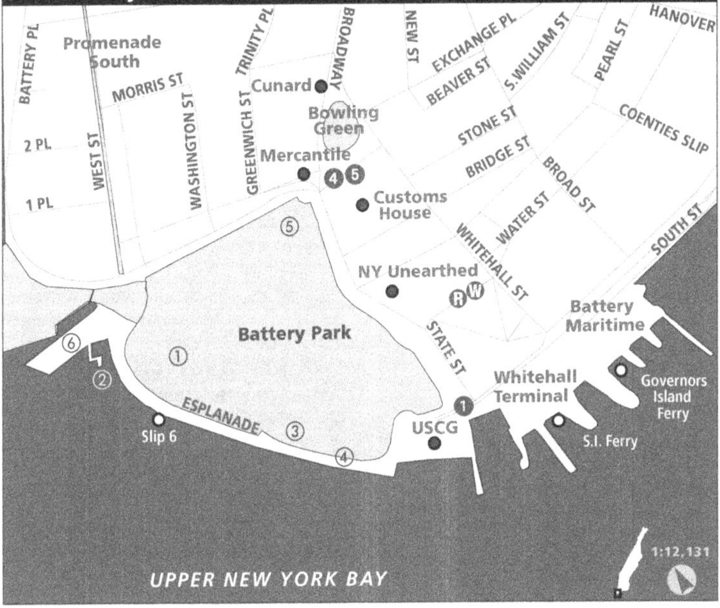

Subway: 4, 5 to Bowling Green; N, R to South Ferry.

Greenway: Manhattan Waterfront Greenway is a 32 mile route around the edge of Manhattan Island. A dedicated bicycle path connects the Hudson and East River esplanades at The Battery.

Blueway: Whitehall Terminal: SI Ferry; Battery Slip 6: NY Water Taxi, Gateway to America Tours, Harbor Cruises; Battery Maritime: Governors Island

**Whitehall Ferry Terminal** The Staten Island Ferry uses Slips 1, 2 and 3 to transport about 60,000 passengers a day between Manhattan and the St. George Terminal. Originally built in the 1950s, the structure was destroyed by fire in 1991 and replaced with a new glass and steel terminal that incorporates green design using solar energy and panoramic harbor views from the waiting room and the rooftop deck. 718-727-2508 siferry.com

**Battery Maritime Building** 10 South St. at Whitehall. Restoration of the cast iron facade of the landmark four story Beaux-Arts ferry terminal, built in 1908, was completed in 2006. Plans for the interior include refurbishing the Great Hall as a specialty food market, and the addition of a boutique hotel and roof top restaurant. Seasonal free Governors Island ferry service.

**Bowling Green** This little oval-shaped park fronting the old customs house was America's first public park. The green plot, located at the start of an ancient Indian trail —present-day Broadway— has been a cattle market, parade ground, and an actual bowling green.

**Alexander Hamilton Customs House** (1899-1907) One Bowling Green, foot of Broadway. The grand seven story Beaux-Arts building, designed by Cass Gilbert, stands like a temple facing Bowling Green. Base figures sculpted by Daniel Chester French represent the continents and 12 statues represent ancient and modern sea powers. At the time it was built, customs duties accounted for 90% of the U.S. economy's revenues, there were no other taxes. Shippers paid duty in a large rotunda beneath murals of harbor scenes by Reginald Marsh. After being vacant for two decades, the great building was reincarnated as the Smithsonian's National Museum of the American Indian. Admission is free. 212-514-3700 nmai.si.edu

**Cunard Building** 25 Broadway. Opened in 1919, Cunard Line's former headquarters, now the Bowling Green Station Post Office, confirms its grandeur in the limestone building's main booking hall, which features 65 foot high Cathedral ceiling and shipping themed murals by Ezra Winter.

**International Mercantile Marine Co.** One Broadway. The entryway to the former United States Lines ship office is still marked "First Class" and "Cabin Class." A Citibank now occupies the old booking room, its marble floor dominated by a large compass and its walls by murals portraying trading routes.

**New York Unearthed** 17 State St. An urban archaeology center started when a judge sentenced the building's owner to set up the museum as penalty for digging a foundation without proper review. The space destroyed without review was the birthplace of Herman Melville. Managed by South Street Seaport Museum, open by appointment. southstreetseaport.org

**Battery Park** State & Whitehall St. 23 acres. The city's oldest public space is one of its most visited. There are historic and spectacular harbor views, 21 monuments and memorials gracing lawns, a town green, and Bosque Gardens framed by the Admiral Dewey Promenade at water's edge. Anglers cast from the eastern edge of the bulkhead. 212-344-3491 thebattery.org

**Battery Park Points of Interest:**

① **Castle Clinton** Built as the West Battery in 1811, the round fortress has served as harbor defense, an enclosed entertainment space (Castle Garden 1824–1855), immigration depot (1855-1890), and the city's first aquarium (1896-1941). The public came to the old fort's rescue when threatened with demolition by the construction of the Brooklyn-Battery Tunnel. Now a National Monument administered by the National Park Service, a diorama exhibit depicts the development of the Battery. 212-344-7220 nps.gov/cacl

② **American Merchant Mariner's Memorial** The names of 6,700 merchant seamen lost in both WWI and WWII are encased in the sculpture of two sailors looking out to sea, while

# Hudson River

The Hudson River is the majestic heart of a beautiful, rich landscape. It is the world's largest tidal river, originating 315 miles north of New York City at spring-fed Lake Tear of the Clouds on Mount Marcy, the highest peak of the Adirondack Mountains. Native Americans called the Hudson "Muhheakunnuk" meaning the river that flows two ways because the waters flow both north and south with each changing tide. Saltwater floods upstream with the incoming tide, freshwater flows down from the mountains to the ocean.

From New York Harbor 155 miles north to the Federal Dam at Troy, the Hudson is not a true river, but a broad saltwater tidal estuary called a "drowned" river. It has two high and two low tides each day with a mean tidal flow of about 400,000 cubic feet per second. The highest freshwater flows are in spring and fall from snow melt and rain. The river runs through land carved out by glaciers and than drowned by rising sea levels after the retreat of the Wisconsin glacier, and the ancient riverbed cuts a gorge in the ocean floor stretching to the continental slope. It is a true fjord near Highlands, NY at its deepest around 175 feet.

The Hudson River is called the North River along the western shore of Manhattan Island, below the George Washington Bridge. It is a name given by early settlers to mark the northern reach of Dutch territory, which extended south to the Delaware (South) River. The width of the river averages 1.5 miles. It is a federal waterway navigable by ocean vessels to Troy. The Lower Hudson has a natural depth of about 16 feet and is continuously dredged to a 45 foot depth to maintain shipping lanes in a straight, deep channel.

The Hudson River watershed is home to 12 million people, drains 13,400 square miles of land in five

a third is reaching down to grasp the outstretched hand of a drowning seaman, who is only visible at low tide.

③ **SeaGlass Nautilus Pavilion** Hi-tech aquatic-themed carousel of sea creatures, fiber optic lights and interactive experience designed to recall the aquarium's original home here. ✖

⑤ **East Coast Memorial** A bronze eagle is perched in the midst of eight granite tablets etched with the names of 4,601 American servicemen who died in the Atlantic during WWII. It is sister to a West Coast Memorial at the Presidio of San Francisco for the men lost in battle in the Pacific.

⑥ **The Seawall** 37 cast iron panels by artist Wopo Holup display a narrative about the Hudson River tides titled *The River That Flows Two Ways*.

⑦ **The 'Sphere'** Designed by Fritz Koenig as a symbol of peace, it stood in the plaza of the World Trade Center for 30 years and was salvaged after the 9/11 attacks.

**Pier A** The oldest covered pier in Manhattan was built in 1886 for the Dept. of Docks & Ferries and later served as a Fire Dept. Marine Station. The clock tower and chimes were erected in 1919 as a WWI memorial. After lying derelict for years, the pier is scheduled to be readapted as a tourist attraction with dining and ferry boarding facilities. ✖

states, and contains hundreds of waste treatment plants. The New York side of the Hudson is a no discharge zone for even treated waste from boats. The waterway supports populations of protected Atlantic and shortnose sturgeon and more than 200 species of fish. Shad and striped bass journey upriver to spawn each year. A New York State saltwater license may soon be required to fish in the brackish Hudson River, and is necessary to cast in its freshwater tributaries.

The Hudson is a National Heritage River and the nation's largest federal Superfund site, covering 200 miles. PCBs (Polychlorinated biphenyls) were dumped decades ago by General Electric's upstate plants; small amounts continue to seep into the river from bedrock beneath the old plants. Water quality and quality of life along its banks are improving due to legislation like the Pure Waters Bond Act of 1965 and the Clean Water Act of 1972, which restricts dumping waste in waterways.

## Battery Park City

The banana boats of the United Fruit Lines used to tie up at piers along the lower Hudson River. The piers were filled with dirt from the World Trade Center excavation in the 1970s. During that dig, workers uncovered the prow and keel of a vessel believed to be Dutch captain Adriaen Block's *Tyger*, which burned and sunk in the Hudson in 1613. The artifacts are now at the Museum of the City of New York. Today the 92 acre Battery Park City extends 1,000 feet into the river, the exact length of the old piers. A strip of picturesque parks, the World Financial Center, Winter Garden, and one of the nation's top high schools, it is home to 9,000 residents, 2 hotels, 22 restaurants, American Express, Dow Jones, Merrill Lynch, and the Mercantile Exchange, the world's largest commodities trader. The complex, bounded on the east by West Street, Battery Park City is a "green" community, from the naturalistic edge of South Cove

## Battery Park City

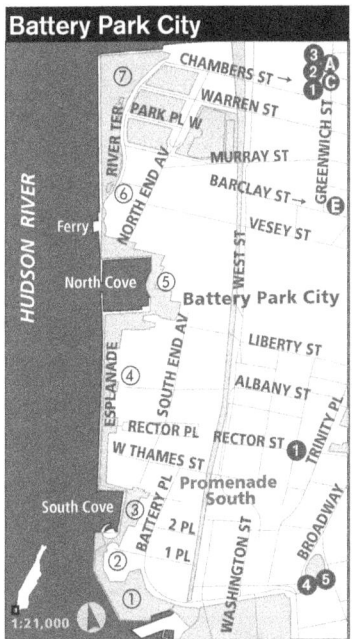

to the ecologically friendly anchorage system at North Cove Marina. The nation's first "green" high-rise is the luxury residential tower Solaire, which consumes less energy and conserves more water than traditional buildings.

Subway: 4, 5 Bowling Green; 1, 2, 3, 9 to Chambers St.

Greenway: Hudson River Greenway runs 13 miles from Battery Park to Ft. Washington Park.

Blueway: World Financial Center Terminal commuter ferry landing; Liberty Landing water taxi.

**Battery Park City Parks** 35 acres. A beautifully landscaped collection of distinctive parks and gardens hug the water's edge around the luxury housing and commercial development embellished with 20 art installations, ball fields, bikeways, picnic areas, playgrounds, dog runs, and tennis courts. 212-267-9700 bpcparks.org

### Battery City Park Points of Interest:

① **Wagner Park** Wide grassy lawns spread out from the Park Pavilion, featuring a restaurant and roof deck.

② **Museum of Jewish Heritage** 36 Battery Pl. The pagoda-shaped living memorial to the Holocaust designed by Kevin Roche has harbor views from the third floor. 646-437-4200 mjhnyc.org

③ **South Cove** 1 Pl. to 3 Pl. Paths wind through three natural acres edging a small inlet, around a rock outcropping, jetties, and a wooden bridge to an island overlook.

④ **The Esplanade** A mile long pedestrian walkway along the entire edge of the Battery Park City complex.

⑤ **Dennis Conner's North Cove** 385 South End Ave. The marina was originally built by Mexican media mogul Emilio Azcarraga Milmo in 1989 as the first port of call for mega yachts in the Big Apple. It has been under the direction of four time America's Cup winner Dennis Conner since its rebuilding in the aftermath of 9/11. Twelve slips accommodate vessels of up to 180 feet. The Manhattan Sailing School's 22 boat fleet, *Ventura* and *Shearwater* tall ships, and the Manhattan Yacht Club are on site. The yacht club's floating clubhouse with full bar and spectator views, designed by acclaimed yacht builders Sparkman & Stephens, is moored in the harbor just north of Ellis Island. 212-786-1200 thenorthcove.com

⑥ **Irish Hunger Memorial** An authentic fieldstone cottage dismantled in Ireland and reconstructed on-site commemorates the Great Famine of the 1840s.

⑦ **Rockefeller Park** Chambers St. Big lawns, playgrounds, and the Real World, sculptor Tom Otterness' miniature bronze figures playing amid piles of giant pennies.

# Hudson River Park

The Hudson River Piers encompass miles of docks that once accommodated more than 100 steamship companies during the port's boom years. That ended in the 1960s with the advent of containerized shipping and air transport. The Miller Elevated Highway, also known as the West Side Highway, veiled the waterfront, until it was dismantled after a section collapsed in 1973. Now, the city could finally see its riverscape, and development of the waterfront soon followed. After decades of neglect, the historic finger piers, numbering over 100, and the adjoining shorefront have been transformed into linear parkland in the largest open space project in the city since Central Park. No pier can be longer than the historically mandated 1,000 feet, so new piers are built over the frames and pilings of old ones.

Hudson River Park is a five mile stretch of greenway, esplanades and piers from Battery Place to West 59 Street. It is a place to stroll, rollerblade, bike, sunbathe, catch a water taxi, or sit and gaze down river to the harbor. The 550 acres of waterfront parkland, about 50% complete, will eventually comprise 13 pier parks and four piling fields for fish habitat as well as 400 acres of estuary waters designated the Hudson River Park Estuarine Sanctuary, the only urban estuary reserve in the United States. Reconstruction and operations are administered by Hudson River Park Trust, a state-city agency. The park has a 1am closing time. Swimming in the Hudson River within park boundaries is only permitted during organized events, like Manhattan Island Foundation races. There are numerous boathouses for human-powered boating activities, as well as a state of the art marina and mooring fields for transient boats. 212-627-2020 hudsonriverpark.org

# Tribeca Esplanade

Tribeca (Triangle Below Canal Street) was once wetlands commonly called Lispenard Meadows. Trinity Church, which owned a significant portion of Hudson River frontage in lower Manhattan, leased the land to Leonard Lispenard. The house at 504 Canal Street was built in 1841 by Robert Stewart, an heir of the Lispenard family. The area was later known as St. John's Park, referring to a fashionable residential development around St. John's Chapel. Landowners were granted water lots that they filled in extending the shoreline into the river. Trinity Church sold this land to Cornelius Vanderbilt who built St. John's Freight Terminal, the original terminus of the West Side Freight Line. What remains of the elevated rail, the High Line which was torn down below Bell Labs, today's Westbeth building.

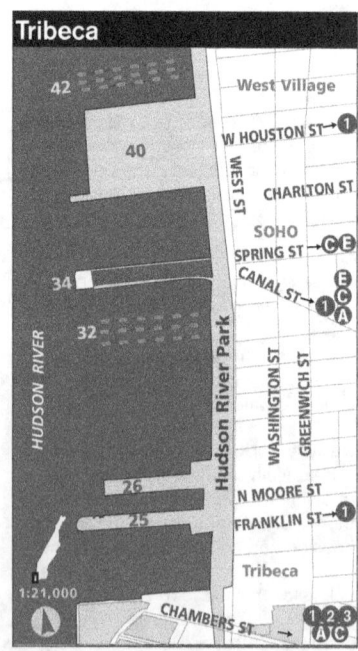

Subway: 1 to Canal St. or 1, 2 or 3 to Chambers St. A, C or E to Canal St.

Greenway: A divided bicycle and pedestrian path stretching from North Moore to W 59 St. There is a pedestrian overpass at Chambers St.

Blueway: Water Trail Pier 40

**Pier 25** North Moore St. Pier reconstruction includes a town dock, mooring field, and water taxi stop and recreations such as sand volleyball courts, miniature golf, a playground, and a patch of artificial turf on the western extreme. ✖ (2010)

**Pier 26** Hubert St. The pier rebuilt and extended to its original footprint will include an estuarine marine interpretation and research facility along with a café and community boathouse for non-motorized craft. ✖ (2010)

**Pier 32** Canal St. All that remains of the Moore-McCormack Line's pier is a pile field which serves as an ecology pier attracting fish and birds.

**Pier 34** Two narrow piers lead to the ventilation towers of the Holland Tunnel, Clifford M. Holland's engineering marvel completed in 1927 linking Manhattan to Jersey City, all made possible by enormous fans to circulate air. The south finger is open to the public with benches for enjoying the view.

**Pier 40** W Houston St. 14 acres. A two-story box-shaped pier, built in 1954 for Holland America Lines passenger and commercial shipping, has a wide public promenade wrapping around the entire pier, rooftop soccer fields, and a central courtyard of athletic fields. The pier is also a parking garage and home to a picnic house, community rowing program, kayak outfitters, and excursion boats. River Project and Hudson River Park Trust are based there. In the building lobby, a mural by Frank Nix depicts a map of Europe with Holland America's ports of call and the four vessels that sailed under the name *Rotterdam*. The park's largest pier is under review for repurposing, which combines commercial and recreational components. Downtown Boathouse operates free kayaking on weekends and Village Community Boathouse has youth rowing programs. A mooring field on the south side of the pier serves up to 40 vessels under 40 feet.

### Greenwich Village Esplanade

After his duel with Aaron Burr in New Jersey, the wounded Alexander Hamilton was rowed to the Greenwich Village shore. He died soon after at the Jane Street home of his friend William Bayard. From here, Robert Fulton launched the famous steamboat *Clermont* up the Hudson all the way to Albany in 1807, forever changing the world of shipping. At the turn of the last century, the Hudson River surpassed the East River in commerce and Greenwich Village piers were the busiest in the port. A few rare seamen's hotels survive along West Street, including the 1898 Keller Hotel (Barrow St.), 1904 Holland Hotel (W 10 St.) and the altered Great Eastern Hotel (180 Christopher St.). Further uptown at Perry Street the river path is shadowed by Richard Meiers' modernist glass towers encasing celebrity lofts and the block-long artists' complex Westbeth (55 Bethune St.) in the former home of Bell Telephone Labs where innovations such as the vacuum tube, radar, transistor, and the digital computer were invented.

The esplanade is buffered by flower beds, grass lawns and seating areas. An information kiosk, snack bar, and comfort station are located near Christopher Street. North of Pier 45, a bridgeway crosses a bow notch, which is a semi-circular cut in the bulkhead originally constructed to

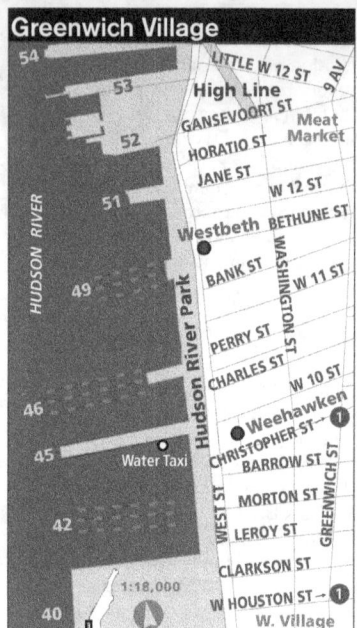

### Greenwich Village

accommodate the prows of ships too long for the piers.

Subway: 1 to Houston St or Christopher St.; C, E to Spring St.; A, C, E, or L to W 4 St.

Blueway: Water Taxi stop Pier 45

**Pier 45** Christopher St. A fountain frames the threshold of the popular 800 foot long pier adorned with an open sun deck, natural grass lawn, and boardwalk with seating areas topped with canvas shade tents. The pier has a water taxi stop. One block from the pier, the 1892 U.S. Appraisers' Warehouse was the place where customs inspectors set duties on imported goods; it's now The Archives residential lofts.

**Weehawken Block** A slender enclave of 14 historic buildings between Christopher and W 10 Streets, on land that was once part of New York State's first prison–Newgate, which was built to the Hudson River bulkhead in 1797. It closed in 1829 when its inmates were sent "up the river" to Sing Sing. The block has seen a sanatorium, a brewery, the Greenwich Market, and maritime-related industries, like Meier & Oelhaf Marine Repair (1920-1984) at 177 Christopher Street.

**Pier 46** Charles St. An active 400 foot long pier decked with an Astroturf lawn encircled by walkways and seating areas. A pile field marks the outline of the original footprint off the western half of the pier, providing marine habitat.

**Pier 49** A viewing balcony provides an overlook to a piling field that serves as a fish nursery, where juvenile striped bass winter.

**Pier 51** Horatio St. A nautical-themed playground pier shaped like a boat hull faces seaward with seashell embedded sidewalks, sand boxes, water sprays, and telescope.

**Gansevoort Peninsula, Pier 53** W 12 St. Herman Melville worked for 19 years as a customs agent on the docks named for his grandfather, Peter Gansevoort. The block long landfill is slated to be a marine waste transfer station for recyclables. The picturesque station house of Manhattan's last active

marine fire company, Marine Co. #1, was demolished in 2008 to make way for a more modern facility on the pier.

**The High Line** Gansevoort to W 30 St. An elevated freight rail, built a block from the river by New York Central Railroad in the 1930s was originally part of a waterfront improvement project that replaced a perilous street grade railroad on 10 Avenue, which came to be called Death Avenue. It originally stretched from St. John's Park Terminal at Spring Street north to W 35 Street, but was severed to 1.5 miles, now anchored on the southern end by the Gansevoort Market, the city's longtime slaughter and meat packing center. The cobblestone streets below the weed covered steel carcass of the abandoned railway are shared with trendy restaurants and designer shops. The High Line is to be transformed into a 22 block long public park two stories above street level capturing river views. Although not yet open to the public, occasional tours are conducted. thehighline.org

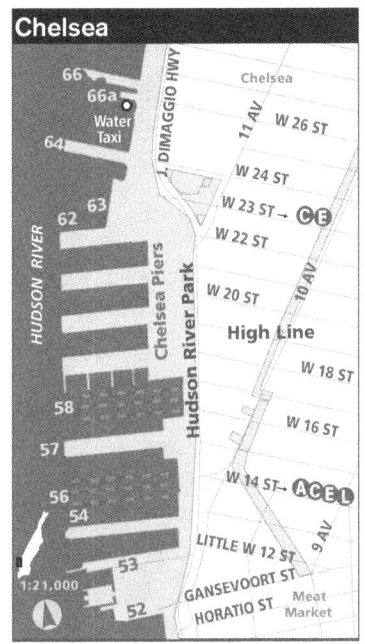

## Chelsea Esplanade

Much of the Chelsea waterfront belonged to the estate of Clement Clarke Moore, author of *A Visit from St. Nicholas* and a professor at the General Theological Seminary, to which he donated the block between W 20 and W 21 Streets. By 1910, the waterfront was dominated by piersheds, designed by Warren and Wetmore and built to accommodate transatlantic liners. The development of the Chelsea Piers complex reclaimed a group of the abandoned piers. Ship of Glass, the hulking headquarters of media mogul Barry Diller designed by acclaimed architect Frank Gehry rises on the eastside of the West Side Highway. The shimmering facade of a new tower by Jean Nouvel rises beside Gehry's. On the esplanade near W 29 Street, the art installation *Tables and Chairs* by Allan and Ellen Wexler beckons visitors to sit and enjoy the cityscape, the views of the Hudson, the High Line, and Empire State Building.

<u>Subway</u>: A, C, E or L to W 14 St.; C, E to W 23 St.

<u>Greenway</u>: Divided path runs on the east side of Chelsea Piers.

<u>Blueway</u>: Water Taxi Stop Pier 66a; Water Trail: Pier 66

**Pier 54** W 13 St. A steel arch marks the threshold to the open pier deck of this former Cunard White Star Line dock where the *Carpathia* landed survivors of *Titanic* in 1912, and the *Lusitania* departed in 1916, to be torpedoed by a German U-Boat, the incident that sparked America's entry into WWI. *Titanic* survivors were taken to the nearby American Seamen's

Friend Society Hotel at Jane Street, now the Hotel Riverview. The flat top pier, used for concerts, movies, and other events, is to be rebuilt.

**Pier 57** W 15 St. An Art Deco pier built for Grace Lines in 1952, the oldest unaltered pier on the waterfront is actually a floating pier supported not by wood piles but by buoyant caissons. Its historic western façade and innovative design by Emil Praeger gained it a listing on both the State and National Registers of Historic Places. Bids to restore the pier are in early development, including access to the underwater caissons, marina, and rooftop park. ⚒

**Chelsea Piers, Piers 59, 60 & 61** W 17 to W 22 St. The piers, originally built to handle the Cunard White Star Line's longest ships, retain the original pier sheds and connecting headhouse. They are now a public recreation mecca, featuring a golf driving range, ice rink, bowling alley, gymnastics center, gym and spa, marina, and waterfront cafes and catering spaces. Public esplanades wrap around the perimeter of each pier for waterside access and a closer look at the excursion boats, dinner cruises, and private yachts berthed at the piers. Enter the complex at W 24 Street, exit at W 17 Street. Ample parking. 212-336-6099 chelseapiers.com

**Chelsea Waterside Park** W 23 St. East of the highway, the park contains athletic fields, ball court, water play area, and one of the city's best dog runs.

**Chelsea Cove, Piers 62 & 63** W 23 St. Measuring more than nine acres, trim gardens provide a segue from Chelsea Piers to an oval skate park and carousel on Pier 62, adjacent

to a large bowl lawn, wide esplanade and seating area on Pier 63. ✷ (2010)

**Pier 64** W 24 St. A landscaped boulder field embellishes the doorstep of the former Panama Lines Pier, reborn as a long high green space with manicured lawns, a grove of shade trees, and superb river views from this pier at a bend in the Hudson.

**Pier 66A Maritime** W 26 St. The wooden Baltimore and Ohio Railroad Float Transfer Bridge, used from 1954 to 1973 for transferring railroad cars to barges has been restored as a reminder of the maritime commerce that once dominated this waterfront. The old bridge was raised from the river bottom in 2001 and restored; it is listed on the State and National Register of Historic Places. A Lackawanna Railroad Barge car float, moored west of the float bridge, features an eatery and berths for such historic ships as the 1929 lightship *Frying Pan* and the fireboat *John J. Harvey*. An old rail caboose on the barge is home to Going Coastal's Waterfront Center. 212-989-6363 fryingpan.com

**Pier 66** W 26 St. This New York River Sports community dock and hand launch features a boathouse offering a thrilling diversity of water sports including kayak trips and lessons, kayak polo, outrigger canoe, and youth sailing. On the western side *Long Time*, a 26 foot stainless steel water wheel by local artist Paul Ramirez Jonas turns with the ebb and flow of the tides. In addition, Pier 66 Lab conducts environmental educational programs in the boathouse. Pier66nyc.org

## Midtown Maritime Esplanade

Long a neighborhood of gangsters, slaughterhouses, rail yards, docks, dockworkers and crusading labor priests, Hell's Kitchen inspired Budd Schulberg to write *On the Waterfront*. Today, a 33 block landscaped stretch of commercial piers serves commuter ferries, sightseeing boats, yacht charters, ocean liners and dinner cruises. A riverside heliport at the bulkhead at W 30 Street offers sightseeing flights. A broad public plaza with fountain, comfort station and eateries is located near 42 Street. Further north near Pier 95 the art installation *Private Passage* by Malcolm Cochran is a 30 foot long wine bottle with a ship's stateroom inside. There is a bow notch north of Pier 96, an inland cut for the prow of vessels too large for the 1,000 foot long piers.

Subway: A, C, E to W 42 St. or W 50 St.

Greenway: Hudson River Park Greenway continues, but has heavy tourist, bus, and taxi traffic crossing the path. There is an overpass at W 42 St.

Blueway: Ferry Pier 79; Water Taxi stop: Pier 84; Water Trail: Pier 84

**Pier 72** W 32 St. A pile field that may be rehabilitated with a new pier to contain heliport services, removing it from the esplanade.

**Pier 76** W. 36 St. The huge former United States Lines Pier, across the highway from Javits Convention Center, is occupied by the NYPD auto tow pound and mounted police unit stables. Future plans anticipate half the pier will become parkland. ✷

**Pier 78** W 38 St. The privately owned docks extend more than 300 feet west toward what in 1837 was going to be a 13 Avenue and contain the terminal for New York Waterway sightseeing vessels and bus lot, plus the boat ramp for NY Duck Tours the city's first land-sea service to splash in the Hudson River.

**Pier 79 Midtown Ferry Terminal** W 39 St. A glass pavilion with six slips for commuter ferries, sightseeing boats and charters straddles the 145-foot high ventilation towers of the Lincoln Tunnel and features a public viewing balcony. NY Waterway operates free shuttle buses to midtown locations and up and down the waterfront. To catch a ride, hail one of the red, white, and blue buses. 800-533-3779 nywaterway.com

**Piers 81** W 41 St. Berth to World Yacht dinner cruises. 212-630-8100 worldyacht.com

**Pier 83** W 43 St. Homeport to the famous Circle Line, which has operated Manhattan circumnavigation sightseeing boats since 1944. There is parking, souvenir stand and a snack bar. 212-563-3200 circleline42.com

**Pier 84** W 44 St. The best riverside access in midtown includes a huge plaza, sunbathing lawns, waterside cafe, water spray area, dog run, boathouse, floating docks, water taxi stop, and a wooden boardwalk at the end of an 800 foot long pier. Floating the Apple maintains the docks, offering rowing and boat building programs from the boathouse. Seasonal free fishing, movies, live music, and educational programs are presented; bike rentals available from Bike & Roll. 212-564-5412 floatingtheapple.org

**Pier 86 Intrepid Sea, Air & Space Museum** W 46 St. Opened as a museum in 1982, the WWII Essex-

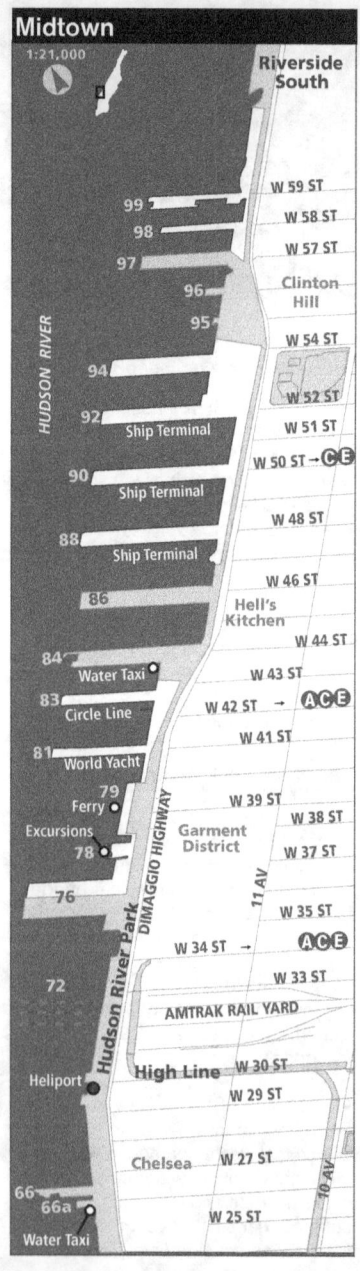

class aircraft carrier is decked with an extensive military aircraft collection and features the submarine *Growler* berthed nearby. Admission fee. 212-245-0072 intrepidmuseum.org

**Piers 88, 90 & 92 Manhattan Cruise Terminal** W 48 to W 52 St. Once port of call to the world's largest cruise liners, the former Passenger Ship Terminal, known as Luxury Liner Row, was built in the 1930s and renovated by the Port Authority in the 1970s. The terminal is one of the busiest in the country, accommodating a growing cruise market at five berths, three levels of operation, and glass enclosed exhibit space atop each pier. Rooftop parking and an on site U.S. Customs Office. 212-246-5450 nycruise.com

**UnConvention Center, Pier 94** W 54 St. Built in 1959 as a Cunard freight terminal and later used as a garage, the pier shed serves as exhibit space for trade shows. 212-399-4247

**Clinton Cove Park, Piers 95 & 96** W 55 to 57 St. The former docks of the Furness and Furness-Bermuda Lines' "honeymoon ships" offer two acres of wide lawns, a river overlook, boathouse, and "get down" allowing visitors to get close to the water. Hudson River Park's free education programs at the pier include fishing, river biology, and ecology. Downtown Boathouse runs free walk-up kayaking and skills clinics. downtownboathouse.org

**Pier 97** W 57 St. The pier is slated to be rebuilt as part of Clinton Cove Park, upon relocation of the NYC Sanitation truck parking.

**Pier 98** W 58 St. Con Edison depot for barge delivery of fuel oil.

**Pier 99** Marine Transfer Station W 59 St. Sanitation pier with a large neon lighted façade framing the entrance where garbage barges load.

## Riverside

Hudson River Park links with Riverside Park South north of W 59 Street, and continues to Riverside Park at W 72 Street providing excellent river access in the Upper West Side. This was not always the case. The once shabby waterfront was riddled with squatters' lean-tos and rail lines cordoning off the river until Robert Moses began construction of Riverside Park and the Henry Hudson Parkway in the 1930s. Donald Trump's 16 tower residential development was built atop the remainder of the New York Central Rail Yards. The rails once carried freight from ships and barges to the North River piers and beyond to Albany and the trunk line to Chicago. The Art Deco viaduct of the old Miller Highway, the last section of America's first elevated highway, casts a shadow on the river from 57 to 72 Streets.

One of the city's top scenic drives and most desirable addresses, Riverside Drive was designed by Olmsted as part of the parkscape from W 72 Street to W 181 Street; the route passes many of the park's sights. The Harlem shore was once a lively place of day liners ferrying people to New Jersey's long gone Palisades Amusement Park. The neglected water's edge, where a succession of road and rail viaducts isolates the river, has been re-imag-

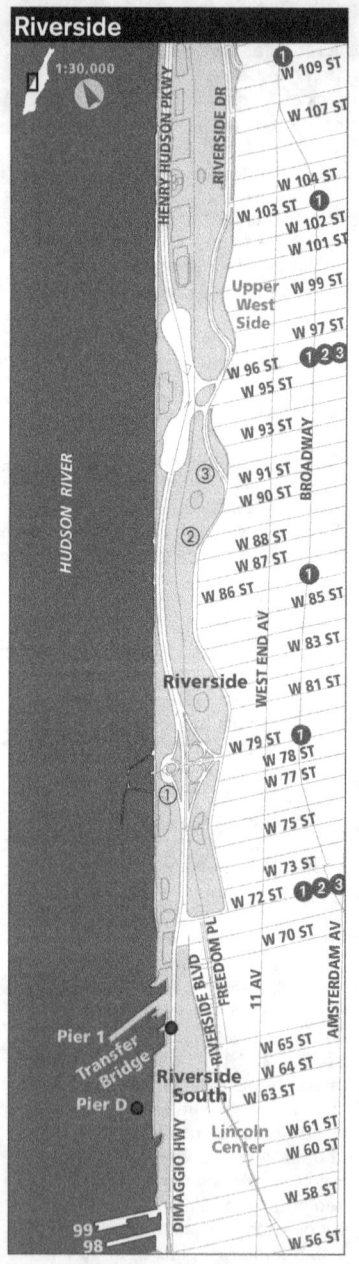

ined and redeveloped for recreation and public access. Farther north, a one of a kind park is planted on top of a municipal water pollution plant.

Subway: 1, 3 to W 72 St. & Broadway; 1 to W 79 St. or W 86 St.; 1 to W 125, W 137 or W 145 St.

Greenway: The bikeway continues from W 69 to W 72 St. through Riverside Park South, Riverside Park Esplanade, then Cherry Walk for a mile (W 100 to W 125 Sts.) to the new West Harlem waterfront. Bikes are not allowed in Riverside State Park.

Blueway: Water Taxi stop at W 125 St; Water Trail: Riverside S, Boat Basin, & W Harlem Piers

**Riverside Park South** W 59 to 72 St. 35 acres. At the former New York Central's yards lighters once barged rail cars across the Hudson to the Westside freight lines. The piers had letter designations with Piers B through I taking up ten blocks of shore. Now an esplanade weaves along the riverbank through diverse ecologies that include boardwalks, terraces, and promontories overlooking natural areas and reminders of the waterfront's industrial past, such as a refurbished 1940's Alco S-1 switcher steam locomotive. Pier I, a 715 foot long slanting recreational pier, is erected atop the remains of an original wooden lighterage pier. The foundation of Grain Elevator A (1877-1939) can be seen near the twisted carcass of the shed on Pier D, destroyed by fire in 1971. The historic W 69 Street Transfer Bridge and gantry are undergoing restoration for use as a ferry landing. A shore side sitting area is made up of large granite slabs aligned to trace the old piers and rail lines inscribed with railroad company logos. Downtown Boathouse hosts free introductory kayaking here on weekends. Park amenities include a cafe of the pier, comfort station, basketball courts and soccer fields.

**Riverside Park** W 72 to 158 St. 323 acres. If Central Park is New York City's backyard, Riverside is definitely the front, with its manicured lawns and gardens sloping down to meet the Hudson River, hospitable to all who pass, whether by boat, bike, foot or car. A designated scenic landmark, this attractive park encompasses four miles of magnificent landscapes conceived by Frederick Law Olmsted and features monuments and sculptures honoring Eleanor Roosevelt, Joan of Arc, the Woman's Health Protective Association, and others. There are wide open lawns descending to the water's edge, natural areas, a bird sanctuary (W 116 St.), and plenty of gardens (W 83, W 91 & W 138 St.). The park has recreational facilities of every variety, including three dog runs, 14 playgrounds, water sprays, clay (W 96 St.) and asphalt (W 119 St.) tennis courts, baseball, basketball, soccer, handball, sand volleyball, and skateboard areas. 212-870-3070 riversideparkfund.org

**Riverside Park Points of Interest:**

① **79 Street Boat Basin** W 79 St. Built by Robert Moses in 1937, the marina has 110 slips, moorings, kayak storage, and two fixed piers. TA-Dock, the north side pier, is open to the public and offers a canoe and kayak launch. The nearby Boat Basin Cafe offers casual dining from a vantage overlooking the yacht docks.

② **Soldiers & Sailors' Monument** W 89 St. Corinthian columns encircle this temple-like landmark installed in 1902 to commemorate soldiers and sailors who served the Union in the Civil War.

③ **Marine Heroes Tablet** W 93 St.

④ **Grant's Tomb** W 122 St. The nation's largest mausoleum and the final resting place of Ulysses S. Grant and his wife, Julia, overlooks the Hudson from Morningside Heights. A national monument managed by

the National Park Service, it is open daily. 212-666-1640 nps.gov/gegr

⑤ **Amiable Child Monument** W 123 St. "Erected to the memory of an amiable child, St. Clair Pollock," reads the marker on the grave of a five-year-old boy who fell to his death from the nearby cliffs in 1797. Over time, as the Pollock family's farm changed hands each new owner agreed to maintain the marble monument.

**Riverside Church** 490 Riverside Dr. Soaring above Riverside Park, the 392 foot high Gothic tower of the nondenominational church (built 1926-1936) is home to the world's second largest and heaviest carillon bell (74 bells), donated by John D. Rockefeller, Jr. Tours are available. theriversidechurchny.org

**Cherry Walk** W 100 to 125 St. A cherry tree lined esplanade offers great strolling and bicycling on the banks of the Hudson River. The trees were a gift from the Committee of Japanese Residents in honor of the 1909 Hudson-Fulton Celebration.

**West Harlem Piers** St. Clair Place. W 125 to W 135 St. 42 acres. About a block west of the Cotton Club a Harlem waterfront renaissance is happening on a narrow strip of shoreline where new piers extend into the Hudson River adjacent to bike paths, an open plaza, and natural habitat plantings bounded by a wide esplanade adjacent to the Fairway Market. The recreational piers contain benches, fishing stations, water taxi landing, and kayak launch.

**Riverbank State Park** 679 Riverside Dr., W 137 to W 144 St. 28 acres. Manhattan's only state park rises 69 feet above the river, built atop the North River Sewage Plant, which processes 125 million gallons of wastewater every day. The beautifully landscaped park, inspired by Japanese roof gardens, offers stunning views. There are playgrounds, a water spray, skating rink, and an amphitheater theater, as well as the signature Totally Kid Carousel. The upper level has tennis courts, running track, and athletic fields, while the building houses a pool and fitness center. 212-694-3600

# Upper Manhattan

The northern Manhattan landscape of Washington Heights and Inwood Hill is shaped by ancient glaciers. Along here, bluffs rise high above the shore making it difficult to access the water. To the south, Morningside Park is on a ridge that rises steeply above the Harlem Valley. There are still many places on the hillside to enjoy views of the Hudson River and Palisades in New Jersey.

The lofty 24 acre estate of John James Audubon is now occupied by the Audubon Terrace Museum Group (W 155 St. & Riverside Dr.), where a Renaissance style courtyard designed by Charles Pratt Huntington holds The American Academy and Institute of Arts and Letters, The American Numismatic Society, Boricua College, The Hispanic Society of America, and The Church of Our Lady of Esperanza.

The riverside greenway meets Fort Washington Park at W 158 Street, an excellent vantage for observing Peregrine falcons that nest in the George Washington Bridge towers. Fort Washington Park also utilizes a naturalistic underground water filtering system which removes pollution from runoff and storm water overflow. At W 184 Street Bennett Park is the highest elevation on Manhattan Island, 265 feet above sea level. The park marks the original site of Fort Washington, where Hessian mercenaries stormed Harlem Heights in November 1776, forcing Washington to retreat to Delaware. Margaret Corbin Circle in Fort Tryon Park commemorates the first woman killed in battle, a Patriot bride who took up her fallen husband's fire arms in the battle. Below the Park, the Dyckman Street waterfront is also known as Tubby Hook, after the Dutch "Tobbe Hoeck" or cape of the tub, for the original barrel shaped outline of the shore. An 1880 construction dig here yielded fossilized bones of a mastodon, now

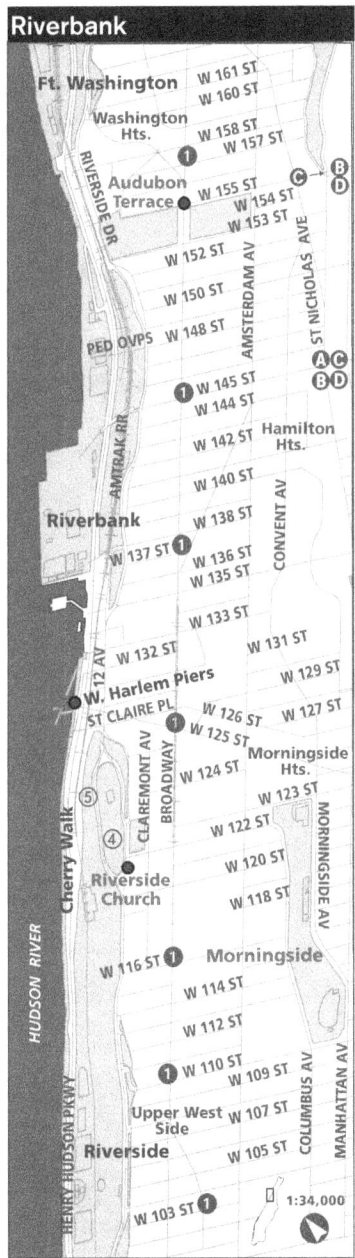

29 Manhattan

part of the collection of the American Museum of Natural History.

<u>Subway</u>: A to W 181, W 190 or W 207 St.; 1, 9 to W 215 St.

<u>Greenway</u>: The greenway extends from W 145 St. to Manhattan's northern tip, narrowing at W 155 St. to meet the lit path through Fort Washington Park and parallel with Henry Hudson Pkwy. from W 181 St. to Dyckman St.

<u>Blueway</u>: Water Trail: Inwood Hill Park

**Fort Washington Park** W 158 to Dyckman St. 159 acres. A former Native American fishing camp, trading post, Dutch farmland, and Revolutionary War outpost, the site was first mapped for parkland in 1894. Sloping lawns descend to a natural shore at the river's edge, where an outcropping of boulders under the George Washington Bridge support a lighthouse. The park includes barbecue areas, dog runs, tennis courts, and baseball fields. Enter along the shore or from the pedestrian bridges at W 155 St. and W 181 St. and Lafayette Place.

**Little Red Lighthouse** W 178 St. Rescued and made famous in 1947 by Hildegarde Swift's children's book *The Little Red Lighthouse and the Great Gray Bridge*, the Jeffrey's Hook Light has stood on the banks of the Hudson River since 1921. The interior is open to the public for tours conducted by the Urban Park Rangers and the annual Little Red Lighthouse Festival held each September.

**Inspiration Point** W 190 St. One of the most impressive views of the Hudson River is from a roadside rest stop situated 136 feet above the water, the Greek temple designed by architect Gustave Steinacher in 1925.

**Fort Tryon Park** Riverside Dr. W 192 to Dyckman St. 67 acres. The heavily forested upland park overlooking the Hudson River is named for the last colonial governor of New York, William Tryon. It was the former estate of

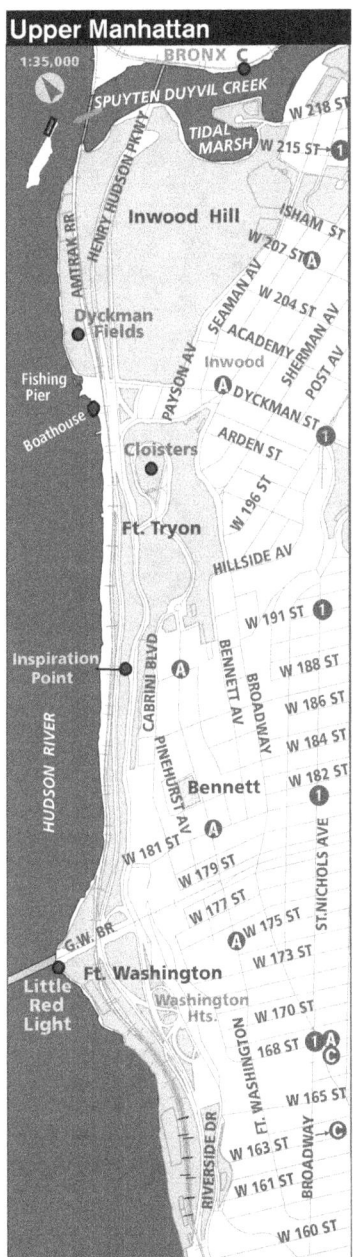

Cornelius Billings and later of John D. Rockefeller Jr. who gave it to the city in 1931. The philanthropist even purchased the land across the river to preserve the Park's view of the Palisades. Frederick Law Olmsted Jr., son of the master designer, landscaped the site for birding, hiking, and unspoiled views. The Heather Garden runs along the bluff and the charming New Leaf Café occupies the former stables of the estate. hhoc.org/fftp

**The Cloisters** Assembled from five French medieval monasteries, the Cloisters and its three gardens house 5,000 works of art from the Metropolitan Museum of Art's medieval collection, all donated by John D. Rockefeller, Jr. 212-923-3700 metmuseum.org

**Dyckman Street Boat Basin** The cross-town street ends at the water's edge, which is occupied by a wooden fishing pier, kayak and canoe beach, and marina with public boat ramp (under construction). It is named for the family of Jan Dyckman, an early Dutch settler who owned the surrounding lands, including Manhattan's only intact 18th century farmhouse, now a museum overlooking the river from Broadway at W 204 Street. The red boathouse of Inwood Canoe Club, located down the service road past the marina, offers free kayaking on summer Sundays. The service road also provides fishing access to the river.

**Dyckman Fields** North of Dyckman St. Waterside baseball and soccer fields located between the active rail line and the river. The park's location affords terrific vantage for early morning bald eagle sighting and night stargazing.

**Inwood Hill Park** W 218 St. & Indian Rd. 196 acres. High above the confluence of the Hudson and Harlem Rivers sits the city's hilliest, greenest, and only unsullied parkland, known as

Cox Hill to colonists. Hiking trails, built by WPA workers during the Depression, amble through primeval forest, meadows, archeological sites, Indian cave shelters, glacial potholes, tidal marsh, and tall ridges of Manhattan schist and Inwood marble. Lenape Indians inhabited the rocky hills for thousands of years. Peter Minuet's bargain purchase of Manhattan took place under a tulip tree in 1626, its location (until 1938) marked by a bronze tablet on a boulder near W 214 Street in the park. There are 136 acres of Forever Wild Area allocated as Shorakapok Preserve—the name the Lenape called the banks of Spuyten Duyvil, containing the last natural forest and salt marsh on Manhattan Island. The park attracts waterfowl, wading birds, and birds of prey. Inwood Hill Center sidles a small cove with a promenade and pier, where Urban Park Rangers offer a variety of outdoor activities, including fishing, canoeing, and nature study.

## Harlem River

The Harlem River is a tidal strait separating Manhattan from the mainland of the Bronx and connecting the Hudson and East Rivers. The passage to the Hudson River had originally run through the turbulent Spuyten Duyvil Creek, which snaked in an S-curve around Marble Hill. In 1895, the Army Corps of Engineers cut the Harlem River Ship Canal straightening the waterway and creating a shortcut for shipping between Long Island Sound, the Hudson, and ports north.

The 7.5 mile long Harlem River bends westward at W 208 Street. The high bluffs make water access difficult. A vein of marble running through the hills as far north as Tuckahoe was mined for headstones at Trinity Church Cemetery and for the construction of St. Patrick's Cathedral. At Broadway and W 215 Street is one of the largest surviving examples of the marble, the Seaman-Drake Arch (1855), which previously served as the guard house of a hilltop estate.

Columbia University's crew team drills on the 2,000 meter sculling course between Henry Hudson Bridge and Sherman Creek. The Harlem River Speedway, stretching 2.5 miles along the riverside from W 208 Street south to W 155 Street, was built for horse racing in 1898. In 1922, the drive was paved and opened to traffic; by 1934 it connected to Manhattan's circuit highway. The legendary Polo Grounds stood near the end of the speedway from 1911 to 1964 at Coogan's Bluff near W 158 Street. The ball park, home to Yankees, Giants, Mets, and 13 World Series, was demolished in 1964 and replaced by the Polo Ground Towers. Yankee Stadium sits directly across the river.

Broadway is the old Kingsbridge Road, stretching the entire length of Manhattan. The Inwood waterfront east of Broadway to Dyckman Street on the Sherman Creek Peninsula is inaccessible because of industrial uses, including municipal garages, Con Edison substations, and subway yards.

<u>Subway</u>: A to W 207 St.; 1 to Dyckman St., W 207, or W 215 St.; 4, 5, 6 to W 125 St.

## Spuyten Duyvil to Sherman Creek

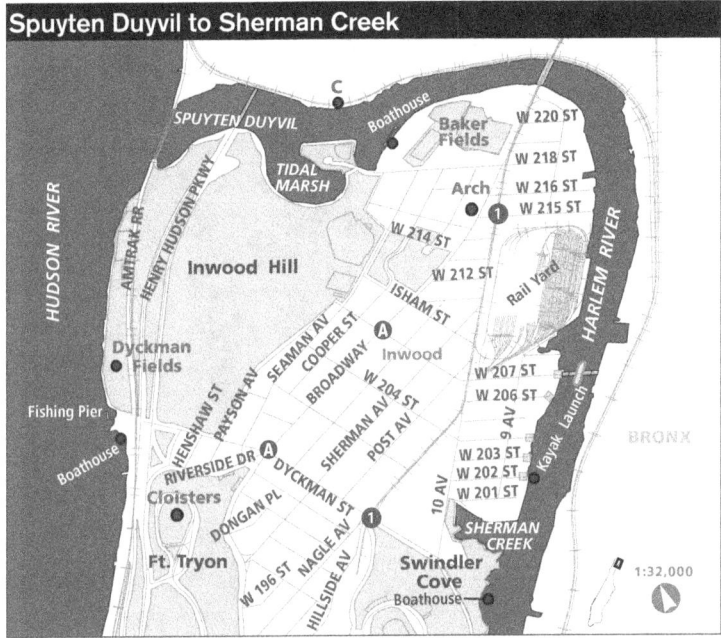

Greenway: Manhattan Waterfront Greenway picks up at Harlem River Speedway, stretching from Dyckman St. to W 155 St., the path's only two entry points. Segments of the greenway are complete from Dyckman to W 164 St., then travels on street to W 155 St. and W 145 to W 132 St.

Blueway: Water Trail: W 202 St.

**Baker Field Athletic Complex**
W 218 St. 26 acres. Lou Gehrig once played baseball and Columbia beat Stanford in the 1934 Rose Bowl at Baker Field. Built in 1922, it is named for its financial sponsor George Fisher Baker (1840–1931).

**Class of 1929 Boathouse** W 218 St. Crew is Columbia University's oldest organized sport. The old, unused Gould-Remmer Boathouse is on a cove beside the new boathouse named for the class of 1929, the last to win the national rowing championships. On race days, free shuttle buses transport spectators from the boathouse to the finish line at Sherman Creek. The team paints the blue "C" on the rock face across the river.

## Sherman Creek Inlet

Sherman Creek is the truncated waterway that becomes a mud flat exposed at low tide. It is fringed by wetlands that once extended inland to present-day Nagle Avenue. The creek was originally called Half Kill by the Dutch, later taking its name from a family that lived on its shores in 1807. One hundred years later, the creek was trafficked by barges delivering coal. "Sculler's Row" occupied the south shore of Sherman Creek; its boathouses included Union (first women's crew), Atalanta, Lone Star, Dauntless, First Bohemian, Harlem

Rowing, Friendship, and NY Athletic Club. Fordham University's boathouse burned in 1978. A rickety collection of old motor boat clubs were recently dismantled on the shore, a short distance from the first new rowing boathouse to be built in the city in 100 years. The coastline of the creek is being restored little by little. At the Academy Street strip a waterfront esplanade is planned.

**Sherman Creek Park** Five street-end parks from W 207 St to W 202 St. feature water viewing areas, a picnic grove, water spray, fishing access, barbecue pits, and kayak launch.

**Swindler Cove Park** Dyckman St. at 10 Ave. 5 acres. Restored wetlands, native plantings, a garden, freshwater pond, and a promenade built on an illegal dump by Bette Midler's NY Restoration Project. nyrp.org

**Peter Jay Sharp Boathouse** Swindler Cove Park. A two-story floating boathouse designed by Robert A.M. Stern was built in Connecticut and floated to its home on Sherman Creek. The boathouse provides storage for racing shells, locker rooms and exercise training facility. The dock is not a public launch, but offers rowing programs for youth and adults.

**Highbridge Park** Dyckman St. & W 155 St., Amsterdam and Edgecombe Ave. 119 acres. A 2.5-mile bucolic park situated 200 feet above the Harlem River, where steep hills, rocky outcroppings, and Harlem River Drive separate it from shore. Rising over Sherman Creek, Fort George Hill was the site of a Revolutionary era defense, now a playground. An outdoor pool, built in place of the old High Bridge Reservoir in 1936 by Works Progress Administration, is one of the City's largest. New York City's first legal mountain bike trails opened here.

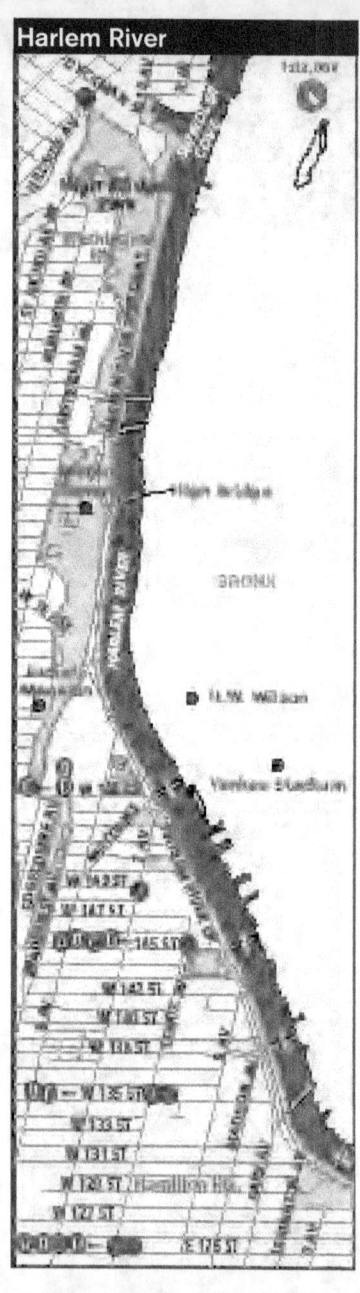

Harlem River

**High Bridge & Water Tower** W 174 St. The pedestrian footbridge is the city's oldest bridge, connecting Highbridge Park to the Bronx. Built in 1848 to carry the Old Croton Aqueduct over the Harlem River as part of an innovative water supply system running 41 miles from Croton Reservoir into New York City, High Bridge is today part of the Old Croton Aqueduct Trail and a link in the East Coast Greenway system that will stretch from Maine to Florida. The Water Tower, built in 1872, equalizes water pressure. The bridge, closed since the 1970s, is being renovated.

**Morris-Jumel Mansion** 65 Jumel Terrace at W 160 St. Manhattan's oldest residence offers stunning views of the Harlem River. The Georgian-style mansion, built in 1765 by Col. Roger Morris as a summer retreat, served as headquarters of Gen. Washington in 1776, and was most famously the home of Madam Eliza Jumel, a prostitute who became the wealthiest widow in the city. Jumel wed Aaron Burr in the parlor of the house in 1833 and died there in 1865 at the age of 90. 212-923-8008 morrisjumel.org

**Harlem River Speedway Esplanade** Dyckman St. to W 155 St. 20 acres. There are few ways to access the tree lined lane squeezed between the river and Harlem River Drive, stretching from Sherman Creek to about the RFK Bridge. Enter at the north or south ends. The path narrows at the Hamilton Bridge, runs under the historic High Bridge, and through landscaping of cherry and crabapple trees.

**Harlem Lane** W 154 to W 150 St. On the west side of Harlem River Drive, swatches of open space with a playground and ball courts are wedged around bridge ramps.

**Harlem River Park Esplanade** W 145 to W 125 St. 20 acres. The existing greenway was extended to include new landscaping, spray shower, bike path connections, and upland parks, such as the *Crack is Wack* playground featuring a handball court with a Keith Haring mural. Nearby, the salt pile (W 125 St.) is to be relocated opening waterfront access for recreational uses.

## Hell Gate

Hell Gate, or Helegat meaning "bright passage," was named by Dutch navigator Adriaen Block in 1614. It is where the East River meets the Long Island Sound tide from the east and the ocean tide from the south, causing strong currents and frequent whirlpools. Hell Gate is one of the deepest and most dangerous spots in the channel. It runs from about E 100 Street to E 90 Street, An estimated 1000 ships have run aground or sunk here. The greatest single explosion in history, prior to the atom bomb, was ignited in Hell Gate in the 1880s, when over 300,000 pounds of dynamite were blasted to clear such obstructions as Pot Rock, Hog's Back reef, Nigger's Head boulder, Frying Pan Reef, Hallet's Cove Reef, and the nine acre Flood Point Island, the main obstacle to navigation. Though somewhat tamer today, its turbulent waters subject boaters to small whirlpools and currents moving at a swift seven knots.

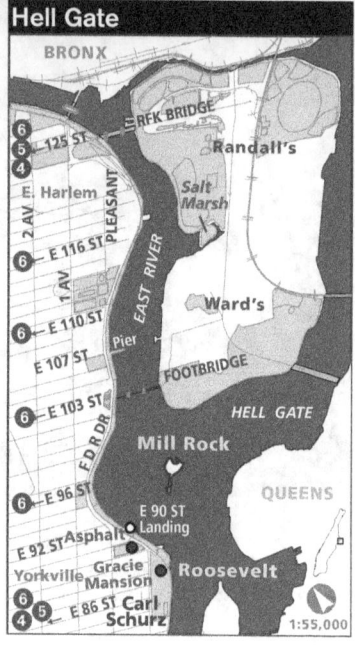

Subway: 4, 5, 6 to E 125 St. transfer to Bus 35 to Randall's Island.

Greenway: Ward's Island Footbridge is open dawn to dusk, April to November.

Blueway: Water Taxi: Randall's Island (events only).

**Randall's & Ward's Island** E 103 St. Footbridge. 272 acres. Really three islands, Ward's, Sunken Meadow, and Randall's, joined by landfill in the 1930s in Robert Moses' Triborough Bridge construction. Three branches of the big bridge merge here and the Hell Gate Bridge trestle bisects the island. A boardwalk crosses swampy Little Hell Gate Inlet to a waterfront path on the west shore, which will become part of an island wide shoreline pathway along areas of habitat restoration and a re-naturalized edge. The Randall's Island Sports Foundation is host to a variety of facilities, including a track and field stadium, baseball diamonds, many soccer fields, and cricket pitches, as well as a state psychiatric hospital, sewage treatment plant, and one of the city's largest homeless shelters. The park offers horseback riding, golf driving range, picnic areas, and nature trails. 212-830-7721 risf.org

**Mill Rock Island** Only accessible by boat, the tiny 2.5 acre island located 1500 feet off Manhattan's E 96 Street housed a tide mill in the 1700s, a fort in 1812, and an Army Corps of Engineers explosives staging area in the late 1940s. Sold to the city in 1953 for $25,000, it is uninhabited today. Its old dock on the south shore was once used to stage events. Mill Rock has returned to a natural state, as an avian habitat and pit stop for kayakers circumnavigating Manhattan Island.

# East River

The East River is not a true river, but a 16 mile long tidal strait flowing through the center of New York City. From Throgs Neck in the Bronx and Fort Totten, Queens, to Brooklyn Heights and Manhattan's Battery, the passage covers 91 miles of shoreline connecting the Upper Bay with the Long Island Sound and linking four of the five boroughs. The East River is a major transportation route with federal channel depths of 35 to 40 feet and a mean tidal range of four to five feet.

The Franklin D. Roosevelt (FDR) Drive, built in 1930s, flanks the river for 9.5 miles, from the Robert F. Kennedy/Triborough Bridge to the Battery. The roadway paved over Sutton Beach, which once provided river bathing just south of the Queensboro Bridge. The shoreline bends at Horn's Hook and Corlear's Hook; "Hook" is Dutch for angle. Much of the FDR Drive is built on landfill. The section from E 30 to E 23 Street is built on the rubble of bombed British cities that arrived as ballast in returning battleships during WWII. Sea termites threaten the wooden pilings supporting parts of the drive and the bulkhead along East River Park. The group East River CREW organizes free Whitehall rowing and youth fishing programs at its shipping container boathouse and davit launch (E 96 St.).

Subway: 4, 5, 6 to E 86, E 96 or E 125 St. Bus: M86 to E 86 St. & York Ave.

Greenway: Manhattan Greenway returns to the waterfront from E 125 to E 63 St. All East River crossings are bike friendly.

**East River Esplanade/Bobby Wagner Walk** E 125 to E 63 St. 3 acres. The oldest section of the walkway, built in 1939 as part of FDR Drive construction. Anglers cast over the rail into the fast currents of the East River. Waterside access at E 120, 111, 103 & 96 streets.

**E 107 Street Pier** A 270 foot long fishing pier with roof and lighting, originally built in 1931 as one of seven commercial piers serving the then industrial waterfront, later converted to a public recreational pier in 1936 as part of Triborough Bridge construction.

**Stanley Isaacs Park** E 95 St. An upland recreational area with a playground and roller hockey rink named for the Manhattan Borough President serving from 1938-41 who oversaw the construction of the East River Drive.

**E 90 Street Landing** Striped bass, weakfish and fluke are said to collect off Horn's Hook, an old fireboat pier converted to an environmental center in the 1980s, and destroyed by fire ten years later. A portion of the pier is used as a ferry and water taxi landing, and seasonal ferry to Yankees and Mets games.

**Asphalt Green** E 90 St. 5.5 acre. A nonprofit state of the art aquatic and athletic center housed inside a former Municipal Asphalt Plant, which at onetime also utilized little Mill Rock Island for youth environmental education programs. The parabolic arch shaped building overlooks FDR Drive from the westside of the roadway. asphaltgreen.org

**Carl Schurz Park** East End Ave., E 90 to E 83 St. 15 acres. The park, built over the East River Drive (FDR Drive), was named in 1910 for the German revolutionary, American soldier, statesman and *New York Tribune* editor (1829–1906). Mature plane trees and garden-lined paths lead to Gracie Mansion and sweeping views of Hell Gate. John Finley Walk is the name given the waterfront esplanade, which is marked by a silhouette of a walking figure with a pole. There is a playground and dog run. A bronze sculpture of Peter Pan erected at E 87 Street was created in 1928 for the old Paramount Theater in Times Square. The NYPD Scuba Unit had to rescue the 1000 pound statue after vandals threw it into the East River in 1998.

**Gracie Mansion** East End Ave. & E 88 St. The elegant Federal style mansion, originally built in 1799 on the country estate of shipping magnate Archibald Gracie, has been the official mayoral residence since Fiorello LaGuardia in 1942. Open Wednesdays, tours by reservations. 212-570-4773

## Turtle Bay

Edgar Allen Poe wrote of afternoons spent rowing in a little cove named for the large population of turtles inhabiting it. Turtle Bay and a creek that emptied into the East River were filled in 1868. A cluster of renowned medical centers, including Memorial Sloan-Kettering Cancer Center, New York-Presbyterian Hospital, Weill Cornell Medical Center, and Rockefeller University, partition much of the waterfront. A few of the centers extend over six lanes of FDR Drive. The neighborhoods of Sutton Place (E 59 to E 53 St.) and Beekman Place (E 51 to E 49 St.) are wealthy enclaves on a rocky bluff above the swift currents of the East River. The locales owe the names to Effingham B. Sutton, a shipping merchant and prospector who built roughhouses at E 58 Street in 1875, and James Beekman, who built his mansion, Mount Pleasant, on the river at E 50 Street in 1764. A parlor and bedroom from the original Beekman house is on exhibit at the New York Historical Society.

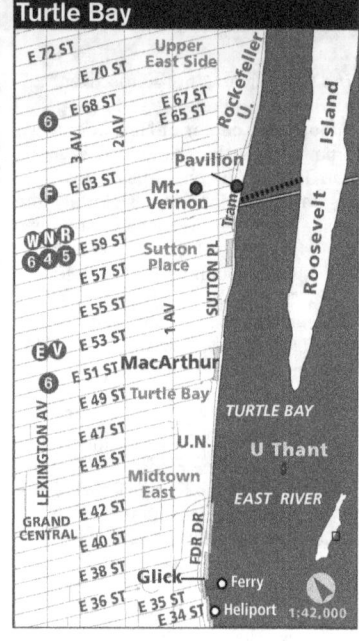

Slums by the early 1900s, the short streets ending at the river were notorious for gangs, and later immortalized Sidney Kingsley's 1935 play and film *Dead End* and by the Dead End Kids movies. Animals were barged to slaughterhouses that once occupied the site of the United Nations complex. Across First Avenue, Tudor City was built by Fred F. French in the 1920s on a former shantytown on Corcoran's Bluff, cliffs named for a local gang. Its apartments were faced inland to avoid the industry that then dominated this waterfront.

The Morgan's and Vanderbilt's migrated east from Fifth Avenue to Sutton Place in the 1920s, to the neighborhood fostered by shipping merchant Effingham Sutton who built brownstones in the midst of coal yards, tenements, and breweries. The prominent residents anchored their yachts in the East River for speedy sail to Wall Street. In the 1940s, gardens that once sloped downhill to private docks were bulldozed for construction of the East River Drive built underneath Sutton Place. The gardens were replanted on decking atop the highway and leased back to residents for $1 a year. Dead end streets have been rehabilitated into small parks. East River Drive separates the waterfront from inland neighborhoods.

Ongoing reconstruction of the bulkhead and the roadway promises to improve water access, eventually completing a continuous paved greenway along the entire riverfront. New sections of the riverside esplanade run from E 60 to E 63 streets, while planned future phases extend the path south to E 54 Street.

Subway: 4, 5, 6 to E 59 St. or Grand Central Terminal/E 42 St.

Greenway: The greenway is interrupted by FDR Drive from E 63 to E 38 St., when cyclists must travel on 2 Ave. street lanes to E 37 St.

**Rockefeller University** York Ave. & E 66 St. 15 acres. Enjoy the landscaped public gardens and river views from one of the foremost biomedical research centers in the world, founded by John D. Rockefeller in 1901. The campus is home to 23 Nobel Prize recipients and 15 Beaux Arts buildings. rockefeller.edu

**Mount Vernon Hotel** 421 E 61 St. Once the carriage house of the Abigail Adams riverfront estate built in 1795, the stone building provided accommodation for travelers journeying into the wilds of uptown from 1826 until 1833. It opened as a museum in 1939 operated by Colonial Dames of America. 212-838-6878 mvhm.org

**East River Pavilion** E 60 St. 2 acres. A former garbage transfer

station, readapted with an open deck exposing the steel superstructure and topped by Alice Aycock's sculpture *East River Roundabout*, being revamped. ⚒

**Sutton Parks** York Ave. E 59 to E 53 St. Five vest pocket, street-end parks overlooking the East River. The brick courtyard of Sutton Place Park (E 57 to E 56 St.) offers classic Woody Allen *Manhattan* views of the Queensboro Bridge. A bronze replica of *Porcellino*, a wild boar statue by Renaissance sculptor Pietro Tacca centers the little park. The E 54 Street park features an Armillary Sphere by Albert Stewart.

**Peter Detmold Park** E 49 to E 51 St. An elegant garden, sitting area, and dog run west of the FDR Drive with a footbridge over the roadway to a tiny riverfront sitting area, fishing spot and esplanade.

**MacArthur Park** E 49 St. The upland park, named for General Douglas MacArthur, offers a playground, spray shower, and unobstructed views.

**United Nations Headquarters** E 46 to E 42 St. Designed by a team of eleven architects from around the world, the three building complex on 18 acres of waterfront, includes the tall glass Secretariat, the sloping General Assembly hall, and the Conference Building on land donated by John D. Rockefeller. On "international territory" since 1951, flags of the 192 member states decorate U.N. Plaza. The north lawn overlooking the river has a public sculpture garden and memorial to Eleanor Roosevelt. One interesting work is the Evgeniy Vuchetich sculpture *Let Us Beat Swords into Plowshares*, a gift from the Soviet Union in 1959. Tours are offered daily, providing access to an outdoor promenade and the General Assembly lobby to see Foucault's pendulum. The property is getting a major overhaul, and when completed in 2014 will include a new park cantilevered over the Franklin Delano Roosevelt (FDR) Drive along the East River Esplanade from E 51 Street to E 41 Street. 212-963-8687 un.org

**Con Edison Waterfront** E 41 to E 38 St. A new section of East River esplanade and park are promised by the developers of the huge former Con Edison plant real estate site. ✸

# Roosevelt Island

Roosevelt Island is a 2.5 mile long narrow strip of land with over 140 acres of parkland about 300 yards offshore in the East River. Native Americans called it Minnehanak, meaning "a great place to live," and the Dutch colonists called it Hog Island. John Manning, Sheriff of New York, was exiled there in disgrace for cowardice after surrendering Fort Amsterdam on Governors Island back to the Dutch in 1673. The island was inherited by his step-daughter and his son-in-law Robert Blackwell in 1686 and was called Blackwell's Island for many years. In 1828, the City of New York purchased the property for $32,500 and began moving institutions, such as the penitentiary, insane asylum, debtor's prison, and contagious disease hospital to the remote island. The horror of the lunatic asylum was described by Charles Dickens in 1842 and years later by journalist Nellie Bly in *Ten Days in a Mad House*. Among

the State Penitentiary's inmates were anarchist Emma Goldman, birth control advocate Margaret Sanger, actress Mae West, and singer Billie Holiday. Renamed Welfare Island by 1921, its institutional populations reached 10,000 by the 1940s. In the 1970s architects John Burgee and Philip Johnson began transforming it to their idea of a utopian community; the island was then renamed for Franklin D. Roosevelt. Though part of the borough of Manhattan, Roosevelt Island is governed by a state agency, the Roosevelt Island Operating Corporation under a lease arrangement with the city.

The river splits around the island. Boats must navigate the swift waters of the west channel because the east channel has only 40 feet of clearance. There is bridge access from Queens, but by far the best and most interesting way to get to the island is by aerial cable car, North America's only commuter tram. Providing magnificent skyline views since 1976, it carries riders 250 feet above the East River. The world's first energy delivery from tidal turbines was demonstrated in the east channel by hydropower energy to Roosevelt Island's supermarket. Another uniquely Roosevelt Island utility is the only automated vacuum trash collection system in the country, whereby garbage is transported at 55 mph through underground tunnels to a compactor. The islet also boasts six landmark structures on the National Register of Historic Places, including Octagon Tower, Renwick Ruins, Blackwell Lighthouse, Strecker Lab, Blackwell House, and Chapel of the Good Shepherd, most built with island quarried Fordham gneiss stone. 212-832-4540 rioc.org

Subway: F to Roosevelt Island

Aerial Tramway: Departs from E 59 St. at 2 Ave. every 15 minutes.

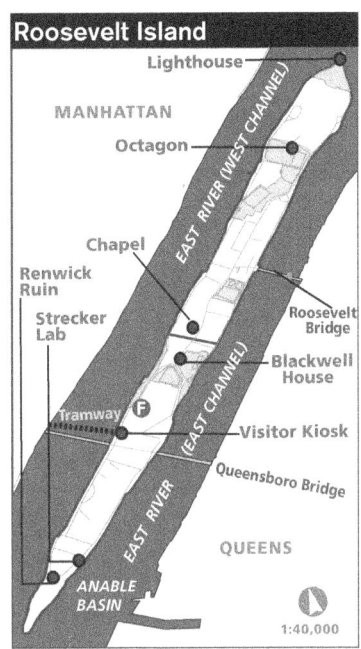

Greenway: Bicycles are permitted on the tram, avoid rush hours. The island has 4 miles of bike path.

**Waterfront Esplanade** A broad esplanade runs along the seawall fringing the island's perimeter offering spectacular views of the Manhattan skyline. On the western shore, Tom Otterness' whimsical bronze sculpture installation The *Marriage of Money and Real Estate* is revealed at low tide.

**Lighthouse Park** 2.8 acres. On the northern tip of the island, broad green lawns and picnic grounds around Blackwell Lighthouse, the 50 foot tall Gothic structure built by convict labor in 1872 to guide ships through the choppy waters of the East River. The light was designed by James Renwick Jr., architect of St. Patrick's Cathedral and Grace Church.

**Octagon Ecological Park** 15 acres. An octagon tower is all that remains of America's first municipal lunatic asylum, designed by Alexander Jefferson Davis, architect of Federal Hall on Wall Street. The eight sided structure is now the entrance lobby for a "green" apartment building and the adjoining park features native plants, and soccer fields on the western shore.

**Capobianco Field** Baseball fields, playground, and ball courts on the east side of the island, just south of the Roosevelt Island Bridge.

**Blackwell Park** A new little park and playground on the western shoreline flanking the pale-blue, two-story clapboard Blackwell Farmhouse, the island's oldest house (1796) that was home to the Blackwell from 1686 to 1828. Amazing river views can be had from the back porch.

**Visitor Kiosk** A restored 1909 trolley kiosk, from the old Queenboro Bridge trolley line which made stops midway on the bridge to let passengers descend by elevator to Roosevelt Island. The information center is operated by the Roosevelt Island Historical Society. rihs.us

**Southpoint Park** 12 acres. Surrounded by water on three sides, the south end of the island is unsurpassed for watching the Fourth of July fireworks display over the Manhattan skyline and East River bridges. Community planners hope to reuse the historic remains of the small pox hospital and the mostly buried foundation of the old City Hospital, next to new natural areas, waterfront promenade and boathouse. An old plan calls for a Louis Kahn designed Franklin D. Roosevelt Memorial that critics claim will obstruct views and destroy much of the natural shore.

**Strecker Memorial Lab** The façade of the old lab, opened in 1892 as the nation's first pathological and bacteriological research center, has been salvaged as a subway substation.

**Renwick Castle** At night, lights illuminate the landmark "picturesque" ruin of the 1856 Gothic Revival smallpox hospital designed by James Renwick, Jr. Currently inaccessible, but planners hope to readapt it as a cafe and gardens. It is best viewed from the East River Esplanade at E 51 Street.

**Belmont Island** An artificial island built up on Man-o'-War reef by landfill from the Steinway Street trolley tunnel dig under the river, a project completed by August Belmont in 1907 and used for the 7 Subway line. The island has commonly been called U Thant Island because of the large metal "oneness arch" placed by Sri Chimnoy as tribute

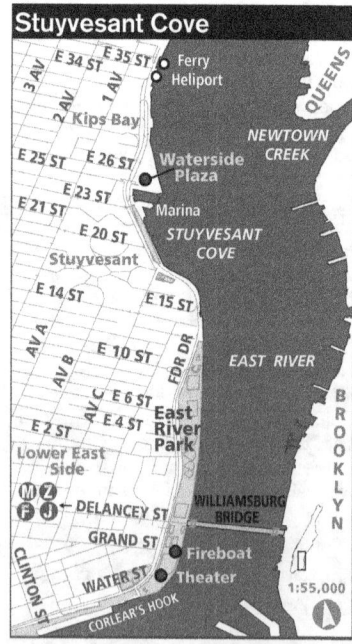

**Stuyvesant Cove**

to the late U.N. Secretary-General. Green navigation buoy #17 sits on top of an antenna tower. No public access, but observers can delight in a colony of the Double-crested Cormorant nesting on the rocks.

## Stuyvesant Cove

Farms and estates once occupied the land on the Midtown East waterfront. The neighborhood of Kips Bay is on top of a small embayment that was named after 17th century Dutch farmer Jacobus Kip who owned the land around the inlet. The bay was filled, but kept the name. The shoreline, dominated by Con Edison's Waterside Steam Plant (E 41– E 37 Sts.) for over 100 years, is undergoing significant change. The 10 acre property has been cleared for development, and sooner or later high residential towers will overshadow this shore, but will include riverside park space. A biotech incubator billed as "harbor views and world-class medical science," is being built farther south as part of the East River Science Park with a public waterfront esplanade.

The famed gashouse district occupied the East River shore starting at E 34 Street, named for large coal burning power plants. In recent years, extensive repairs have been done to the East River seawall, recreational facilities, and other infrastructure. The area, also notorious for its red light district, was once the busiest shipbuilding center in the nation, with thirty yards in operation by 1832. The schooner *America*, for which the America's Cup is named, was built at William H. Brown Shipyard on the East Village shore. An anchor pulled from the river is displayed in East River Park as a memorial to the local shipbuilding legacy. The opening scene of Moby Dick takes place in a shanty town in Corlear's Hook, where the East River curves south at the Lower East Side. Before WWII, 25 working piers lined the river from East River Park south to Brooklyn Bridge.

Subway: 6 to E 34, E 23 or Union Square/E 14 St.; F to Delancey St.; J, M, Z to Delancey/Essex; L to 1 Ave.

Greenway: The path picks up at E 37 St. on the service road, then narrows near the E 15 St. Con Edison fuel docks.

Blueway: E 35 St. Ferry Terminal supports a water taxi, commuter ferry, and express ferry to Yankees and Mets games.

**East River Esplanade** E 41 St. to East River Park. The shore walkway follows the marginal road from E 30 to E 25 Street, past the E 34 Street Heliport, ferry terminal, parking lots, Water Club seafood restaurant, Skyline Marina, and Waterside Plaza to Stuyvesant Cove.

**Glick Park** E 38 to E 36 St.
A fragment of riverside esplanade, plantings, and seating below the elevated E 42 Street exit ramp.

**Waterside Plaza** E 28 to E 25 St.
An isolated windswept rooftop garden with six acres of landscaping amid the four towers of the only residential complex east of the FDR Drive, constructed in 1974 on 2,000 cement pilings driven 80 feet deep into the river bed. Steps go down to the water. The open space offers public programs like outdoor movie nights and youth fishing clinics. Access by footbridge at E 25 Street. watersideplaza.com

**Skyport Marina Pier** E 23 St.
A 36-slip marina hosting big excursion boats, the NY Health & Racket Club Yacht, *Rocket* sportfishing charters, and pleasure craft alongside amphibious seaplanes, which take-off and land on the river is on the north side of the six story parking garage.

**Stuyvesant Cove Park** E 23 to 18 St. 2 acres. Curvy paths wind through natural landscaping by Solar One, a sun-powered environmental center. A sandy little beach has formed in the cove on top of pier pilings and debris dumped off docks once occupied by a cement plant. Human powered boaters hope to utilize the space for launching a community boating program. stuyvesantcove.org

**East River Park** (John V. Lindsay Park) E 12 St. to Montgomery St. 57 acres. The breezy waterside park, originally built in 1939, features views of the river and the industrial Brooklyn waterfront. A wide tree-lined esplanade

## East River Piers

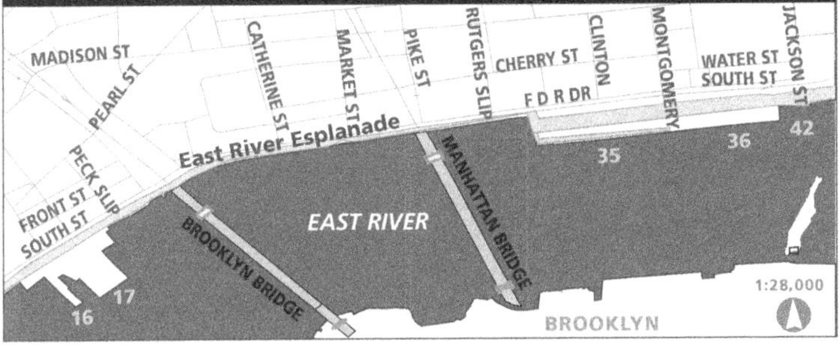


spans 20 blocks flanking baseball diamonds, tennis courts, running track, athletic fields, playgrounds, barbecue pits, and water sprays. The riverside promenade closed for over three years due to bulkhead and seawall reconstruction to repair damage to wooden pilings from ship worms and marine borers is scheduled to reopen in 2010. Footbridges over FDR Drive are at E 10, E 6, Houston, Delancey, and Cherry Streets.

**Fireboat House** Grand St.
An historic fireboat house re-purposed as an environmental center, the building and nearby community gardens are operated by the Lower East Side Ecology Center. 212-477-4022 lesecologycenter.org

**Corlear's Hook Amphitheater**
The original home of Joseph Papp's Shakespeare in the Park offers summer concerts and performances in the landmark theater.

**Piers 42, 36 & 35** Jackson St. to Rutgers Slip. The old coffee and banana piersheds run parallel to the East River Esplanade. The piers will be enhanced with plantings, boardwalks, and viewing decks. Pier 42 is envisioned as a future urban beach. A 16 foot wide public promenade with sitting area and picnic tables travels the waterside of the shed of Pier 36, where Basketball City has plans to occupy a portion of the pier shed now used by the Sanitation Department. Pier 35, the 80 by 400 foot structure at Rutgers Slip is being rebuilt with a new esplanade. Transient docks will rim the new wharf. ⚒

## Seaport District

The South Street Historic District is an area of restored 18th and 19th century buildings encompassing 11 square blocks from Pearl Street east to South Street and Peck Slip south to Burling Slip. It was the city's first port, called "The Street of Ships" where soaring masts were its "skyscrapers." The East River, protected from wind and waves and free of ice, provided an ideal port for sailing ships. The shore here was swampy when the Dutch began re-shaping the coast, digging boat basins or "slips" that extended inland about two blocks. By the turn of the century, ships had outgrown the little basins and tied up at piers and wharves. In time, the slips were filled.

Herman Melville sent Ahab to sea on this crowded riverfront. At one time, the sailing ships on this stretch of piers moved one third of the world's merchant tonnage. A public

market operated on the site of the Tin Building since 1836, later occupied by Fulton Fish Market until 2005. Thomas Edison's first power plant was located at 40 Fulton Street. The historic district was drawn in 1977, extended in 1989, and is on the State and National Registers of Historic Places. The district's oldest building is at 45 Peck Slip.

<u>Subway</u>: 2, 3, 4, 5, J, Z or M to Fulton St.; A, C to Broadway-Nassau, 1 to South Ferry; N or R to Whitehall St.

<u>Greenway</u>: A divided bike lane extends from East River Park to the Seaport and Pier 11, tapering from Old Slip to the Battery Maritime Building then linking with Battery Park and westside paths. The tight path is being made wider to as part of pier rehabilitation including glass pavilions under the FDR Drive viaduct.

<u>Blueway</u>: Commuter Ferries Pier 11/Wall St.; Water Taxi Pier 17

**The Slips** Expectations for Rutgers Slip and Peck Slip include "get-down" steps down leading into the water. In addition, a redesigned Peck Slip features a green park and broad Belgian-blocked piazza. A children's playground devised for Burling Slip will be completed in 2010.

**Two Bridges Beach** On the esplanade below the Manhattan and Brooklyn Bridges, a landscaped path and sitting area feature interpretive signage describing the history of this storied waterfront. A 250 foot long mud flat has built up under the Brooklyn Bridge. Broader access is sought to the little beach, which is used as a rest stop by kayakers.

**New Market Building & Tin Building** Fishmongers sold as much as a million pounds of fish a night at the nation's oldest wholesale fish market, which occupied the 1939 New Market and 1903 landmark Tin Building from 1835

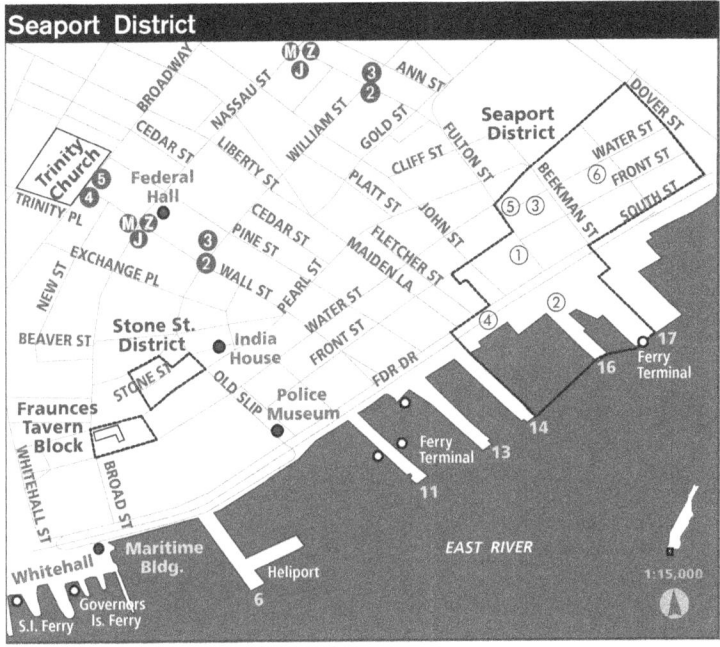

to 2005, when the 180 year old Fulton Fish Market moved to Hunts Point in the Bronx and became the world's second largest fish market.

**Pier 17 Seaport Mall** The pier, conceived as a "festive marketplace" was converted to a shopping mall in the 1980s, hosting national retailers, viewing decks, and a food court looking out on the East River and Brooklyn Bridge. The owner, General Growth, has floated plans to redevelop the space, but economic downturns have left the future to speculation. The north face of the pier will become a seasonal Water Taxi Beach complete with sand and cabana bar. 212-SEA-PORT southstreetseaport.com

**South Street Seaport Museum** 12 Fulton St. Established in 1967 by a group of maritime enthusiasts, the museum occupies a complex of restored buildings housing several galleries in the Seaport District and historic ships berthed at Pier 16. It recreates and chronicles the history of the Port of New York, hosts historic tours, and conducts numerous programs recounting days of China clippers, merchant schooners, and sailing packets. Museum docents have an opportunity to learn maritime trades and seamanship first-hand aboard the historic vessels. 212-748-8600 southstseaport.org

**Seaport Points of Interest:**

① **Schermerhorn Row** The row of Georgian-style red brick counting houses on Manhattan's oldest block was constructed in 1812 and was the first in the country to be lit by electricity. This was once the site of the Fulton Ferry Hotel and Sloppy Louie's eatery so pungently recalled by Joseph Mitchell in *Up in the Old Hotel*.

It's now occupied by the main gallery and offices of the Seaport Museum.

② **Pier 16 Historic Ship's Pier**
The largest private collection of historic vessels in the nation are berthed here, such as the schooner *Pioneer*, 1885 square rigged iron-hulled *Wavetree*, and the lightship *Ambrose*.

③ **Bowne & Co.** 211 Water St. A re-created full service letterpress and stationers of one founded in 1775 by Robert Bowne.

④ **Maritime Crafts Center**
Watch museum master craftsmen carve figureheads and build ship models in their dockside studio.

⑤ **Titanic Memorial Park** Pearl & Water Sts. The triangle park holds the lighthouse monument that pays tribute to those who died aboard *RMS Titanic* in 1912. It has marked the gateway to the Seaport Historic District since 1976, and was originally on top of the Seamen's Institute at South Street and Coenties Slip from 1915 to 1967.

⑥ **Seaman's Church Institute Gallery** 241 Water St. Established in 1834. A model ship gallery on the ground floor is open to the public. 212-349-9090 seamenschurch.org

**Pier 15** Maiden Lane. The piling field will be replaced by a new two-tiered pier for historic vessel docking and a rooftop park with cafes and open space. ✯ (2012)

**Piers 13 & 14** Rehabilitation of the former tennis bubble piers includes pile replacement and new decking. ✯

**Pier 11** Wall St. A busy commuter ferry landing with glass terminal, snack bar, and seating along the deck enroute to the gangways.

**Pier 6 Downtown Heliport.** One of three city skyports offering helicopter sightseeing rides and passenger transit. 212-943-5959

## Stone Street District

Before the Dutch began shifting the shore with landfill and artificial inlets, Manhattan's ancient waterfront rimmed the cobbled streets of what is now the Stone Street Historic District. Waves lapped the storefronts on Pearl Street and the eastern edge of Hanover Square in the 16th century. A narrow stream on present day Broad Street was dredged for a canal with a wide promenade and bridge reminiscent of Amsterdam. The shoreline was pushed out by piling rubble on top of the hulls of sunken ships. In 1982, an old British merchant frigate was excavated at 175 Water Street.

The historic district encompasses the area bounded by Stone, Pearl, Hanover Square, and South William Streets. These are some of New York City's most notable streets, first laid out by the Dutch more than 350 years ago. Stone Street was the first paved street in New York. The Stock Exchange was founded in 1792 under a buttonwood tree at the foot of Wall Street.

The Tontine Coffee House where the seed of revolution brewed in colonial New York stood at the northwest corner of Pearl and Wall. The pirate Captain William Kidd lived in the neighborhood keeping a pew at Trinity Church and Herman Melville was born at a house at 6 Pearl Street on August 1, 1819. William Bradford established New York's first printing press, "The Sign of the Bible," at 81 Pearl Street making Hanover Square the center of the city's publishing and printing industries. Delmonico's, America's first restaurant, was founded by a Swiss sea captain at 23 William Street in 1827, later relocating to Beaver Street. Jews settled on Mill Lane and built the city's first synagogue and ritual baths from natural springs.

The area was devastated in the Great Fire of 1835 with over 500 buildings destroyed. Downtown was quickly rebuilt of brick and granite rather than wood. Many of the buildings erected after the fire still stand. In the 1990s the crooked old Dutch alley Stone Street was renovated with gray cobblestone and bluestone sidewalks duplicating the original paving. The district was landmarked, preserving this part of old New York.

**India House** 1 Hanover Square. Private club India House founded by merchant shippers interested in foreign trade in 1914 is still active in the landmark Italianate palazzo, originally built as Hanover Bank in 1854. Bayard's restaurant takes over the space in the evening, when diners can enjoy the club's outstanding maritime collection. 212-269-2323 indiahouseclub.org

**NYC Police Museum** 100 Old Slip. Plaza in the shape of a police badge next door to the historic building designed as the NYPD's First Precinct. 212-480-3100 nycpolice-museum.org

**Fraunces Tavern Museum** 54 Pearl St. The 1719 yellow brick house where Washington said farewell to his officers is also the site of the founding of the New York Yacht Club. The museum, dedicated to the history of American liberty, also comprises four adjacent 19th century buildings saved from demolition by the Sons of the Revolution. Open to the public with exhibits. 212-425-1778 frauncestavernmuseum.org

**Federal Hall National Memorial** 26 Wall St. George Washington was inaugurated here in 1789. The first Congress met here in 1790 to draft the Bill of Rights in Federal Hall in the new nation's first Capitol. Today's Greek Revival landmark was erected on the site in 1842 as the Customs House. The Federal Reserve System was established here in 1913. Open to the public with exhibits administered by the National Park Service. 212-825-6888 nps.gov/feha

**Trinity Church & Cemetery** 74 Trinity Pl. The 140 foot spire of the Anglican church was once the tallest sight on the island. The church owned all the land from Broadway to the Hudson River, which then washed up against the cemetery retaining walls. Columbia University was founded in 1754 as King's College in rooms borrowed from the church. The present church was consecrated in 1846 and is now surrounded by skyscrapers. Trinity Parish still owns some downtown properties. The cemetery holds the remains of many prominent Americans, including: Alexander Hamilton, first Secretary of the Treasury; Robert Fulton, inventor of the steamboat; Navy Capt. James Lawrence who cried "Don't give up the ship" in the War of 1812; Silas Talbot, Commander of the *USS Constitution*; William Bradford, printer; John Jacob Astor, fur trader; and John James Audubon, artist.

# The Bronx

The only borough that is not an island, the Bronx is a peninsula bounded on three sides by 75 miles of shoreline—on the west by the Hudson and Harlem Rivers, on the south by the Bronx Kill and East River, and on the east by Long Island Sound. Named for Swedish sea captain Jonas Bronck, who settled land between the Harlem River and "Bronck's River" in 1638, the Bronx offers a rich variety of environments, from bucolic cliffs over the Hudson in the west to a rustbelt waterfront to the east. It's all worth exploring.

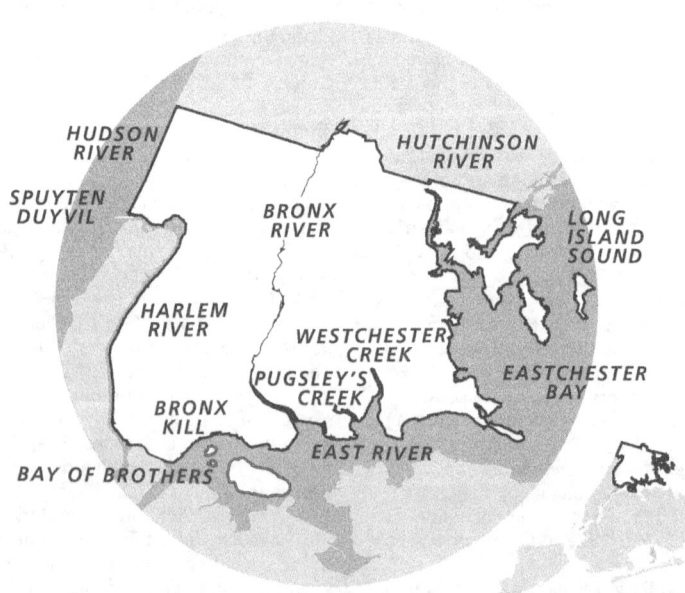

# Hudson River

The Hudson River edges three miles of shoreline in the northwest corner of the Bronx. Here Riverdale and its attractive streets and parkland sit on a high-forested bluff commanding superb views of the river and the New Jersey Palisades. Steep slopes descend to the Hudson, overlooked by rock outcrops. Along the high ridge, landscaped open spaces like the private 70 acre campus of the College of Mount St. Vincent and the grounds of the Passionist Monastery Retreat take in spectacular views. The gardens of Wave Hill are the only public access at this vantage.

The green, hilly northwest corner of the Bronx has long been a favored suburb of Manhattan. Since the New York Central Railroad built the Hudson Line five feet above the high tide mark in the 1860s, the community has been effectively cut off from the water. In 1852, the day liner *Henry Clay* burned on the banks of Riverdale when a fire broke out in the steam boilers after the captain of the side-wheeler raced a rival vessel from Albany to New York City. At least 80 were lost in the disaster. The elegant Riverdale Yacht Club, founded in 1931, affords members water access, riverside dining, swimming pool and tennis courts. Recently, Metro-North has created small parks providing shore access at its stations in Riverdale and Spuyten Duyvil.

The Spuyten Duyvil Creek was a narrow channel that separated Manhattan Island from the Bronx mainland and connected the Hudson to the Harlem River. The city's first bridge, Kings Bridge, once spanned the creek, whose Dutch name means "in spite of the devil" and recalls the fate of a brave 17th century colonist who swam across its rough waters to warn of an English attack. He drowned sounding the alarm trumpet to his last breath.

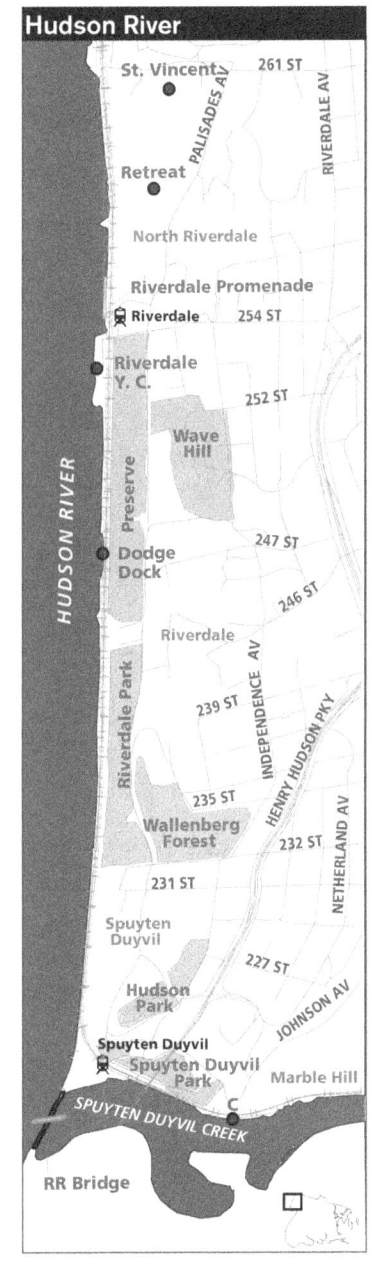

Subway: 1 to W 231 St.; A to W 207 St. ; Metro-North to Riverdale.

Greenway: Palisades Ave. has an onstreet bike lane. There are plans to open a bike trail in Riverdale Park.

**Riverdale Station Promenade** W 254 St. Metro-North provides Riverdale's only direct access to the Hudson River by way of a bridge over the rail tracks to a tiny promenade with fishing platforms.

**Riverdale Park Preserve** Palisades Ave. from W 232 to W 254 Sts. 97 acres. From a rustic high ridge sloping down to the river, trails pass through deep ravines, wetlands, dense forests of oak, black birch, hickory, 100-foot-tall tulip trees, and a freshwater stream. Two old lime kilns and the oldest extant pier on the Hudson −19th century Dodge Dock (W 247 St.) −are located here. Rail tracks block river access. Across the street is the Rauol Wallenberg Forest. The preserve is a Forever Wild Site. riverdalenature.org

**Wave Hill** 675 W 252 St. 28 acres. Beautiful gardens, rolling lawns, and scenic vistas from a bluff above Riverdale Park in a country estate once home to Theodore Roosevelt, Mark Twain and Arturo Toscanini. The arboretum property was deeded to the city in 1960. wavehill.org

**Henry Hudson Memorial Park** Kappock St. & Independence Ave. 9 acres. The explorer's namesake park sits on a hill with scarcely a water view just above a spot where he anchored the *Half Moon* in 1609. A bronze statue of Hudson by Karl Bitter faces the river from atop a towering Doric column, a memorial completed in 1936.

**Spuyten Duyvil Shorefront Park** Edsall Ave. & Spuyten Duyvil Metro-North Station. 6.5 acres. A little triangle at the confluence of the Hudson and Harlem Rivers extending to the northern foot of the Henry Hudson Bridge with wooded trails winding to an overlook high above the river.

# Harlem River

The city's early passion for rowing was nurtured on the flat waters of the Harlem River in the 1800s. Rival clubs built boathouses along the shore, on summer weekends hundreds pulled oars as more watched from the grand promenade on the High Bridge. The first female crew rowed the Harlem in the 1930s. Today, it is home to Columbia University's Crew, whose Class of 1929 Boathouse sits across the river from Columbia Rock, a cliff of Fordham gneiss ancient bedrock, painted with a blue varsity "C" 60 feet tall, on the Bronx side.

Separating the Bronx and Manhattan, the river is a 7.5 mile long tidal strait joining the Hudson River at Spuyten Duyvil and the East River at Hell Gate. Depths vary from 12 to 26 feet, and widths from 400 to 620 feet, widest at the High Bridge. It is spanned by 15 bridges, including six swing, three arch, and one lift, all providing at least 24 feet of clearance. The Spuyten Duyvil Railroad Swing Bridge provides only five feet of clearance and is opened about every 20 minutes to allow the Circle Liner to pass. Boats on the river must observe "no wake" zones for much of its length.

The Harlem River was once much wider and bound by intertidal marshes. There has been extensive filling, bulk heading, and commercial development along both banks, and the Harlem River Ship Canal set straight the river and cut 14 miles off the route around Manhattan from Long Island Sound. In 1895 the building of the canal transformed the landscape here. With the Spuyten Duyvil Creek filled, the former island of Marble Hill became an appendage of the Bronx, though it retains a Manhattan address.

Access to the Bronx shore is blocked by the Major Deegan Expressway and railroad tracks. Since 1929, a highly visible marker has been

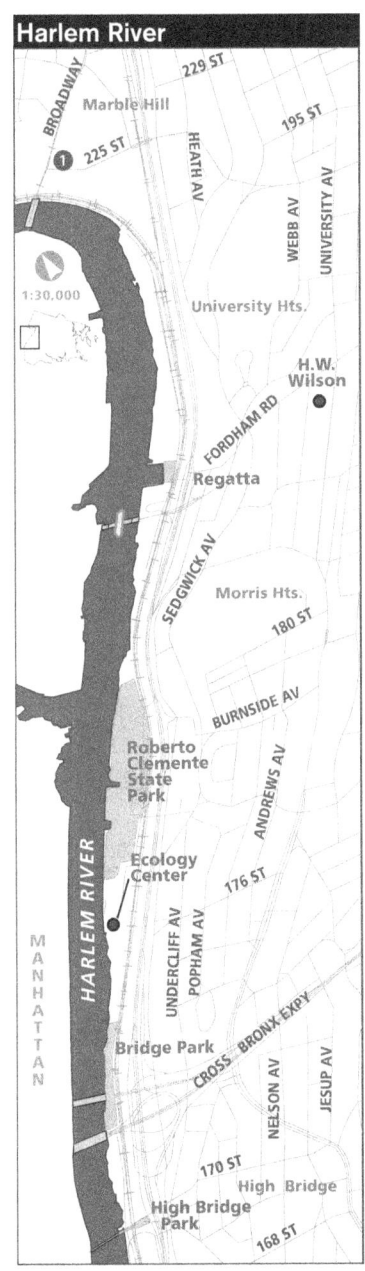

the publisher H.W. Wilson Company's ornamental lighthouse. The Macombs family mill and dam operated on these shores, not far from the "House that Ruth Built," razed to make way for a new modern Yankee Stadium.

Subway: 1 to W 225 St. Marble Hill; 4 to 138 St. Grand Concourse; W 161 St. for Yankee Stadium; 4 to Burnside. Metro-North to Yankee Stadium.

Greenway: Harlem River Greenway is a 3.5 mile path adjacent to the Major Deegan linking Roberto Clemente State Park to Depot Place, which can be reached from High Bridge Park by the W 170 step-street, one of the Bronx's many step streets, consisting of 171 stone stairs.

Blueway: Yankee Stadium Landing ferry service from N.J. and Manhattan during baseball season.

**Regatta Park** End of W Fordham Rd. 1 acre. A parcel just north of University Heights Bridge will provide much needed waterfront access and open space when completed. ✘

**Roberto Clemente State Park**
W Tremont Ave. & Mattewson Rd. 25 acres. Honoring the Puerto Rican baseball star, the waterfront park features a 1.25 mile long bike path, swimming pool, riverside esplanade, ball fields, playgrounds, and barbecue areas. There are plans for a new boathouse to accommodate several local crew teams. 718-299-8750 nyparks.state.ny.us

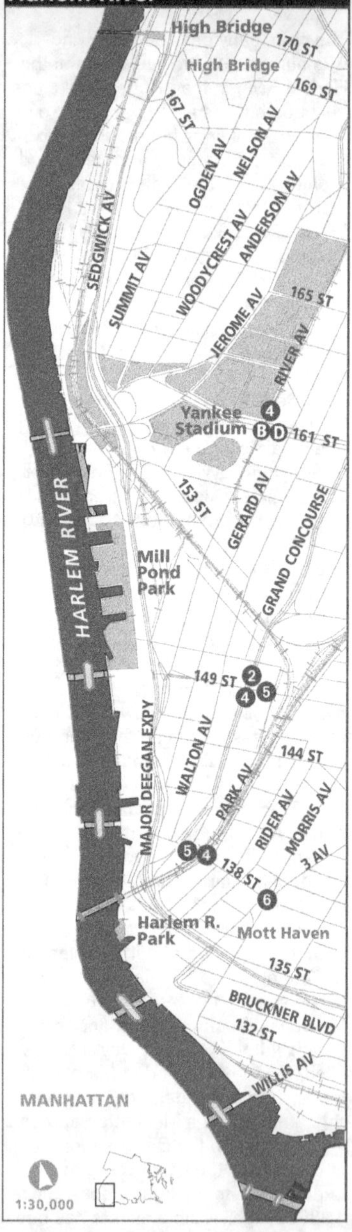

**Bridge Park** W 174 St. to Depot Pl. 3.4 acres. A small park under the Hamilton Bridge connects to the Harlem River Greenway and offers exceptional views of the High Bridge and cliffs across the river. ⚒

**High Bridge Park** University Ave. at W 170 St. 1 acre. A small green space on a ridge above the river at the Bronx base of the pedestrian only High Bridge. The landmark 1838 crossing is the city's oldest standing bridge; part of the Old Croton Aqueduct system that carried water from upstate reservoirs. Under restoration, it is due to reopen in 2012.

**Mill Pond Park** Harlem River & E 149 St. 10 acres. The new park sports a public esplanade, sand beach, and new piers providing significant river access alongside a tennis center, café, and ice rink housed in an old Power House, as part of redevelopment of Yankee Stadium and Gateway Center, the long derelict Bronx Terminal Market, once the busiest wholesale market in the country. (2010)

**South Bronx Harlem River Waterfront Park** Foot of Park Ave. 1 acre. Rare open space and community boating access in the Mott Haven/Port Morris neighborhoods is envisioned at this spot below the rail bridge, near the Harlem River Yard waste transfer station where rail cars are loaded with city garbage bound for landfills in neighboring states. ⚒

## Bronx Kill

A slender mile-long strait connecting the Harlem to the East Rivers, Bronx Kill separates the South Bronx and Randall's Island. The Hell Gate and Triborough (now Robert F. Kennedy) Bridges span the tiny passageway. The Kill touches the banks of the city's heaviest industrial district, the Port Morris and Mott Haven neighborhoods.

The neglected watercourse runs almost dry at low tide, making it possible to wade across rocks (and debris) to Randall's Island, which is part of the borough of Manhattan. It is navigable by kayak or canoe only at high tide, but paddlers warn of extremely low clearance under decaying concrete beams carrying Con Edison electrical feeder cables to the islet. There is no legal waterfront access along the Bronx shore and a fence hampers passage to the island from the shallow channel. Advocates are working to create public open space and access, including a proposal to open a connector bridge to the athletic fields on Randall's Island using a path under the Hell Gate Bridge railroad trestle, which will tie into the South Bronx Greenway. This planned conduit over the channel at grade level will make the Bronx Kill completely unnavigable. Canoers and kayakers need at least six feet of clearance at mean high tide to continue to enjoy this quiet little waterway in which many see so much potential.

# East River

The Bronx shore of the East River is a classic urban industrial waterfront, stretching six miles from the Harlem River to Long Island Sound, and a total of 14 miles from the Sound to Upper New York Bay. Technically a strait, the river is subject to tidal flow from both the Sound and New York Harbor. The river is shallow near shore, but there is a 35 foot channel between Port Morris and the Throgs Neck Bridge; beyond, depths reach 100 feet between the Throgs Neck and Whitestone Bridges.

The worst maritime disaster in New York City history occurred off the Bronx East River shore in 1904, when the steamboat *General Slocum* burst into flames while carrying German immigrant families from the Lower East Side to an annual church picnic. By the time the poorly equipped boat beached on North Brother Island, just east of Port Morris, more than 1,000 lives were lost, mostly women and children. The Captain was blamed for the tragedy and "sent up the river" to Sing Sing Prison. The tragedy is remembered by a *General Slocum* memorial in Manhattan's Tompkins Square Park.

The East River here is also the place of a two-century-old treasure hunt for the British frigate *HMS Hussar*, which was alleged to be carrying British Navy gold and American war prisoners when it sank in 65 feet of water after striking a rock in the Hell Gate in 1780. Divers continue to search these waters for the lost fortune.

Many of the river's former industrial sites are to be converted to parks. Rehabilitation of a derelict pier at the end of E 132 Street and the old Riker's Island ferry dock at E 134 Street may open access for fishing, small boat launching, and new ferry service. Hunts Point Terminal Market, the world's larg-

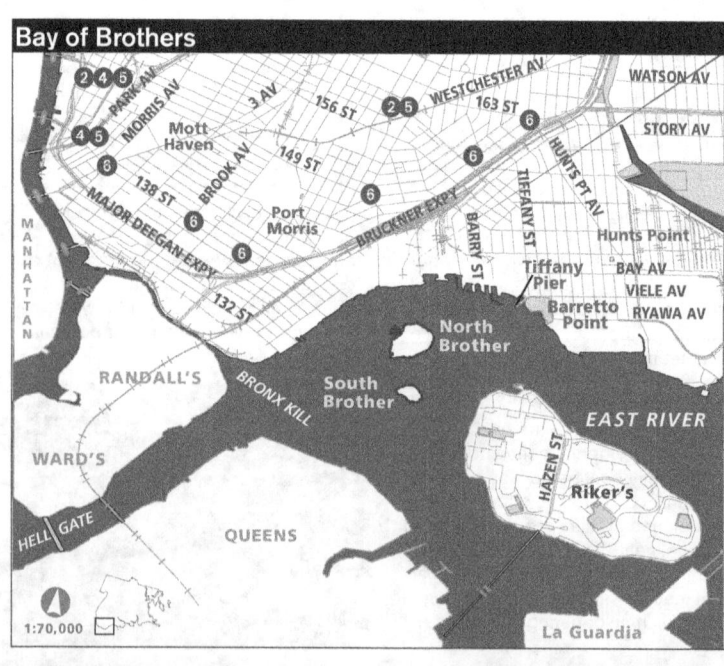

est food distribution facility, is located on the South Bronx riverbank. The city-owned wholesale market distributes meat, produce, and fish, the last since the closing of the Fulton Fish Market.

## Bay of Brothers

Along this busy coast, the few patches of green are penned in by the Hunts Point Water Pollution Control Plant, the Vernon C. Baines Floating Correctional Facility, and the inactive South Bronx Marine Transfer Station. There's fishing from the end of Farragut Street and a short greenway, ferry slip, and kayak put-in are envisioned within the Food Center at the foot of Halleck Street.

Subway: 6 to Longwood or Hunts Pt.

Blueway: Water Trail: Barretto Point

**North Brother Island** A 13 acre city owned island occupied by the ruins of former municipal buildings that were once home to Mary Mallon, the typhoid carrying cook who was held there in quarantine without trial for 26 years. Typhoid Mary died on the island in 1938. It is now protected bird habitat offering no public access.

**South Brother Island** The former summer retreat of beer baron and Yankee owner Colonel Jacob Ruppert (who brought Babe Ruth to the Bronx), this disused island is a key wading bird rookery. The City Department of Parks and Recreation (DPR) began managing the seven acre property as a wildlife refuge in 2007.

**Rikers Island** 413 acres. 1,000 feet off the Bronx coast, the "Rock" houses America's largest jail where about 15,000 men and women are interned in ten buildings and a floating barge docked at the end of Halleck Street in Hunts Point. Inmates till the soil as part of a Farm Project. No access, save for a bridge from Queens.

**Tiffany Street Pier** Foot of Tiffany St. & Viele Ave. The pier made of waste plastic was twice destroyed by fire. There is a kayak launch to the west.

**Barretto Point Park** Barretto St. & Viele Ave. 5 acres. The park on the edge of the Bronx River delta replaces an abandoned brownfield with open grass lawns rimmed by a waterfront promenade. Facilities include a little sand beach called La Playita, a community boathouse, water spray, and ball courts. *The Floating Lady* swimming pool moors here during the summer months.

## Bronx River

The Bronx River is the only true river within city limits. It flows for 23 miles from Davis Creek and Kensico Dam in Westchester County to drain in the East River. Streaming swiftly through the Bronx for eight miles, the river is named for Jonas Bronck, a 17th century Swedish sea captain who settled the region. The Mohegan Indians called the river Aquehung, or "River of High Bluffs."

The Bronx River runs through Woodlawn Cemetery, an ancient forest, the New York Botanical Garden, and the Bronx Zoo before reaching the industrial South Bronx. In 1880s, public parkland was created along the river, which was straightened when Bronx Park was built in the 1920s as part of construction for the Bronx River Parkway, the country's first auto parkway. The result was a wider, shallower channel with faster flowing water. More than 75 bridges span the river's width, which runs from 15 feet at the narrowest point to 2,000 feet at the mouth. It has several waterfalls through the Botanical Gardens and Bronx Zoo, which canoes must portage around. As the river flows south the shoreline becomes more industrial and less accessible.

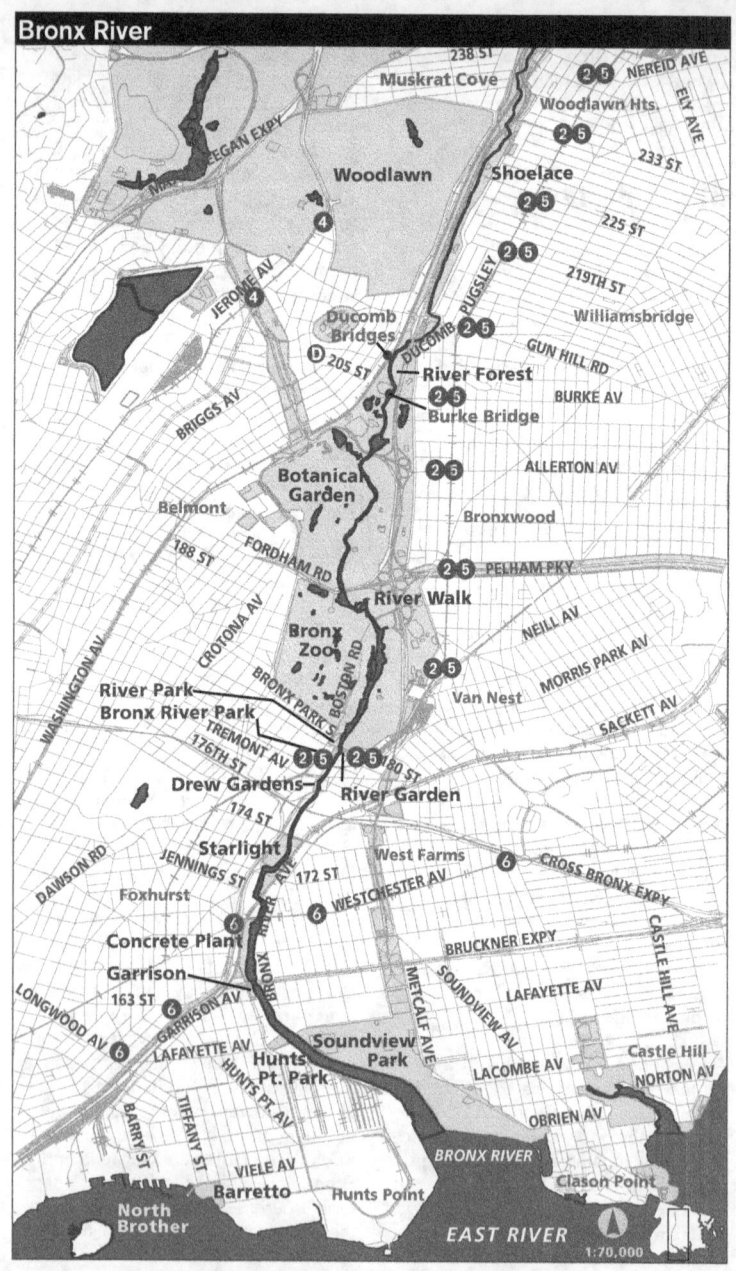

A pre-glacial river, it is thought to have emptied into the Hudson before glaciers forced it to alter its course. The Bronx River Valley splits the hills of the western Bronx from the coastal plains to the east, its watershed draining more than 57 square miles in Bronx and Westchester Counties. The river ecosystem becomes an estuarine environment below E 180 Street where it meets the East River at Hunts Point. There are three dams in Bronx Park originally built to power grist mills in the 17th century. The installation of fish passageways helps restore the natural connection between the marine and freshwater environments. In recent years, alewives (river herring) have been reintroduced and native flora restored to its shore. The river has a dredged channel that is navigable by motor boat for about two miles above the entrance to E 172 Street. The best way to experience the river in its entirety is by canoe. A New York State license is required to fish the river.

Subway: 2 to E 233 St. Pelham Pkwy. or Bronx Park E; 5 to 180 St.; 6 to Hunts Point.

Greenway: The Bronx River Greenway is in place below Bronx Park to Soundview Park, where a 1.5-mile off-road path extends around the lagoons from Lafayette St. to the O'Brien St.

Blueway: Water Trail: Shoelace Park, Hunts Pt. Riverside Park

**Muskrat Cove** E 238 St. A half-mile wedge of greenery and paved path trailing under the Nereid Avenue Bridge originally named for the muskrats that once inhabited these shores.

**Shoelace Park** E 233 St. to Gun Hill Rd. 1.5 mile narrow segment of park on the east bank of the river as it meanders to E 211 Street. A stairway at Duncomb Avenue leads under the stone-arched Duncomb Bridges along the riverside. There is a canoe put-in at E 219 Street.

**Woodlawn Cemetery** Webster Ave. & E 233 St. 400 acres. Built in 1863 along the west bank of the river, the landscaped lawns, tree-lined roads, and rolling hills contain more than 300,000 gravesites and ornate mausoleums, including that of Herman Melville. Maps are available for self-guided tours. 718-920-0500 thewoodlawncemetery.org

**Bronx Park** Bronx Park E & Brady Ave., Gun Hill Rd. to E 180 St. 710 acres. Journeying south, the river cuts through the park, which encompasses a hardwood forest and enters a deep gorge at the Botanical Gardens before flowing under Fordham Road and cascading in double waterfalls in the Bronx Zoo.

**Bronx River Forest** Duncomb Ave. to Kazimiroff Blvd. In one of the last stands of old-growth forest in the city, the river reveals its primeval condition alongside woodlands of tulip trees, sweet gum, and beech. This natural floodplain features riverside paths to the Burke Bridge scenic overlook. The Forest is a Forever Wild Area.

**New York Botanical Gardens** E 200 St. & Kazimiroff Blvd. 250 acres. The first botanical garden in the country is built on the former Lorillard Estate, of the tobacco family. It contains a two mile stretch of Bronx River, which runs through a deep, lushly forested, 40 acre gorge. The picturesque Snuff Mill Trail meanders along the river over the 100 year old Hester Bridge. Admission is free on Wednesdays and from 10am to noon Saturdays. 718-817-8700 nybg.org

**Bronx Zoo** Fordham Rd. & Bronx River Pkwy. 265 acres. The country's largest urban zoo is home to more than 4,000 animals. Originally established as the New York Zoological Society in 1895, it was renamed the Wildlife Conservation Society in 1993. The Bronx River

courses all the way through the bison pasture and rain forest exhibit. The Wild Asia monorail offers terrific aerial views of the river. Free admission on Wednesdays. 718-367-1010 wcs.org

**Riverwalk** In the Zoo, an interpretive trail on the east bank where waterfalls, shallow beaches, and viewing stations offer close access to the restored river. Entry is near the first gate at the Bronx River entrance (Gate B). The walk is free and open to the public during regular zoo hours.

**River Park** E 180 St. & Boston Rd. 5 acres. An attractive picnic and barbecue spot just below the zoo that overlooks the weir at so-called DeLancey's Falls. About a block below the park is a reclaimed sliver of land located where the fast flowing estuary portion of the river starts.

**River Garden** E 180 St. & Devoe Ave. A recently shaped patch of green on the eastern shore.

**Drew Gardens** E Tremont Ave. 1 acre. A community botanical and vegetable garden (gated) built on a former dump at the West Farms rapids.

**Starlight Park** E 174 St. 15 acres. The park, named for an old amusement area, sits on contaminated land. Reconstruction plans call for a greenway, boathouse, and launch. ✖

**Concrete Plant Park** Between Westchester Ave. & Bruckner Blvd. 2.7 acres. The river channel widens to about 200 feet off an abandoned cement plant now partially reclaimed with salt marsh restoration, native plant nursery, greenway link, and boat launch. The steep slope of the western shore, rusty concrete hoppers, and a restored Italian palazzo-style train station designed by Cass Gilbert will be part of the future redesign. ✖

**Garrison Park** Edgewater Rd. 1 acre. This overgrown lot on the river's west side is to be a sculpture park. ✖

**Hunts Point Riverside Park**
Lafayette Ave. at Edgewater Rd. A neglected dead-end street at the edge of the Hunts Point Market has been made over to provide river access from a lush green park featuring picnic and barbecue spots, a kid's water spray with giant seashells and boats, a floating dock, and amphitheater.

**Soundview Park** Lafayette Ave., Metcalf Ave. & O'Brien Ave.
205 acres. Views are plentiful from this former landfill at the mouth of the Bronx River. A steep riverbank encircles restored tidal wetlands, coastal meadows, and upland forests containing nature trails, a 1.5 mile greenway, athletic fields, and fishing areas. At the southeastern end of the park, 7.4 acres of lagoons offer respite for migrating brandt and quarry for a host of wading birds, counting egret, black-crowned night heron, great blue heron, and double-crested cormorant.

# Westchester Creek

Westchester Creek is a 2.6 mile long tributary of the upper East River. The shallow tidal creek averages depths about one to five feet, other than a 12 foot deep channel dredged for about 2000 feet. Average widths range from 60 to 170 feet, and up to 600 feet at its mouth. There is no freshwater flow. The creek is between Zerega and Commerce Avenues on the west and the Hutchinson River Parkway on the east. Its heavily industrialized shore supports marine transport of fuel oil and one surviving recreational marina.

A large Siwanoy Indian village once stood at its eastern lip. The undeveloped and uncared for parkland on Pugsley's and Westchester Creeks is surrounded by public housing. Nearby, Harding Park, a converted summer bungalow colony, is the city's first cooperatively owned low income community.

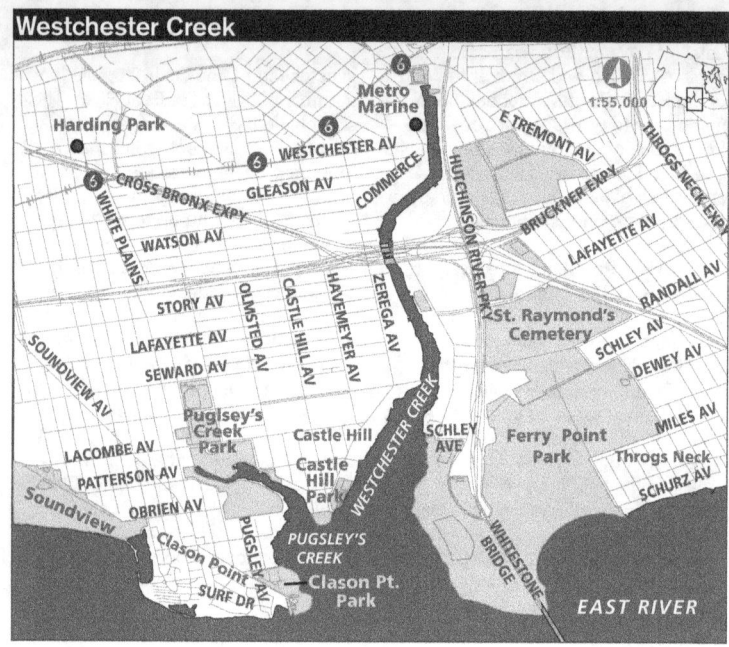

# Westchester Creek

Subway: 6 to E 177 St., then Bx6 bus to Clason Point.

Greenway: Eight miles of greenway are planned between Soundview and Ferry Point, there is a completed 1.5 mile section in Soundview Park.

Blueway: Water Trail: Clason Point Park

**Clason Point Park** Foot of Soundview Ave. 4.25 acres. Clason Point is surrounded on three sides by water between the Bronx River and Pugsley's Creek. It is named for a Scottish merchant who purchased the land in 1720 was later a military academy, and amusement park. The park's few facilities include seating overlooking the East River and a concrete boat ramp.

**Pugsley's Creek Park** Lacombe Ave., Pugsley Rd. 78 acres. The undeveloped parkland consists of freshwater wetlands framing the head of the rivulet. Osprey dive for fish from as high as 150 feet into nearby waters.

**Castle Hill Park** Castle Hill Ave. & Hart St. 4.25 acres. Anglers cast from the unimproved shore at the tip of Castle Hill Neck at the convergence of Pugsley and Westchester Creeks. The peninsula was named by explorer Adriaen Block for the Siwanoy Indian fortification that resembled a castle on a hill overlooking the river.

**Ferry Point Park** Schley Ave., Balcolm Ave. 414 acres. The Bronx-Whitestone Bridge carves up the parkland built atop a garbage dump. The western half has over 100 landscaped acres and sports fields open to the public. The Baxter Creek inlet still runs about 10 feet beneath the eastern acreage, which is to be turned into a world-class 18 hole golf course framed by waterfront promenade.

# Long Island Sound

An estuary touching 300 miles of shore in New York and Connecticut, the sound runs from the Bronx coast in the west out to Block Island and the Atlantic Ocean in the east. In the Bronx, it supports the most recreational boating in New York City. Its salt marshes and rocky intertidal environment provide habitat for a variety of plants and wildlife, including small populations of oysters at the juncture of the East River and the Sound. Enormous glacial boulders mark the seashore, which is the most southerly extension of the rocky New England coastline extending north as far as Maine.

The entrance from the East River to Long Island Sound is marked by a long neck of land named for John Throckmorton who originally settled it in 1642; here the Throgs Neck Bridge spans the East River narrows linking the Bronx to Queens and separating the river from the sound. The picturesque cliffside neighborhood of Silver Beach sits on land in Throgs Neck formerly occupied by the estate of sugar baron Frederick C. Havemeyer Jr. Nearby Edgewater Park has 650 bungalows packed into 55 acres north of the Bronx approach to the Bridge.

Under the Bridge, Hammond Cove is a sheltered anchorage nestled in what was once a safe harbor for rum runners. The small skeletal tower of the Throgs Neck Lighthouse shines beside the old keepers' quarters at SUNY Maritime College. The first keepers operated a bar in the house. Here the mean tidal range is seven feet. Sandy Hook Pilots keep a pilot boat stationed at City Island in order to guide commercial vessels into New York harbor through the East River entry.

Subway: 6 to Westchester Sq, Express bus from Manhattan to Throgs Neck, NY Bus Service 718-994-5500

**Silver Beach Green Grass** A small bucolic park at the head of a long footpath called Indian Trail, which runs along bluffs with magnificent water views. A stairway leads down to a resident-only beach.

**Fort Schuyler** SUNY Maritime College, 6 Pennyfield Ave. The college grounds are open to the public. The old Fort ramparts house a museum and offices. The school's training vessel, *Empire State IV*, is berthed at a 550-foot wharf. Community programs include aquatic training and offshore sailing lessons. Fishing from the seawall surrounding the campus is by permit only, obtained at the security gate. 718-409-7200 sunymaritime.edu

**Maritime Industry Museum** Inside Fort Schuyler, the museum houses a large collection of artifacts, including model ships and a scale model of the 1942 Brooklyn Navy Yard. 718-409-7218 maritimeindustrymuseum.org

# Eastchester Bay

Eastchester Bay stretches for one mile between the Throgs Neck peninsula and City Island. It has a depth of about seven feet where it opens to the East River and Long Island Sound and four feet in the northern reach where the Hutchinson River empties. A slim channel links the bay to the remaining lagoons of Pelham Bay. The Bay was filled by the formation of Orchard Beach. A sand bar under the City Island Bridge hampers tidal flow and shoals, rocky shore, and several wrecks impede navigation. Cuban Ledge is a small reef formed from ballast rocks chucked overboard by Cuban sailors during the Spanish-American War.

Much of the coast is restricted to private residences with personal deep-water docks and many old beach clubs, like the Danish American, White

Cross Fishing, Locust Point Beach, and American Turners clubs on Clarence Avenue. In the Country Club neighborhood, Jennifer Lopez's alma mater Villa Maria Academy has overlooked the bay since 1927, but the old Bronx Beach and Pool and Golden Beach Clubs, and Shelter Cove Marina have succumbed to condo development.

The foreshore, a nursery for aquatic life and habitat for shorebirds, is an Essential Fish Habitat. New York City's largest park, Pelham Bay Park dominates the northeastern shore between the Hutchinson River and Long Island Sound. In 1654, Thomas Pell bought the land from the Siwanoy Indians. Since the city took control of it in 1888, community groups have ensured that the parkland preserves its natural beauty and public access.

Subway: 6 to Pelham Bay (last stop), Bx29 bus.

Greenway: Pelham Bay Park offers miles of paved bike lanes.

Blueway: Water Trail: Lagoons.

**Bicentennial Veteran's Memorial Park** Ellsworth Ave. 9.25 acres. Located on the westside of Eastchester Bay overlooking City Island, the park is laid over Weir Creek, a once navigable stream. A "weir" is a dam or an enclosure built across a brook for catching fish. It is a rich archeological site that once held a freshwater spring.

**Palmer's Inlet** End of Lucerne St. 7.5 acres. A small cove bound by restored marshland once part of the Lorillard Spencer estate is now encircled by Griswold Avenue's residential neighborhood and Outlook Point Condominiums.

**Bayshore Avenue** The bay side of the scenic little drive has a sandy beach popular for shore fishing and a few surviving boatyards, like Ampere and Evers Marina.

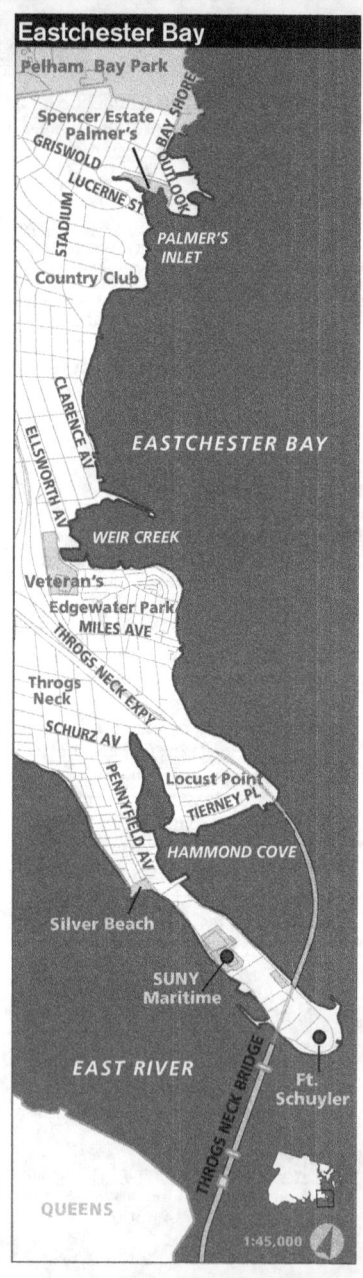

Eastchester Bay

1:45,000

# Pelham Bay

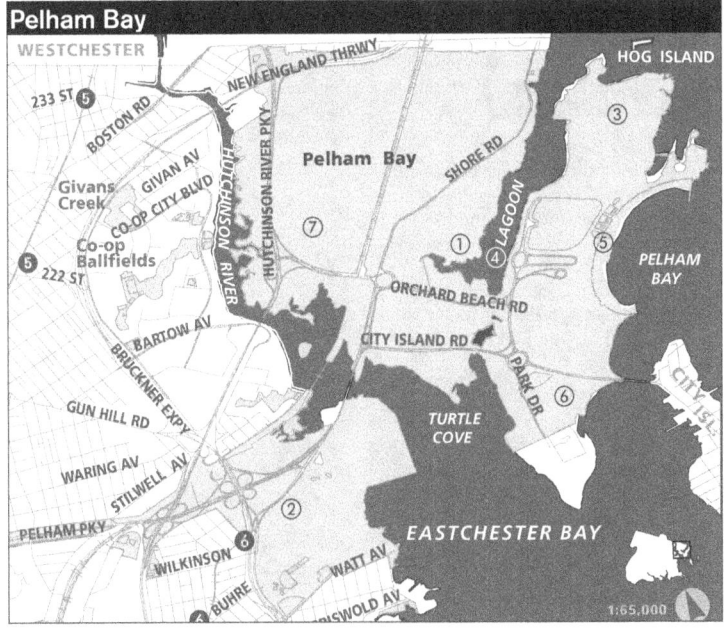

**Pelham Bay Park** 2,766 acres. The Park's magnificent 13 miles of coast are bursting with natural beauty— the rocky foreshore, man-made sand beach, lagoons, 200 acres of salt marsh, and hundreds of acres of woodland. About a quarter of the park comprises two wildlife sanctuaries. This is a key bird-watching area in every season of the year. The city's largest park contains incomparable recreational facilities, including golf, horseback riding, miles of hiking trails, and athletic facilities. Urban Park Ranger programs are conducted at the Pelham Bay Nature Center and Orchard Beach Nature Center.

**Pelham Bay Park Points of Interest:**

① **Bartow-Pell Mansion & Museum** 895 Shore Rd. 9 acres. Built between 1836 and 1842, this landmark Greek revival mansion sits amid splendid grounds and gardens and once served as a retreat for underprivileged youth, and later as the summer office of Mayor Fiorello LaGuardia, before opening as a museum in 1946. Open to the public. 718-885-1461 bartowpellmansionmuseum.org

② **Bronx Victory Memorial** Shore Rd. A 75 foot tall Corinthian column topped by a bronze statue of winged victory is set in the middle of a Memorial Grove commemorating Bronx soldiers who died in WWI.

③ **Hunter Island Marine Sanctuary** 125 acres. Formed from a group of islands during the creation of Orchard Beach, this important sanctuary features the Kazimiroff Nature Trail looping around its rocky outcroppings, tidal wetlands, and mature oak forest on the Sound.

④ **Orchard Beach Lagoons** A small bay behind Orchard Beach with a small craft launch accessing the Sound. The lagoon was widened for the 1960 Olympic trials and is used as a rowing basin by local intercollegiate teams. Seasonal canoe trips are offered by the Urban Park Rangers.

⑤ **Orchard Beach** 115 acres. The mile long crescent famous as the "Bronx Riviera" was built in the 1930s by Robert Moses. A promenade edges the 13 section beach of sand barged from Rockaway to Pelham Bay. Facilities include a bandshell, food pavilion, playgrounds, picnic areas, nature center, and courts for basketball, volleyball, and handball.

⑥ **Rodman's Neck** The place to detonate explosives in city limits has been used as a firing range by NYPD, FBI, and the armed services since the 1900s. Plans call for relocating the range to Queens.

⑦ **Thomas Pell Wildlife Refuge** 371 acres. Split Rock Trail winds through saltwater wetlands and forest of oak and hickory on the Eastchester Bay and Hutchinson River side of the park, a Forever Wild Area.

# Hutchinson River

The Hutchinson River is a small tidal estuary coursing for five miles from its source in Scarsdale through the northeast Bronx to Eastchester Bay. It has a dredged midchannel for about three miles with a depth of six feet. The Hutchinson River Parkway parallels the river. It takes its name from the religious exile Ann Hutchinson who established a settlement in 1642 after being banished from the Massachusetts colony. She was killed here in an Indian massacre. The 330 acre residential towers of Co-op City rise where Ann's cottage stood. The shore is inaccessible and the river barely visible except from the bridges crossing it or trails in Pelham Bay Park from which bird sanctuary Goose Island is visible.

**Givans Creek Woods** Co-op City Blvd. 10.5 acres. Givans Creek flowed into the Hutchinson River before Co-op City covered it. This natural area north and west of the giant housing complex preserves a rich early habitat

of wetlands, meadows, and forest that was once the site of the Scottish Givan's family tidal mill.

**Co-op City Greenway & Ballfields**
Co-op City Blvd. 60 acres. A strip of marshy parkland, formerly the site of a cucumber farm and town dock, on the west bank of the Hutchinson River.

# City Island

City Island is a 230 acre enclave of Victorian homes, yacht clubs, boatyards, and seafood restaurants just off Pelham Bay Park in Eastchester Bay and Long Island Sound. Its 4,600 residents live within two blocks of the water on the 1.5-mile-long island. Once a Siwanoy summer habitation, the island was settled by the English in 1685, and has thrived as a maritime center, home to oyster farms, salt works, an amusement park, world-renowned shipyards, and quiet streets.

Public waterfront access is limited to a short promenade, a waterside cemetery, and a rare patch of wetlands. The housing landscape is rapidly changing as attached townhouses crowd out vintage cottages and historic boatyards succumb to condo development and expansive restaurant parking lots. A new mast-type Cable Stayed Bridge will soon replace the more than 100 year old City Island Bridge. City Island Avenue runs the length of the atoll from the City Island Bridge to Belden Point. Most streets end in small private beaches. The City Island wetlands are a mostly submerged tract of restored salt marshes from Bay Street to Williams Street on the Eastchester Bay shore, which once supported a thriving oyster farming industry and a solar salt works.

Legendary local yards designed and built five America's Cup victors. Marine supply, sail lofts, and boat yards linger, but economic activity today centers on tourism and recreation. The century-old Victorian clubhouse of the Morris Yacht and Beach Club originally built by William Randolph Hearst was destroyed by fire in 2006. Katharine Hepburn filmed Eugene O'Neil's *Long Day's Journey into Night* at 21 Tier Street.

The boulders, reefs, and shallow flats around City Island have been the cause of many shipwrecks. Execution Light guards these waters in the northeast and Stepping Stone Light

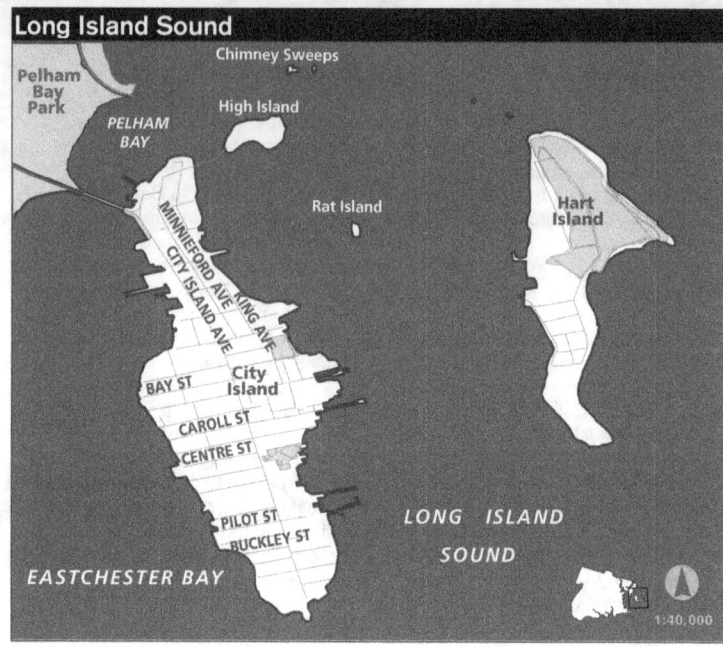

in the southeast. The waters between City Island and Rodman's Neck are a popular anchorage for pleasure boats and a "no wake" area. On the island, anglers can easily rent rowboats at tackle shops or join party boats. City Island Harbor is a sheltered anchorage between City Island and Hart Island. All of the islands in surrounding waters have restricted access.

**City Island Promenade** City Island Ave. A small bayside walkway with sitting areas located just off the bridge.

**Ambrosini Fields** Centre St. 6 acres. Baseball diamonds and playing fields on the east coast of the island.

**City Island Nautical Museum** 190 Fordham St. Exhibits preserve the island's illustrious yacht-building past in the old Public School 17, built in 1897 on one of the highest points on the island. Recently reopened after fire damage to the building. 718-885-0008 cityislandmuseum.org

## The Pelham Islands

The group of under utilized islands in western Long Island Sound once belonging to Thomas Pell include City Island, Hart Island, Hunters Island, Twin Island, Goose Island, Davids Island, High Island, Rat Island, and the Chimney Sweeps, all part of the Bronx, and the Blauzes and Travers Island in New Rochelle.

**Hart Island** The mile-long, 101 acre island lies about a half mile west of City Island and is accessed by ferry from the City Island Harbor pier at the end of Fordham Street. It is currently uninhabited, though the Department of Corrections once used it as a prison. The island also houses defunct Ajax missile silos from the 1960s and almost 800,000 indigent dead buried three-deep at a Potter's Field established here in 1869. A lone deer on the island is shot by a hunter in William Stryon's *Lie Down in Darkness*.

**Chimney Sweeps** In the early 1900s, a German tavern operated on one of these two small outcroppings in the northern part of City Island Harbor. Also, uninhabited.

**High Island** A narrow steel bridge leads from City Island to the eight acre islet a one-time summer resort colony and present-day home to the transmitter and AM radio towers over 500 feet tall for stations WFAN and WCBS, owned by CBS.

**Hog Island** This northernmost part of the Bronx was once claimed by female squatter, Marion Laing who lived on

the island until her death in 1930. A marker to her memory on this vacant and inaccessible island reads: "This island was her paradise."

**Rat Island** An artists' colony took up residence on this two-acre island in the late 19th century. It is now privately owned and uninhabited.

# Brooklyn

Brooklyn is the second largest borough in size and the largest in population, its 2.5 million people making it the equivalent of the fourth largest city in the country. Located at the western end of Long Island, Brooklyn is practically surrounded by water and almost 80% of the waterfront is publicly owned. From its rustbelt north shore and sprawling port facilities along the Upper Bay to parks and beaches of the Atlantic Coast and the wild waters of Jamaica Bay, Brooklyn's got coastline enough for everyone.

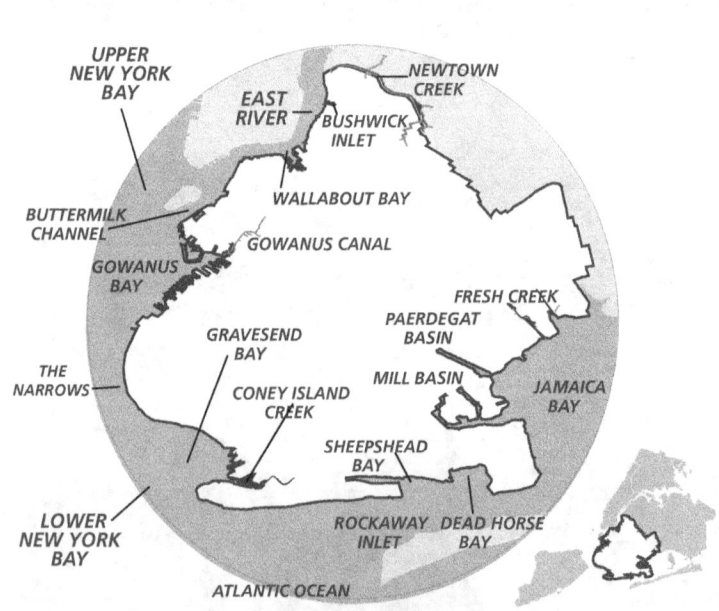

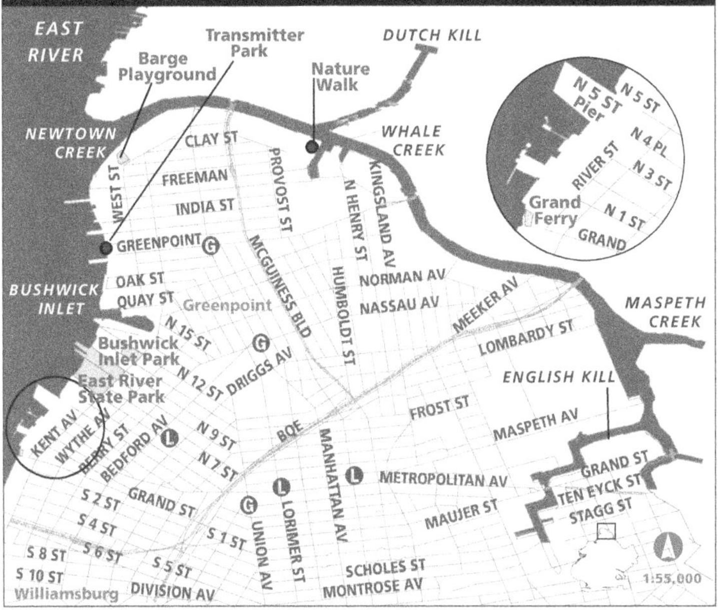

## East River

Separating Brooklyn from Manhattan, the East River is not a true river but a tidal strait that reaches from Upper New York Bay to Long Island Sound. It was first called the East River by early navigators because it took them east toward Long Island and New England. A federal channel and part of the Intercoastal Waterway, it ranges from one half to three and a half miles wide and from 22 to over 100 feet deep. The river has two mouths and a hydraulic current that causes a strong tidal flow of water from one end to the other and back again. Tidal currents are swifter here than in the Hudson, running about four knots at the Brooklyn Bridge. The tide may be ebbing on the East River while flooding on the Hudson River. A small natural cove has developed on the shore between the Brooklyn and Manhattan Bridges, two of the three great spans that link the boroughs and the define the Lower East River. North America's longest auto tunnel runs from Brooklyn to the Battery under the river where it meets the Upper Bay.

When the early settlers arrived on Brooklyn's north shore it had a natural sandy beach rising to bluffs as high as 100 feet. Newtown Creek was surrounded by a vast salt marsh. The Canarsee tribe of the Algonquin Nation hunted and fished its shores. A grassy appendage jutting into the East River at the foot of today's Freeman Street was a familiar sailor's landmark dubbed Green Point.

Brooklyn's industrial waterfront along the East River has been named one of the 11 most endangered places in America by the National Trust for Historic Preservation. Rezoning of vacant commercial parcels on the water's edge has unlocked miles of waterfront for the promise of much needed open space. At the same time, long stretches of shoreline will eventually be occupied by high rise residential towers fronting public waterfront esplanades. South beyond the Brooklyn Bridge, city and state are transforming the massive Brooklyn Piers into an 85 acre park. A greenway is planned to link the entire Brooklyn coast, which here provides one of the most spectacular views of the Manhattan skyline, especially at sunset.

## Newtown Creek

Newtown Creek is a tidal creek forming a natural boundary between Brooklyn and Queens. Flowing west for about four miles into the East River between Greenpoint and Hunters Point, it's an active commercial waterway that once rivaled the Mississippi River as one of the country's busiest industrial channels. Tributaries include Dutch Kills, Whale Creek, Maspeth Creek, and English Kills. Newtown Creek is a federal channel with a turning basin for vessels just above the Kosciusko Bridge. One of the city's six Significant Maritime and Industrial Areas, the creek's banks are lined with oil tanks, concrete plants, scrap metal recycling yards, and the city's largest waste treatment plant. Newtown Creek holds the record for the largest oil spill in U.S. history when, in 1978, a 55 acre petroleum plume believed to be from Exxon-Mobil, Chevron/Texaco, and BP refining operations leaked about 17 million gallons of oil underground. About half the spill has since been mopped up, and lawsuits have been filed to speed the remedial efforts. The full cleanup will take many more years.

The old building at the foot of Manhattan Avenue was rehabilitated in the late 1990s for small manufacturing enterprises and a floating dock is used for small craft access. Vest pocket parks are planned along the creek at street ends and under bridges.

Subway: G to Greenpoint Ave.; L to Bedford Ave.; J, M, Z to Marcy St.

Greenway: The Brooklyn Waterfront Greenway is a planned 14 mile long continuous off-street bike route along the East River. brooklyngreenway.org

Blueway: Water Trail: Newtown Creek Nature Walk

**Newtown Creek Nature Walk** Whale Creek Canal. 320 Freeman St. 53 acres. The Newtown Creek Treatment Plant, the largest wastewater treatment facility on the East Coast, features eight huge stainless steel "digester eggs," dramatic views of the city skyline, and a quarter mile esplanade with installations depicting the history of the creek. Granite slab steps descend right into the water for canoe and kayak access.

**Newtown Barge Playground** Dupont & West St. Ball courts and a baseball diamond are just a few feet from the water. No access here.

**WNYC Transmitter Park** Foot of Greenpoint Ave. 1.5 acres. Ground breaking is scheduled for 2010 to turn a lot containing a former radio station transmitter into a lush garden park with a fishing pier. ✵

# Bushwick Creek Inlet

Bushwick Creek Inlet separates Greenpoint and Williamsburg. The creek, which attracts wading birds and offers a secure harbor for kayakers, was originally called the Norman Kill and extended inland as far as McCarren Park. The watercourse was pruned and surrounding marshlands filled for industrial and manufacturing use. The north side of the creek was once home to Continental Iron Works, where the hull of the first ironclad warship *Monitor* was built and launched on January 30, 1862. A monument to the revolutionary ship's designer, John Ericsson, is in nearby McGolrick Park.

Thanks to a 2005 rezoning of its once blighted industrial shore the Williamsburg coast has been rapidly covered in large scale residential developments, many 20 to 40 towering stories high, from Palmer's Dock and The Edge to Northside Piers and Schaefer Landing. Landmark designation has protected a few historic buildings. At 184 Kent Street, the former Austin Nichols warehouse guards its 1915 Cass Gilbert designed exterior from the wrecking ball. Looming over the river, the Domino Sugar Refinery, built in the 1880s and once the world's largest, will keep its landmark smoke stacks intact, after it becomes the New Domino condominium development. The project vows accessible waterfront stretching from South 5 Street to Grand Street.

<u>Subway</u>: M, Z Marcy Pl.; L to Bedford Ave.; G to Nassau Ave.

<u>Greenway</u>: A public esplanade is to be built piecemeal as part of developer incentives on Kent Ave. from N 6 to N 4 St. Not much progress, yet. Williamsburg Bridge has paths connecting with the Lower East Side.

<u>Blueway</u>: Water Taxi: Schaefer Landing

**Bushwick Inlet Park** Kent Ave. A 28 acre park encircling the whole inlet is planned for the currently fenced waterfront once environmental testing and remediation is complete. The park will include a beach, gardens, concert space, and wetlands. Phase 1 encompassing athletic fields between N 9 and N 10 Streets will be completed by summer 2010. ✵

**East River State Park** Kent Ave. between N 9 St. to N 7 St. 7 acres. Stunning views of midtown Manhattan are rewards from the open lawns at this somewhat barren state park on the former Brooklyn Eastern District Terminal, the terminus of the Erie Railroad. The site was abandoned in 1983 after almost 150 years of operation. Open only until sundown.

**North Fifth Street Pier** Northside Piers, Kent Ave. at N 5 St. A 400 foot long recreational pier located behind the condo development.

**Grand Ferry Park** Kent Ave. at W River St. 2 acres. The riprap shore protects this small park's promenade and lawns from erosion caused by the river's rapid currents. A red brick smokestack in the park is all that remains from the original Pfizer Pharmaceutical plant.

# Wallabout Bay

Wallabout Bay, or the "bay of foreigners," is named for the French speaking Walloons from Belgium who settled here. Across the river from Corlears Hook in Manhattan this semicircular bay is framed by the Williamsburg Bridge to the north and the Manhattan and Brooklyn Bridges to the south. Here in 1776 Washington and his troops launched their retreat to Manhattan from the British forces.

These two miles of waterfront were purchased for $40,000 by the federal government in 1801 for a U.S. Navy Yard, later called the New York Naval Shipyard and more commonly known as the Brooklyn Navy Yard, shut down in 1966 and long one of Brooklyn's proudest treasures. Among the many ships built here were Robert Fulton's steam frigate *Fulton*; Ericsson's *Monitor*; the battleship *Maine*,

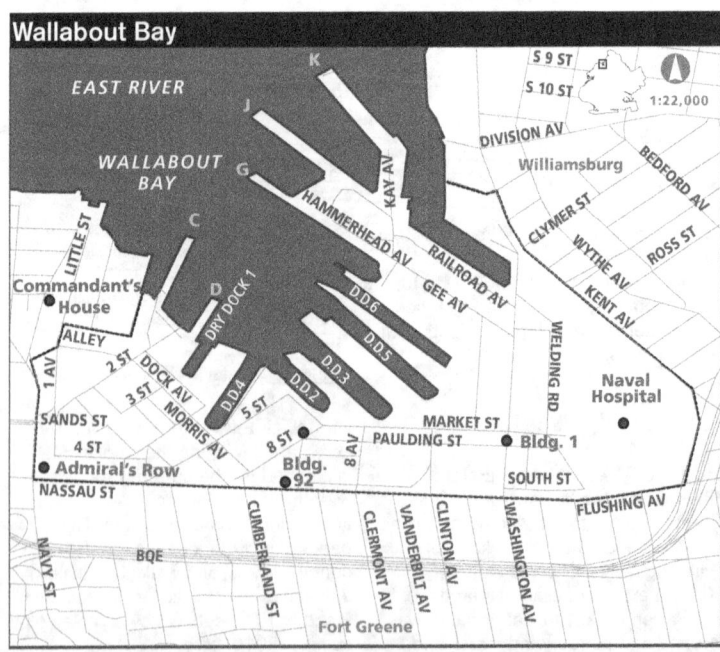

whose sinking in 1895 started the Spanish-American war; the battleship *USS Arizona*, the most famous casualty of Pearl Harbor on December 7, 1941; and the battleship *USS Missouri*, on whose deck the Japanese surrendered in 1945. At its peak, 60,000 worked at the Yard. The original 1807 Commandant's House is now a private residence behind a gated driveway at the end of Evans and Little Streets. Beyond, Yard walls block public access to the waterfront.

During the Revolution, as many as 11,000 soldiers perished aboard British prison ships moored in the little bay, more fatalities than in all of the battles of the war. In 1808, their remains were discovered in the bay's muddy bottom and are interred in the Prison Ship Martyrs memorial, a 149 foot Doric column with an eternal flame overlooking the bay from a summit in Fort Greene Park (Hudson Ave. at Front St.).

The city reopened the Brooklyn Navy Yard as a mixed use industrial park. There are plans to demolish "Admiral's Row", the officers' quarters built between 1864 and 1901, to make room for a supermarket. The old Naval Prison built across from the Yard in 1940s is planned for reuse as residential housing. On the south shore of Wallabout Bay, a pocket of well preserved brownstone homes on Belgian-block streets make up the small but atmospheric Vinegar Hill Historic District, named for a famous battle for Irish independence.

Con Edison's massive Kent Avenue Powerhouse (at Division St.), built in 1905 to power street cars cordoned off the bulkhead of Wallabout Channel. It has been razed, but plans for the site are not public.

Subway: A or C to High Street; F to York St.; G to Clinton/Washington Ave.

Greenway: An on-street path runs along the walled perimeter of the Yard, Kent & Flushing Aves. to Navy St.

**Brooklyn Navy Yard** Flushing & Cumberland Ave. 300 acres. The Yard's industrial park is home to more than 200 small businesses, including the world's largest exporter of shark fins, the nation's first LEED-certified industrial building, and the 15 acre Steiner movie studios. The city landmark Naval Hospital and Surgeon's House are to be redeveloped as part of the media studio complex. The Yard's first dry dock, No. 1, a huge granite structure built in 1850, is a city landmark now used by GMD Shipyard as the city's largest. The fleet of Fire Department's Marine Co. 6 is berthed here, including the fireboat *Kevin C. Kane*, which made more runs than any fireboat in the world. Building 92, the former Marine Commandant's house built in 1857, is being renovated as an exhibit and visitor center. Tours are offered monthly. brooklynnavyyard.org

# Fulton Landing

Ferry operations between Brooklyn and Manhattan began in 1642 at the foot of Old Fulton Street, where, in 1814, Robert Fulton launched steam service with the *Nassau*. The street itself was an Indian Trail and later part of the King's Highway crossing the entire borough. The surrounding neighborhood of DUMBO, an acronym for "Down Under the Manhattan Bridge Overpass," is dominated by the huge granite blocks of the Manhattan Bridge anchorage. The tracks of a railroad that once carried supplies to the many factories along the waterfront still score the cobbled streets. Brooklyn Bridge defines the view from the south and provides a high perch for the Peregrine falcons, which have taken up residence in the east tower. The deep vault of the Brooklyn Bridge anchorage is a performance and exhibit space. Adjacent to the Bridge, a gigantic neon clock illuminates the hour on the Watchtower Building, the national headquarters of the Jehovah's Witnesses.

Fulton Ferry Landing is flanked on each side by converted railroad barges. One hosts classical music concerts and the other is home to the renowned River Café. Nearby, in the massive Eagle Warehouse at 28 Old Fulton Street, Walt Whitman edited the *Brooklyn Daily Eagle* from 1846 to 1848. The poet set type for *Leaves of Grass* at a print shop at 70 Old Fulton Street.

Subway: A, C to High St.; F to York St..; G to Clinton; 2, 3 to Clark St.; 4, 5 to Jay St./Borough Hall

Greenway: Manhattan and Brooklyn Bridges both have bike lanes.

Blueway: Governors Island Ferry; Water Taxi: Fulton Ferry Landing

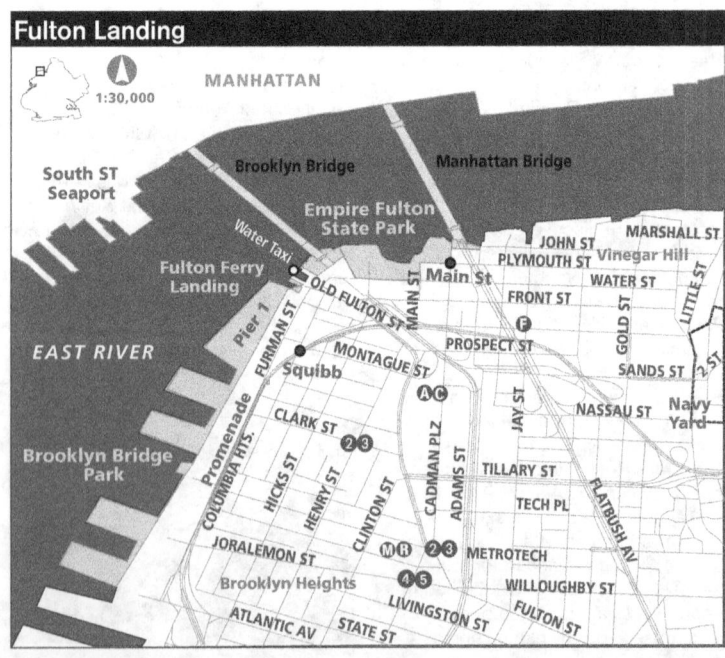

**Brooklyn Bridge Park** Only 12 acres of the future 85 acre park are complete. It will eventually stretch from the old Con Edison lot at John Street just north of the Manhattan Bridge to Atlantic Avenue. It includes the Main Street Park, Empire-Fulton Ferry State Park, and Brooklyn Piers 1 – 6 along 1.3 miles of continuous public space. Future plans for the long abandoned piers envision recreational facilities and athletic fields mixed with natural landscapes, a beach, and secure waters for mooring and kayaking. The park is slowly taking shape as pier sheds and the Purchase Building (under the Brooklyn Bridge) are demolished. 718-802-0603 bbpc.net

**Main Street Playground** Plymouth at Washington St. 1.5 acres. The dense little park between the Bridges packs in native flora, lawns, a small tidal cove, sandy beach, and salt marsh as well as a nautical-themed playground. brooklynbridgepark.org

**Empire-Fulton Ferry State Park** 26 New Dock St. 9 acres. An open grassy ramble with shade trees, picnic areas, and riverside boardwalk surrounds the roofless shell of an old tobacco warehouse originally built by the Lorillard family. The perimeter is framed by the red brick Civil War era Empire Stores, which are to be adapted for commercial use. Open 8am to dusk. brooklynbridgepark.org

**Fulton Ferry Landing** Foot of Old Fulton St. A beautifully restored public pier at the site of the city's first ferry landing. The pier is inscribed with verse from Walt Whitman's poem "Crossing Brooklyn Ferry." The former fireboat house of Marine Co. 7 from 1924 with fire hose drying tower is now an ice cream parlor. Olga Bloom's floating concert hall on an old coffee barge, Bargemusic is permanently docked on the south side of the Fulton Ferry pier. The famed River Café dining barge takes up the north side.

**Pier 1** Furman St. 9.5 acres. An enormous lawn covers the wharf, which contains a small boat ramp and toddler playground.

# Brooklyn Heights

Situated on a high bluff above the East River, Brooklyn Heights was the city's first suburb and the first federally recognized historic district. The neighborhood is defined by elegant brownstone homes and a broad promenade offering incomparable vistas of the harbor, especially the Statue of Liberty, the lower Manhattan skyline, South Street Seaport, and the Brooklyn Bridge. The Promenade's view is protected under city law. The surrounding streets have a long tradition as a literary enclave, one time home to Truman Capote, Carson McCullers, W.H. Auden, Hart Crane, Thomas Wolfe, Richard Wright, Arthur Miller, and Norman Mailer.

**Brooklyn Heights Promenade** Columbia Heights, Remsen St. to Orange St. 1/3 mile. Gotham's most romantic walkway, built in 1950, is cantilevered 50 feet above the water, projecting over two tiers of the Brooklyn-Queens Expressway (BQE) and the Brooklyn Bridge Park piers. There are playgrounds at Pierrepont and Middagh Streets. At Montague Street, a stone marks the site of Washington's headquarters during the Battle of Long Island.

**Squibb Park** Foot of Middagh St. A closed playground and basketball court is to be reactivated as a pedestrian bridge to Brooklyn Bridge Park.

**The Fruit Street Sitting Area** Cranberry St. A narrow esplanade taking in the panorama of river, bridge, and skyline.

# Upper New York Bay

The East River opens into the sheltered harbor of Upper New York Bay, which here measures about 5.5 miles across. Brooklyn is the closest city port to the open sea. Along its west coast, from Red Hook to Sunset Park, stretch long abandoned and decaying industrial structures being reclaimed by developers. Rich in maritime history, the area, long known as South Brooklyn, is also a working waterfront of basins, wharves, cranes, and warehouses—and streets once home to longshoremen and seafarers. The arrival of containerized shipping and air transport in the early 1960s sank Brooklyn's port economy. In recent decades, however, a renewed waterfront is again a vital manufacturing and maritime center. The port still defines the shore and limits access to it, while the notorious Gowanus Expressway and Brooklyn-Queens Expressway further isolate its old residential neighborhoods.

Buttermilk Channel, Gowanus Bay, and Erie Basin are the coasts of the mile square peninsula of Red Hook, named for the red clay soil and hook shape of the land. Loved for the light of its enormous skies and its endless harbor views, the once thriving maritime community sees its fortunes ebb and flow as industrial protectionism competes with demands for open space and residential redevelopment.

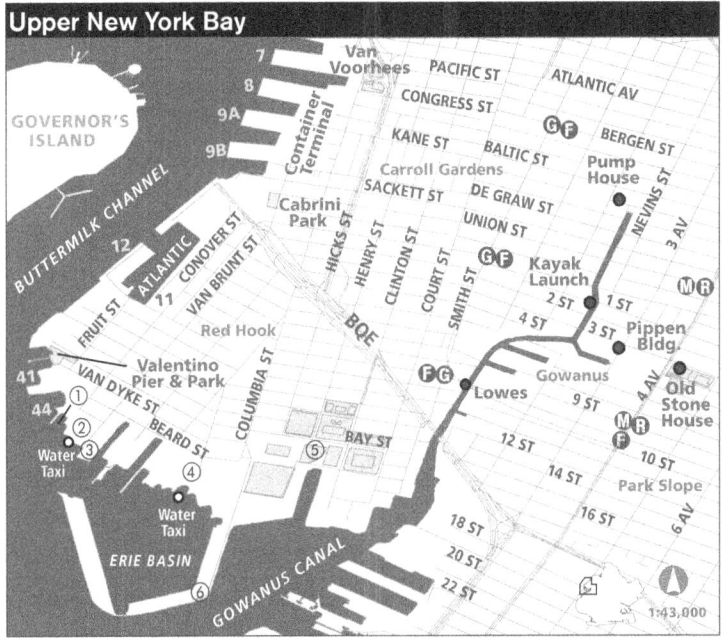

Al Capone began his criminal career in the gritty Red Hook immortalized in films like *Last Exit to Brooklyn*. The biggest property in the isolated neighborhood is the Red Hook Houses, built by the WPA in 1938 for dockworkers and their families. The vast public housing complex is today home to about three quarters of Red Hook's population.

## Buttermilk Channel

The Brooklyn waterfront bends south along Buttermilk Channel, a quarter mile long, half mile wide strait between Brooklyn and Governors Island. Before being dredged for port traffic the channel could be crossed on foot at low tide. According to folklore, the name stems from a time when cattle were driven across the salt marshes to the island to graze. In one story, milk being barged to market was turned to buttermilk by the channel's turbulent waters.

Bulk cargo and container ships enter Buttermilk Channel to unload at Red Hook Container Terminal and Atlantic Basin. Even though Ports Newark and Elizabeth across the harbor handle the vast majority of New York's shipping, Brooklyn longshoremen still work bulk cargo at the Brooklyn wharves. And container ships offload bottles and kegs of Heineken to warehouses at Piers 7 and 11, leased by the city's largest beer distributor, relocated to the Brooklyn working waterfront in 2009. Atlantic Basin is the nation's first man-made, protected harbor, 17 acres surrounded by Piers 10, 11, and 12. Brooklyn Cruise Terminal at Pier 12 welcomes 40 ship calls a year, including Cunard's colossal *Queen Mary 2*. Norwegian and Carnival Lines have leased berths through 2017 at the modern, $56 million terminal. A plan for the surrounding property envisions public waterfront access and maritime uses. On the shore, the decaying carcass of the 1911 New York Dock Company, a six-story storage facility at 160 Imlay Street, awaits rebirth from years of litigation by rival developers.

<u>Subway:</u> F to Smith/9 St.; A, C, F, 2, 3, 4, 5 to Jay St./Borough Hall; B61 bus.

<u>Greenway:</u> On-street ride Columbia St. to Van Brunt St. There is a steady stream of traffic on the narrow cobbled streets and heavy truck traffic.

<u>Blueway:</u> Water Trail: Valentino Beach

**Van Voorhees Park** Columbia St. 5.25 acres. Upland tennis, handball and basketball courts in sight of the working docks and Upper Bay.

**Mother Cabrini Park** President St. at Van Brunt St. In this half acre park, named for the first American saint, watch cargo ships from a playground cooled by water sprays.

**Valentino Park** Pier 39, Coffey St. 2.2 acres. A popular fishing, strolling, and viewing pier at the mouth of Buttermilk Channel, features one of the best views of the harbor and Statue of Liberty. The park has a grassy lawn and pebble beach used by rowers and kayakers, called Fort Defiance Esplanade after the Revolutionary War redoubt.

# Erie Basin

Erie Basin was developed as the southern terminus of the Erie Canal, 524 miles of connecting rivers, lakes, and canals stretching north to Albany and Lake Champlain and west to Buffalo and the Great Lakes. The completion of the canal in 1825 ushered in an era of incredible growth for Red Hook, making it one of the busiest ports in the country and a center of ship repair, a distinction it carried until WWII. The largest man-made harbor on the East coast, Erie Basin is sheltered by a 2,500 foot breakwater that provides moorage for barges, tugs, and small ships. It is homeport to the large open barges of Hughes Brothers Marine and the fuel transport tugs of Reinauer.

In the mid 1800s, William Beard developed the marshlands of Red Hook into the most modern shipping facility of the age. Three of Beard's old warehouses, built cheaply of discarded ballast from arriving ships, have been reclaimed: Beard Street Stores, Pier 41, and Red Hook Stores. Red Hook was cut the off from the rest of Brooklyn by construction of the Gowanus Expressway in 1946. This and the loss of port traffic, led to a rapid decline as the once bustling waterfront grew derelict. A revival began in the 1990s when a retired police detective purchased the dilapidated Beard warehouses from the Port Authority of New York-New Jersey and set about rehabilitating them for new uses. Today, their arched windows framed by black iron shutters open on small businesses and artisan studios drawn to large spaces and wide views. The big Fairway supermarket occupies the ground floor of the 1869 coffee warehouse known as Red Hook Stores (480-500 Van Brunt St.) with luxury lofts on higher floors. Built of local gray schist, the 1859 Brooklyn Clay Retort and Fire Brick Works

Storehouse at 76 Van Dyke St. is the neighborhood's first city landmark.

Many extraordinary industrial structures have succumbed to development. The Revere Sugar Refinery, located just across the quay from the Beard Street Pier and well known for its conical silo, was leveled in 2007 to free up prime waterfront real estate for a big box store. Further down the shore, the world's largest Ikea store has replaced the 48 acre Todd Shipyard compound. It's Graving Dock No. One, operating since the Civil War when the *Monitor* was repaired there, was plowed under for parking lots. The shadow of a massive silo and concrete grain elevator, built in 1922, looms 10 stories high in Gowanus Industrial Park at the head of Erie Basin's docks.

Subway: F, G to Smith/9 St.; A, C to Jay St./Boro Hall to B61 bus.

Greenway: The Columbia St. Esplanade on Erie Basin has a bike lane.

Blueway: Water Taxi: Fairway & Ikea

**Pier 41** Van Dyke St. The large red brick warehouse is occupied by artisan manufacturers, including glassmakers, cabinet makers, a key lime pie baker, and a large nursery, one of the few public areas where you can wander among tall plants and trees.

**Pier 44 Jetty** Foot of Conover St. The landscaped garden park is part of a half mile boardwalk from Pier 41 to the Beard Street Warehouse promenade. Built along a gravel beach, it yields magnificent harbor views from several angles.

① **Waterfront Museum & Showboat Barge** Pier 44. Docked at the rock jetty, the restored red *Lehigh Valley #79*, a wood covered lighter barge built in 1914, houses a small museum presenting public programs, exhibits, tours, and seasonal music series. 718-624-4719 waterfrontmuseum.org

② **Fairway Market Esplanade** 80 Van Brunt St. Behind the market, a walkway with benches is a quiet place to take in stunning harbor views. It connects from Pier 44 and looks out on two neglected trolley cars

that once were planned to travel the waterfront from Red Hook to Atlantic Avenue. There's an outdoor café attached to the market and a water taxi landing.

③ **Beard Street Stores Promenade** 499 Van Brunt St. 7.5 acres. The enormous 1869 warehouse is in fact 21 connected storerooms on a pier with a harborside public walk. The pier is homeport to NY Water Taxi, a glassworks, and the annual Brooklyn Waterfront Artists Coalition (BWAC) Pier Show. Open dawn to dusk.

④ **Ikea Esplanade** One Beard St. 5.5 acres. Turn your back on the bright blue and yellow megastore and look out on the harbor from a long public esplanade ornamented with preserved maritime structures, such as an old gantry, shipyard tools, and a portion of the dry dock. Submerged pier pilings provide good fishing grounds. There are free water taxi runs from Pier 11/Wall Street and shuttle buses from Brooklyn's Jay Street/Borough Hall and Smith/9 Street subway stations. info.ikea-usa.com/Brooklyn

⑤ **Red Hook Park** Bay St. 58 acres. In this active park, about a block off the water there's constant motion on the athletic fields, ball courts, running track, and picnic areas where in season local vendors serve delicious Latin favorites. Close by are a community farm and an Olympic size public swimming pool.

⑥ **Columbia Street Esplanade** Foot of Columbia St. A 500 foot wide pier extending the full length of the Erie Basin breakwater has a broad bike lane and gives local anglers plenty of room to cast a line into the bay.

## Gowanus Canal

The Gowanus Creek was a tidal inlet named for Chief Gowanes by the local Canarsee Lenape tribe that once flowed through saltwater marshes in the small valley between present day Park Slope and Carroll Gardens. It was a famous fishery that boasted of giant oysters the size of dinner plates. The Battle of Brooklyn was waged on these shores. In the mid 1860s, the marshes were drained and the creek dredged by the Brooklyn Improvement Company. The man-made canal travels inland 1.5 miles from Gowanus Bay, winding northward and branching off into Fourth Street Basin. This short stretch of industrial waterway was once an important link in the Erie Canal system but quickly became polluted from sewage and manufacturing waste. It was branded "Lavender Lake" because the waste from commercial dyes had tinted its waters.

Cleanup began in 1999, when a circulating pump was reactivated to flush fresh seawater from Buttermilk Bay through the stagnant waterway. Originally installed underneath Butler Street in 1911, the pump had not worked since the 1960s. The cleaner water and reduced odor helped to revitalize the surrounding neighborhood, where artists have taken up residence in old factories and oysters have been reintroduced. Just upwind from the historic pump house, the landmark 1888 Carroll Street Bridge is the oldest one of only four retractile bridges left in the country, operating by rolling backward on steel wheels along tracks. Four other drawbridges cross the canal at

Union, Third, and Ninth Streets, and Hamilton Avenue.

Although industry crowds the bulkheaded shore, new development is slated to transform lethal brownfields into visions of a "Venice on Gowanus." Water quality has a long way to go, however: the canal is loaded with pathogens and industrial contaminants and 12 overflow outlets spew sewage directly into the waterway with every rainfall. A green roofed Whole Foods market is planned for the eastern bank complete with a new waterfront esplanade, but the site's toxic soil has proven complicated to cleanup. At the corner of the property (3 St. & 3 Ave), the former headquarters of the developer of the Gowanus Canal, the Brooklyn Improvement Company, is now a landmark. Known as the Pippen Building it is one of the first concrete structures built in the nation, cobbled locally in the 1870s by the Coignet Stone Company of Red Hook.

Subway: F, G to Smith/9th St. or Carroll St.; N, R to Union St.

Greenway: Onstreet bike lanes on the bridges spanning the Gowanus Canal.

Blueway: Water Trail: 2 St.

**2nd Street Landing** Foot of 2 St. A little street end park with plantings and a boat launch on the west side of the canal maintained by the Gowanus Dredgers Canoe Club, which offers free canoe tours of the waterway. gowanuscanal.org

**Lowes Promenade** 9 St. west of 2 Ave. A stark mini esplanade with benches at the edge of the store's parking lot on the east side of the canal.

**Public Place** Smith St. & Gowanus Canal. 6.5 acres. A highly toxic city owned brownfield that's been slated for environmental remediation and planned for open green space and affordable housing. ✗

**Old Stone House** 336 3 St. In Washington Park, this 1933 reconstruction of a Dutch farm house was built from the stones of another farmhouse on the old banks of Gowanus Creek. The house commemorates the bloody battle of the Revolutionary War in which 400 patriots of the Maryland Brigade valiantly held off thousands of British soldiers. The building later served as the first clubhouse of the Brooklyn Dodgers, whose early stadium was across Fourth Avenue. historichousetrust.org

## Gowanus Bay

Gowanus Bay is bound by the heavily industrialized Sunset Park waterfront stretching for three miles south from the Gowanus Canal to the Belt Parkway at 66 Street. The Sunset Park neighborhood takes its name from a hilltop park overlooking waterfront and harbor. The hilly terrain runs down the center of Brooklyn's terminal moraine – slopes of rocky debris left behind from Ice Age glaciers. In the heart of the neighborhood, the manicured lawns, and great mausoleums of historic Green-Wood Cemetery take Brooklyn's highest ground. Among its neo-Gothic arches and spires, the figure of the goddess Minerva waves across a protected sightline to the Statue of Liberty.

Sunset Park has been a maritime center for over a hundred years. About 440 acres of industrial waterfront in

South Brooklyn are separated from residential streets by the elevated lanes of the Gowanus Expressway. This working waterfront has begun to come back in recent years, thanks to port modernization and the growth of light industry. It is homeport to the Police Department's Harbor Unit, a federal prison, the New York Power Authority's clean power plant, and a marine transfer station. They are served by the Bay Ridge Channel which connects the main Anchorage Channel to South Brooklyn Terminal, a state of the art facility occupied by a marine based recycler, an automobile processing facility, and the city's largest scrap metal processor. Lafarge, one of the world's largest cement distributors, operates 25 Street Pier where products to upstate plants are transported by barge.

The 100 acre Bush Terminal complex (32-37 Sts.) contains 18 piers, 15 industrial lofts, and a waterfront railroad. Developed in 1890 by Irving T. Bush, and operated as Industry City until 1974, it is now a growing center for light manufacturing. The vast Brooklyn Army Terminal (53-66 Streets), designed by Cass Gilbert and built in 1919, sent millions of G.I.s and tons of supplies overseas during WWII. The Terminal closed in the 1970s; Building B has been readapted for small industry and affordable artists' lofts. A rail line runs at grade level along First Avenue linking South Brooklyn Marine Terminal with Brooklyn Army Terminal and the 65 Street Rail Yard terminus of the Long Island Rail Road's freight branch. The yard has two rail transfer bridges to convey freight cars to and from floats for transport across the harbor. A large waterfront park is envisioned, but plans have yet to materialize. One improvement plan, active since the birth of the Port Authority, is for a 2.5 mile long cross harbor freight tunnel under the Upper Bay from Sunset Park to the New Jersey docks.

Subway: D, M, N, R to 36 St. & 4 Ave.

Greenway: Sunset Park Connector, on- and off-street bicycle lanes that link Owl's Head Park, Greenwood Cemetery, and Prospect Park.

Blueway: Pier 4 commuter ferry

**Brooklyn Army Terminal Pier 4**
58 St. The only public waterfront access on this industrial stretch, the pier is used by fishermen and as a water taxi dock offering breathtaking views of the Upper Bay and Lower Manhattan. There is parking at the pier.

## The Narrows

The mile wide Verrazano Narrows strait, the entrance to New York Harbor, connects Upper Bay and Lower Bay. The name honors Italian explorer Giovanni da Verrazano, the first European to enter the harbor. The Narrows is rich in American history. British forces landed here to crush the patriots in the Battle of Brooklyn from a fleet of 300 ships, twice the size of the Spanish Armada. Robert E. Lee and Stonewall Jackson served at Fort Hamilton and attended its little chapel replaced by St. John's, known as the Church of Generals. Fort Lafayette once guarded the Narrows from a small reef. The fort razed, the reef became an anchor of the tower of the Verrazano-Narrows Bridge that spans the strait from Fort Hamilton in Brooklyn to Fort Wadsworth in Staten Island. The world's longest suspension bridge when it was built in 1964, it remains the longest in the United States.

While farther north the waterfront is all about shipping and industry, the leafy neighborhood of Bay Ridge was once summer home to some of New York's wealthiest citizens who built ornate mansions on the bluff overlooking the Narrows. The only 19th century home left standing, the onetime residence of Diamond Jim Brady, is today a prep school for girls at 9901 Shore Road. The neighborhood,

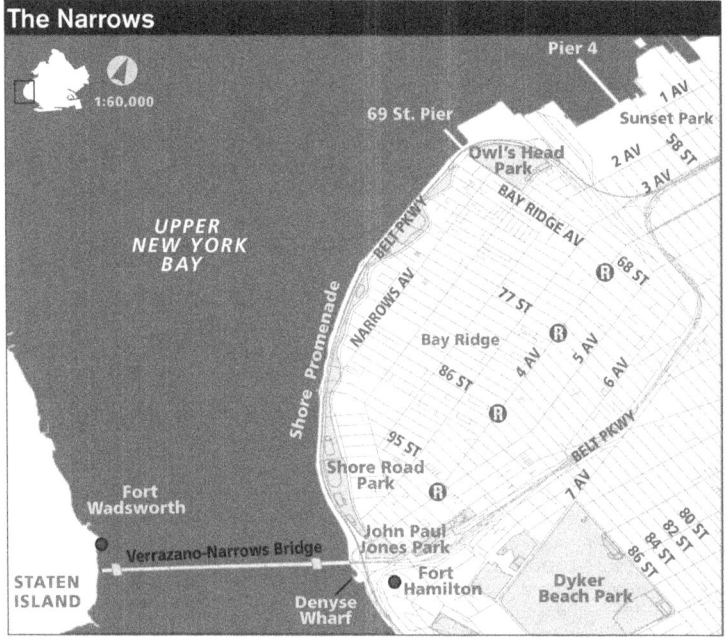

## The Narrows

originally called Yellow Hook after the blonde tint of its sand, was renamed in 1853 as a real estate response to a yellow fever epidemic. Long a quiet, conservative residential neighborhood, Bay Ridge was made famous as the setting for John Travolta's *Saturday Night Fever*.

The Belt Parkway hugs the shore of West Brooklyn along the Narrows and Lower Bay; beginning at Owl's Head Park; part of the 36 mile Belt Parkway System running through Brooklyn and Queens, this stretch is also known by its official name, Shore Parkway. A Robert Moses project, it opened in 1940. The limited access road intertwines miles of esplanade and green parks, both on the water and upland margins. There are a couple of parking lots along the thruway. Shore Road, on a ridge above the water, is one of City's most scenic drives, taking in the mansions of Bay Ridge, the majestic Verrazano, and the full reach of New York Harbor.

Subway: R to 86 St. at 4 Ave. or Bay Ridge Ave.

Greenway: Shore Parkway Greenway, a section of the East Coast Greenway, begins at the 69 Street Pier and continues south for 7 miles along the waterfront to Bensonhurst Park. No access on the Verrazano-Narrows Bridge, except during the Marathon when runner's start the race on the big bridge 295 feet above the water.

**Owl's Head Park** 69 St. & Colonial Rd. 27 acres. The park, next to a sewage treatment plant, is set on a verdant hilltop overlooking the harbor, an ideal spot to watch ship arrivals and also one of the city's top skateparks.

**69 Street Pier** Shore Rd. & 69 St. The 600 foot long pier, once the site of a ferry terminal, attracts crowds of anglers and picnickers with incredible views of the Bridge, the Narrows, Lower Manhattan, and beyond to the mouth of the Hudson River. Brooklyn's 9/11 Memorial is here. Local advocates are petitioning to restore commuter ferry service at the wharf. The pier, lit after dark, is open dawn to 11pm.

**Shore Parkway Promenade**
Shore Rd. & 69 St. to Bay Pkwy.
A four mile long paved walkway and bicycle path at the water's edge runs alongside the Belt Parkway from Owl's Head Park passing under the Verrazano-Narrows Bridge, past Fort Hamilton to Bensonhurst Park.

**Shore Road Park** Shore Rd. between 68 St. & Colonial Rd. 58 acres. Across the parkway from the waterfront, tree lined walkways wind through parkland around ballfields, tennis courts, playgrounds, and a modest botanical gardens (72 St.). Get there from the water side across footbridges at 69 Street, 92 Street, Bay 8 Street, and 17 Avenue. Above the park at 81 Street, the Old Glory Lookout flagstaff commemorates Admiral Dewey's victory in the Spanish American War.

**John Paul Jones Park** 4 Ave. & 101 St. 5 acres. A rolling lawn on the high ground above Fort Hamilton, named for the Revolutionary War Naval hero who declared "I have not yet begun to fight," is dominated by a Rodman gun and a Parrot cannon, placed as a war memorial surrounded by 50 cannonballs and other monuments.

**Denyse Wharf** This 18th century remnant of a concrete dock forms a tiny beach under the Verrazano-Narrows Bridge, where British troops under General Howe came ashore in 1776 Battle of Brooklyn. The Denyse family operated a ferry to Staten Island from the wharf until the bridge opened. The decaying dock is the property of

the U.S. Army at Fort Hamilton and there is no access. Local educators have proposed establishing a science lab on a refurbished pier for hands-on learning about the harbor estuary.

**Fort Hamilton** 8302 Colonial Rd. 155 acres. The Army's "Boots on the Ground" in New York City was built by the Army Corps of Engineers for coastal defense in 1825. Its garrison, the nation's second oldest after West Point, is home to the Armed Forces Reserve Center and Army Corps of Engineers, North Atlantic Division. The original Officer's Club, now a popular event space, overlooks the beautiful Narrows. Notable landmarks include Colonel's Row, the Fort Hamilton Community Club, Lee House, and the Harbor Defense Museum building, all on the National Register of Historic Places. hamilton.army.mil

**Harbor Defense Museum**
Fort Hamilton Bldg. 230 Sheridan Loop. Inside the old Fort's caponier, a freestanding guard house in the fort's moat, a unique collection of shore battery and other artifacts. Tours offer a close look at the pre-Civil War fortifications. Admission is free. 718-630-4349 harbordefensemuseum.com

# Lower New York Bay

Much larger than the Upper Bay, Lower New York Bay measures 100 square miles and encompasses the harbor below the Narrows, from Gravesend to the tip of Rockaway. Waters are usually shallow, ranging from six to 35 feet deep, with federal channels dredged to 45 and 50 feet. The Brooklyn shore faces south at this point, as the Shore Parkway Promenade rims Gravesend Bay. This coast was once part of the town of New Utrecht, one of Brooklyn's original Dutch settlements, which now contains the residential neighborhoods of Dyker Heights, Bath Beach, and Bensonhurst. These communities were fashionable seaside resorts in the 19th century. Bensonhurst is named for potato farmer Robert Benson. When speculators began buying up waterfront lots, Benson refused to sell. His patch is today's Bensonhurst Park.

The Lower Bay has several coves, inlets, creeks, and inner bays, many of which have harbored ship wrecks, pirates, and smugglers. The inlets once protected the notorious rum-running boat *The Cigarette*, owned by Bay Ridge mobster Vannie Higgins and the fastest boat in New York waters during Prohibition. The shad fishing industry flourished here at one time. In the late 1800s, the spring shad run saw hundreds of fishermen cast nets in Gravesend Bay and fishing shacks crowded the shore. Pollution led to the collapse of the industry. Big box stores first colonized the city on the Bensonhurst shores at Caesars Bay, an impervious site at the end of Bay Parkway that was formerly a giant flea market. The Lower Bay is nesting grounds for bird populations and winter home to a growing colony of harbor seals inhabiting two man made islands under the Verrazano Bridge.

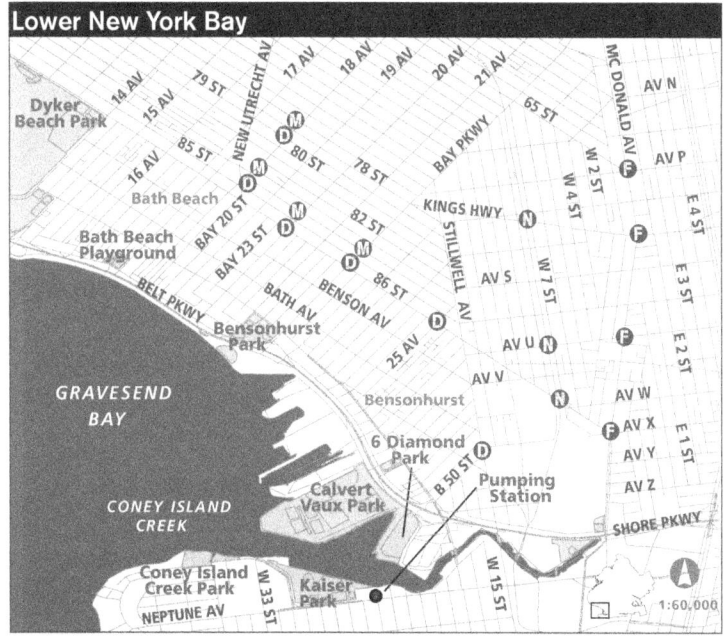

## Gravesend Bay

South of the Narrows the shore bends southeast to form Gravesend Bay, stretching three miles across at the edge of Lower New York Bay. The bay is a federal anchorage, a fish nursery, and a harbor for recreational boaters, and fishermen. It is named for one of the original Dutch towns of Brooklyn, the only one founded by a woman, Lady Deborah Moody, an Anabaptist refugee from Massachusetts who settled here in 1643 when the coast was salt marshes and sand dunes. The Dyker Beach neighborhood (there's no beach) takes its name from dikes built by Dutch settlers to reclaim these vast seaside expanses. Several parks straddle the Belt Parkway (here, also called Leif Ericson Drive) on the knolls of Dyker Beach and next door Bath Beach. The bayside is a mix of marinas, the Nellie Bly Amusement Park, bus garages, a sanitation truck facility, fuel oil tanks, and the toxic site of a dismantled incinerator proposed by the city as a marine waste transfer station. The scheme, which requires dredging the bay, is strongly opposed by many in the community. Among its potential dangers may be live antiaircraft shells at the bottom of the bay.

Subway: D, M to 86 St. to B1 Bus.

Greenway: Shore Greenway runs from Bay Ridge Ave. to Dreier-Offerman Park with pedestrian overpasses at 17 Ave., Bay 8 St. & Bay Pkwy. Eastbound riders travel on-street on Shore Rd. south to Cropsey Ave., then cross the Cropsey Ave. Bridge to Neptune Ave.

Blueway: Water Trail: Marine Basin

**Dyker Beach Park** Shore Pkwy., 86 St. 7 to 14 Aves. 216 acres. One of Frederick Law Olmsted's final landscapes, the upland park contains recreational facilities and athletic fields. On the water's edge, the Shore Promenade becomes a wide, grassy, windswept field favored by kite flyers.

**Dyker Golf Course** 7 Ave. & 86 St. Not far from the coast, the lush fairways of this public course, built as a private club in 1897, are some of the city's most affordable and scenic. Tiger Woods' father Earl sliced balls here while stationed at Fort Hamilton. 18 holes, 71 par.

**Bath Beach Playground** Shore Pkwy. & 17 Ave. 3 acres. A marine theme playground with water spray and playing fields, linked by footbridge to the Promenade.

**Waterwalk** The promenade between the Bath Beach playground and Bensonhurst Park is a narrow passageway with a divided foot and bike path, called Waterwalk. Its seaside handrail is decorated with models of marine creatures and a series of educational panels about marine life and ecology installed by the New York Aquarium.

**Bensonhurst Park** 21 Ave. & Bay Pkwy. 17.5 acres. A shady spot at the eastern terminus of the Shore Promenade features ball fields, tennis courts, handball courts, and a playground on the bay.

## Coney Island Creek

Coney Island Creek is a tidal inlet about one and a half miles long originating at a storm drain near Shell Road and emptying into Gravesend Bay. It once formed a channel connecting Gravesend Bay to Sheepshead Bay, but was filled, reshaping the barrier island into a peninsula in 1910. Not navigable for most of its length, the mucky creek is only about one foot to 10 feet deep. The skeletons of wood barges are visible at low tide in the mudflats on the north bank across from Kaiser Park on the coast of popular Dreier-Offerman Park. Towed here in 1945 to help prevent shore erosion at the

Coney Island Creek Boat Basin, today the decaying remnants are habitat for aquatic species. More dilapidated wrecks were scuttled at the mouth of the creek creating a small graveyard of ships. These include the rusting hulk of an abandoned 45 foot long yellow submarine, *Quester I*, built in 1963 to salvage the sunken *Andrea Doria* off the coast of Nantucket Island. Improperly balanced, the submarine never made it beyond its test run on Coney Island Creek.

On the northwest bank, the small bungalow colony of White Sands, about 41 homes, was razed to make way for a Home Depot store. The Coney Island Creek shore along Neptune Avenue is largely commercial, ending at Shell Road. Its waters are heavily polluted from low tidal activity and hazardous waste from the former Brooklyn Gas Company plant on the north shore, which is due to be cleaned up by the present owner. The contaminated 16 acre parcel abuts Coney Island Rail Yards, which handles about 5000 subway repairs each year.

Subway: D to Bay 50 St; Bus B74

Greenway: Shore Parkway Greenway exists through Calvert Vaux Park to the Home Depot path, Cropsey Ave. Bridge has a bike lane, though the ride is on street to the boardwalk.

Blueway: Water Trail: Calvert Vaux Park in planning. ✷

**Calvert Vaux Park** (or Dreier-Offerman Park) Shore Pkwy., Bay 44 to Bay 49 Sts. 73 acres. The park is named after landscape architect Calvert Vaux, who in partnership with Frederick Law Olmsted designed Central and Prospect Parks; he mysteriously drowned while walking the shore of Gravesend Bay in 1895. The fork of landfill initially developed for the Coney Island Creek Boat Basin was built from the Verrazano-Narrows Bridge excavation and a small parcel donated by the Dreier-Offerman Home for unwed mothers. The parkland contains baseball diamonds, soccer fields, bocce courts, a model airfield, and restored wetlands. Future improvements include a kayak launch, nature trail, and sports fields.

**Six Diamond Park** W 22 St. 37 acres. On the south fork of the Coney Island Boat Basin, ball fields connect to a path through restored wetlands behind the Home Depot parking lot.

**1938 Fire Pumping Station** Neptune Ave. at W 23 St. 15 acres. The landmark station, which provided water pressure to Coney Island, is surrounded by vegetable gardens that are part of the city's Green Thumb program. Fishermen access the creek from its embankment.

**Leon S. Kaiser Park** Neptune Ave. at W 27 St. 26 acres. Open lawns encircle a playground, running track, athletic fields, tennis courts, and grilling areas adjacent to a concrete fishing pier. As early as 1898, local congregations have performed baptisms in the waters off the small beach on the west end of the park.

**Coney Island Creek Park** Bayview Ave. 9.8 acres. A trail leads through native plants and restored dunes to a sandy shore extending from the mouth of the creek to Sea Gate, a popular fishing and seining spot.

# Atlantic Ocean

Coney Island, a four mile long sandbar, is the western most barrier island in a chain extending along the southern shore of Long Island. The Dutch named it "konijin" for the rabbits that overran its high dunes and cedar forest. Shortly after the Civil War, the beach became a high end summer resort, which by the 1920s was attracting millions more drawn to its shores by the new subway lines. America's iconic beach playground, Coney Island is the birthplace of many national firsts, from the large-scale amusement park and the roller coaster to winter bathing, self-serve cafeterias, and the hot dog.

"If Paris is France, then Coney Island, between June and September, is the world." declared George Tilyou, the visionary entrepreneur who built the first grand amusement park, Steeplechase Pier, in 1897. Coney would later be known as "Sodom by the Sea." In 1916, Nathan Handwerker opened a nickel hot dog stand on Surf Avenue calling it Nathan's Famous long before it was.

The big three amusement parks –Luna Park, Steeplechase Park, and Dreamland– had all closed by the 1960s, when Coney Island was being engineered into a more residential– and often poor–community. Luna Park was plowed under for Luna Park Houses. The Aquarium sits on the grounds of Dreamland. And after decades as a barren lot, the site of the former Steeplechase Park next to the defunct Thunderbolt roller coaster welcomed KeySpan Park, home of the Mets' Brooklyn Cyclones farm team. The smaller Astroland on the boardwalk closed in 2008, on the old site of Feltman's Restaurant, the inventor of the hot dog.

The landmarks stay. The classic Parachute Jump towers over the ball park and a few homey arcades and amusement rides keep the honky-tonk spirit alive. The Cyclone roller coaster continues to thrill, even as its companion rides at Astroland were sold off. Deno's Wonderwheel turns slowly high above the beach. The 1923 Child's Restaurant building, famous for ornate terra cotta sea scenes decorating its façade, was preserved as a landmark in 2003.

As Coney Island gears up for its next incarnation, millions still crowd its wide beaches each summer. Some "carny" traditions endure at Sideshows and at the annual springtime Mermaid Parade. Planners and developers keep looking for ways to transform the rundown amusement district, usually dreaming of a grandiose Vegas by the sea entertainment complex with high tech arcades, a glossy hotel, beachfront condo towers, and a water park.

<u>Subway</u>: D, F, N, Q to W 8 St. or Stillwell Ave.; B, Q to Brighton Beach; B1 Bus to Oriental Blvd. Manhattan Beach.

<u>Greenway</u>: Ocean Parkway Greenway is the nation's first dedicated bike path stretching for five tree-lined miles from Prospect Park to Coney Island.

**Sea Gate Beach** Surf Ave. & 37 St.
A gated community on the western end of Coney Island, covering about 43 square blocks and 900 homes. Enter through the guard gate on foot or by bike only to see the lighthouse.
• **Sea Gate Beach Club**
A private pool and surf club on a private beach. seagatebeachclub.com

**Coney Island Lighthouse**
Beach 46 St. Sea Gate. America's last civilian lighthouse keeper, Frank Schubert, served here from 1960 and died here at his last post in 2003; now automated, the light still guides mariners into Lower New York Bay from Norton Point. It is owned by the USCG and licensed to the Seagate Association. The property is closed to the public.

**Coney Island Beach** W 37 St. to Seabreeze Walk. One of the world's best and best known urban seashores is also America's first public and completely free beach. The signature Riegelmann's Boardwalk, 2.7 miles long and 80 feet wide, offers a colorful stroll past clam shacks and arcades. Comfort stations, showers, beach volleyball, and children's play areas dot the beach and boardwalk.

**Steeplechase Pier** W 17 St. The 700 foot pier, lined with fishermen catching herring and setting nets for blue crab, has a distinctly Latin beat. Scuba divers explore below for artifacts from the vanished amusement park's heyday.

**Coney Island Points of Interest:**

① **KeySpan Park** 1904 Surf Ave. Home field of the Brooklyn Cyclones, whose season starts in late June. Great views abound from all seats—of the Parachute Jump, Cyclone Roller Coaster, Wonder Wheel, and the Atlantic Ocean. brooklyncyclones.com

② **The Parachute Jump** Steeplechase Plaza. 2.2 acres. The restored landmark's 250 foot steel tower, an icon of Coney Island since 1941, was originally built as the Lifesaver exhibit for the 1939 World's Fair. No longer in use, future improvements include a public promenade of shops, restaurants and exhibits at its base.

• **Bischoff & Brienstein (B&B) Carrousel** Steeplechase Plaza. One of the last classic carousels in the country features elaborate hand carved horses by Brooklynite

Charles Carmel. The historic 50 horse ride, built in 1919, acquired at auction by the city for $1.8 million is to be refurbished and installed beside the Parachute Jump.

③ **Cyclone Roller Coaster** 1000 Surf Ave. & W 10 St. The famed wooden roller coaster, thrilling riders since 1927, is the centerpiece of the emerging amusement district.

④ **Deno's Wonder Wheel** W 12 St. A small amusement park centers around the world's tallest Ferris wheel, 150 feet high, with 16 swinging seats and an unusual double-ring structure designed in 1920 by Charles Herman and operated by his son Freddie until the 1980s. wonderwheel.com

⑤ **Sideshows By the Seashore** 1208 Surf Ave. at W 12 St. Exhibits of amusement park memorabilia housed in a 1917 historic building overlooking the Cyclone and Wonder Wheel, upstairs from a circus sideshow of freaks and other human curiosities. Drinks are served at the Freak Bar. 718-372-5159 coneyisland.com

**New York Aquarium** (part of the Wildlife Conservation Society) 602 Surf Ave. at W 8 St. 14 acres. The nation's oldest aquarium and Brooklyn's most popular tourist draw presents William Beebe's Bathysphere, Alien Stingers jellyfish, shark, dolphins, walruses, and more than 8,000 marine creatures on exhibit. California sea lions perform in four shows daily at the Aquatheater, while a new 4D digital show explores coastal waters and coral reefs. A 300 foot long sculpture wall, called *The First Symphony of the Sea* by artist Toshio Sasaki, fronts the boardwalk. 718-265-4740 nyaquarium.com

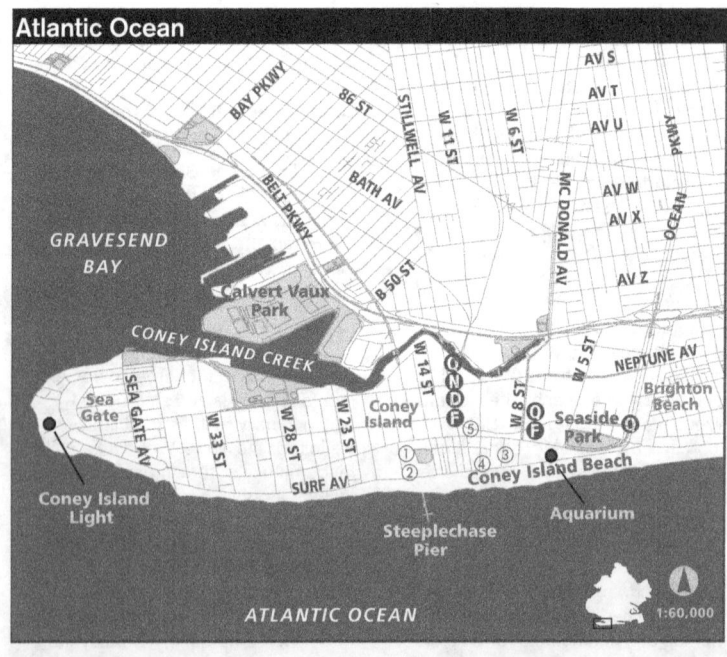

**Asser Levy Seaside Park**
Ocean Pkwy. & Seabreeze Ave. 22 acres. The park is named for an early champion of Jewish rights who arrived in New Amsterdam in 1654 with 23 refugees from Brazil. Across from the beach, an open lawn and small bandshell plays host to free summer concerts. Residents are at odds over borough plans to remake the simple music venue into a large amphitheater.

**Brighton Beach** Seabreeze Walk to Corbin Pl. Home to a salt marsh, a racetrack, a hotel, and a public bath house, the beach developed in 1878 is named for England's famed seaside resort. It contains one of the largest Russian speaking populations in the country. The boardwalk here is lined with outdoor cafes, and the wide sandy beach is often less crowded and lower key than its neighbors.

**Manhattan Beach** Oriental Blvd. 40 acres. The former summer resort was built by railroad financier Austin Corbin on the eastern heel of Coney Island between the Atlantic coast and Sheepshead Bay. It features a compact family beach, a boardwalk, picnic areas, ball fields, playgrounds, tennis courts, and parking.

**Kingsborough Community College**
2001 Oriental Blvd. 70 acres. On Orient Point, the far eastern tip of Coney Island, the former WWII Merchant Marine and Coast Guard training station offers a major in maritime technology. The campus has a public esplanade, private beach (pass required), marina, and a functioning lighthouse atop the Marine and Academic Center. There's a large shark tank in the lobby. 718-368-5069 kbcc.cuny.edu

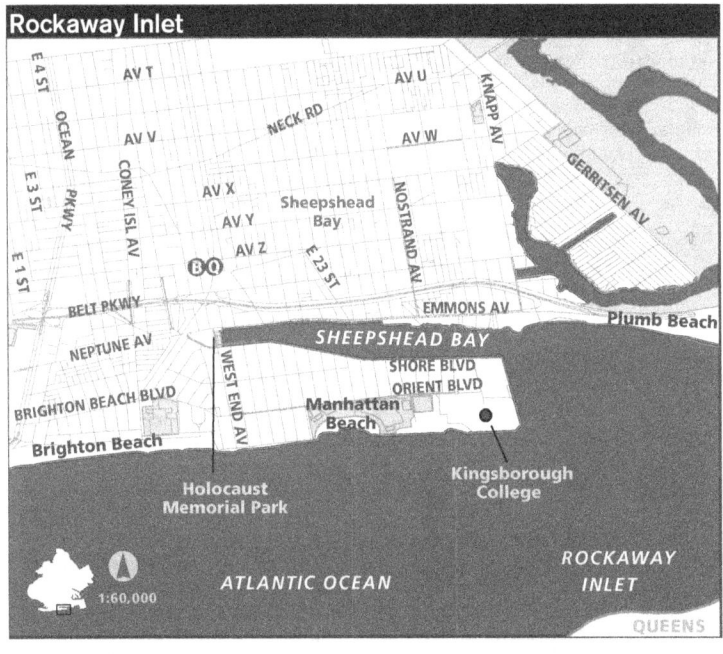

# Sheepshead Bay

This long time fishing village is named for the sheepshead fish, a member of the porgy family once plentiful in local waters. It is a well protected anchorage with depths of 14 feet. Sailboats bob at moorings in the narrow inlet, swans paddle in pairs across the calm water, and a fleet of deep sea sport fishing boats dock along the main drag, Emmons Avenue, which runs the length of the bay. A flotilla of charters, eco tours, and dinner excursions on Jamaica Bay also sail from here, and all vessels participate in Fourth of July fireworks cruises.

A few alleys of simple summer bungalows remain amid the yacht clubs, seafood joints, and new condo developments. Lundy's landmark fish house, which started as a clam shack on the family's pier in the 1880s, is being revived as a gourmet market and restaurant catering to the area's growing Eastern European population. Austin Corbin developed Sheepshead Bay, building the enormous Manhattan Beach Hotel, and the 420 foot long wooden footbridge across the bay in 1880s. The slender bridge, a popular spot for fishing and netting crabs, links the commercial strip with the showy mansions of Manhattan Beach.

Subway: B, Q to Sheepshead Bay.

Greenway: Shore Parkway Greenway connection at Brigham Rd. at the east end of Emmons Avenue.

**Holocaust Memorial Park** Shore Blvd. & West End Ave. At the head of the bay, New York's first public memorial to victims of the Holocaust tells its story through a field of inscribed granite markers.

**Sheepshead Bay Esplanade & Piers** Emmons Ave. between Ocean Ave. & E 26 St. A broad esplanade links ten slanting piers, built by the WPA in 1937, for party boats that tender half day and full day ocean fishing or all night trips for blues and porgies, gear and bait provided. Around four o'clock each afternoon the day's catch is sold on the docks. Moorings for transients and "dock and dine" boaters are available. 718-478-0480

**Tucker Place Park** Emmons Ave. & 27 St. Sandwiched between the Stella Maris bait shop and the piers, this tiny park offers big views.

**Brigham Street Park** Foot of Brigham St. Undeveloped bayside parkland well used by anglers casting from the bulkhead. There is a Department of Environmental Protection dock at the bottom of the street. ✗

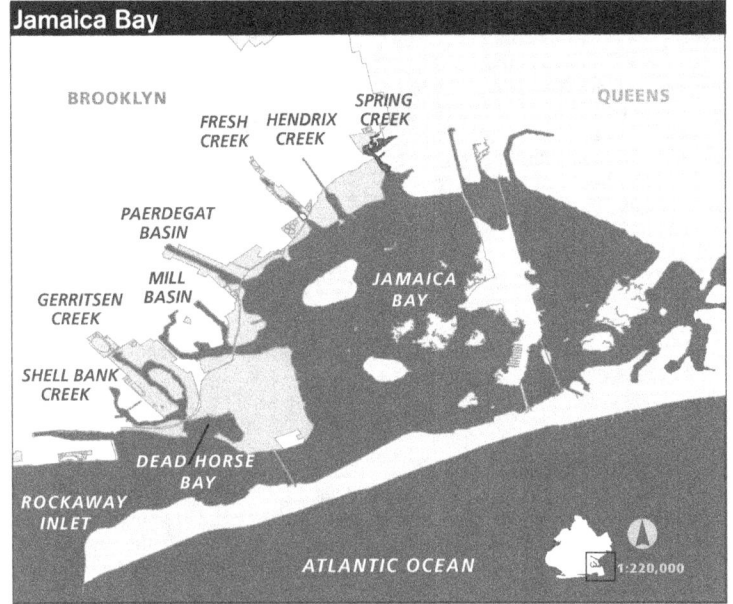

## Jamaica Bay

Jamaica Bay and the Belt Parkway define Brooklyn's southern boundary. Jamaica Bay is a 39 square mile estuarine lagoon filled with hassocks, meadows, freshwater wetlands, barrier beaches, and salt marshes that provide critical habitat for large populations of birds, butterflies, shellfish, and finfish. The largest area of open space in New York City, the Bay straddles Brooklyn and Queens and is separated from the Atlantic Ocean by the Rockaway Peninsula. Jamaica Bay is an active recreational area for boating, fishing, and birding. It provides rich habitat for winter flounder, scup, bluefish, weakfish, American eel, stripped bass, American shad, and black sea bass.

In Brooklyn, 2,000 acres of land surrounding the bay are publicly owned. Floyd Bennett Field, Plumb Beach, Canarsie Pier, Marine Park, and the grass islands lie within Gateway National Recreation Area, 26,000 acres in Brooklyn, Queens, Staten Island, and Sandy Hook, New Jersey under the jurisdiction of the National Park Service. New York City has designated Jamaica Bay a Special Natural Waterfront Area where preservation is a priority, while New York State has identified the bay as a Significant Fish and Wildlife Habitat.

The coast is scored by a number of channels, creeks, and inlets. The two mile long main channel follows the perimeter of the bay connecting at Rockaway Inlet to the Atlantic Ocean. Water depths range from 13 to 20 feet, with some channels dredged up to 50 feet for navigation. In the interior of the bay, wildlife preserves are off limits except for educational and research purposes. These areas carry names originally given by local fishermen and oystermen, like Canarsie Pol, Elders Point Marsh, and Pumpkin Patch Marsh.

No one knows why the salt marshes of Jamaica Bay are shrinking. The marshes protect shore communities, provide habitat and shelter, and defend against coastal flooding. Human encroachments threaten these valuable environments. Roadways encircle the bay, train tracks bisect it, and growing residential development crowds the shore. Channels have been dredged, waterfronts bulkheaded, and deep borrow pits dug in the bay's bottom. Pollution is also a problem, since the only sources of water are the tides of the Atlantic Ocean and outflows from four water pollution control plants.

## Shell Bank Creek

Shell Bank Creek and Gerritsen Creek are the first inlets of Jamaica Bay east of Sheepshead Bay. The approach is through Plumb Beach Channel with serious shoals along the coastline and a mid channel depth of 12 feet. A long neck of land reaching across the mouth of the conduit and named for an indigenous fruit, the beach was first an island of squatters' shacks and beach bungalows. In 1940 the island became a beach, part of construction of the Belt Parkway system. Gerritsen Inlet Bridge provides clearance of 35 feet at mean high water. Several marinas line the west bulkhead of Shell Bank Creek, quietly existing beside a sewage treatment plant, highway, and a big box retailer.

Gerritsen Beach is a peninsula of narrow streets and waterfront homes

with private docks bounded by Shell Bank Creek on the west, Plumb Beach Channel on the south, and Gerritsen Creek on the east. The neighborhood is named for Wolfert Gerritsen, a Dutch settler who built his house and America's first tide powered gristmill here in 1645. The mill burned to the water line, leaving only the pilings visible. The Gotham Avenue Canal cuts the neighborhood in two, separating one story bungalows to the south from newer houses to the north. A private strip of sand called Kiddie Beach is open only to residents.

<u>Subway</u>: B Q to Kings Hwy. to B31 Bus to Gerritsen Ave.

<u>Greenway</u>: The eastern section of Shore Greenway begins at Brigham St. and Emmons Ave. in Sheepshead Bay for 11 miles on the waterfront through Plumb Beach, Marine Park, Floyd Bennett Field, Bergen Beach Park, Canarsie Beach Pier, and Spring Creek Park, ending in Howard Beach, Queens.

<u>Blueway</u>: Water Trail: Plumb Beach

**Plum(b) Beach** (GATE) Belt Pkwy. east of Exit 9, Knapp Street. A gritty little beach composed of a long dune, tidal lagoon, and mudflats where horseshoe crabs lay eggs in late spring. The seashore's handy parking and strong breezes make it a center for kiteboarding and windsurfing and an easy launch access for kayaks into Rockaway Inlet. nps.gov/gate

# Gerritsen Creek

This freshwater creek flows in a straight line through Marine Park at the eastern edge of the protected Gerritsen peninsula to drain in Dead Horse Bay. It originally streamed inland as far as Kings Highway, but was diverted underground to feed freshwater to the salt marsh. The charred wood pilings of the Gerritsen tide mill are still visible at the head of the creek at low tide. Between Gerritsen and Mill Creeks, White Island is a wildlife preserve supporting a wide range of shorebirds, including sandpipers, heron, cormorants and egrets. There are many submerged wrecks and the pilings of an old bridge in the waterway. Gerritsen is a "no wake" zone most of its length north of the Belt Parkway. The west side is a natural area with trails along the marsh next to athletic fields and recreational facilities. The area, the former horse racing estate of the Whitney family, was donated to the city in 1920 as a public park. A picturesque 18-hole golf course takes up the eastern shore of Mill Creek.

Subway: 2, 5 to Flatbush Ave., or N, F, or Q to Ave. U

Greenway: A dedicated bicycle lane extends along Flatbush Ave. from Marine Park past Floyd Bennett Field to Jacob Riis Park in Rockaway.

Blueway: Water Trail: Salt Marsh Center

**White Island** (Mau Mau Island) 73 acres. This onetime city dump on a sandbar in the middle of the creek is now a bird sanctuary accessible by kayak or canoe. Grassland nesting habitats are being extensively restored.

**Marine Park** (GATE) Flatbush Ave. at Gerritsen & Fillmore Aves. 798 acres. The park has over 500 acres of Forever Wild preserve alongside nature trails, a golf course, baseball diamonds, handball courts, and cricket pitches.

**Henrik I. Lott House** 1940 E 36 St. Built in 1792, this rare example of Dutch-American farmhouse architecture served as a working farm until the 1920s and stayed in Lott family hands largely unchanged until 1989. 718-375-2681 historichousetrust.org

**Salt Marsh Nature Center** 3302 Ave. U at E 33 St. A mile long nature trail winds through tall cordgrass to scenic lookouts on the creek and tidal flats. At the nearby nature center park rangers offer exhibits, classes, and explorer programs, such as canoeing, fishing, and bird watching. 718-421-2021

## Dead Horse Bay

Dead Horse Bay washes the eastern shore of the Barren Island peninsula, which merges with Rockaway Inlet to the south and Mill Basin on the northeast. This is a cove of low lying salt marsh and tidal mudflats on the southwest side of what was Barren Island, once the largest island in the bay before being filled to create Floyd Bennett Field. The bay gets its name from the horse rendering industry that occupied its shore in the 18th century. Booty from the notorious buccaneer Charles Gibbs is said to be buried here. A treasure trove of old glass bottles can be seen at "Bottle Beach" on the southern and eastern shore of the landfill. The level acreage has grasslands, woodlands, salt marsh, and coastal dunes which attract shorebirds, hawks, owls, sparrows, and songbirds.

Floyd Bennett Field opened in 1931 as the city's first municipal airport, named for the pilot of Admiral Byrd's faked North Pole flyover. Legendary flights by Amelia Earhart, Wiley Post, "Wrong Way" Corrigan, and Howard Hughes launched from its runways. Italo Balbo landed 24 Italian seaplanes at the field in 1933. It was a Naval Air Station from WWII to 1972, when it was taken over by the National Park Service.

Subway: B, Q to Sheepshead Bay; 2, 5 to Flatbush Ave. to Q35 bus.

Greenway: Shore Greenway passes Plumb Beach, links with the Rockaway Gateway Greenway running adjacent to Floyd Bennett Field, at Flatbush Ave. and over Marine Pkwy. Bridge.

Blueway: Water Trail: Floyd Bennett Seaplane Launch, Mill Basin Outlet

**Floyd Bennett Field** (GATE) Flatbush Ave. 1,448 acres. The old airfield houses the Police Department's Aviation Unit, airship dockage, FAA radar station, a model airfield, and the historic Hangar Row, now the private Aviator Sports and Recreation complex. In Hanger B, volunteers of the Historic Aircraft Restoration Project (HARP) preserve aviation heritage by restoring vintage aircraft, including a PBY-5A Catalina twin engine seaplane. The grounds, attracting more than one million visitors annually, are crisscrossed by original runways and encompass nature trails, kayak launches, public campsites, playgrounds, fishing beaches, community gardens, and acres of reverted grassland habitat. Park rangers offer year round educational and recreational programs, such as free kayak paddles, basic sailing lessons, and shore casting clinics. The historic Ryan Center, the old passenger terminal and control tower, is being refurbished into a modern visitors center with exhibits about the history of the Field. The permit office is housed at the entrance gate until 2010, open daily 8:30am to 5pm. 718-338-3799 nps.gov/gate

**Gateway Golf Center** 3200 Flatbush Ave. A driving range, batting cages, tennis courts, and mini golf located on Dead Horse Bay offers terrific views.

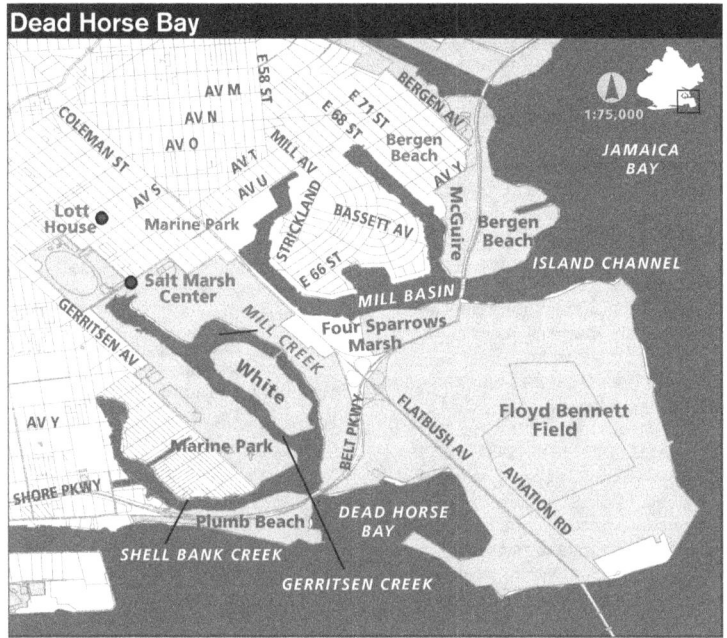

## Mill Basin/East Mill Basin

Mill Basin was first mapped by Adriaen Block as he explored other tributaries in Jamaica Bay. Its name reflects early history, when mills propelled by the tides would grind grain on the shore. The oldest extant house in the United States originally stood here, at E 63 Street, south of Avenue V. Built in 1675 by the owner of Mill Island, the Jan Martense Schenck house was dismantled and moved in 2005 to its current home inside the Brooklyn Museum. There it stands beside the 1775 home of grandson Nicholas Schenck, which had overlooked Jamaica Bay from Canarsie Beach Park.

The man-made promontory is surrounded by Mill Basin and East Mill Basin channels, and connected by landfill to Brooklyn on the north at Avenue U. It is insulated by the northeastern wing of Floyd Bennett Field and the skinny arm of Bergen Beach. Mill Basin and East Mill Basin are about 13 feet deep. The approach through Mill Basin Outlet has sand bars near the base of a drawbridge which is being replaced by a fixed bridge with a clearance of 60 feet.

This was an important industrial center by the early 20th century, transformed again after WWII into a family neighborhood of brick bungalows. The enclave of circular streets and flashy mansions with backyard boat docks has no public waterfront access. Kings Plaza, Toys R Us, and Home Depot parking lots provide a peek at the basin and its boat slips. In recent years, marinas and yacht clubs have been replaced by townhouses.

Subway: Q to the Ave. U, then B3 bus to Flatbush Ave.

Blueway: Water Trail: Mill Basin Marina

**Four Sparrows Marsh Preserve**
Flatbush Ave. at the boundary of the Toys R Us parking lot. 67 acres. The salt marsh, south of Mill Island on the north coast of former Barren Island, is an important migrating bird stopover and vital nesting habitat to four native species, including Song, Swamp, Sharp-tailed and Seaside sparrows. It is an inaccessible Forever Wild Site.

**McGuire Park** Bergen Ave. & Ave. X. 77 acres. An active sports park used for baseball, volleyball, roller blading, and tennis reaches from East Mill Basin to Paerdegat Basin on the north side of the parkway.

**Bergen Beach Park** (GATE) Bergen Ave. 300 acres. The national parkland, originally an island fronted by amusement parks, contains three miles of protected beach stretching from Mill Basin Outlet west to Paerdegat Basin south of the Belt Parkway. It holds marshland and the seaside bridle paths of Jamaica Bay Riding Academy. 718-531-8949 horsebackride.com

## Paerdegat Basin

Paerdegat Basin is a 450 foot wide, mile long bulkheaded channel dredged to 16 feet deep. The name means "horse gate" in Dutch. Bound by Bergen Avenue, Flatlands Avenue, and Paerdegat Avenue North, most of the shoreline is city owned park with marinas and boat clubs. The tributary, originally a tidal creek, is popular for boating and kayaking. Sebago Canoe Club, a club devoted to human powered boating, provides free community kayaking paddles into Jamaica Bay during warmer months. A waste treatment plant anchors the head of the channel. Because of low tidal exchange and outfalls from several combined sewers significantly reduce water quality in the basin, a large holding tank is to be installed to capture runoff in an effort to restore the east side of the Basin.

Canarsie Pier is a municipal dock originally built to develop Jamaica Bay into a major seaport. Dreams of spanning the bay with large commercial wharves were never realized, however over the years unchecked development killed shellfish harvesting and an active shore resort industry.

<u>Subway</u>: L to Canarsie/Rockaway Pkwy. then the free B42 Bus; bus also stops at Canarsie Pier.

<u>Greenway</u>: Shore Parkway multi-use path runs from along the perimeter of the coastal wetlands.

<u>Blueway</u>: Water Trail: Canarsie Pier, Sebago Canoe Club

**Paerdegat Basin Park** Ave. T. 169 acres, 75 acres underwater. There is no access to this Forever Wild Site comprised of natural wetlands and wildlife habitat on the western banks of the creek, north of McGuire Park.

**Canarsie Park** (or Seaview Park) Between Seaview Ave. & Belt Pkwy. 132 acres. Athletic fields north of the parkway accommodate cricket, baseball, soccer, and basketball.

**Canarsie Beach Park and Pier** (GATE) Foot of Rockaway Pkwy. The land below the Belt Parkway consists of natural areas and a reedy beach with access to Jamaica Bay. A broad 600 foot long pier is a favorite fishing spot and good vantage for seeing wildlife on the protected marsh islands. Before the pier, a bungalow colony with a floating bathhouse occupied Canarsie Landing, an area rich with crabs and shellfish, but so heavily polluted by 1920, the Board of Health shut down fishing and swimming in Jamaica Bay. There is a beach kayak launch on the eastside of the pier, picnic area, ample parking, and a ranger station The defunct restaurant and floating docks have been idle for years.

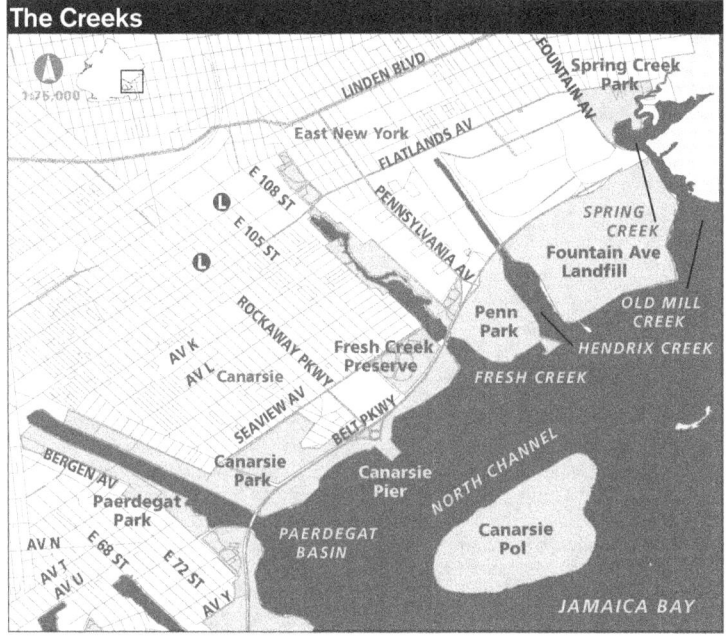

## The Creeks

Of the murky creeks emptying into Jamaica Bay, most are channelized waterways bound by former municipal landfills. Hundreds of abandoned and wrecked boats dumped in these backwaters impede navigation and damage fragile ecosystems. Restoration of the Jamaica Bay ecosystem focuses on eliminating invasive plant species along the shore, unclogging sediment buildup in the creeks, improving tidal flows, and allowing the wetlands surrounding the creeks to revert to a natural state.

Fresh Creek Basin and Hendrix Creek flank the massive Spring Creek Towers (formerly Starrett City), built at the foot of Pennsylvania Avenue in 1976. This is the largest federally subsidized housing project in the country with 20,000 residents in 46 buildings spread across 150 acres of wetlands. Fresh Creek meanders about a half mile beside Louisiana Avenue on its eastern periphery, from 125 feet to 650 feet wide with water depths three to 18 feet. The Fresh Creek Bridge carries the Belt Parkway over the creek at a clearance of 21 feet. The Towers lie on the shared delta of Fresh and Hendrix Creeks, where landfill has created a peninsula piled 30 feet high with refuse and which for years was used to sun dry sludge from the nearby 26th Ward Water Pollution Control Plant. The plant feeds Hendrix Creek, which flows for a mile through the East New York neighborhood before emptying into the bay. At the eastern mouth of Hendrix Creek is the dormant Fountain Avenue landfill. The Gateway Center strip mall has been developed on the upland part of the old garbage dump.

Remediation of the Pennsylvania and Fountain Avenue landfills is the largest restoration project undertaken by New York City. Oyster beds have been reintroduced in Hendrix Creek to serve as natural water filters, able to handle as much as 50 gallons of water a day. Spring Creek, two miles east of Canarsie Pier, marks the Queens border. It is actually three tidal streams, including Old Mill and Ralph Creeks.

<u>Subway</u>: A to Euclid Ave., Q8 Bus to Gateway Mall

<u>Greenway</u>: Shore Greenway: From Pennsylvania Ave. to JFK Airport is six miles and intersects with a one mile path on west side of Erskine St. in Spring Creek Park.

**Fresh Creek Nature Preserve** E 108 St., Louisiana & Seaview Aves. 74 acres. The narrow strip of salt marsh skirting both shores of the creek and the channel itself is designated a Forever Wild Site. The eastern shore has walking paths and a landing at Louisiana Avenue for views of the creek and marshland.

**Penn Park** Foot of Pennsylvania Ave. 110 acres. The park greens the closed landfill with native tree plantings that will over time restore coastal forest. ✘

**Creek Park** Gateway Ave. & Erskine St. A nature walk runs along the wetlands of Hendrix Creek and a cricket pitch at Gateway Mall.

**Fountain Avenue Natural Area** Foot of Fountain Ave. 300 acres. The work of transforming this sealed city dump to a landscaped park has been started by the city's Department of Environmental Protection. ✘

**Spring Creek Park Preserve** 75 acres. The mostly inaccessible Forever Wild Site is the largest undeveloped wetlands in Jamaica Bay, located around the head of Spring Creek and Old Mill Creek. In the northwestern corner, a 20 acre Sanitation Department composting facility handles 15,000 tons of yard waste and discarded Christmas trees each year.

# Queens

Queens, the largest of the five boroughs in area, has more than 7,000 acres of city parkland, a few patches of state property, and large tracts of a unique national park. The borough also contains 30% of the city's waterfront on two coasts, encompassing 196 miles of shoreline on Jamaica Bay, Long Island Sound, Flushing Bay, Little Neck Bay, East River, Newtown Creek, and the Atlantic Ocean.

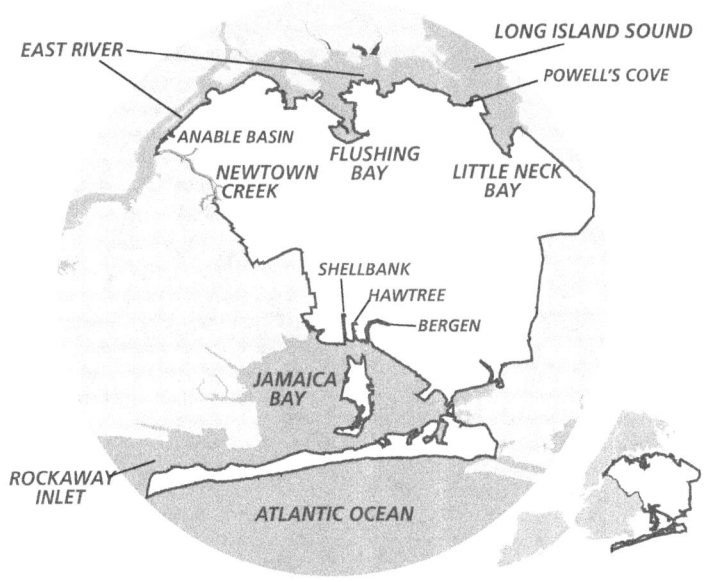

## Jamaica Bay

Jamaica Bay takes its name from the Jamaco Native Americans. It is a tidal estuary covering 18,000 acres of wetlands surrounded by Brooklyn and Queens. Formed by the Rockaway Peninsula the bay, it opens to the west on Lower New York Bay through Rockaway Inlet at Breezy Point—the easternmost tip of a barrier beach system extending 60 miles along the southern Long Island shore. The mean water depth in Jamaica Bay is 13 feet with a tidal range of five feet.

The 1,000 foot wide channel at Rockaway Inlet is dredged to 20 feet. The Marine Parkway (Gil Hodges Memorial) Bridge crosses the inlet between Rockaway Point and Barren Island, where a pair of Peregrine falcons nest in the north tower of the vertical lift span. Vessels entering the bay must pass under the bridge at 55 foot clearance (down) to 152 feet (up). Boat traffic is almost exclusively recreational except for a small number of barges and tankers. Several channels interconnect across the bay winding through marsh islands, including North, Winhole, Grass Hassock, Pumpkin Patch, and The Raunt. To protect sensitive shoreline, a ban on the use of personal watercraft has been in effect in the Gateway National Recreation Area waters of the bay since 2002.

Just 15 miles southeast of the Battery, Jamaica Bay's coastline supports the most productive natural marine ecosystem in the northeast and is the largest coastal wetland and one of the most valuable coastal resources in New York State. Its sheltered waters, marsh islands, and inlets are a major migratory bird stopover on the Atlantic Flyway and an extremely productive fishery for finfish and shellfish. Terrapins and Atlantic Ridley sea turtles reside in the bay. Wetlands buffer the effects of storms and ocean waves on the shore, and protect residential areas from flooding.

Jamaica Bay's fragile ecosystem is over 1,000 years old. It has endured a century of dredging, landfilling, development, and other human encroachments. A watershed of about 85,000 acres drains to the bay and four wastewater treatment plants dump millions of gallons into the water each day. Efforts are underway to control erosion, restore wetlands, and develop riparian buffer zones between the bay and surrounding uplands. Many of the marsh islands in the bay are only visible at low tide, and these ever changing islands are rapidly eroding. Low lying marsh areas are protected sites that can be visited for study by permit only.

Robert Moses rescued the bay's shore from development in 1938 by creating a wildlife refuge and lacing the waters' edge with parks. The parkland is part of Gateway National Recreation Area, a 26,000 acre preserve created by an act of Congress in the 1970s and run by the National Park Service. Gateway National Recreation Area is composed of three distinct units: Jamaica Bay, Staten Island, and Sandy Hook. Jamaica Bay, the largest, comprises a well known wildlife refuge, historic forts and airfields, private beach communities, and outdoor recreational facilities. The Jamaica Bay unit encompasses Frank Charles Memorial Park, Jamaica Bay Wildlife Refuge, Jacob Riis Park, Fort Tilden, and Breezy Point.

## Grassy Bay

Grassy Bay is a labyrinth of inlets and marshland within Jamaica Bay, east of Cross Bay Boulevard along the southwest shore leading to John F. Kennedy International Airport. Winhole is a natural channel extending a mile south through Grassy Bay to Beach Channel. The deep borrow pits originally dug to provide clean fill for airport expansion are being restored to help improve water quality.

Shellbank Basin is a mile long, 250 foot wide, and 10 foot deep canal that drains into Grassy Bay. It runs behind the commercial strip of Cross Bay Boulevard in Howard Beach. The mouth of the basin is skirted to the west by a picturesque portion of Spring Creek Park. Frank

M. Charles Memorial Park flanks the eastern side. The basin is crowded with docks and pleasure craft. Howard Beach is a residential community first established as a fishing camp of squatters' shacks on the eastern banks of Hawtree Basin. The area was transformed in the early 1900s by glove manufacturer Bill Howard who dredged Shellbank Basin and labeled the new community the "Venice of Long Island." Across Hawtree Basin a few fishing shacks remain among the houses on pilings with private wharves in the alleys and dead end streets of tiny Hamilton Beach, bound by Jamaica Bay to the south, and the subway tracks and airport to the east. At 163 Street a pedestrian bridge links Hamilton Beach and Howard Beach.

John F. Kennedy International Airport was built as Idlewild Airport in 1948 over the Idlewild Beach Golf Club, several creeks, and 680 acres of marshland east of Hamilton Beach. Cordgrass, creeks, and wetlands fringe the airfield. Within the airport, Bergen Basin is a 15 foot deep hook shaped channel draining into Grassy Bay. The west bank at its mouth holds vacant parkland and a 40 foot high circular storage tank. A water pollution control plant at the head of the basin and fuel storage tanks on the eastern shore are nearby. On the east end of the airport is Hook Creek, a two mile long freshwater stream through Idlewild Park and Hook Creek Sanctuary. The Hook Creek Canal marks the Queens-Nassau County border. Grassy Bay ends at JoCo Marsh where JFK's runway 22 intrudes on the nesting area of the only laughing gull colony in New York State. Thurston Basin has a depth of about 10 feet at the entrance to two feet at the head. Head of Bay Basin flanks the eastside of JoCo Marsh and marks the end of airport property.

Subway: A to Howard Beach. Q11 Bus to Hamilton Beach.

Greenway: Shore Greenway ends just past the Queens border. There is an onstreet bike lane on Cross Bay Blvd. to Addabbo Bridge linking to Rockaway Gateway Greenway, a 20-mile multipurpose trail circumnavigating the Bay.

Blueway: Water Trail: Idlewild Park

**Frank M. Charles Memorial Park** Shellbank Basin. 165 Ave. 15 acres. Natural wildlife preserve with a half-mile paved perimeter walkway running the entire length of the park to a sand beach with amazing views and to storied tennis courts once home base to Vitas Gerulaitis.

**West Hamilton Beach Park** Hawtree Basin. End of 104 St. & 165 Ave. 5 acres. The park, accessible over a wooden bridge, offers walking paths through marsh, fields, and beach. Recreation amenities include ball fields, playground, and picnic area.

**Idlewild Park Preserve** Thurston Basin. Northwest border of the airport bounded by Rockaway Blvd., Springfield Blvd., 149 Ave., and Brookville Blvd. in Rosedale. 346 acres. A pristine wetland comprised of sandy grasslands, dunes, and freshwater tributaries of Hook Creek. The designated Forever Wild Area encompasses a kayak/canoe launch to explore the preserve at Public Place and Hook Creek Wildlife Sanctuary.

# Broad Channel

Broad Channel is an island in Jamaica Bay situated midway between the Queens mainland and Rockaway Peninsula and linked by the Joseph P. Addabbo Bridge on the north and the Cross Bay Veterans Bridge on the south. The only inhabited island in the bay, it was a Canarsee and Jameco Indian fishing village later populated by homesteaders and squatters. The northern half of the island, Ruler's Bar Hassock, is part of the Jamaica Bay Wildlife Refuge, established by the City Department of Parks and Recreation (DPR) in 1951 under Robert Moses. Thanks to Herbert Johnson, the first refuge manager, the landscape was transformed and is today one of the largest bird sanctuaries in the northeastern United States.

About 3,000 residents live on the southern half of the island. Because of the marshy ground many of the homes are built on wooden stilts and connected by plank gangways. Raunt Channel is a shallow waterway that flows through Big Egg Marsh, Little Egg Marsh, and Yellow Bar Hassock, terminating at Goose Pond Marsh. Smitty's Fishing Station offers boat rentals for fishing and exploring the bay.

Subway: A to Broad Channel.

Greenway: Rockaway Gateway Greenway is a multi use path on the west side of Cross Bay Blvd. extending to the Wildlife Refuge over Veterans Memorial Bridge, then on Beach Channel Dr. along Jamaica Bay, and over the Marine Pkwy. Bridge to Flatbush Ave. and Floyd Bennett Field.

Blueway: Water Trail: North Channel Bridge Beach

**North Channel Bridge Beach** (GATE) Cross Bay Blvd. At the southern foot of the Addabbo Bridge, sand beaches, and parking lots on both sides of the roadway are used by picnickers, anglers, and kayakers.

**Jamaica Bay Wildlife Refuge** (GATE) Cross Bay Blvd. 9,155 acres. Waterfowl and shorebirds flock to these feeding grounds during migration, when more than 300 species have been spotted, including glossy ibis, great blue heron, warbler,

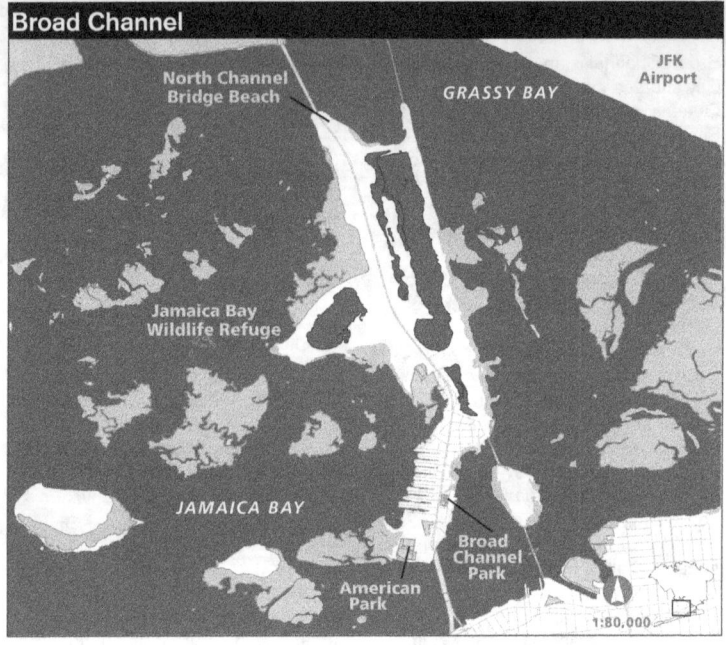

## Broad Channel

and snow geese. From the visitor center, the 1.5 mile West Pond trail loops around 45 acres of habitat. The three mile trail around East Pond is less traveled and more secluded. Open year round, 8:30am to 5pm, except for Christmas and New Year's Day. 718-318-4340 nps.gov/gate

**Broad Channel Wetlands** 188 St to 197 St & Cross Bay Blvd. 33 acres. Protected tract of salt marsh on the west side of the island.

**Broad Channel Park** Cross Bay Blvd. between E 16 & E 18 Rds. 15 acres. This ribbon park on East Broad Channel offers tennis, handball, and basketball courts.

**Broad Channel American Park** Cross Bay Blvd. & 20 Rd. 17 acres. Ball fields on the southern tip of the islet overlooking Jamaica Bay.

## Rockaway Peninsula

The 11 mile long Rockaway Peninsula takes its name from a Delaware/Chippewa term meaning "sandy place." The first European resident on the neck of land was iron master Richard Cornell who built a homestead on what is now Beach 20 Street in 1690, and whose family later founded Cornell University. Their cemetery in Far Rockaway is one of the city's oldest and a landmark. Before the Civil War, the Rockaway shore was a world famous resort, Rockaway Playland amusement park operated from 1901 to 1985. Today, only a handful of older bungalows survive among large public housing projects and seaside condos. At Breezy Point on its western tip, the peninsula has added a mile of new beach, thanks to ocean tides which have deposited sand from barrier beaches farther to the east.

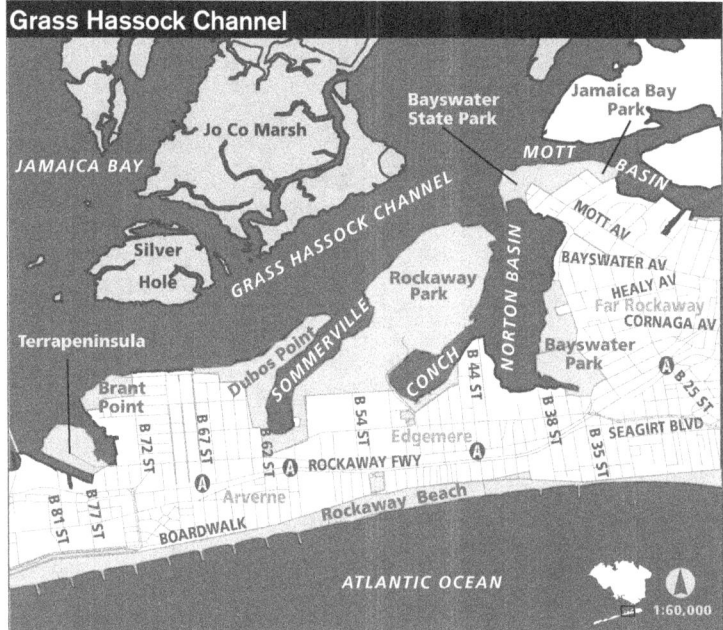

# Grass Hassock Channel

Far Rockaway is the south border of Jamaica Bay. Grass Hassock Channel extends east of JoCo Marsh to Head of the Bay. A 1905 medical report pointed to Grass Hassock Channel oysters as the common cause in the outbreak of typhoid among local residents. A chain of parks now skirt the back bay and afford public access to the water's edge. The Audubon Society and Trust for Public Land helped preserve many of these waterfront parcels fronting Grass Hassock Channel as part of the "Buffer the Bay" project aimed at protecting natural wetlands. One tract was the former estate of investment banker Louis A. Heinsheimer called "Breezy Point." His elaborate 1907 limestone mansion overlooking Jamaica Bay was demolished in 1987 to allow the land to return to a natural state. It is the site of Bayswater State Park.

Subway: A to Far Rockaway/Mott Ave or Wavecrest/Beach 25 St.

Blueway: Water Trail: Bayswater Park

**Jamaica Bay Park** 149 acres. On the northeast edge of Mott Basin, the park takes in several parcels of undisturbed wetland reachable only by a narrow path from Edgewater Road.

**Bayswater Point State Park**
End of Mott Ave. 12 acres. A preserve of marshland, beach, and woodlands at the very tip of Mott Point Peninsula, best for birding, fishing, and hiking. 718-471-2212 nysparks.state.ny.us

**Norton Basin Natural Resource Area**
Foot of Healy Ave. 11 acres. Restored tidal wetlands and dunes managed by the New York State Department of Environmental Conservation offer opportunities for nature viewing and hiking on nature trails.

**Bayswater Park** B 32 St. 30 acres. Marshland and sand beach hugging the head of Norton Basin has views of Lower Manhattan and contains playgrounds, barbecue pits, ball fields, tennis courts, and a kayak launch.

**Rockaway Community Park** Almeda Ave. 253 acres. The former Edgemere landfill is a windswept jut of land located between Conch (Little Bay), Norton, and Sommerville Basins that has been allowed to return to a natural state providing for birding, hiking, and shore casting. Park amenities include ball fields and courts.

**Dubos Point Wildlife Sanctuary** B 63 St. & DeCosta Ave. 34 acres. The finger peninsula of Conchs Hole Point is built of dredged material and is named for the visionary ecologist René Dubos and his wife Jean, who advocated creating the sanctuary. Best access is along the shore.

**Brant Point Wildlife Sanctuary** 17 acres. Bayfield Ave. & DeCosta Ave. Undeveloped wetlands fronted by rocky beach acquired by City Parks to help protect the shore ecosystem.

**Terrapeninsula Preserve** Amstel Blvd. 22 acres. A knob of high coastal dunes, grasslands, and salt marsh jutting in the bay and bound by the silt filled Vernam and Barbados basins.

The Forever Wild Site has plenty of marine plants, such as sea lavender, beach heather, and bayberry which attract a variety of songbirds.

## Beach Channel

A main passage for boat traffic on the bay, Beach Channel is a narrow waterway separating Broad Channel Island from the northside of Rockaway Peninsula. Beach Channel Drive edges the bay traveling from the Nassau County border and connecting the Cross Bay and Marine Parkway Bridges. Cross Bay Veterans Memorial Bridge has a clearance of 55 feet. The bulkhead alongside the bay is a popular fishing spot and provides a pedestrian path beside the bay from bridge to bridge. There are parks, playgrounds, and public access areas along much of this bayside. Jet skis are allowed to operate in the waters closest to the coast of Rockaway, where federal restrictions do not apply. Farther west is the Belle Harbor Yacht Club, established in 1905. Its 500 foot wooden dock was destroyed by a hurricane in the 1930s.

<u>Subway</u>: A to Broad Channel, then S Shuttle to Beach 105 St.

<u>Greenway</u>: Bicycle lanes on all bridges to Rockaway, Beach Channel Dr. and Shore Front Pkwy.

**Beach Channel High School**
Beach Channel Dr. The school offers classes in oceanography and marine sciences, rowing, and a new center dedicated to researching Jamaica Bay's disappearing saltwater marshes. The athletic fields are on the bay.

**Waterfront Tribute Park** B 116 St. Open space and a memorial to 9/11 featuring a mosaic centerpiece *The Heavens over Rockaway* and firefighters memorial by local artist Patrick Clark.

**Beach Channel Park** B 116 to 124 St. Beach Channel Dr. 12 acres. A narrow park and walkway beside the bulkhead is a fine place for fishing and viewing the bay.

**Beach Channel West** B 128 to B 130 Sts. Beach Channel Dr. .75 acre. A grass promontory and seawall on land once owned by the Belle Harbor Yacht Club.

## Rockaway Inlet

Rockaway Inlet connects Jamaica Bay to the Atlantic Ocean. The channel lies between the Rockaway Point breakwater to the southeast and the coast of Coney Island to the northwest, with depths of 15 feet at mid channel. A long stone jetty and 25 foot light tower mark the very tip of the peninsula. West of the channel entrance are shallow shoals of less than one foot.

In 1919, the first transatlantic flight took off from Rockaway Naval Air Station, today's Jacob Riis Park. Gateway National Recreation Area, one of the first national parks, was created in 1972 to administer much of the lands around Jamaica Bay including Fort Tilden and Breezy Point. The largest part of it is protected habitat. The gated 500 acre Breezy Point Cooperative of 2,800 single family homes, including Roxbury, Rockaway Point, and Breezy Point, is

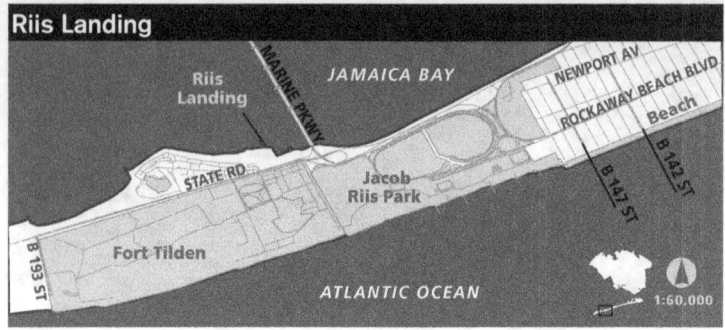

located amid three miles of federally maintained seashore interlaced by pedestrian-only pathways.

Much of the shore west of Jacob Riis Park did not exist before the 1900s, when groins built to protect the beaches of Rockaway caused sand to drift westward extending the beach. Over 100 new acres have been added since 1960. On the bayside near Beach 218 Street the remains of a fire control tower recall the gun batteries built during WWII as part of the harbor defense system. The western end of Rockaway Peninsula is the best city seashore for beachcombing and shelling, its coastal waters offering the finest sailing conditions in the bay. Terns, skimmers, and American oystercatchers swoop down or scurry along the water's edge and parts of the beach are closed each spring to safeguard nests of endangered piping plovers. Wading surfcasters pitch into schools of stripers and blues feeding on bait fish caught in the currents. Party boats drift the inlet's tides setting hooks for bass and fluke.

Shallow bars, dangerous rocks, reefs, and shoals off the coast have caused thousands of shipwrecks. The station of the U.S. Life-Saving Service was established in 1849 in Rockaway Point. In 1856 USLSS merged with the United States Coast Guard and the post stands today as Coast Guard Station Rockaway at Riis Landing. The remains of wrecks attract marine life which in turn draw fishing and dive boats. There are regular trips to the *Black Warrior* beached on Rockaway Bar in 1859 and the *Cornelia Soule* foundered off Rockaway Point in 1902. In 1993, the notorious *Golden Venture*, overloaded with hundreds of Chinese immigrants, went aground off Fort Tilden, where 10 drowned trying to escape.

<u>Subway</u>: 2 or 5 to Flatbush Ave. last stop transfer to the Q35 Bus to Rockaway or the Q22 from Beach 116 St.

<u>Greenway</u>: Rockaway Gateway Greenway runs across Marine Parkway Bridge to Jacob Riis Park. There is a bike lane on Rockaway Point Blvd. to Breezy Point. Fort Tilden has paved trails.

<u>Blueway</u>: Riis Landing: Seasonal ferry service to the beach.

**Jacob Riis Park** (GATE) Rockaway Blvd. at Channel Dr. B 149 St. to B169 St. 220 acres. A deep, mile long sandy beach divided by jetties into 14 bays and bound by dunes, a concrete boardwalk, snack bars, and recreation areas, the first beach developed for urban motorists was built by Robert Moses and transferred to the National Park Service. The park is named for the Danish journalist who uncovered the poverty of immigrant New York in the early 1900s. The Park's recently restored Moorish-style bathhouse

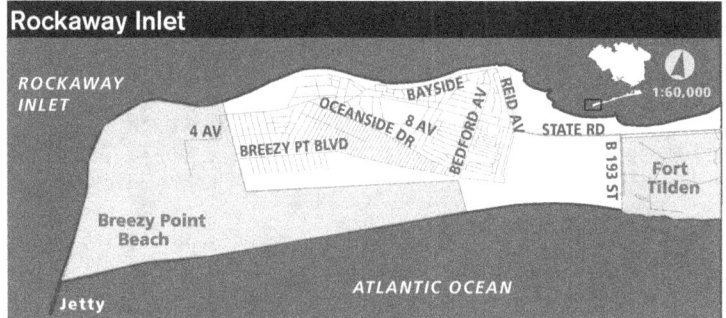

## Rockaway Inlet

and historic clock tower, both city landmarks since the 1930s, are on the National Register of Historic Places. Nude bathing is tolerated at the western end of the beach.

• **Executive Golf Course** B 155 St. 18-hole, Par 3 pitch-and-putt built on the beach promenade in 1935.

**Riis Landing** (GATE) B 169 St. A former U.S. Coast Guard facility comprises a boat basin, ferry dock, and parking lot along a seawall on the south side of Rockaway. It's used for fishing, eco-cruises, and ferry service.

**Fort Tilden** (GATE) B 169 St. & Rockaway Pt. Blvd. 317 acres. A garrison established in 1917, Fort Tilden was once the site of Nike Ajax and Hercules air defense missiles. Named for New York governor Samuel Tilden, the base was decommissioned in 1974 and reassigned to the National Park Service. Scattered across the landscape of 20 foot high dunes and isolated beaches are former weapons installations. One, the old gun site at Battery Harris East, offers great hawk watching. 718-318-4300 nps.gov/gate

• **Silver Gull Club** 1 B 193 St. Made famous by the movie The Flamingo Kid, this members only beach club has a huge pool, tennis, and catering. 718-634-2900 silvergullclub.com

**Breezy Point Beach** (GATE) Rockaway Point Blvd. 200 acres. A half mile wide white sand beach, grasslands, and drifting dunes along two miles of protected national seashore within the exclusive cooperative community. The best parking access is a fisherman's off-road permit ($50), which can be purchased at Fort Tilden Ranger Station.

• **Breezy Point Surf Club** 1 B 227 St. Private cabana club providing nonresidents access to the beach at Breezy Point. Members enjoy 60 acres of beach, a pool, cafe, and bar. 718-634-7200 bpsconline.com

## Atlantic Ocean

Giovanni da Verrazano, exploring the shores of New York Bay in 1542, noted a wampum station crowded with natives at present day Rockaway. Henry Hudson passed Rockaway when he sailed into New York Harbor in 1609. In 1640, the Mohawk sold some of the land to the Dutch; in 1685 the Canarsee sold it to the English. The first Europeans built homesteads in Far Rockaway five years later.

A barrier beach extending from Far Rockaway westward to the tip of Breezy Point, this long, narrow neck is made of sand and sediment pushed along the southern coast of Long Island from other barrier beaches as far east as Montauk. The beachfront is completely engineered, and jetties and groins extend from every block in an attempt to fight erosion. The coast is prone to severe rip tides which cause dangerous swimming conditions. The waters off Rockaway are prime fishing ground. A recordbreaking 735 pound tuna was caught in 1935. In 2006, a six foot blue shark washed up on the beach. About two nautical miles offshore anglers and divers enjoy the artificial Rockaway Reef, made up of old tires, construction rubble, and steel buoys covering over 400 acres at a depth of 40 feet.

## Rockaway Beach

Rockaway Beach once rivaled Coney Island as America's most popular seaside resort. It was known as the "Irish Saratoga" in the late 1800s because of the large number of Irish immigrants who settled there. Generations of Jews and other immigrants also caught ocean breezes from the porches of bungalows and boarding houses around the boardwalk from Beach 112 to Beach 115 Streets. Action centers around Beach 116 Street.

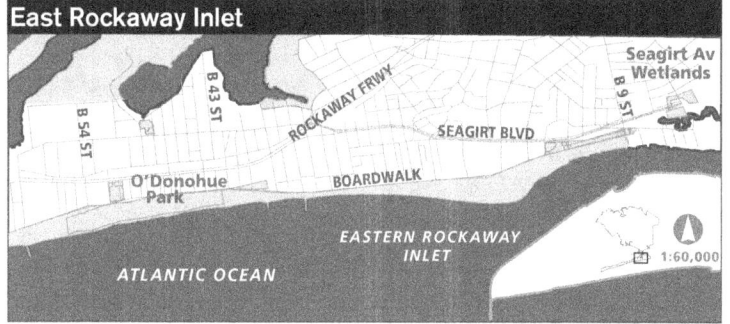

**East Rockaway Inlet**

Rockaway has been a surf destination since Hawaiian legend Duke Kahanamoku first introduced the long board in 1912. The Rockaways beloved icon Whaleamena, a 13 foot high, 19 foot long stucco whale, relocated from the Central Park Children's Zoo to mark the main entrance to Rockaway Beach at Beach 95 Street. On Shore Front Parkway the wave-shaped bus shelters sport murals of aquatic scenes painted by artist Ester A. Grillo. At Beach 116 Street, artist Freddy Rodriguez commemorates the 300 lives lost in the crash here of American Airlines flight 587 on November 12, 2001.

Subway: A to Broad Channel transfer to S shuttle to B 90, 98, 105, or 116 St.

Greenway: The Shore Front Pkwy. bike lane runs 1.6 miles from B 73 to B 109 Sts. and connects with Beach Channel.

**Rockaway Beach & Boardwalk** B 149 St. Neponsit to B 3 St. Far Rockaway. 97 acres. The country's largest urban beach extends for seven miles on the Atlantic Ocean and attracts four million visitors a season. Ocean Promenade boardwalk runs from B 126 to B 129 Streets. There are two surf beaches B 67 to B 69 Sts. and B 87 to B 92 Sts. Barbecuing areas and playgrounds are located all over the seaside. Handicap access at B 17, B 116, and B 131 Sts.

## East Rockaway Inlet

Here in Far Rockaway, public housing projects, speculative development, and the remaining empty acres leveled for urban renewal in the 1970s mark this sadly neglected waterfront. A popular scuba diving spot at Beach 8, near the Atlantic Beach Bridge, has depths of 40 feet in the middle of Reynolds Channel, which teems with marine life. Police and fire department scuba rescue units train here, along with local dive certification outfitters. With new development threatening public water access, scuba divers advocate designating the beach exclusively for diving and snorkeling.

Subway: A to Far Rockaway/Mott Ave.; Wavecrest/B 25 St.; B 67 St.

**Arverne Shorebird Preserve** B 57 to B 44 Sts. 84 acres. Protected dunes and a nature park for piping plover nesting area. Forever Wild Area.

**O'Donohue Park Boardwalk** B 20 – B 17 Sts. 2.5 acres. The boardwalk fronts athletic fields and a grilling area built in 1963 on the site of Roche's private bathing beach which operated here from 1881 to 1931.

**Seagirt Wetlands** B 5 to B 3 St. 6 acres. Just off the boardwalk, this salt marsh restoration provides critical habitat for native wildlife.

# Long Island Sound

Long Island Sound is an estuary of the Atlantic Ocean and several Connecticut rivers. One hundred and ten miles long and an average 21 miles wide, the sound is home to a varied shoreline of about 548 miles. Water depths range from 60 to 120 feet. Navigator Adriaen Block discovered the sound when he sailed up the East River from New York Harbor in 1614. In a village on Little Neck Bay, Matinecoc Indians established a wampum factory making beads made from local shells. The coastal waters were a rich source for oyster and hard clams in the 19th century until over harvesting and pollution closed the beds.

Along the Sound, the North Shore of Long Island is known as the Gold Coast because of its wealthy neighborhoods and stately mansions. A raggedy coast and low hills created by glacial deposits dominate the Queens north shore along the East River and Long Island Sound. Its tiny bays and coves are bound by grand homes, high density condo towers, and waterside parks intersected by the Cross Island Expressway and Northern Boulevard.

# Little Neck Bay

Little Neck Bay is a shallow harbor inlet of about 1,400 acres, less than 10 feet deep at mean low water with a tidal range of about seven feet. It is an important striped bass nursery and waterfowl habitat as well as a bustling recreational boating area. Anglers cast for stripers, blues, scup, menhaden, blackfish, and winter flounder.

Captain Kidd is said to have anchored here where his band of pirates smuggled booty in secret passages dug beneath what is now Bayside. Later, prohibition rum runners navigated the bay. By the early 1900s, Hollywood celebrities W.C. Fields, Norma Talmadge, Rudolph Valentino, and other prominent residents were building estates on the waterfront.

Douglaston Peninsula on the bay's eastern shore is flanked by the protected wetlands of Alley Pond and Udalls Cove. Alley Creek, a freshwater brook, cuts a ravine threw the park draining to Little Neck Bay. Native brook trout were reintroduced here in recent years. Udalls Cove is a 30 acre inlet off Little Neck Bay marked by salt marsh and freshwater wetlands. These freshwater creeks are important spawning areas for American eel. Gabler's Creek flows through a gully known as The Ravine to feed Aurora Pond, which is also fed by natural springs near the Long Island Rail Road embankment. These coastal wetlands, filled in by the WPA in the 1940s in an attempt to control mosquitoes, are being restored to their natural state.

Little Bay is tucked under the southern viaduct of the Throgs Neck Bridge, where, since 1926, the greens of Clearview Golf Course have offered grand views of the Sound and the bridge. A spur at the end of Utopia Parkway at 12 Road offers a short scenic waterside drive. Crowding the western edge of the bay, the massive Le Havre apartment complex takes up 28 acres and the six acre Cryders Point cooperative houses has its own promenade and great water views.

<u>Subway</u>: 7 to Main St. or LIRR to Little Neck, Douglaston or Bayside.

<u>Greenway</u>: Joe Michaels Mile travels 3 miles from Alley Pond Park to Fort Totten and Little Bay Park. There is an access ramp at 35 Ave. and 28 Ave. Vanderbilt Roadway is 2.5-mile bicycle path extending from Alley Pond to Cunningham Park. The Brooklyn-Queens Greenway is to be a 40 mile continuous route, 22 miles are in place, that crosses existing parks from Coney Island to Alley Pond Park.

<u>Blueway</u>: Water Trail: Bayside Marina

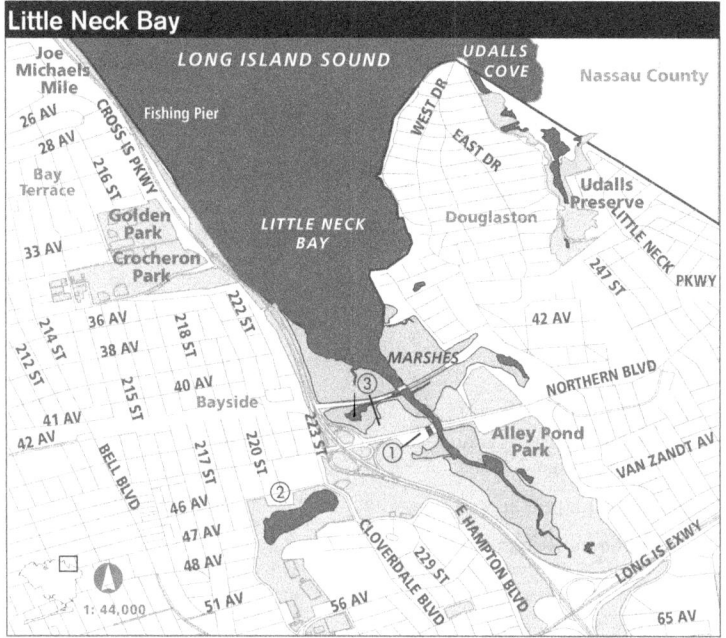

**Udalls Cove Park Preserve** Northern Blvd., 244-247 Sts. & Douglas Rd. 31 acres. 2.5 miles of nature trails offer views of osprey nesting platforms through shallow intertidal flats and swamp. The cove is named for Richard Udall who bought a mill here in 1833. Trails and a viewing platform overlook Aurora Pond (Sand Hill Rd.) a one acre freshwater watering hole newly restored at the center of the park.

**Douglaston Manor Historic District** Douglaston Peninsula. 175 acres. A garden community developed on the former Douglas estate in 1906 whose residents cooperatively own the mile-long waterfront, including a private dock and two private beaches. The first winner of the America's Cup was estate heir William Douglas' yacht, *Sappho*. The historically significant range of architecture includes 31 homes protected as the city's largest group of Arts and Crafts houses and others designed by famed female architect Josephine Wright Chapman. The Landmark district is in the National Register of Historic Places and contains the city's largest collection of imported trees along with Long Island's oldest tree, a 600 year old white oak at 233 Arleigh Road. The square, 1819 mansion of Wyant van Zandt, now the Douglaston Club, sits atop a high peak overlooking an 18-hole golf course and the city skyline.

**Alley Pond Park** 288-06 Northern Blvd. 655 acres. The diverse ecosystem of Queens' second largest park is sand and rock and boulders shaped by glacial moraine 15,000 years ago. A significant natural preserve protected as park in 1929 it contains hardwood forest, meadows, natural springs, and freshwater kettle ponds in the southern end and saltwater wetlands

in the north, all accessed by trails and interpreted at the nature center. New York City park's systems first nature trail opened here in 1935. There are 26 acres of recreational fields featuring a high ropes climbing course, ball fields and courts, playgrounds, bridle paths, and barbecue areas.

**Alley Pond Park Points of Interest:**

① **Alley Pond Environmental Center** (APEC) 228-06 Northern Blvd. The center offers conservation education and youth programming such as bird walks, nature hikes, and workshops. 718-229-4000 alleypond.com

② **Windmill** A working replica of a windmill originally built in 1870 but destroyed by fire in 1988, which pumps water from a well deep in the pond.

③ **Kettle Ponds** were created by melting glaciers in the Ice Age. An esplanade skirts Oakland Lake, a 20 foot deep spring-fed kettle pond offering excellent freshwater fishing. Other kettle ponds in the park include Little Alley Pond, Turtle Pond, Lily Pad Pond, and Decadon Pond.

**Crocheron Park** 33 Rd. to 36 Ave. 46 acres. The former estate of the Crocheron family, built in 1695, is one of the city's prettiest scenic parks. A verdant landscape of meandering footpaths it features a pergola on a bluff above the inlet, an aquatic theme playground, sports fields, and the tennis house.

**John Golden Park** 215 Pl. & 32 Ave. 17 acres. The old John Golden estate of the Broadway producer called "Mr. Bayside" was bequeathed to the city in the 1950s. There are picnic grounds, baseball diamonds, tennis courts, and a goldfish pond.

**Bayside Marina Fishing Pier** 28 Ave. A footbridge crosses Cross Island Pkwy. from Crocheron Park to the pier where fishing and crabbing are permitted. There is a snack bar and small boat moorings. Parking is reserved for boat owners. 718-229-0097

**Joe Michaels Mile** Northern Blvd. to Totten Rd. 2.75 miles. A wide path along Little Neck Bay from Fort Totten running under the Throgs Neck Bridge to Little Bay Park and Shore Road. The path is named for the drummer of the 1906s doo-wop group Jay and the Americans, who was a Bayside resident and avid marathoner.

**Fort Totten Park** Totten Ave. at Totten & 15 Rds. 50 acres. A portion of the Army base was transferred to the City Department of Parks and Recreation in 2005. The landscape serves panoramic views of Long Island Sound along with its granite battery, historic structures, parade grounds, outdoor pool, and athletic fields. At the entrance gate is a parking lot, a small rocky beach where paddlers launch kayaks and a long rock jetty where anglers cast into the bay. The Visitors

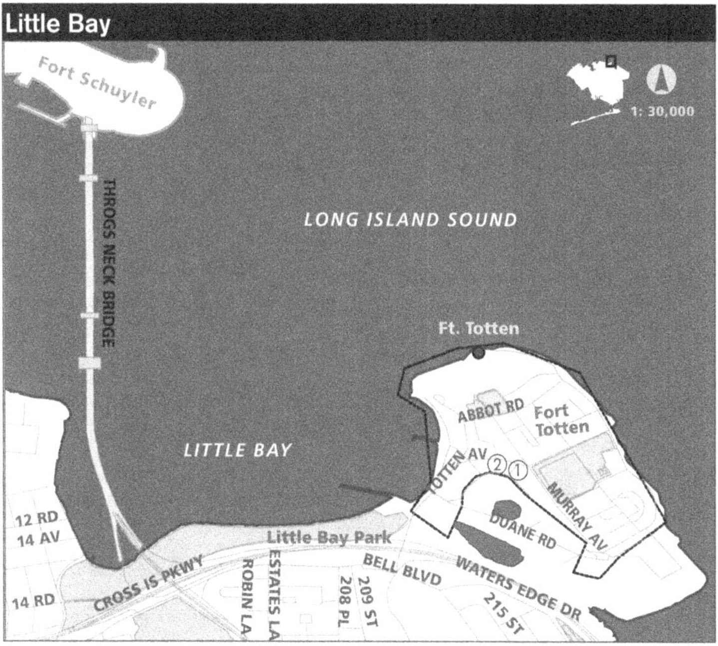

# Little Bay

Center has a museum and Urban Park Rangers offer scheduled guided tours.

Fort Totten was built in 1857 on 136 acres on the western promontory of Willets Point to protect the East River approach to New York Harbor. Meant to mirror Fort Schuyler in the Bronx, it was designed by General Robert E. Lee and named for the engineer General Joseph Totten. It housed the regional headquarters of the Nike Missile Defense system from 1954 to 1974 and is still home to the U.S. Army Reserves 77th Division. It is on the National Register of Historic Places and its Battery and Officers' Club are city landmarks.

**Fort Totten Points of Interest:**

① **Officers' Club** 208 Totten Ave. The castle that inspired the Army Corps of Engineers insignia was built in 1887 and is today home to the Bayside Historical Society.

② **Willets Farmhouse** Totten Ave. Built in 1829, the oldest house in Fort Totten was owned by Charles Willet, owner of one of the early fruit tree nurseries in Flushing.

**Little Bay Park** Cross Island Pkwy. & Utopia Pkwy. 50 acres. A green ribbon park abutting a rock-strewn beach, concrete pier, and wide path that stretches from Fort Totten to the base of the Throgs Neck Bridge.

# Upper East River

The East River is a 14 mile long tidal strait linking Long Island Sound to Upper New York Bay. Powell Cove Boulevard runs through the largely residential communities of Beechhurst, Whitestone, Robinswood, and the discreet enclave of Malba along a three mile stretch of waterfront from the Throgs Neck to the Bronx-Whitestone Bridge. Whitestone is one of the area's oldest European settlements, said to have been named for a large white boulder visible in the water where the East River meets Long Island Sound. Whitestone Point juts into the river east of the bridge where rocky shoals hold a skeleton light tower. The Bronx-Whitestone Bridge was built to carry traffic to the 1939 World's Fair.

The Tropicana company has distributed its Florida orange juice from this coast since the 1950s, when as much as 1.5 million gallons were being shipped here each week aboard the world's only "juice tanker," *SS Tropicana*, which operated until 1961. The shore is changing: waterfront patio homes and large estates are being replaced by crowded multifamily housing, condos, and "McMansions."

Just west of the Bronx-Whitestone Bridge, Powell's Cove is a little bay fronting a preserve of reclaimed salt marsh between Malba and College Point. It provides a rich habitat for birds and fish, and welcomes exploration of its natural areas.

Subway: 7 to Flushing/Main St. transfer to Q14 or Q15 Bus; Q25 Bus to Powell's Cove. Or LIRR to Flushing.

Greenway: QBx1 Bus Bike & Ride shuttle crosses the Bronx-Whitestone Bridge, which along with the Throgs Neck Bridge has no bike access.

Blueway: Water Trail: Francis Lewis Park

**Francis Lewis Park** 3 Ave. at 147 St. 17 acres. Shady green place beneath the Bronx-Whitestone Bridge, named for Whitestone's most famous resident, a signer of the Declaration of Independence. The park offers a waterside esplanade, ball courts, and a gravel beach used as a kayak landing.

**Malba Pier Circle** Foot of Malba Dr. A scenic lookout at the parking circle at the water's edge. The original Malba Field & Marine Club (c.1914) pier, boat docks, and boathouse were destroyed by arson in 1992. Plans are in progress to restore the facility.

**Powell's Cove Park** Located between 9 Ave., 130 St. & 11 Ave. 24 acres. A preserve of restored tidal wetlands with paths cutting through open fields, high saltmarsh cordgrass, and patches of trees to a rocky beach and overlook

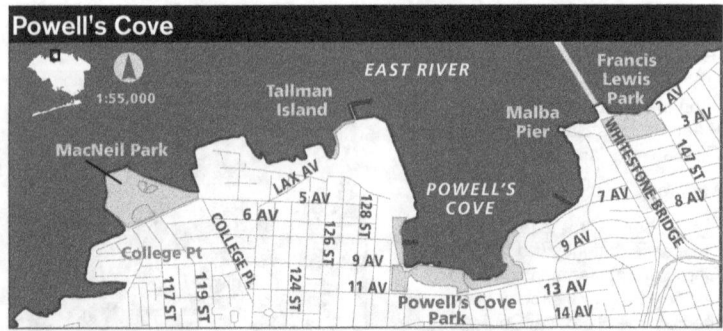

perfect for scoping heron feeding in the cove and watching fiddler crabs scatter on the mud flats at low tide. An iron fence securing the property depicts the skyline of the Whitestone Bridge.

**Tallman Island Park** 127-01 Powell's Cove Blvd. 30 acres. The onetime island home to a large beer garden was joined to Long Island and a wastewater control plant was built in the late 1930s. On its western perimeter, a landscaped public walkway adjoins the property. The dock, used by Department of Environmental Protection vessels, is closed to public use.

**Hermon MacNeil Park** 119 St. & Poppenhusen Ave. 29 acres. A shady hillside park with groomed lawns sloping to winding waterside paths through ball fields, playgrounds, and picnic areas presents spectacular vistas of the distant Manhattan skyline. The park is named for the renowned sculptor of *George Washington as Commander-in-Chief, Accompanied by Fame and Valor* on the Washington Square Arch in Manhattan. The fenced shoreline is all riprap.

# Flushing Bay

Flushing Bay extends four miles inland to the village of Flushing, the geographical center of New York City and the city's fastest-growing business district. The land here once bloomed with fruit trees in America's first commercial nursery, the first apple orchard established by Robert Prince on eight acres in 1737. The site, visited by George Washington and Thomas Jefferson, was the repository of botanical finds from the Lewis and Clark Expedition and home to the Linnaean Botanic Gardens.

Today, industrial pollution, development, sewer overflows, airport runoff, low tidal flow, and silting all contribute to poor water quality in the bay. Dredging is required to maintain a 15 foot deep navigational channel for barging sand, concrete, and petroleum products. Water depth outside of the channel is about six feet. The *Socony 200*, the first barge with a concrete hull, was launched in Flushing Bay by Fougner Concrete Shipbuilding Company in 1918. The last barge manufacturer on the Bay closed shop over 50 years ago.

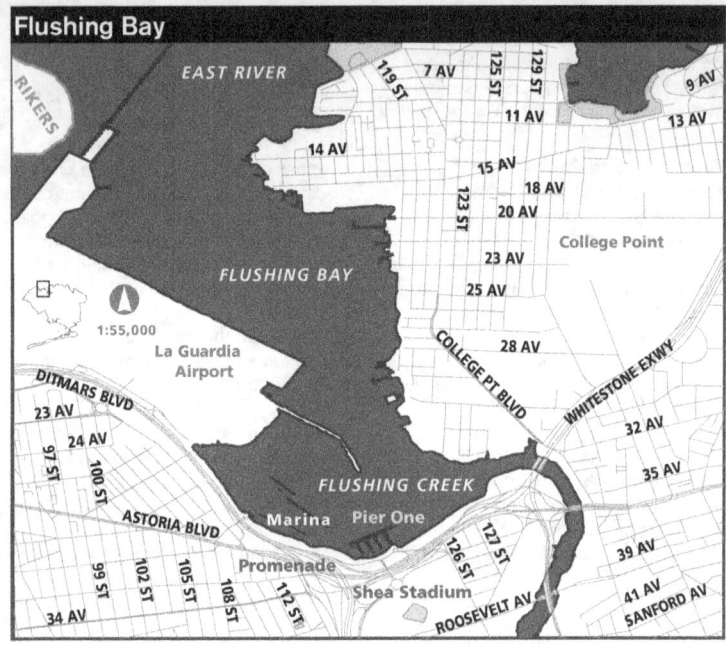

College Point is a hilly peninsula on the northeastern shore and LaGuardia Airport sits on the western rim of the bay. A light marks the College Point Reef just offshore. The landscape was completely transformed in the 1850s by German immigrant Conrad Poppenhusen who built not only a bridge from Flushing to College Point but also the nation's first free kindergarten, today a landmark community center at 114-04 14 Road. College Point became the rubber capital of the region when Poppenhusen bankrolled Charles Goodyear's vulcanization process and began to manufacture combs here. The heavily commercial eastern shore blocks much of the waterfront. The oarsmen of the Wahnetah Boat Club pushed off from these shores in the early 1900s. The green west bank at the mouth of Flushing River offers waterfront access today at parks, marinas, and promenades.

## Flushing Creek

Flushing Creek flows through a valley that bisects Queens, contains Flushing Meadows-Corona Park and downtown Flushing. It drains into the southeast head of Flushing Bay. The waterway is narrow with average depths ranging from five to 16 feet. A dredged channel runs slightly less than a mile to the Roosevelt Avenue Bridge, where there is a turning basin. Other fixed bridges cross the river with clearances of 34 feet. The river is heavily polluted and inaccessible to the public.

By the 1920s, land along the creek was replaced by a 90 foot high pile of ash nicknamed Mount Corona— the Valley of Ashes made famous by F. Scott Fitzgerald in *The Great Gatsby*. Robert Moses transformed the site for the 1939 World's Fair. Remnants of old ash pits and stone silos can be found amid the auto junkyards of the

# Flushing Creek

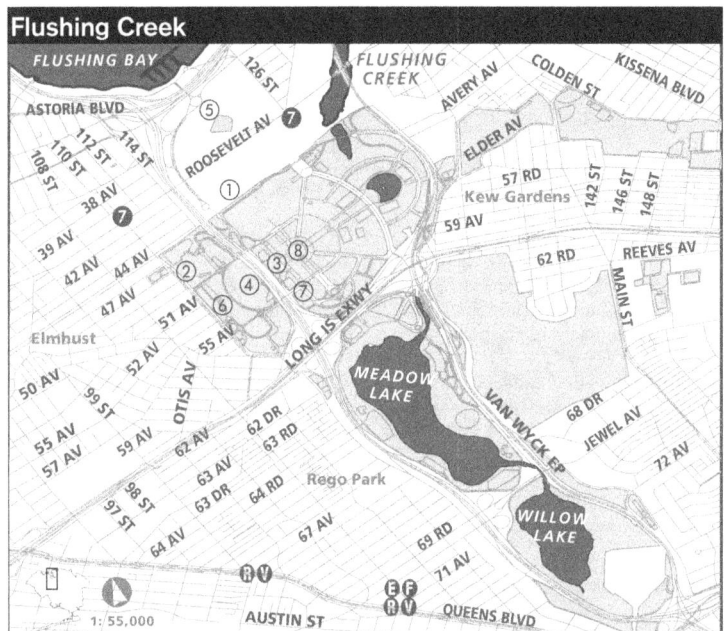

"iron triangle" on the west side of the river on Willets Point, an area that the city has slated for a makeover.

Subway: 7 to Willets Point/Shea Stadium or Main St/Flushing; LIRR to Flushing Station.

Greenway: Flushing Bay Promenade runs from Harpers St. to LaGuardia Airport. A bridge connects downtown Flushing to the Promenade. Flushing Meadow park paths link to Kissena Park and the B-Q Greenway. Bike rentals available at Meadow Lake boathouse.

Blueway: Seasonal Ferry to Shea Stadium & U.S. Open ferry. Water Trail: World's Fair Marina.

**Flushing Bay Promenade** 27 Ave. 28 acres. A 1.4-mile long public walk on Flushing Bay stretching from Flushing River near the site of the former Shea Stadium extends to LaGuardia Airport, offering biking, strolling, and fishing. There is a large city owned marina, paved boat ramp, and kayak launch, parking lot, and waterfront restaurant. There is a parking fee during Met's home games.

**Pier One** World's Fair Marina's public pier and docks offering fishing, kayaking, dragon boat racing, powerboats, transient vessels, Skyline excursion cruises of Long Island Sound, and ferry landing for Mets baseball express ferries arriving at the new Citi Field. A concession on the pier offers snacks

**Flushing River Esplanade** River at 40 Rd. 14 acres. Real estate development, like the troubled Sky View Parc high rise, pair retail and residential with promises of public parks and waterfront promenades on the river at the former Con Ed site. ✘

**Flushing Meadows-Corona Park**
Grand Central Pkwy. & Van Wyck Expwy. 1,225 acres. The sprawling park built atop the old Corona Dump is the city's third largest. It makes use of pavilions leftover from the 1939 and 1964 World's Fairs to house cultural, recreational, and sports facilities. Flushing River feeds the twin man made Willow and Meadow lakes, the latter ringed by a bike path. The Meadow Lake boathouse hosts a sailing school and dragon boat crews, as well as paddle and rowboat rentals in season. Willow Lake is a largely inaccessible natural area. Fishing is currently prohibited after invasive snakehead fish were found in the lakes.

**Flushing Meadows Points of Interest:**

① **Arthur Ashe Stadium** Home to the U.S. Open Tennis Championship.

② **New York Hall of Science** 47-01 111 St. Hands-on learning center.

③ **Queens Museum** Built for the 1939 World's Fair, the former New York City Pavilion has the world's largest diorama of the metropolis. In 1947, the United Nations briefly met here and voted on the creation of Israel.

④ **Queens Zoo** Animals native to North America and a geodesic dome aviary designed by Buckminster Fuller.

⑤ **Shea Stadium** Roosevelt Ave The new home of the New York Mets, replacing Shea Stadium (demolished) which was built next door in 1964.

⑥ **Terrace On The Park** In a 120 foot high building designed as a heliport for the 1964 World's Fair (the Beatles landed here), this catering hall offers East River views.

⑦ **Queens Theatre in the Park** The former New York State Pavilion's Tent of Tomorrow from the 1964 Fair is home to an active performance season. The Pavilion's rusted remaining observation towers were seen in *Men in Black*.

⑧ **Unisphere** At 12 stories, the world's largest globe was the steel centerpiece of the 1964 World's Fair theme "Peace Through Understanding." It is 140 feet high and 120 feet in diameter.

# Bowery Bay

The 680 acres of LaGuardia Airport, built atop the former Gala Amusement Park, dominate the largely industrial waterfront. A bridge crosses Rikers Island Channel to the Bronx prison island, and a Con Edison power plant occupies former Berrian Island across Luyster Creek from the Bowery Bay Water Pollution Control Plant. Facing Rikers Island the Dutch Colonial Riker homestead still stands and is the oldest house in the city owned as a private residence. The Art Deco Marine Air Terminal was the airport's first, welcoming the Boeing 314 Clippers of Pan American Airlines. These classic seaplanes are memorialized in the Terminal's terra cotta frieze of flying fish.

West of Bowery Bay, Steinway Creek can be reached by dirt road off Berrian Boulevard. Timber is still barged down the Creek to Steinway and Sons piano factory established by German cabinet-maker Henry Steinway in the 1880s. The old Steinway mansion rests on a buff over Bowery Bay at 42 Street and Berrian Boulevard, near a row of 19th century worker houses that were part of the company town, Steinway Village.

Subway: N to Ditmars Ave.; R to Steinway St./Astoria.

Greenway: On-street bike lane on 20 Ave. from Hazen St. Bowery Bay to Shore Rd. on the East River.

**Athletic Fields** 19 Ave. at Hazen St. Baseball diamonds in a fenced field near Bowery Bay are blocked from water views and access.

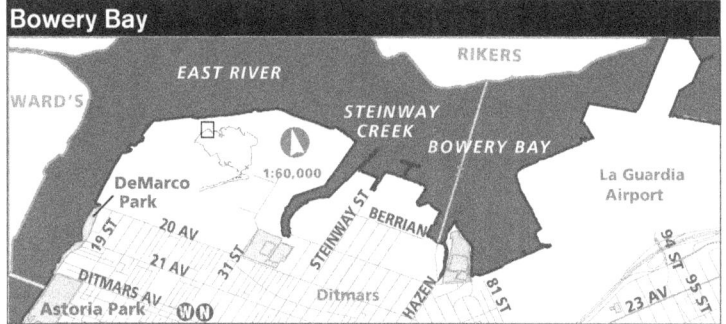

Bowery Bay

## East River

This is one of the East River's most accessible shorefronts, containing over 100 acres of parkland. Its principal neighborhood, Long Island City, is made up of several distinctive villages which merged decades before the consolidation of New York City. Native peoples called the coast Sunswick, or "high woman's place," where a small creek and extensive marshlands drained to Hallets Cove, first filled for farmland and later for development at present day 21 Street. The land elbows south at Hell Gate, the very narrow, heavily trafficked channel separating Ward's Island from Astoria. Named Hellegat (or 'bright passage") by the Dutch explorer Adriaen Block. Here the forces of the East River, Harlem River, and Long Island Sound converge at one of the deepest and most treacherous areas in the harbor. Many ships have sunk in Hell Gate. In 1929, the female daredevil Emilie Neumann Muse swam across its turbulent waters. There is a brief window of calm at slack tide, providing about a half hour when it is best to go through Hell Gate.

Hallet's Point is a knob of land projecting into Hell Gate. It is bound by the shallow waters of Pot Cove and Hallet's Cove and marked by a U.S. Coast Guard navigation light on a stanchion in Whitey Ford Field. Pot Cove is a bend on the north shore of the point, where the huge pyramid topped Shore Towers blocks water views and restricts shore access. Old industrial buildings are finding new uses, such as the Sohmer Piano Factory, now a luxury housing cooperative. There is a vertical lift bridge over the swift currents of the East Channel to Roosevelt Island. The narrow waterway moves so swiftly that it may one day generate electricity–tidal-power trials with submerged turbines are in progress. Dominating the waterfront farther south, the towering red and white smokestacks of Con Edison's "Big Allis," the giant Ravenswood power generating plant are reminders that Queens supplies half of New York City's electricity.

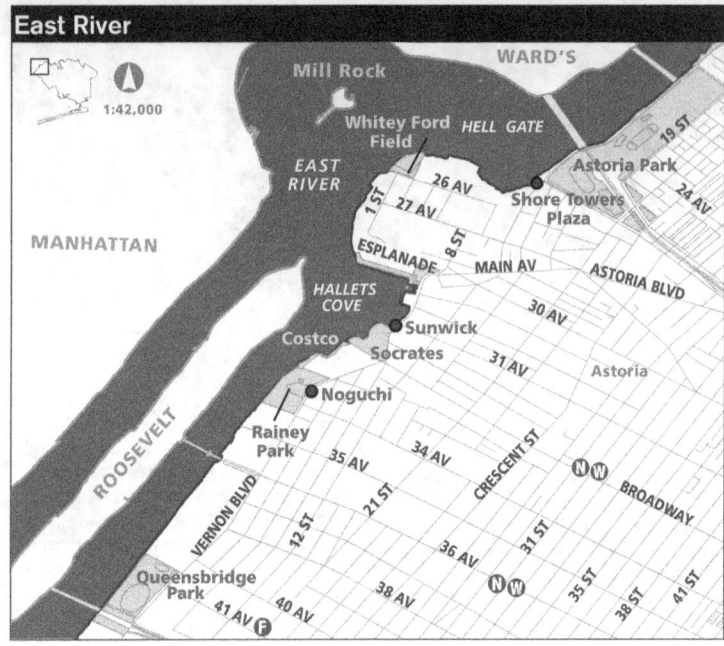

Subway: N/W to Astoria, F to 21 St. & 41 Ave.; N/W to 31 St. & 36 Ave.

Greenway: Vernon Blvd. runs parallel to the river. Access the Triborough Bridge bikeway to Wards Island at Hoyt Ave. Roosevelt Island Bridge (36 Ave.) path links to a lane around the island.

Blueway: Water Trail: Hallets Cove

**Ralph DeMarco Park** Shore Blvd. 20 Ave. to Ditmars Blvd. 6.2 acres. A narrow swatch of grassy parkland with shore path, weeping willows, benches, and extraordinary views.

**Astoria Park** Shore Blvd. from Ditmars Blvd. to Hoyt Ave. 66 acres. A stunning landscape framed by the Hellgate and Triborough Bridges, featuring a riverside esplanade, picturesque lawns, tree lined trails, tennis courts, ball fields, and the city's largest public pool. The huge Art Deco pool was built by Robert Moses and the Works Progress Administration for the 1939 Olympic trials.

**Shore Towers Plaza** 25-40 Shore Blvd. A short public promenade on Pot Cove open from dawn to dusk, but the gate is usually locked.

**Whitey Ford Field** 26 Ave. & 2 St. 3.5 acres. The ballpark named for the Yankees' star pitcher, Edward "Whitey" Ford, has seating for viewing the fast moving river and holds the Coast Guard's Hell Gate Light.

**Hallet's Cove Esplanade** 27 Ave. A wide public walkway and playground skirts the Astoria Houses overlooking Blackwell's Lighthouse on Roosevelt Island and Hallet's Cove, on land where the Englishman William Hallet received a Dutch land grant for his household in 1652.

**Sunswick Beach** Vernon Blvd. A pebble beach on the southern nook of Hallet's Point, where Sunswick Creek once flowed, accessible over a seawall. A large elm tree shades the shore where seasonal free kayaking is offered by the Long Island City Community Boathouse.

**Socrates Sculpture Garden** Vernon Blvd. at Broadway. 5 acres. A former dump on Gibbs Point transformed in 1986 and designated a park in 1998 is used chiefly for exhibiting large-scale sculptures and other public programs. 718-956-1819 socratessculpturepark.org

**Noguchi Museum** 32-37 Vernon Blvd. The 13 galleries of Japanese sculpture Isamu Noguchi are in an old factory across from the water. noguchi.org

**Costco Walkway** 32-50 Vernon Blvd. A public path on the riverfront goes around the building and parking lot. It is open to the public during store hours. No fishing.

**Rainey Park** 34 Ave. & Vernon Blvd. 9 acres. The scenic landscape contains a promenade, playground, and ball fields.

**Queensbridge Park** Vernon Blvd. & 41 Ave. 20 acres. Open fields and trees under the Queensboro (or 59 Street) Bridge made famous by Simon and Garfunkel's *Feelin' Groovy*. Restoration of the seawall after its collapse has made the esplanade inaccessible for several years. The park's many recreational facilities include athletic fields, ball courts, playground, and a barbecue area.

**Silvercup West Esplanade** Vernon Blvd. at 43 St. 6 acres. The film studio's expansion is slated to overhaul the landmark Terra Cotta Works, which made the bricks for Carnegie Hall, and create a waterfront esplanade and public plaza. (2010) ✯

## Anable Basin

Anable Basin is a 500 foot long canal constructed in 1868 and used today by cargo and oil tankers. The sprawling Queens West complex monopolizes the shore south of the canal. What remains of the public pier next to the barge restaurant Water's Edge at 44 Drive is in poor shape and inaccessible. A 12 block cluster of landscaped parks will eventually hem the East River shoreline from Anable Basin to Newtown Creek.

<u>Subway</u>: 7 to Vernon/Jackson; G to Court Sq.; E/V to 23 St./Ely Ave.; Q102 Bus runs on Vernon Blvd.

<u>Blueway</u>: Water Taxi Stops: Hunters Point, Schaefer Landing; Water Trail: LIC Community Boathouse

**LIC Community Boathouse** 46 Ave & 5 St. Community dock of the kayak club offering free paddle trips, events, and public programs. licboathouse.org

**River East** 5 St. at 47 Ave. 9.5 acres. A public park will front a large residential development at the old Pepsi plant, where the bottler donated acreage in exchange for preserving its iconic (1937) red neon sign. ✗

**Peninsula Park** Center Blvd. & 47 Rd. 1 acre. A short promontory featuring an open lawn and walkway through a naturalized riverscape.

**Gantry Plaza State Park** 48 Ave. 2.5 acres. The restored scaffolds of two historic barge gantries that once lifted railcar floats are the centerpiece of this state park preserving the shore's industrial past. The gantries are flanked by recreational piers for viewing, dining, sunning, and fishing. In the plaza, paths weave

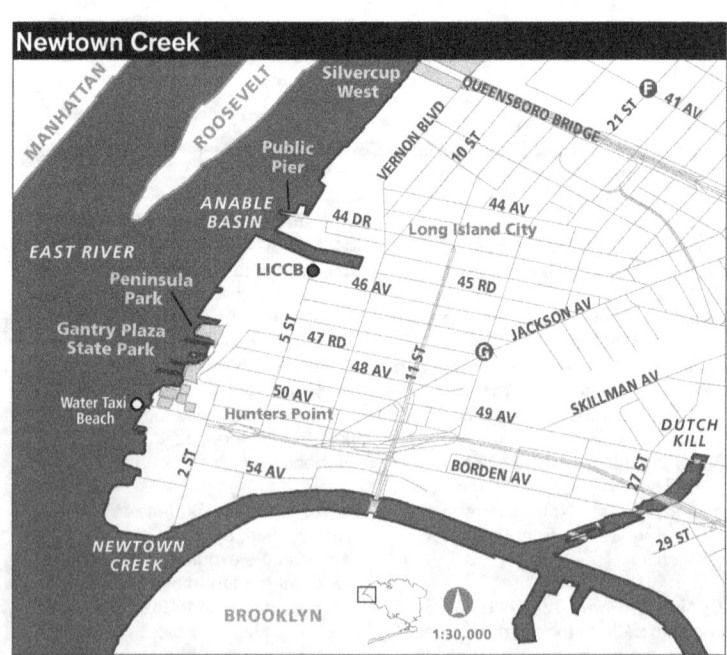

through manicured lawns and an interpretive garden. Facilities include basketball courts, handball courts, and playgrounds.

**Water Taxi Beach** 2 St. & Borden Ave. 400 tons of white sand were imported from the Jersey shore to fill a vacant lot creating a riverside beach with seasonal offerings. No swimming or water access. harborexperience.com

# Newtown Creek

Newtown Creek is a 3.5 mile long tidal flow separating Queens and Brooklyn. Legend holds that Captain Kidd buried treasure on the Queens shore of the creek. From the late 19th century until the mid 20th century, Newtown Creek was one of the nation's busiest and most polluted waterways. It remains today a heavily industrialized bulkhead lined corridor with little public access, one of six designated Significant Maritime and Industrial Areas in the city.

With depths ranging from 10 to 40 feet the 300 foot wide creek is navigable to the Grand Street/Metropolitan Avenue Swing Bridge. Headwaters are on the Maspeth Plateau, the high ground of West Maspeth. Tributaries Dutch Kill and Maspeth Creek flow north into Queens, while English Kills, East Branch, and Whale Creek lie entirely in Brooklyn. There is little tidal action and no natural freshwater flows, beyond stormwater and sewage overflow. Leaking since the 1950s, a massive oil spill under Greenpoint in Brooklyn causes a greasy slime on the surface water. Pleasure craft occasionally wander into the waterway and the practically flat water draws neighborhood kayakers. The Pulaski Bridge spans the creek and marks the midway point in the NYC Marathon, offering a commanding view of almost the entire Manhattan skyline from its narrow pedestrian path.

Dutch Kills ("kill" is Dutch for a small stream) is an arm of Newtown Creek that flows a half mile north as far as Queens Plaza. Its shore was home to the earliest Dutch settlements in Queens and the site of its first industry, a tidal gristmill. The original 1657 mill stones are the borough's oldest European artifacts, now preserved underfoot in a traffic triangle at Queens Plaza North and 41 Avenue. Industrial development has redirected the watercourse and filled adjoining wetlands. The verdant landscape of Calvary Cemetery occupies drained marshland once known as Wolf Swamp, named for the packs of wolves that once roamed it.

Maspeth Creek is a 2,000 foot long, 100 foot wide branch of Newtown Creek, which has depths of 20 feet and was filled beyond 49 Street. Maspeth is derived from the name of the native Mispat tribe and means "bad water place," referring to snake infested swamplands. Governor DeWitt Clinton drafted his ambitious plan for linking New York Harbor to Lake Erie by canal at his home near the head of the creek by the town dock. He also surveyed a canal linking Newtown Creek to Flushing Bay. In the mid 1800s, a profitable trout farm operated in the streams and ponds that fed Maspeth Creek. Today, it is one of the most polluted limbs of Newtown Creek. The Phelps-Dodge copper smelting plant (42-02 56 Road) is a 35 acre brownfield and Superfund site where decades of chemical wastes contaminate land and groundwater.

The proposed cross harbor tunnel linking port, rail, and freight facilities in New Jersey to Brooklyn and Queens would recycle Phelps into a new West Maspeth Yards dramatically altering the north bank of Newtown and Maspeth Creeks.

<u>Subway</u>: 7 to Vernon/Jackson or Hunters Point Ave.; G to 21 St.

**Street-end Parks** There is no access to Newtown Creek in Queens. New waterfront parks are proposed at the ends on 2 St. and Vernon Blvd. ✗

# Staten Island

Staten Island has been a part of New York City since 1687 when the Duke of York offered the island as prize in a sailing contest won by the team from Manhattan. The borough encompasses five islands: Staten, Hoffman, Swinburne, Prall's, Isle of Meadow, and half of Shooters Island. It has twice the land mass of Manhattan, and the lowest population of the five boroughs. At Wards Point, it is the southern-most spot in New York State and at Todt Hill, the highest point on the eastern seaboard south of Maine. The island is 17 miles long and 11 miles wide, with 35 miles of waterfront.

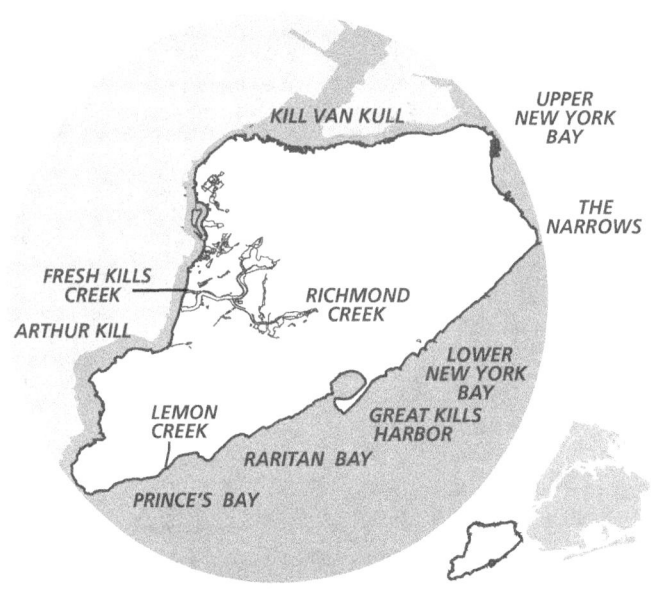

## Upper New York Bay

Staten Island offers the city's most stunning views of the inner harbor and Manhattan skyline from its shore and from its hilltop summits. Upper New York Bay extends from St. George at the north end of the island to the Verrazano-Narrows Bridge in the south. The first stop for most visitors is the ferry terminal at St. George, Staten Island's downtown named, not for the dragon slaying saint, but for real estate investor George Law, who owned this waterfront and consolidated ferry and rail terminals. Within a short walk of the ferry, the landmark St. George Historic District is notable for its terraced landscape and the rich variety of architecture, counting Victorian, Tudor, and Arts & Crafts houses. The Richmond County seat is located on Richmond Terrace with the distinctive Borough Hall and Court House designed by Carrère and Hastings set above the waterfront. The old 1929 vaudeville theater with pipe organ has been restored to its former glory.

The seeds of Cornelius Vanderbilt's fortune were sown on the coast of the Upper Bay at Stapleton, where the young entrepreneur started his ferry service between Staten Island and Manhattan. The unoccupied Naval Station New York, known as Homeport, was the site of the nation's first Free Trade Zone in the 1930s and later the port of embarkation for the Army and Navy during WWII. The Fire Department's Marine Unit 9 and its landmark vessel *Fire Fighter* operate from Homeport. Offshore is a federal anchorage used by containerships awaiting berth or a favorable tide.

In 1831, a hospital for sailors, Seamen's Retreat, opened on Bay Street in Stapleton, financed by a tax collected from all mariners entering New York Harbor. The National Institute of Health began in a one-room laboratory at the hospital in 1887. Later converted to Mariners Hospital, then

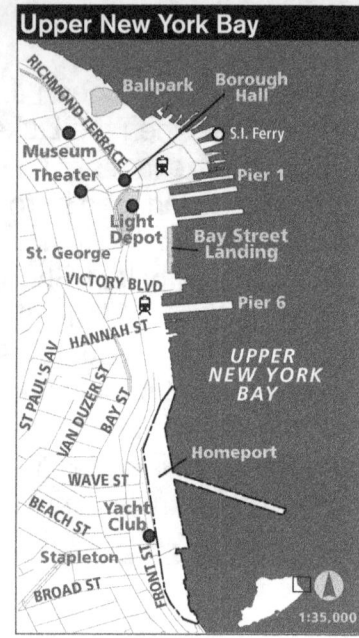

Bayley Seton Hospital, the large facility half-abandoned since 2004, may be demolished and replaced by a Salvation Army owned recreation center.

<u>Transit</u>: SIRT (Staten Island Railway) 14-mile, 21 stop commuter rail running parallel to Hylan Blvd., from St. George to Tottenville. The $2 fare is paid at St. George. 718-966-SIRT

<u>Greenway</u>: Bikes are allowed on the ferry at no charge. Exit right to North Shore Esplanade to Snug Harbor or left to St. George Esplanade and Bay Street Landing.

<u>Blueway</u>: The Staten Island Ferry carries over 60,000 passengers a day on its free 25 minute voyage from the tip of Manhattan to St. George, 24 hours a day. nyc.gov/html/dot

**St. George Terminal** 1 Bay St. The 1940s brick terminal has been modernized with a "green" roof, improved open space, huge saltwater aquariums in the waiting area, and a landscaped

waterfront plaza affording full view of the harbor and Lower Manhattan.

**Staten Island Museum** 75 Stuyvesant Pl. One of the city's oldest cultural institutions has an exhibition about the Staten Island Ferry right in the waiting room at the terminal. The museum itself is located two blocks away and holds a vast group of locally collected specimens, including 10,000 shells. 718-727-1135 statenislandmuseum.org

**North Shore Esplanade** Borough Pl. to Westervelt Ave. This mile long park and multi-use path extending along the north shore from the ferry connects recreational, cultural, and historic sites. The footpath leads to the Staten Island 9/11 Memorial *Postcards*, designed by architect Masayuki Sono. The older, narrower path reaches around the bayshore to the Kill Van Kull. The new, wider, section of the Esplanade runs from the ballpark past the terminal to Bay Street Landing by way of Siah Armajani's sculptural 65-foot-high *Tower and Bridge*, with Wallace Stevens' poem "A Bridge Above the Bright and Blue of Water."

**Richmond County Bank Ballpark** 75 Richmond Ter. The stadium, built atop the railroad tracks, hosts New York Yankees minor league play and major views of the bay from the seats. 718-698-9265 siyanks.com

**National Lighthouse Museum** A seaside plaza skirts the decaying buildings and underground vaults of the former Third District Lighthouse Depot, where new-fangled fuels, lamps, and lenses were tested from 1862 until the 1960s. The defunct 10 acre compound was selected in 1997 to be home of the National Lighthouse Museum. However, plans have stalled and its future is undecided. Four of the six Federal style buildings are listed on the National Register of Historic Places. *Nantucket LV-112*, the museum's historic lightship and the biggest ever built, sits deteriorating at a dock in Oyster Bay, while renovated building #11 awaits new uses.

**Pier One** A restored pier once meant for historic lightships, now a popular fishing spot, is under restoration from damage by ship worms.

**Bay Street Landing** A wide promenade, offering beautiful harbor views fronts the 40 acre former American Dock & Trust Company where abandoned brick warehouses were converted to co-ops in the 1980s. An inaccessible piling field is all that remains of the old piers.

**Pier 6 Cromwell Center** Murray Hulbert Ave. 5 acres. A city park's recreation center, built in 1936 on a large enclosed pier, features the Joseph P. Lyons outdoor swimming pool, largest in the borough. 718-816-6172

**Homeport** Front St. 35 acres. A chain link fence topped with barbed wire has barred access to this mile long coastline for years, idle since the Navy deserted the site after spending $200 million to build its military base. The facility was decommissioned in 1995 after only five years. Successive plans have envisioned an auto racetrack, a movie studio, a sports complex, and lately the familiar theme of highrise glass residential towers with a public esplanade. Within the port, the 1,410-foot *USS The Sullivans* Pier, which commemorates the five "Fighting Sullivan" brothers killed in WWII, may remain a permanent site for decommissioned Naval ships.

**Ocean Yacht Club** 370 Front St. A 100 year old clubhouse across from the fenced Homeport enclosure, originally stood at the water's edge, but lost its water rights when the base was built. It's now a yacht club in name only, featuring a bar and wall to wall photos of racing sailboats on the Upper Bay.

# The Narrows

The Narrows is the tight reach that connects Upper New York Bay and Lower New York Bay. Bluffs high above the mile wide strait offer good public access and unobstructed water views. A few maritime support services still command this coast; they include the Reynolds Shipyard and the Sandy Hook Pilots, escort navigators who board oceangoing ships to guide them into the harbor, a task that has been done since 1692. Coast Guard Station New York operates search-and-rescue and a boat maintenance facility at a pier in Rosebank. From these shores Alice Austen honed her photography skills and the New York Yacht Club successfully defended the America's Cup for the first time.

The deepest part of the harbor in here under the Verrazano-Narrows Bridge, where Fort Wadsworth guarded the entrance to the inner harbor for over 200 years. Although the last military tenant left in 1995, the campus still includes a motel for current and former Navy personnel. The Coast Guard is remains active at the garrison where the control room for

vessel traffic monitors harbor and port activity. Fort Wadsworth is part of the National Park Service's Staten Island Unit of Gateway National Recreation Area, which also encompasses Miller Field, Great Kills Park, and Hoffman and Swinburne islands.

Transit: SIRT to Clifton, Fort Wadsworth; Bus S51 (from Ferry)

Blueway: Water Trail: Buono Beach

**Buono Beach** Foot of Hylan Blvd. A pebble beach and small boat launch named for Mark Buono, a local resident killed in the Vietnam War. A bed and breakfast looks at the water across from the beach, where anglers shore cast for stripers, bluefish, flounder, and porgy, and horseshoe crab lay eggs on full and new moon nights in May.

**Alice Austen Park** 2 Hylan Blvd. 14 acres. The Victorian cottage and garden home of self-taught photographer Alice Austen, who named it "Clear Comfort" and lived there until 1945. The restored house, a city and national landmark, operates as a museum presenting photography exhibits. Open March to December, Thursday to Sunday 12 to 5pm. 718-816-4506 aliceausten.org

**McFarlane-Bredt House** 30 Hylan Blvd. The former quarters of the New York Yacht Club (1868-1871) is a clapboard house built in 1845 overlooking the harbor where in 1870 the first defense of the America's Cup took place. The city landmark is in need of extensive repair and not accessible.

**Arthur Von Briesen Park** Foot of Bay St. 10 acres. A beautifully landscaped park with winding paths offering the best vantage for seeing ships passing through the Narrows and spotting the Peregrine falcons nesting there. The park is named for the founder of the Legal Aid Society and author of the book *First House on the Left, America* about his estate on the bluffs overlooking the Narrows.

**Fort Wadsworth** (GATE) 1580 Bay St. One of the oldest military installations in the country was first a blockhouse in 1663, and later fortified as Flagstaff Fort, captured by the British in 1776. The complex of seacoast defense batteries strategically located on the terminal moraine high above the Narrows is named for Brigadier General James Wadsworth, who was killed in the 1864 Battle of the Wilderness. Battery Weed sits directly on the harborfront, its lighthouse restored as a solar-powered beam in 2005. The canons of Fort Tompkins loom from the bluff above the Battery. A little beach located near the old Torpedo Pier is a prime fishing spot. The National Park Service offers programs at the museum and ranger led tours, and plenty of places to take in the spectacular view. Admission is free at this Gateway National Recreation Area site. Open Wednesday to Sunday, 10am to 5pm. 718-354-4500 nps.gov/gate

## Lower New York Bay

Lower New York Bay is a vast body of water drained by the Hudson River as it flows from the Narrows to the open sea. Long stretches of barrier beach, nature preserves, and public parks face the wide bay. South and Midland are big public beaches that once drew tens of thousands of summer visitors to Happyland Amusement Park and other seaside resorts and gambling houses in the early 1900s. It is possible to walk the six mile long continuous beach from the Verrazano Bridge to Great Kills. The entire shore is a natural beach, extending past the cottages at private Cedar Grove Beach to the restored dunes at Oakwood Beach.

The coast was inhabited by the Raritan tribe when the Dutch first attempted a settlement. British commander General Howe established his headquarters in New Dorp at the Rose and Crown Tavern. New Dorp

Lighthouse, a clapboard cottage with square tower rising 192 feet above sea level, served as an aid to navigation since 1854 and is today a private residence. Narrow streets ending at the shore are packed with old summer cottages modified into year round homes. Much of the bay's flotsam washes up on the beaches here. There is no saltwater license needed to fish from the shore, but city beaches have seasonal restrictions and Gateway National Park Service properties require a special parking sticker for fishing that can be purchased at the nearby Miller Field ranger station.

Transit: Bus S51 serves Fr. Capodanno Blvd. Bus S76 from ferry.

Greenway: Beach Greenway, a 6 mile path from Fort Wadsworth to Great Kills Park, still has many on-road gaps.

Blueway: Water Trail: South Beach & Midland Beach

**Hoffman Island & Swinburne Island** (GATE) 10.25 acres. The islands, created by landfill in 1872, are about a mile offshore. Both have served as quarantines for immigrants detained from Ellis Island, for soldiers carrying venereal disease, and as a training school for merchant marines from 1938 to 1947. The islands, once home to quarantined parrots, are now sanctuaries for wading birds within the Harbor Herons Project under the Staten Island Unit of Gateway National Recreation Area and closed to the public. The islands are also home to a growing population of wintering harbor seals. The shoals between the islands are popular fishing waters.

**South Beach** Father Capodanno Blvd. A wide, brown sand beach on the Atlantic Ocean, positioned between Fort Wadsworth and Midland Beach, best for sunbathing and gazing across the bay. The illuminated Dolphin Fountain sculpted by Steven Dickey sits at the north entry point, at the

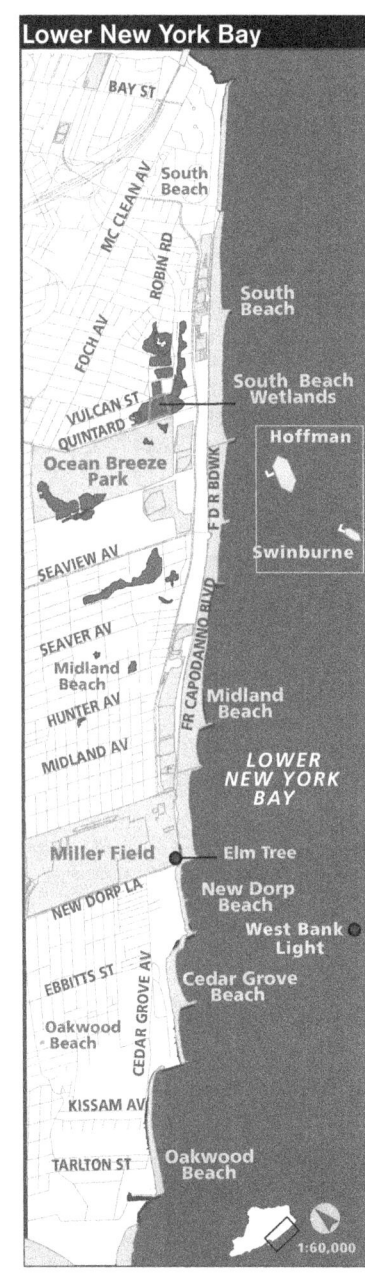

Lower New York Bay

137 Staten Island

start of the Franklin Delano Roosevelt Boardwalk, which stretches south for 2.5 miles. Built by the WPA in 1939, the boardwalk is interspersed with benches and bocce courts, play areas, handball courts, and baseball fields. At the terminus of the boardwalk, adjacent to Ocean Breeze Park and the Freedom Circle Memorial, Ocean Breeze Pier is an 835 foot long T-shaped deep-water wharf, a fishing base for striper and fluke.

**South Beach Wetlands** Vulcan St. 5 acres. This undeveloped swampland is protected as one of three Staten Island Bluebelt preserves designed for stormwater control using natural drainage corridors.

**Ocean Breeze Park** Quintard St. & Mason Ave. 110 acres. A low lying area of the New Creek Bluebelt, these protected freshwater wetlands and coastal grasslands were restored as natural habitat to alleviate flooding and storm damage. Nature trails offer wildlife viewing and future upgrades include active recreation facilities and a nature center at the designated Forever Wild Site.

**Midland Beach** Fr. Capodanno Blvd. The seashore, bounded by sports and recreation fields, is centered by a giant sea turtle water spray midway on the beach. A handicap access mat is located near Jefferson Avenue. Fishing is permitted from October to May.

**Miller Field** (GATE) New Dorp Ln. 187 acres. Once the farm of William H. Vanderbilt, son of the "Commodore," the property opened as an Army airfield in 1919, later serving as a seaplane base during WWII. Charles Lindbergh and Admiral Byrd landed on the grass airstrip. It has served as a Nike missile repair depot and Army Special Forces base. The historic airfield is named for James Ely Miller, the first U.S. aviator killed in combat. It's now occupied by ball fields, but still contains defunct hangars, the old Elm Tree beacon, a submarine lookout tower, and seaplane ramp. Its forest of swamp white oak is a pretty place for birdwatching. 718-351-6970 nps.gov/gate

**New Dorp Beach** Cedar Grove Ave., between New Dorp Ln. to Ebbitts St. 40 acres. A pair of mussel coated rock jetties frames this largely inaccessible wild beach, which was obtained by the city through eminent domain. The Britton Cottage, home of botanist Nathaniel Britton, stood on this shore for more than 200 years before being dismantled and reassembled in Historic Richmond Town.

**Cedar Grove Beach** Cedar Grove Beach Pl. A public access path runs along one of the shore's last summer bungalow colonies, established in 1911. cedargrovebeachclub.com

**Oakwood Beach** Tarlton St. The shore is also known as Fox Beach, named for Emiel R. Fox, inventor of the Fox Police Lock, who built a dozen beach bungalows and other seaside amenities here in 1912. Flood walls, a tide gate, and levees protect the shore from erosion. The watershed surrounding the water pollution control plant is part of the Bluebelt natural drainage area.

# Great Kills Harbor

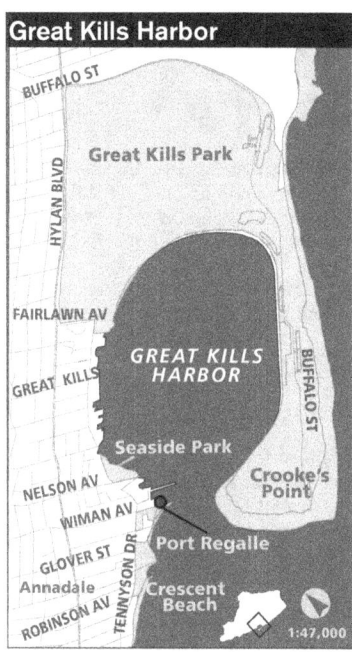

Great Kills is a protected natural harbor and "no wake: area with small craft anchorage, and moorings managed by the NYC Department of Parks and Recreation. The 6.3 foot deep channel into the shallow bight is marked by the Great Kill Light, a skeleton tower east of the harbor entrance. Great Kills Park, part of Gateway National Recreation Area, encircles the southeastern edge of the harbor. Marinas and yacht clubs crowd the eastern shore, the best place on the island to board a party boat, fishing charter, or dive boat. Developers and conservationists are in a tug-of-war over the fate of open space on the waterfront. Most of the shore is below sea level in a 100 year floodplain. Residential complexes like the Port Regalle Mediterranean-style village with boardwalk and marina and Sailor's Key townhouses straddle newly designated parkland.

Transit: SIRT to Amboy Rd. Great Kills; Bus S78 (30 min. to St. George)

Greenway Onstreet ride on Hylan Blvd. Great Kills Park offers miles of paths.

Blueway: Water Trail: Great Kills Harbor

**Great Kills Park** Hylan Blvd. 960 acres. Built on artificial fill, the park encompasses acres of woodlands, marshes, mud flats, dunes, a mile of white sand beach, and a wide esplanade along the edge of Great Kills Harbor. It is an important bird and monarch butterfly migration landing spot. Boaters have access to a kayak/canoe launch, trailer boat ramp, and a 1,000 slip marina. The park has nature trails, picnic areas, swimming beaches, athletic fields, and a model airplane field. The White Trail is a moderate 7.5 mile hike that connects with trails in the Greenbelt at its northern end. The Ranger Station is open year-round and there is no fee to enter the park. A parking permit ($50) is required for the boat ramp lot, off-hour fishing, and parking access at Crooke's Point. 718-987-6790 nps.gov/gate

**Crooke's Point** A mile long sand spit at the southern tip of Great Kills Park was a small island before landfilling formed the current harbor. The Labyrinth Trail, a 1.5 mile loop, winds through the coastal scrub from bay to beach to the rock jetty at the point, a great spot for birding and fishing.

**Seaside Wildlife Nature Park** Nelson Ave. 15 acres. A vacant lot turned into parkland with winding paths, woods, wildflowers, and a boardwalk approaching an overlook to harbor views. About three acres have been improved and future plans include a playground, promenade, and fishing pier.

**Port Regalle Boardwalk** Foot of Wiman Ave. A public walkway rims the private community linking Seaside Nature Park with Crescent Beach.

**Crescent Beach Park** Tennyson Dr. 68 acres. Patches of woodlands, coastal grasslands and beaches at the entrance to Great Kills Harbor make up this diverse waterfront park, named for a crescent-shaped sandbar visible at low tide.

# Raritan Bay

Raritan Bay is an arm of Lower New York Bay that extends from the confluence of the Raritan River in New Jersey and the Arthur Kill to the Atlantic Ocean. It is about 12 nautical miles in length and eight nautical miles wide. The seashore contains beaches, dunes, wetlands, freshwater ponds, and subtidal mudflats protected from the open sea by the Sandy Hook bar. Raritan Bay, named for the Lenape tribe, is shallower than the waters of the Lower Bay, with depths of seven to 18 feet. It is rich in marine life and prime fishing grounds for striped bass, fluke, blue fish, and flounder. Horseshoe crabs spawn on the beaches in late spring and threatened sea turtles feed in bay waters during the summer.

# Raritan Bay

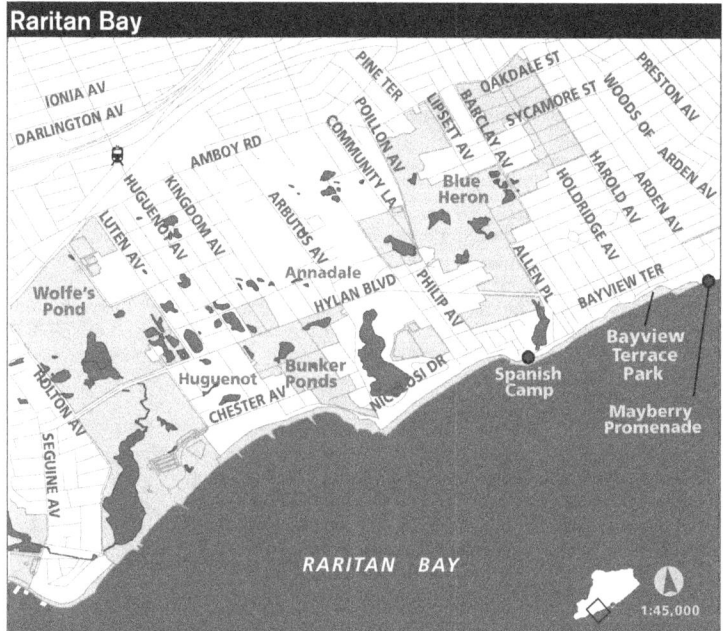

The Raritan Reach marks the middle of the main shipping channel and is the accepted boundary line between New York and New Jersey. Fishing regulations of both states apply in the Bay. About 100 baymen (commercial clammers) still ply the waters of Raritan Bay harvesting over half of the clams produced in New York State, about 80,000 bushels a year. Hard clams seeded in the bay are relocated to cleaner waters about three weeks prior to harvest and sale.

Facing the bay, the south shore of Staten Island was shaped by the final stop of the Wisconsin glacier during the last ice age, about 90,000 years ago, when ice pushed materials to form the Harbor Hill Terminal Moraine. These low hills that make up the high spine of Staten Island are a continuation of a ridge that travels across the Brooklyn Narrows. Glacial outwash and coastal beaches front the moraine where the receding glacier cut the eastern shore north of Great Kills. The northern extent of the island is reddish-brown glacial till. The shore, encompassing the communities of Eltingville, Princes Bay, Annandale, and Tottenville, was originally settled by Dutch and French Huguenots.

Transit: SIRT to Annadale; Bus S78

Greenway: Wolfe's Pond Park has eight miles of multi-use mountain biking trails through hilly terrain.

**Mayberry Promenade** Foot of Arden Ave. A short scenic drive and narrow slip of public waterfront with water access at Strawberry Lane.

**Bayview Terrace Park** Bayview Ter. 19 acres. Perched 17 feet over the water, where the old roadway,

Boardwalk Avenue washed away, the reclaimed vacant lot holds a naturally cultivated garden that attracts over 30 species of butterfly and a rich mixture of birds, including purple martins drawn there by brightly colored birdhouses.

**Blue Heron Park Preserve** Poillon Ave. 236 acres. The quiet preserve is a refuge for waterfowl and wading birds, viewed along nature trails through woodlands, meadows, and swamps. A Forever Wild Area and part of the Bluebelt, the wetlands contain six freshwater ponds draining to Raritan Bay, including 1.75 acre Spring Pond and 1.4 acre Blue Heron Pond, with wooden footbridge for close up wildlife viewing. Naturalists provide guided walks and Urban Park Rangers present programs at the Nature Center.

**Spanish Camp** Poillon Ave. & Spanish Colony. 18 acres. The colony, located on a bluff overlooking Raritan Bay, was begun in 1929 as a summer retreat of the Spanish Naturopath Society, a group of vegetarian, nudist Communists. Dorothy Day, founder of the Catholic Worker movement, lived here in a bungalow that was illegally bulldozed in 1999 by a developer using forged permits just days before the property was to be landmarked. Today, the developer is bankrupt and the site is vacant. Day is buried nearby at Resurrection Cemetery.

**Bunker Ponds Park** Hylan Blvd. between Arbutus & Huguenot Rds. 33 acres. A wedge of beach skirts this beautiful natural preserve containing a glacial kettle pond, woods, and swampland.

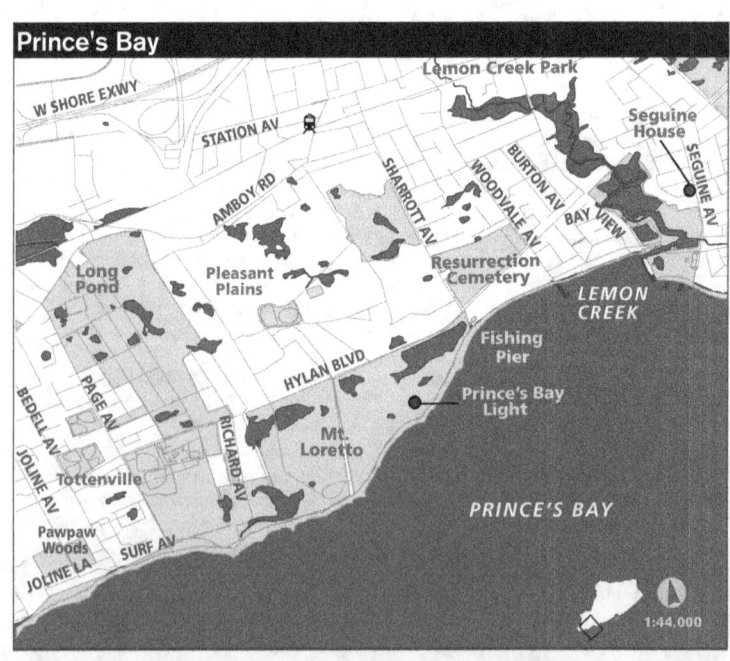

**Wolfe's Pond Park Preserve & Beach** Hylan Blvd. & Cornelia Ave. 341 acres. The park, named for Joel Wolfe who farmed here in 1857, spans both sides of Hylan Boulevard. A preserve of old growth forest, swampland, ravines, and kettle holes like Acme Pond are on the north. The beachside, once quarantine station and burial ground for immigrants with contagious diseases, has been a popular recreation spot since the 1920s. Wolfe's Pond is a freshwater pool formed when sand and clay dammed the original tidal inlet. Near the cobble beach, recreational amenities, such as a dog run, ball fields, and tennis courts, as well as the Battle of the Bulge Memorial take up 20 developed acres. The park offers first-rate fishing, sunbathing, and harbor views. Salt water fishing is permitted from October through May, and freshwater fishing is allowed year-round with a license.

## Prince's Bay

Prince's Bay is one of the City's most rural corners. A narrow strip of beach trims the shoreline stretching from Wolfe's Pond Park to Conference House Park. Open space acquisitions by the state and city have preserved over 625 acres of continuous parkland, including Mount Loretto and Butler Woods. The high bluffs mark the farthest advance of the glacial ice sheets.

Prince's Bay (also known as Princes and Princess Bay) boasts some of the Northeast's best striper fishing. Once the hub of the island's oyster trade in the 1800s, employing over 1500 watermen who raked the bay, its plots of harbor bottom were leased from the state and staked with long poles. Pollution and a typhoid outbreak closed the beds in 1916. After 2005, the oyster beds were reopened. Seguine Avenue along Prince's Creek takes its name from Ann Seguine, a

descendant of the Huguenot settlers who fled religious persecution in France to the colony of Staaten Eyelandt in the late 1600s.

Lemon Creek is tidal freshwater creek draining into the small cove of Prince's Bay. The watershed extends 2.5 miles inland to the creek's source at Porzio's Pond, near Woodrow Road. These are the south shore's last remaining wetlands and tidal ecosystem. A stopover for migratory birds during spring and fall, the creek is summer home to a colony of purple martin, the largest members of the swallow family in North America. Martins nest in special multi-family birdhouses built atop 20 foot high poles near a freshwater pond. Some of their elaborate perches were constructed by Riker's Island prison inmates of mahogany donated by piano maker Steinway & Sons. A small cluster of marinas and piers occupies the mouth of Lemon Creek. The Reach Channel, a federal shipping lane just off the beach, offers close-up views of containerships, barges, and tugboats entering the Arthur Kill. Stripers begin to show up in the shoals beyond the channel in early spring.

Tottenville, on the southwest tip of Staten Island, is the southernmost point of New York City and New York State. The town is named for the Totten family, who built the wharf at Totten's Landing and founded Bethel Church in 1822. In recent years, new development has encroached on undeveloped natural areas along the shore.

Transit: SIRT Princes Bay, Pleasant Plains; Bus S74 & S78.

Blueway: Water Trail: Lemon Creek Park; Conference Park

**Lemon Creek Park** Hylan Blvd., Sharrott, Bayview, Seguine Aves. 106 acres. The park encompasses the largest salt marsh on Staten Island alongside marinas and a paved boat ramp at the end of Bayview Avenue. A preserve of forest and freshwater wetlands is in the northern portion of the park. Kayaks launch from either Seguine or at the foot of Sharrott Avenue, where anglers cast from a fishing pier to popular striper and flounder grounds.

**Seguine House** 440 Seguine Ave. 2 acres. Its rolling lawns and horses pasturing over the waters of Prince's Bay, this Greek revival mansion was built in 1838 by bay oysterman Joseph H. Seguine, who managed a large salt hay farm on the land. The property is administered by the Historic House Trust, with tours offered by appointment. 718-667-6042 historichousetrust.org

**Sandy Ground** 1538 Woodrow Rd. The oldest free black community in the country, Sandy Ground was settled upland, near the headwaters of Lemon Creek in the 1830s by oystermen who came from Maryland to rake the shell beds in Prince's Bay. The National Historic Site houses a library and museum dedicated to preserving its heritage operated by the Sandy Ground Historical Society. 718-317-5796

**Mount Loretto Unique Area** 6450 Hylan Blvd. 194 acres. Sea cliffs ascend 85 feet above a mile long beach on the last undeveloped land in the state. Opened in 1883 as a Catholic orphanage, Mount Loretto became the largest such institution in the country before closing in 1995. The grounds are now a sanctuary for wildlife administered by the State Department of Environmental Conservation. Prince's Bay lighthouse and keeper's quarters overlook the bay from the high bluffs of Mount Loretto, where for years a statue of the Virgin Mary stood in for the navigational light. A newer beacon

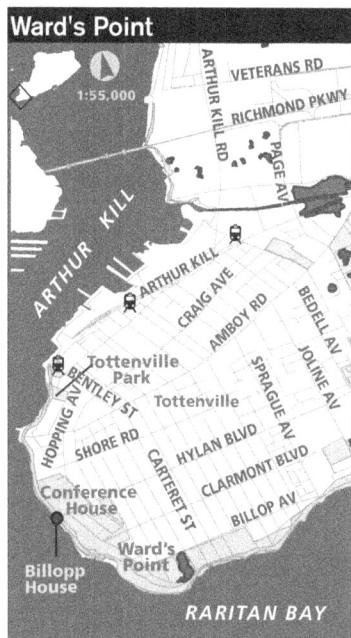

### Ward's Point

**Conference House Park** End of Hylan Blvd. 267 acres. The park starts next to Mount Loretto at a patch of forested wetlands between Richards and Page Avenues. Tiny Surf Avenue runs parallel to Tottenville Beach giving access and parking at Page Avenue and an overlook at Sprague Avenue. A narrow two mile long shoreline strand extends around the "South Pole" of New York State at Ward's Point, best for beach-combing or fishing. The site of an 8,000 year old Lene Lenape Indian settlement and ancient burial ground, the park takes its name from the failed peace conference between John Adams, Benjamin Franklin, Edward Rutledge, and Admiral Lord Howe on Sept. 11, 1776 that might have prevented the Revolutionary War. The beach fronts a heavily wooded park of historical and natural interest. Hiking and biking trails flank stunning panoramic views from the Pavilion that overlooks the confluence of the Arthur Kill and Raritan Bay.

tower is located on the beach. The grounds comprise old growth forest with 200 year old American beech trees and five distinctive ecosystems, including marine-coastal, grassland, forest, tidal, and freshwater wetlands. They can be explored by three trails: Wetlands Trail, Grasslands Trail, and Beach Loop. Butler Manor Woods and Camp Saint Edward have been added to the preserve. dec.ny.gov/outdoor

**Long Pond Park/Cozzens Woods** Cozzens Blvd. 97 acres. Upland from Mount Loretto, the uncultivated park, part of the Bluebelt, is a delight for bird-watchers in its forest and swampland habitat encircling spring fed ponds.

**Pawpaw Hybrid Oaks Woods** Joline Lane. 9.6 acres. Rescued from development, a rare forest, this is the only place in the state where hybrid oaks grow, flanking streams and footpaths to the beach.

**Billopp House** The 1680 fieldstone manor house of British Loyalist Capt. Christopher Billopp where the famous peace conference took place is a national and New York City landmark. Legend has it that Billopp won Staten Island for New York City by winning a bet to sail around the island in just a day. The property, confiscated by the state after the Revolutionary War, includes the Conference House and three other historic homes: the Biddle House, the Ward House, and Rutan-Beckett House. 718-984-2086 conferencehouse.org

## Arthur Kill

The Arthur Kill (or Stream, in Dutch) connects Raritan Bay to Newark Bay and separates Staten Island from New Jersey. The natural landscape of Staten Island's westside was all salt marsh. Over half of the wetlands have been filled by bulkhead, first for agriculture and shipping and later

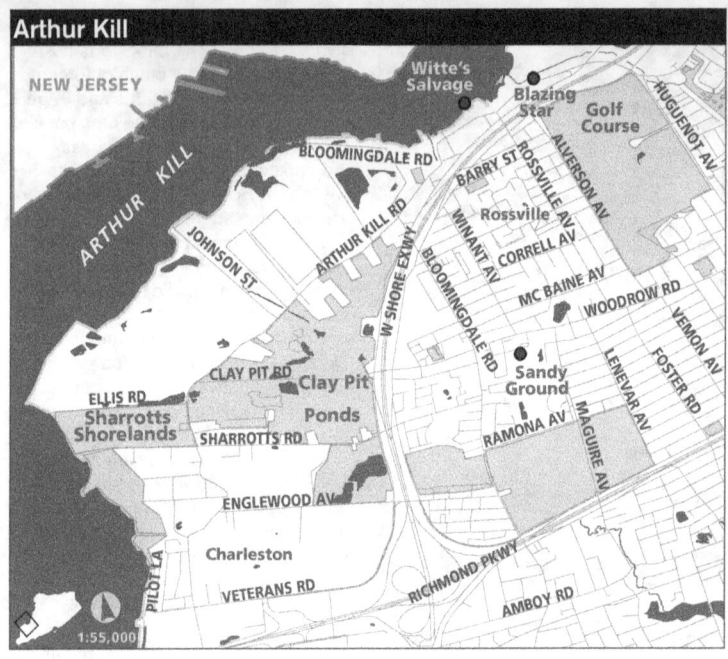

### Arthur Kill

for oil refineries and industrial plants. In 1900, Tottenville was the western terminus of the Staten Island Railroad and home to eight shipyards. During WWI, Cossey Shipyard here produced more than 1,000 large vessels. Today, Garpo (John Garner's) shipyard at Tottenville Marina carries on the maritime tradition repairing many of the harbor's historic ships. With an average of 50 ships transiting it daily, Arthur Kill is a major shipping channel, 14 miles long, 500 feet wide and dredged to a depth of 41 feet. Vulnerable to pollution because of weak water currents, it holds one of the largest oil refineries in the world on its banks. A spill in 1990 leaked more than a million gallons of fuel oil into the water. Restoration is ongoing to repair the damage to natural shore areas and rebuild habitat.

Even though roads in the towns of Charleston and Rossville often end at dirt paths that lead through cordgrass to the water, there are few places to access the Arthur Kill coast. Over the past decade, new residential development has taken up many of the undeveloped lots along this shore. Tottenville Station, the last stop on the SIRT, terminates right at the waterfront. Ellis Street is a backroad that runs parallel with the Arthur Kill. The old Perth Amboy Ferry slip was located at the end of Bentley Road. The shore at Kreischer Cove contains Port Mobil, a large oil tank farm that separates Clay Pits Pond from the Arthur Kill. Balthazar Kreischer operated the city's largest brick factory on the cove from 1854 to 1930. The landmark Kreischer mansion and leftovers of the company town's workers' houses are near the shore's rich clay deposits on Kreischer Street.

The eroding pilings of old wooden piers and the corroded hulls of hundreds of derelict vessels crowd the

shallow shore. The ghost fleet is known as the "Graveyard of Ships," towed there by admiralty lawyer J. Arnold Witte who established the scrapyard on the banks of the Arthur Kill in 1967. At the foot of Victory Boulevard, an old pier marks the Blazing Star Ferry and Inn, an important stage coach stop between Manhattan and Philadelphia in the early 19th century. Rossville, previously called Blazing Star, was renamed for Colonel William Ross who built a replica of Windsor Castle on bluffs above the ferry stop in the 1830s. Jasper Cropsey, the Hudson River School landscape artist was born here in 1823. His painting *Looking Oceanward* made famous the Joseph J. Holka Overlook on the Greenbelt blue trail at Todt Hill.

Some 16 tributaries flow into the Arthur Kill. Tidal creeks penetrate vast wetlands and protected breeding grounds for wading birds and a one time city garbage dump Fresh Kills that is due for an extreme makeover to park- land. About 8,000 acres of wetlands have been preserved along the channel and its tributaries. The Outerbridge and Goethals Bridge crossings con- nect Staten Island with New Jersey.

Transit: SIRT Tottenville (last stop); Bus S74 & S78 to end of Hylan Blvd.

**Tottenville Shore Park** Hopping Ave., Arthur Kill Rd. & Bentley St. 9 acres. A scenic park and shell scattered beach provides rare water access on the Arthur Kill.

**Sharrotts Road Shorelands** Foot of Sharrots Rd. 25 acres. The open space with tidal and freshwater wetlands is part of a state preservation effort.

**Clay Pit Ponds State Park Preserve** 83 Nielsen Ave. 260 acres. The upland park's spring-fed creeks drain to Arthur Kill. Nature trails join five miles of bridle paths for horseback riding (no rentals) through freshwater wetlands, pine barrens, and woodlands. Guided walks and educational programs are offered year round. Pets are prohibited. 718-967-1976 nysparks.state.ny.us

**Blazing Star Burial Ground** Arthur Kill Rd. east of Rossville Ave. 12 acres. One of Staten Island's oldest public cemeteries contains 41 graves dating from 1750, half of them members of the Seguine family. It is a city landmark that offers the only landside views of the half submerged wrecks of Witte's Salvage.

**Harbor Herons Complex** 2,195 acres. A protected rookery encompassing the Isle of Meadows, Pralls Island, Gulfport Marsh, Goethal's Bridge Pond State Preserve, Saw Mill Creek, Old Place Creek, Mariner's Marsh, Shooter's Island, Granitville Swamp, and Teleport Woods. Often called the "Everglades of New York City," the complex of tidal and freshwater marshes, ponds, creeks, and islands supports the largest breeding population of colonial water birds in the northeastern United States, including great, snowy and cattle egrets; glossy ibis; and blue, green, black-crowned, and yellow-crowned night herons.

**Isle of Meadows Preserve** 100 acres. An uninhabited island at the mouth of Fresh Kills Creek that is a nature preserve in the Harbor Herons Wildlife Refuge and rest stop for kayakers paddling the Kill.

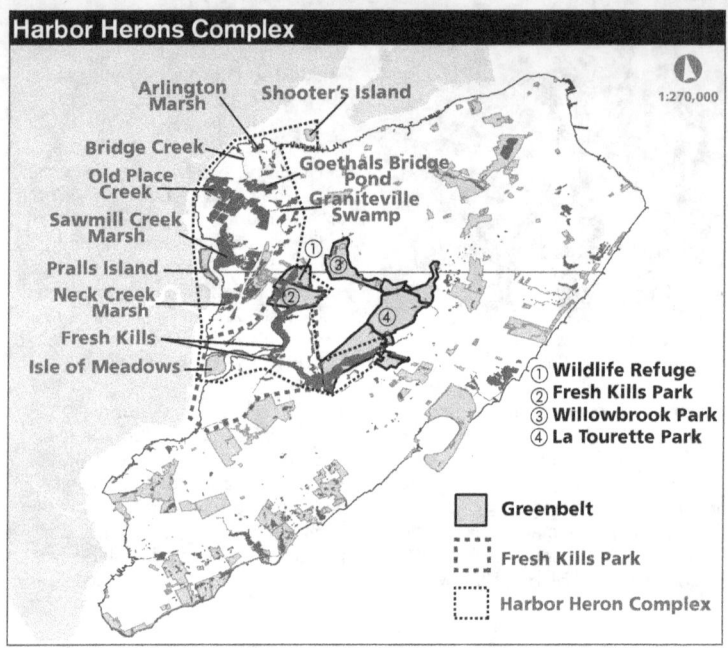

## Harbor Herons Complex

- Arlington Marsh
- Shooter's Island
- Bridge Creek
- Goethals Bridge Pond
- Old Place Creek
- Graniteville Swamp
- Sawmill Creek Marsh
- Pralls Island
- Neck Creek Marsh
- Fresh Kills
- Isle of Meadows

① Wildlife Refuge
② Fresh Kills Park
③ Willowbrook Park
④ La Tourette Park

- Greenbelt
- Fresh Kills Park
- Harbor Heron Complex

1:270,000

## Fresh Kills Creek

The Fresh Kill Estuary is one of the island's largest tidal ecosystems, its brackish wetlands designated as a New York State Significant Coastal Fish and Wildlife Habitat. Fresh Kills Creek flows three miles inland through the Fresh Kills Landfill, the world's biggest landfill and one of the largest constructs on the planet. Opened in 1948 and closed in 2001, the dump compressed household waste into mounds that are now taller than the Statue of Liberty and visible from outer space. It can take decades after the mounds are capped before the refuse decomposes completely. In the process, it leaks methane gas. The recovery and sale of methane gas harvested at the site is sold to local energy companies, generating about $11 million a year to the city.

Main, Springville, and Richmond Creeks are tributaries of Fresh Kills Creek. Main Creek is navigable at high tide flowing through Travis and the southern reaches of the serpentine ridge, a greenish rock from the earth's core pushed up when Africa and North America collided over 300 million years ago to form a high crest down the center of the borough. In the mid-1800s, the mineral was mined for asbestos by Johns Manufacturing, which later became Johns-Manville, the world leader in the manufacture of asbestos. The creek branches into Willow and New Springville Brooks.

**Fresh Kills Park** 2252 Richmond Ave. 2,200 acres. The park, divided into five distinct areas, is to be built in stages over 30 years, featuring boat launches, esplanades, great lawns, gardens, and natural areas. A community kayak and

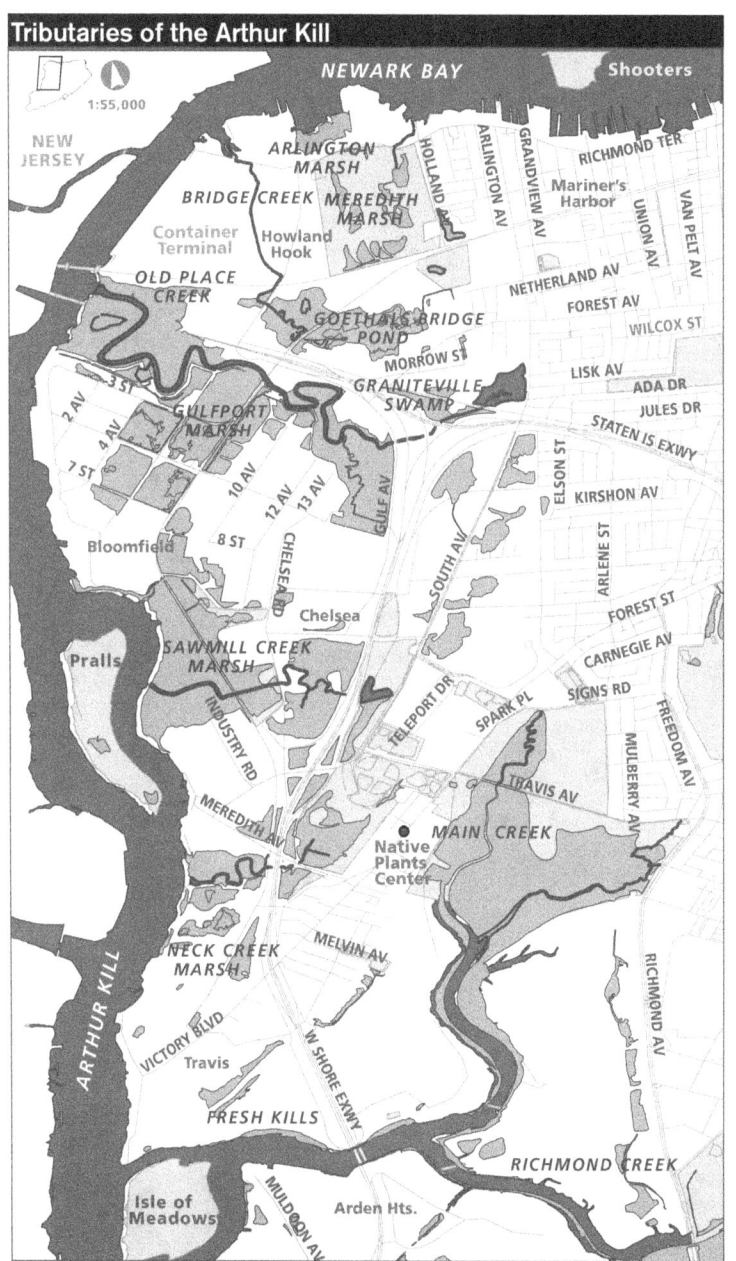

canoe center is planned for Creek Landing, the centerpiece of the park located where Richmond Creek and Main Creek merge with Fresh Kills Creek. On the south side of the Fresh Kills Creek, a waterfront promenade will frame sports fields and open lawns. Guided bus tours are offered monthly. nycgovparks.org. ✲

**Owl Hollow Fields** Arthur Kill Rd. & Muldoon Ave. 28 acres. At the head of Main Creek on the perimeter of the landfill, picnic areas and soccer fields have opened alongside Schmul Park.

**William T. Davis Wildlife Refuge** Victory Blvd., Signs Rd, Travis Ave. & Arthur Kill Rd. 428 acres. At the head of Main and Springville Creeks, the former site of America's first linoleum plant was reclaimed in 1928 as New York City's first wildlife and bird sanctuary. The preserve bears the name of a renowned local naturalist whose 1892 memoir *Days Afield on Staten Island* documented the borough's plants and wildlife. Water from the refuge's natural springs was once bottled. A trail winds through wetlands and woodlands. Canoe access is at Signs Road. A Forever Wild Site and in the Greenbelt.

**Greenbelt Native Plant Center** Travis Ave., near Richmond Ave. 10 acres. A greenhouse and nursery preserves native plants, trees, and shrubs, as well as seed stock and flora rescued from construction sites that is used in habitat restoration.

# Richmond Creek

Richmond Creek has its source at Orbach Lake, a fishing hole for black bass, pickerel, and carnivorous bluegills in Pouch Camp. It meanders through the Staten Island Greenbelt passing alongside La Tourette Park and Historic Richmond Town into Egbertville Ravine. The creeks 950 acre watershed flows through Historic Richmond Town and is part of the 18 acre Richmond Creek Bluebelt, protected wetlands of a city-owned natural drainage area. The creek is canoeable its entire length at high tide. Early settlers arrived by water paddling up Richmond Creek to establish Richmond Town as the seat of government for the Staten Island colony, and goods once moved to Arthur Kill on the creek. One of the old mills has been restored at Historic Richmond Town, with water directed from the creek to power the mill. A 19th century stone arch bridge carries Richmond Hill Road over the creek. Looming above the creeks and landfill, Todt Hill is the second highest

# Richmond Creek

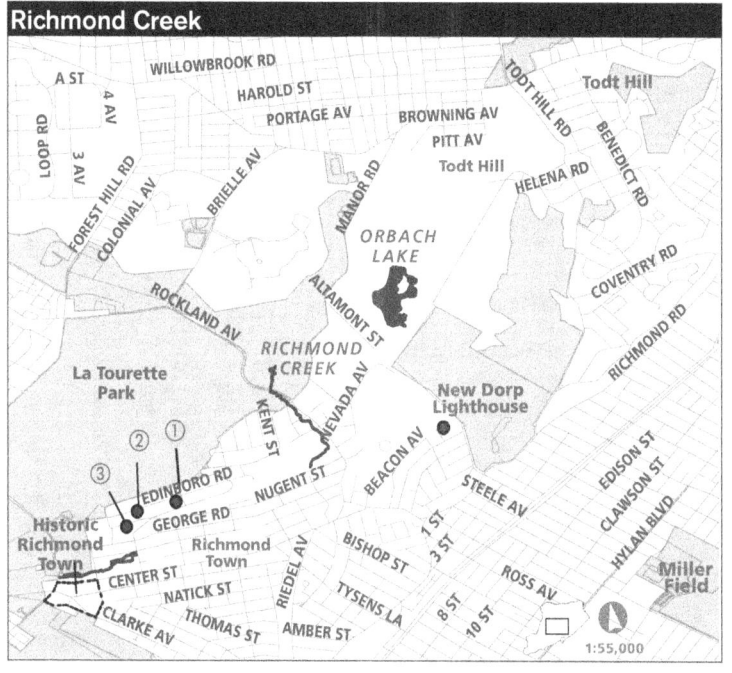

peak on the East Coast, at 410 feet above sea level.

Transit: Bus S74 to Richmond Hill Rd.

**Staten Island Greenbelt** 2,800 acres. A preserve encompassing 12 parks interlaced with 35 miles of foot trails in mixed terrain that includes woodlands, wetlands, and meadows. The Greenbelt contains historic and recreational sites in natural areas and city parks, including Latourette, W. T. Davis Refuge, Willowbrook Park, Clove Lakes Park, and High Rock Park – Staten Island Greenbelt headquarters. 718-667-2165 sigreenbelt.org

**La Tourette Park** 1001 Richmond Hill Rd. 540 acres. The park has five sections, including Richmond Town, woods, marsh, hills, and a golf course. The La Tourette family settled this land in the 1600s, and their Federal style mansion built in 1836 by David La Tourette is now the clubhouse of the 18 hole golf course. 718-351-1889

**Historic Richmond Town** 441 Clark Ave. 100 acres. A museum village containing 27 restored buildings dating from the late 17th to early 20th centuries was established in 1958 on the site of the three century old Richmond County seat. The complex is a City landmark and on the National Register of Historic Places. Tours, exhibits, and educational programs are offered by interpreters costumed in Colonial dress. historicrichmondtown.org

**Lighthouse Hill** A summit upland from the headwaters of Richmond Creek provides dramatic water views and holds several historic and cultural sites.

**Lighthouse Hill Points of Interest:**

① **Jacques Marchais Museum of Tibetan Art** 338 Light House Ave. The museum holds the largest collection of Himalayan art outside of Tibet. 718-987-3500 tibetanmuseum.org

② **Staten Island Lighthouse** The active 1912 Ambrose Channel Range Light sits at the top of the hill, 200 feet above sea level.

③ **Crimson Beech House** 48 Manor Ct. The privately owned red brick prefab is the only Frank Lloyd Wright designed residence in the city.

# Arthur Kill Tributaries

Freshwater and tidal wetlands envelop the brackish tributaries of the northern reach of the Arthur Kill, including Chelsea, Saw Mill, Merrell's, and Old Place creeks. The marshes are home to one of the state's only populations of southern leopard frogs. Extensive shoreline restoration is returning abandoned waterfront to viable fish and wildlife habitat. From Granitville Swamp, Old Place Creek snakes for three miles through wetlands alongside the Staten Island Expressway to drain just north of the Goethals Bridge. Gulfport Marsh on the Bloomfield shore formerly held bulk oil storage.

**Meredith Woods** Meredith Ave. 15 acres. Undeveloped tidal salt marsh drained by Neck Creek, originally called Neck Creek Marsh.

**Pralls Island Preserve** 80 acres. The uninhabited island, once a key farming hub, is a wading bird rookery inhabited by heron, ibis, and egrets. It is a Forever Wild Area and part of the Harbor Herons Complex. Asian Longhorned Beetles, a destructive invasive species, infested trees on the island in 2007, prompting parks officials to destroy over 3000 trees in its effort to eradicate the pest and prevent its infecting surrounding regions.

**Sawmill Creek Marsh** Chelsea Rd. 166 acres. A large tract of salt marsh bisected by Saw Mill Creek provides valuable fish and bird habitat. A Forever Wild Site and part of the Harbor Heron Complex.

**Old Place Creek Wetlands** 70 acres. The creek winds through tidal marshes to forested woodlands and a rare grove of persimmon trees that are part of the Harbor Herons Complex. The headwaters reach Granitville Swamp and a narrow tributary drains the 33 acre Goethals Bridge Pond.

# Kill van Kull

A four mile long tidal strait, the Kill van Kull is the main shipping lane linking Newark Bay to Upper New York Bay. An endless flotilla of barges, tugs, and container ships navigate the federal channel each year. The half mile wide channel separates Staten Island from the Bayonne Peninsula in New Jersey. It is spanned by the Bayonne Bridge, the third longest steel arch bridge in the world. The Bayonne Bridge clearance will be raised by 32 feet and the channel dredged to 50 foot depths by blasting through bedrock to accommodate the growing fleet of giant Post-Panamax vessels.

Kill van Kull is the main route for ships unloading at New York Container Terminal and New Jersey's Port Newark and Port Elizabeth. Nearby, the 124 acre Port Ivory site where Procter & Gamble made ivory soap until 1991 has been purchased by the Port Authority for containerport expansion and an intermodal transportation center linking freight lines from the Staten Island Railroad with the national freight network.

Industrial areas flank wetlands at Arlington Marsh and Mariner's Marsh. There is a long tradition of ship building in the coastal communities of Mariner's Harbor, Port Richmond, and West Brighton. Downey Shipyard built *Meteor III*, the German imperial yacht of Kaiser Wilhelm and United Shipyards was bought by Bethlehem Steel in 1938. The Bethlehem site is now occupied by May Ship Repairs, a drydock and builder of barges. Marine support services, tug, and barge companies, drydocks, and other traditional maritime businesses populate the shore. Tugs of the East Coast's top towing companies – Moran, McAllister, K-Sea, and Reinauer – work from the shores of the Kill van Kull. Caddell Dry Dock, at the foot of Broadway, has been an important shipyard for 100 years. It is where South Street Seaport's historic ship *Wavetree* was restored and is the repair yard for Staten Island ferries.

Water views are limited and direct access is blocked by railroad tracks and industrial structures. There are few places to view the water, with the exception of street ends at Harbor Road and Nicolas, Broadway, Port Richmond, and Bard Avenues. Richmond Terrace, running parallel to the waterfront, was once lined with the homes of ship captains, complete with widow's walks. A short row of captain's houses still stands between Van Name and Van Pelt Avenues. West Brighton is home to ancient Lenape Native American burial grounds and a number of historic cemeteries. Aaron Burr died at the waterfront St. James Hotel on Richmond Terrace in Port Richmond in 1836. Herons and seagulls perch atop old pilings on shores that also serve as fish nurseries. An abandoned gypsum plant, now a brownfield site in need of cleanup, takes up 29 acres of waterfront.

Transit: Staten Island Ferry to (Ramp D) Bus S40, which runs on Richmond Terrace. The North Shore Railroad may be reactivated as a lightrail system connecting to PATH trains and the ferry.

Greenway: The North Shore Waterfront Greenway extends from Snug Harbor to St. George Ferry Terminal. The Bayonne Bridge has a narrow path ending in a steep stairway on the New Jersey side.

Blueway: Snug Harbor Dock

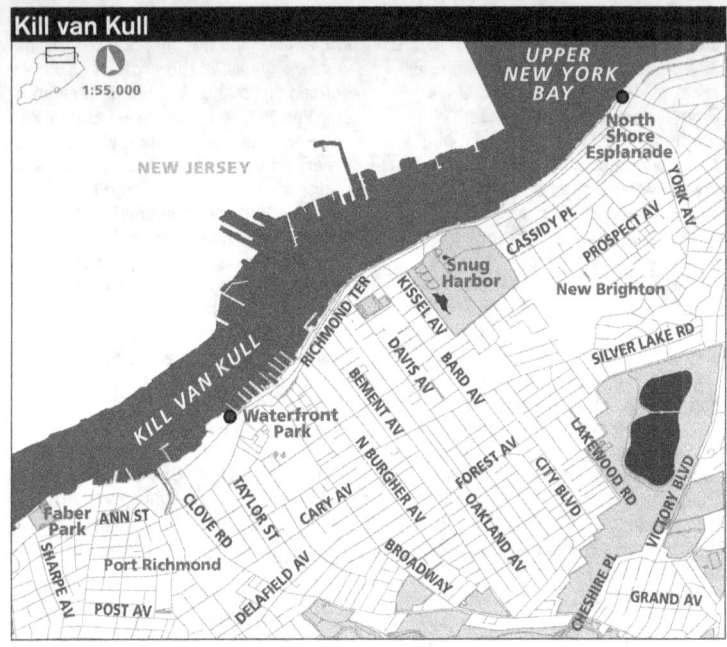

**New York Container Terminal**
300 Western Ave. Howland Hook.
187 acres. The three berth terminal is the largest container port in the state and the fastest growing terminal in the Port of New York - New Jersey. From here, freight moves directly from ship to rail over the Arthur Kill lift bridge to the national freight network in New Jersey. nycterminal.com

**Shooter's Island** A bird rookery in the Harbor Heron Complex, located both in New York and in New Jersey, this one time hunting preserve is an island created from the dredging of Newark Bay. Remnants of a shipyard and oil refinery are still evident and there is a vessel graveyard on the western shore

**Arlington Marsh** 90 acres. Protected city owned tidal salt marsh lodged amid a heavily industrialized coast on the Kill van Kull.

**Mariner's Marsh Park** Richmond Ter. at Holland Ave. 107 acres. Upland freshwater wetlands encompassing ten ponds, sweet gum trees, and the only known patch of American bittersweet vine along its nature trails. The former Lenape camp and burial grounds were later a steel plant and shipyard.

**Faber Park** 2175 Richmond Ter. 4.25 acres. The best waterfront access on the north shore offers picture postcard views of the Bayonne Bridge from an impressive swimming pool, landscaped lawns, and esplanade along the seawall at the former home of the Faber pencil making family.

**North Shore Waterfront Park**
Richmond Ter. & Tompkins Court. 10 acres. A new park and marina development at the former Blissenbach Marina opens valuable Kill van Kull waterfront to public use. ✶

**Snug Harbor Cultural Center**
1000 Richmond Ter. 83 acres.
A thousand feet from the Kill van Kull, Sailor's Snug Harbor was the country's first home for retired and disabled merchant mariners when it opened in 1833. Herman Melville's brother, Thomas, administered the institution from 1867 to 1864. The campus has served as an arts and cultural center since the 1970s and contains a National Register Historic District of 26 landmark buildings. Five splendid Greek revival structures, dormitories that housed the "Snugs," face the channel and August Saint Gaudens's bronze statue of benefactor Captain Robert Randall. An iron fence encircles the campus and there is a boat dock on the Kill van Kull. Admission to the campus is free, although there is a fee to enter most of the attractions. 718-448-2500 snug-harbor.org

**Snug Harbor Points of Interest:**

① **Governor's House & Cottage Row** The large house and five Victorian cottages on the western side of the campus that once housed staff have been restored to provide extended stays for visiting artists.

② **Neptune Fountain** Designed by J.W. Fiske, the 1893 zinc statue is on view at the Visitor's Center. A bronze recast adorns the grounds.

③ **Newhouse Center** The oldest building, constructed in 1833, retains the original skylight dome and ceiling murals. The former administration building is now a contemporary art gallery.

④ **Noble Maritime Collection** A museum featuring the works and studio barge of noted maritime artist John. A. Noble, who worked to preserve these grounds. Plus, ship models and a recreated "snug" dorm room. 718-447-6490 johnanoble.com

⑤ **Staten Island Children's Museum** The Block Harbor exhibit in the museum helps kids explore the waterfront. 718-273-2060

⑥ **Staten Island Botanical Garden** The Carl Gillo Glass House is famous for its rare collection of flowers and regional plants. The Chinese Scholars Garden was constructed in China by master gardeners, shipped and assembled on site at Snug Harbor. The archival collection of the horticultural library includes early landscape plans and maps. 718-273-8200 sibg.org

# ANNUAL EVENTS

## January
ALS New Year's Day Beach Walk
NY National Boat Show
One Hour National Postal Swim
Polar Bear New Year's Plunge
Sail NY Frostbite Sailing Series

## February
Great Backyard Bird Count
NYRA Indoor Rowing Championships
NYAC St. Valentine's Erg Regatta

## March
Beneath the Sea Scuba Show
NY-NJ PaddleSport Show

## April
Cyclone Coaster Opening Day
Bronx River Flotilla & Golden Ball
Earth Day
Gowanus Canal Earth Day Flotilla
Manhattan College Invitational Regatta
RYC Annual Flounder Tournament
Sailors Ball
The Big Swim

## May
Horseshoe Crab Spawning
Sheepshead Bayfest
Beaches Open Memorial Day

Bike Month
BWAC Pier Art Show
Manhattan Cup Bass Tournament
Fleet Week
Great Five Boro Bike Tour
Great Hudson River Swim International
Migratory Bird Day
Jamaica Bay Kayakfishing Tournament
National Maritime Day
National Safe Boating Week
NYC Audubon Birdathon
River to River Festival
Rockaway Beach Kite Festival
Shadfest
Shorewalker's Great Saunter
Surfrider Beach Cleanup

## June
Aquarium Month
CircusSundays at Waterfront Museum
City of Water Day
Coney Island Mermaid Parade
Clearwater Hudson River Revival
Free Fishing Days
General Slocum Memorial Ceremony
Hudson River Park Blessing of the Fleet
Hunts Point Fish Parade
International Surf Day
Liberty Island Swim
Liberty World Challenge Outrigger Race
Manhattan Island Marathon Swim
National Fishing & Boating Week

---

**Bernarr MacFadden**, Physical Trainer & Publisher (1868-1955) An advocate of winter bathing as a tonic for health and vitality, MacFadden founded the Coney Island Polar Bear Club in 1903. He arrived in New York City 9 years earlier with only $50 cash, changed his name from Bernard, set up shop as a personal fitness trainer and was the first person to become a millionaire in the alternative health field. His magazine, Physical Culture remained in publication for over 50 years and his publishing empire survives today under the name Sterling MacFadden. He also discovered Charles Atlas who mythologized the Coney Island beach bully to sell mail-order weight training courses.

NYC Powerboat Poker Run
Rockaway Beach Bicycle Race
Rockstock & Barrels Surf Rockaway
Staten Island Junefest
Stonewall Sails Regatta
Tour de Cure
World Ocean Day

## July

Around Long Island Regatta
Brooklyn Bridge Park Outdoor Movies
Coney Island Sand Sculpting Contest
Cove to Cove Swim
Fireworks at City Beaches, July 4th
Great Hudson River Paddle
Ladies Fluke Tournament
Macy's Fishing Contest
Macy's 4th of July Fireworks
Movies Under the Stars, Riverside Park
NYC Triathalon
NYRA Summer Club Classic Regatta
Riverflicks at Hudson River Piers
Rockaway Beach Sandcastle Contest
Shad Creek "It's a Fluke" Tournament
Siren Music Festival, Coney Island
Socrates Sculpture Park Film Festival
South Beach Sandcastle Contest
SI Tuna Club Shark Tournament
Tamaqua Shark Tournament

## August

AVP Coney Island Open-Beach Volleyball
Coast Guard Day
Harrison Street Kayak Regatta
Hong Kong Int'l Dragon Boat Fest
Ken Killian Ocean Mile Swim
Park to Park One Miler Swim
MidAtlantic $500,000 Fishing Tournament
National Marina Day
NY Ship & Boat Model Festival
NY Stunt Kite Championships
Sebago Canoe Club All-Club Invitational
SEA Paddle Around NYC
Snapper Fishing Derby, Bayside Marina
Tamaqua Bass & Bluefish Tournament

### Seaside Concerts

Castle Clinton, Battery Park
Clinton Cove Park, Pier 84
Kingsborough Community College
River to River Festival
River Rocks, Pier 54
Seaport Concerts
Seaside Concert Series
Siren Music Festival
Wagner Park Sunset Jams

## September

Brooklyn Bridge Swim
Environmental Bike Ride
Head of the Harlem Regatta
Coastal & Underwater Cleanup Day
Lady Liberty Sail Regatta
Little Red Lighthouse Festival
Little Red Lighthouse Swim
Mayor's Cup Race for Schooners
National Estuary Day
NYC Century Bike Tour
NY Super Boat Grand Prix
Richie Allen Memorial Surf Classic
Surf Film Festival
Tugboat Challenge

## October

Mayor's Cup Kayak Championship
MS Bike Tour
National Seafood Month
NY State Surfing Championships
Red Bull Flutag
Soldiers, Sailors, Marines Club Fair
Staten Island Waterfront Festival
Tour de Bronx

## November

Metro Championship Crew Regatta
Surf Film Festival

## December

American Star Rowing Race
Audubon Christmas Bird Count
Seamen's Church Christmas-at-Sea

## Seaside Attractions

**Astrotower** Coney Island. Featuring views from 275 feet above the beach, the landmark ride is one of the last remnants of Astroland, closed in 2008.

**Bargemusic** Fulton Ferry Landing. Year-round chamber music concerts aboard a converted railroad barge that offers spectacular views of Lower Manhattan and the Brooklyn Bridge. 718-624-2083 bargemusic.org

**Cyclone** 1000 Surf Ave. Coney Island. The most famous and most copied roller coaster ever built, the amusement ride was built on the site of the world's first roller coaster, the Switchback Railway. The Cyclone was designed by Vernon Keenan and built by Harry C. Baker in 1927 at a cost of $100,000. Three cars carry 24 passengers over 2,640 feet of wooden track for 1:50 minutes of ride-time that reaches speeds of 60 miles an hour, heights of 85 feet and has 12 steep drops. In the New York State Register of Historic Places and a National Historic Landmark. Open weekends in April-June, and daily June to Labor Day.

**B&B Carousel** Surf Ave. Brass ring, band organ and antique horses, the famous Coney Island carousel purchased by the City in 2006 for almost $2 million will reopen near the Parachute Jump upon restoration. ✘

**Deno's Wonder Wheel** Boardwalk at W 12 St. Built of Bethlehem Steel forged right on site by the Eccentric Ferris Wheel Co. in 1920, the landmark wheel stands 150 feet high and holds 144 people on 16 swinging cars and 8 stationary cars that give riders a panoramic ocean view. 718-372-2592 wonderwheel.com

**Parachute Jump** An old amusement ride originally built for the 1939 World's Fair, stands 262 above the beach at Keyspan Park.

**Sideshows By The Seashore** Surf Ave. Sideshow freaks and human curiosities perform at Coney Island theater. 718-372-5159 coneyisland.com

**Totally Kids Carousel** Riverbank State Park. A unique carousel designed by 36 kids who drew animals that were then fashioned into the ride by Milo Mottola. 212-694-3600 hoopla.org

**Whaleamena** Rockaway Park. Boardwalk at Beach 95 St. A 13-foot-high, 19-foot-long sculpture of a whale that was originally part of the Children's Zoo in Central Park.

# AQUATIC LIFE

New York has a diverse and very interesting population of sea life in an area that mixes the East Coast's longest river with a deep-water canyon that falls off the continental shelf very close to shore. This area is ever changing with tides fighting the river's flow and temperature fluctuations that can range from near freezing in winter to sub-tropical in summer.

Animal life comes and goes, visiting briefly to spawn and retreat, like the Atlantic shad, or others, taking residence permanently, to move about from shallow or deep adjusting to season and temperature.

This sample of New York sea life gives a snapshot at best, one that's completely different at another time of year. Many animals can be listed as residents of New York since they so influence our impression of New York sea life; others are exotic visitors, up from the south, carried into the bay on a wayward swirl of the Gulf Stream.

**Harbor Seals** (*Phoca vitulina*)
Harbor seals are making a comeback in New York. Sightings around the city are becoming more common, even some distance up the Hudson. This seems strange to many New Yorkers, but they're not called harbor seals for nothing! At one time they were so commonplace and such a competition to fishermen, that a bounty was placed on their noses. Hunters would get a cash reward for every nose presented. This practice and hunting for their skins eliminated them almost completely from areas around humans. Their population shrank to strongholds further north and offshore islands. The Marine Mammal protection Act now protects them from any human interference or hunting. They are now in New York waters every year. They can often be seen "hauled-out" and sunning themselves on Hoffman and Swinburne Islands, a few hundred yards off Midland Beach, Staten Island.

**Whales** are infrequent visitors, but sometimes do pass through the maze of shipping traffic that crisscrosses the harbor. Recently, the Aquarium staff spotted a humpback in Caesar's Bay, just south of the Verrazano Bridge and in easy view of the Belt Parkway. This whale was swimming strongly and with purpose. What purpose could it have so close to Gotham? We can only guess, but it was an exception to other incidents of sick or injured whales washing in or straying into New York City disoriented or dying. These offshore animals happen in only by chance or ill luck. With the busy traffic, it is probably just as well.

**Seahorse** (*Hippocampus erectus*)
Many would not believe it, but the seahorse is native to New York. Most people think of seahorses in tropical waters, but we have a species that survives our cold winters and can be found in estuaries and along the piers in the Hudson River. In fact, scientists used to call this species, Hippocampus hudsonius. The scientific name being derived from the Greek: hippo = horse, campus = wriggling monster, and hudsonius for the river where it is found. Like the flounder, sea horses are "normal" fishes just oriented in a different way. Stretch out a seahorse, and it looks just like a pipefish, and pipefish are not too far from "normal"- Gills on both sides. Pectoral fins on each side (the ears of a seahorse). Dorsal fin on the back and vent underneath. Both pipefish and sea-horses have an exoskeleton that look like armor plate. Seahorses have a prehensile tail that they wrap around plants or hold onto pilings. Seahorses eat small shrimp, which they snap up as they swim by.

**Horseshoe crab** (*Limulus polyphemus*) Like a relic from prehistoric seas, the horseshoe crab lives much the same as its ancestors must have over 250 million years ago. It is not actually a "crab" It is an arthropod, that has the characteristic jointed legs like the crabs, but have feeding appendages called chelicerae that group it to the spiders and scorpions. Horseshoe crabs are common along the Atlantic coast and can be found along the NYC shore all summer. So common in many places that they used to be harvested by the ton for fertilizer. Today they are recognized as an essential element in the ecology of the shore, especially because their eggs are such an important food source for shore birds. Horseshoe crabs are collected for medical research where their blood is used in tests for detecting bacterial contamination. Their blood happens to be "blue" because oxygen is carried by a copper-based, hemocyanin, rather than the iron based, hemoglobin, that colors human blood red. The dangerous looking tail of the horseshoe crab is actually a harmless tool that it uses to right itself when it is flipped over. In the surf, this is a common occurrence.

**Moon jelly** (*Aurelia aurita*) Educators no longer refer to these animals as jellyfish so that they are not confused as being "fish". The confusion is unlikely, particularly as they are most commonly seen- as a gelatinous blob washed onto the beach. Sometimes they proliferate the waters and swimmers bump into them in the surf. This usually sends them screaming back to shore. While some species are, in fact, very dangerous, the common moon jelly is harmless and if it could be observed; is quite beautiful. Aquariums are now displaying these animals so that the public can appreciate their delicate beauty. The moon jelly is a clear and transparent disk, something like a glass Frisbee. It has small tentacles that while they do have stinging cells, they are completely harmless to humans. Sea turtles eat moon jellies. Sometimes the nearsighted turtles will consume plastic bags that resemble a transparent jelly—one more reason to prevent such trash from entering our waters.

*Paul L. Sieswerda Curator, NY Aquarium & author of* Sharks

## Stranded Animals

It is illegal to capture, harass, or kill marine animals and sea turtles. Sea Cliff Training Division of the NY Aquarium rescues and rehabilitates stranded marine mammals. If you come across a sick or injured animal, do not intervene. Call the NY Aquarium 718-265-3441 or the 24-hour Rescue Hotline of the Riverhead Foundation 631-369-9829 riverheadfoundation.org

# Aquariums & Zoos

## Manhattan

**Central Park Zoo** 830 5 Ave. at E 64 St. A variety of coastal creatures reside in natural habitats in the five acre zoo, such as California sea lions in the pool, Antarctic penguins in the Ice Pack Zone and Arctic polar bears; part by the Wildlife Conservation Society. 212-439-6583 centralparkzoo.com

## Bronx

**Bronx Zoo** Wildlife Conservation Society. Bronx River Pkwy. at Fordham Rd. Over 4,000 animals reside on 465 natural acres on the Bronx River shore at the country's largest urban zoo, working to save wildlife since it opened in 1899. Sea lions greet visitors at the main entrance and the aviary is home to shorebirds. 718-220-5100 bronxzoo.com

**Cornell Cooperative Extension** 965 Longwood Ave. One of only two aquaculture education centers in New York State, the facility is a leader in recirculating aquaculture technology. 718-328-4800 nyc.cce.cornell.edu

## Brooklyn

**Aquatic Research and Environmental Assessment Center** (AREAC) Brooklyn College. In the basement of one of the city's most beautiful college campuses is an aquatic eco-center where researchers study marine life, such as horseshoe crabs and urban aquaculture. brooklyn.cuny.edu

**Brooklyn Aquarium Society** Aquaria hobbyists meet 2nd Friday of each month at the New York Aquarium. brooklynaquariumsociety.org

**Kingsborough Community College Shark Tank** 2001 Oriental Blvd. A 5,000 gallon shark tank in the lobby of the Marine & Academic Center at KCC. kingsborough.edu

**New York Aquarium** Wildlife Conservation Society, Surf Ave. & W 8 St., Coney Island. The oldest continuously operating aquarium in the country and Brooklyn's most heavily attended attraction. Originally located in Castle Clinton in Manhattan when it opened in 1896, it relocated to 14 acres of Atlantic beachfront in 1957, where it is home to 8,000 fish and other marine creatures, including Beluga whales, sharks, sea lions and jellyfish. 718-265-3474 nyaquarium.com
• **Bathysphere** The record-breaking submersible that transported Will Beebe and Otis Barton 3,028 feet beneath the ocean on August 15, 1934 can be visited at the aquarium.
• **Osborn Lab of Marine Sciences** Marine research arm of the WCS explores white shark migration, dolphin cognition, and coral reefs.

**Prospect Park Zoo** Flatbush Ave. & Empire Blvd. Sea lions hold court from a pool in the center of the zoo. 718-965-6560 prospectparkzoo.com

## Queens

**Queens Zoo** Wildlife Center 5351 111 St. A 12 acre zoo with species from the across the Americas, including sea lions. 718-271-1500 queenszoo.com

## Staten Island

**Staten Island Ferry Aquariums** Two 8 ft. tall 10 ton saltwater fish tanks, each with over 400 tropical fish swimming around a coral reef, located in the St. George Terminal.

**Staten Island Zoo Aquarium** 614 Broadway. 15 tanks hold marine life from around the globe, in addition to a world class collection of reptiles, including snakes. 718-442-3100 statenislandzoo.org

# Nature Centers

Nature Centers situated at parks throughout the city offer a variety of environmental education programs and activities for all ages. Programs ranging from canoe trips and birding to beachcombing and water monitoring are conducted by the Urban Park Rangers at city park centers while the National Park Service administers the programs at Gateway National Recreation Area.

## Manhattan

**Charles A. Dana Discovery Center** Central Park Harlem Meer, E 110 St. & Lenox Ave. Catch & release fishing on the shores of the 11-acre freshwater lake. 212-860-1370 centralpark.com.

**Henry Luce Nature Observatory** Central Park. Nature center and exhibits dedicated to the park's wildlife located inside Belvedere Castle. 212-772-0210 nycgovparks.org

**Inwood Hill Park Nature Center** W 218 St. & Indian Rd. Seaman Ave. Explore Manhattan's last extant salt marsh and forest and ancient Indian caves with Urban Rangers. 212-304-2365 nycgovparks.org

**Lower Eastside Ecology Center** East River Park at Grand St. Riverside gardens and ecology in a former Fireboat House. 212-477-4022 lesecologycenter.org

**River Project** Hudson River Park. Marine research field station currently located at Pier 40. 212-233-3030 riverproject.org

**Solar One** East River. FDR Dr. at E 22 St. An eco-classroom in a riverside solar-powered pavilion. 212-505-6050 solar1.org

## Bronx

**Crotona Park** A freshwater pond eco-system, huge swimming pool and views of the New Jersey Palisades from the hills. 718-378-2061 nycgovparks.org

**Harlem River Ecology Center** A small estuarium with a variety of interpretive exhibits operated by Urban Divers Estuary Conservancy. urbandivers.org

**Orchard Beach Nature Center** Pelham Bay Park. Learn about life on the beach. 718-885-3466 nycgovparks.org

---

**Charles William Beebe**, Naturalist, Scientist & Ocean Explorer (1877-1962) Beebe was the first person to observe deep sea life when he made his world record descent 3,028 feet beneath the ocean in the submersible Bathysphere with Otis Barton on August 15, 1934. Born in Brooklyn, Beebe began exploring under water with a homemade diving helmet constructed out of wood in the 1920s. He attended Columbia University in 1899, became Assistant Bird Keeper at the new Zoological Park (Bronx Zoo), and was later named director of the Department of Tropical Research. He first drafted a sketch for a deep-sea vessel when dining with his friend Teddy Roosevelt. The final design for the 5,400 pound spherical Bathysphere was accomplished by Otis Barton, an engineer and Beebe's dive partner. Their expedition was sponsored by the New York Zoological Society and National Geographic Society.

**Pelham Bay Nature Center**
Pelham Bay Park. 660 acres of saltwater marsh, 13 miles of shoreline, and acres of forest. 718-885-3467 nycgovparks.org

**Van Cortlandt Nature Center**
Broadway at 246 St. The largest freshwater lake in the Bronx. 718-548-0912 nycgovparks.org

**Wave Hill** W 249 St. Botanical gardens, arboretum and greenhouses overlooking the Hudson River and hills of the Palisades. 718-549-3200 wavehill.org

## Brooklyn

**Dead Horse Bay Ecology Village**
Jamaica Bay. Floyd Bennett Field. Youth group overnight camping and nature exploration. 718-338-4306 nps.gov

**Jamaica Bay Institute** Jamaica Bay. Floyd Bennett Field. Scientific research and stewardship program. 718-338-3338 nature.nps.gov/jbi

**Prospect Park Audubon Center**
Boathouse, Prospect Park Lake. Overlooking the Lullwater, where visitors enjoy guided nature programs including fishing, birding, and lake tours aboard an electric boat. 718-287-3400 prospectpark.org

**Salt Marsh Nature Center** Gerritsen Creek. 3302 Ave. U. Canoeing, kayaking, hiking, and nature exploration along five miles of marshy shore, upland meadows and tidal flats. The building is also home to a honeybee hive, observable behind plexiglass. 718-421-2021 saltmarshalliance.org

## Queens

**Alley Pond Nature Center** (APEC) Alley Creek. 228-06 Northern Blvd. Urban park ranger activities include camping, canoeing, and nature study. 718-229-4000 alleypond.com

**Jamaica Bay Wildlife Refuge** Jamaica Bay. Cross Bay Blvd. One of the northeast's largest bird sanctuaries, containing trails along 9,000 acres of coast and two freshwater ponds. 718-318-4340 nps.gov/gate

## Staten Island

**Blue Heron Park** 222 Poillon Ave. Wetlands, streams, and a nature library, along with handicap accessible trails. 718-967-3542 preserve2.org/blueheron

**Clay Pit Ponds Nature Center**
83 Nielson Ave. Birding and ecology on trails passing spring-fed streams, sand barrens, bogs, and ponds. 718-967-1976 nysparks.state.ny.us

**Greenbelt Nature Center** Rockland Ave. Center for exploring the Greenbelt trail system encompassing 2,800 acres of glacial ponds, wetlands, forests, meadows and streams. 718-351-3450 sigreenbelt.org

# BEACHES

Rockaway Peninsula and Coney Island are barrier beaches that defend the coast from Atlantic storms. These long, narrow sandy spits are part of one of the largest coastal barriers in the world, stretching from Maine to the Gulf of Mexico. The sand is never in one place very long, as wind, waves, tides, and storms keep it in constant motion. Most of the action occurs in the fall and winter when storms carry sand to offshore bars. In summer, the sand migrates back, renourishing the beaches.

Breezy Point is shaped by wave action moving sand east to west along the entire length of Long Island, all the way from Montauk. The land west of Jacob Riis Park formed since the Civil War and in recent decades a mile of new growth has been added to the peninsula.

The sand on most city beaches is a blend of Fordham gneiss, quartz pebbles, and Manhattan schist remnants, such as hematite, magnetite, and small garnets. On Staten Island, the sand comes from brown stone sediment washed down Newark Basin. Jetties, seawalls and groins disrupt the natural flow of sand causing extensive erosion down current. One

example is Coney Island's natural supply of sand, which has been cut off by the Breezy Point jetty. In 1922, it was the nation's first beach replenishment project with sand pumped from offshore bars.

Urban beachcombers will find surf clams, quahogs, Atlantic slippers, common jingles, bay scallops, blue mussels, Atlantic ribbed mussels, cockle shells, razor clams, oyster, and moon snails. The Official Shell of New York State is the bay scallop. The best beach for shell collecting is Breezy Point. Treasure hunters using a metal detector need a permit on city park beaches and it is not permitted in Federal and State parks or historical sites where relics might be of archeological significance.

| | |
|---:|:---|
| New York City Parks: | 14 miles of beaches |
| Gateway National Recreation Area: | 17 miles of beaches |
| Beach Season: | Memorial Day to Labor Day |
| Swimming Beaches: | Lifeguard on duty 10am - 6pm |
| Summer Average Air Temps: | 75° F 24° C |
| Summer Average Water Temp: | 67° F 19° C |
| Handicapped Access: | City Park beaches have Mobimats |
| Bicycles: | Boardwalks only, 5am - 10am |
| Dogs Friendly: | Off-season, on leash only |

# Beaches

## Bronx

**Orchard Beach** Long Island Sound. Pelham Bay Park. This crescent-shaped mile-long beach features a promenade and band shell near the Pelham Bay salt marshes. In addition to playgrounds, tennis and basketball, the AeroBalloon pilot offers rides in a wicker gondola lifting 350 feet into the air. 718-885-2275 nycgovparks.org Getting there: 6 to Pelham Bay Park then BX12 or BX5 Bus (summer only).

## Brooklyn

**Brighton Beach** Atlantic Ocean. E. Seabreeze Walk to Corbin Place. A wide stretch of white sand beach with rock jetties, a boardwalk and several waterside Russian cafés. 718-946-1350 nycgovparks.org Getting there: B, Q to the Brighton Beach; Bus B1, B68.

**Coney Island Beach** Atlantic Ocean. Surf Ave. America's first beach features two miles of sand framed by Riegelmann's Boardwalk, amusement rides, clam shacks, ball courts, the NY Aquarium and Steeplechase Pier. 718-946-1350 nycgovparks.org Getting there: D, F, N, Q to Stillwell Ave.

**Manhattan Beach** Atlantic Ocean. Oriental Blvd. A compact family beach and promenade featuring ball fields, grills, picnic area, playground, and fee parking. 718-946-1373 nycgovparks.org Getting there: B, Q to Brighton Beach; Bus B1 Eastbound.

**Plum(b) Beach** Dead Horse Bay. A rest stop on the Belt Pkwy. provides access to a stretch of beach, sand dunes and mudflats that are part of Gateway National Recreation Area. The calm waters are favored by wind surfers and kite boarders. The Shore Greenway bike path edges the dunes.

## Swimming Advisories

The NYC Department of Health tests water quality at public and private beaches and advises of beach closures due to pollution. The general rule is to refrain from swimming at beaches for at least 12 hours after heavy rainfall when pollution levels are high due to stormwater runoff and combined sewer overflow. A wait of up to 48 hours is advised at Eastchester Bay beaches in the Bronx. For details, visit nyc.gov/health/beach.

| Beach Amenities | Beach Bathing | Boat Ramp | Concessions | Fishing | BBQ Grills | Launch | Marina | Nature Center | Parking | Restrooms | Showers | Surfing | Volleyball |
|---|---|---|---|---|---|---|---|---|---|---|---|---|---|
| Breezy Point | • |  |  | • |  |  |  |  |  |  |  | • | • |
| Brighton Beach | • |  | • | • |  |  |  |  |  | • | • |  | • |
| Coney Island Beach | • |  | • | • |  |  |  |  |  | • | • |  | • |
| Fort Tilden Beach |  |  |  | • |  |  |  | • | • | • |  |  | • |
| Great Kills Beach | • | • | • | • | • | • | • | • | • | • | • |  | • |
| Jacob Riis Park | • |  | • | • | • |  |  |  | • | • | • |  | • |
| Manhattan Beach | • |  | • | • |  |  |  |  | • | • | • |  | • |
| Midland Beach | • |  | • | • | • |  |  |  | • | • | • |  | • |
| Orchard Beach | • |  | • | • | • | • |  | • | • | • | • |  | • |
| Plumb Beach |  |  |  | • |  |  |  |  | • | • |  | • |  |
| Rockaway Beach | • |  | • | • |  |  |  |  | • | • | • |  | • |
| South Beach | • |  | • | • |  |  |  |  | • | • | • |  | • |
| Water Taxi Beach |  |  |  |  | • | • |  |  |  | • |  |  | • |
| Wolfe's Pond Beach | • |  | • | • | • |  |  |  | • | • |  |  |  |

nps.gov/gate <u>Getting there</u>: D, Q to Sheepshead Bay.

**Sea Gate Beach** Atlantic Ocean. W 38 St. Resident-only beach in gated community located on the western end of Coney Island accessible at low tide from Coney Island Creek Park. <u>Getting there</u>: D, F, N, Q to Stillwell Ave., B36 bus.
• **Sea Gate Beach Club** 3700 Surf Ave. Cabana club. 718-372-4477 seagatebeachclub.com

## Queens

**Breezy Point** Atlantic Ocean. Beach 222 St. 1,000 acres of protected beachhead reaching to the jetty at the tip of the Rockaway Peninsula with access along the beach from the parking area at Jacob Riis Park. 718-318-4300 nps.gov/gate <u>Getting there</u>: A to Beach 116 St. to Q35 Bus.
• **Breezy Point Surf Club** B 227 St. 718-634-7200 bpsonline.com
• **Silver Gull Beach Club** B 193 St. The setting for the movie "The Flamingo Kid." 718-634-2900 silvergullclub.com

**Fort Tilden Beach** Atlantic Ocean. A former Army Base with a big expanse of unguarded and unspoiled beach primarily used by fishermen. It has one of the city's last surviving dune ecosystem, protected and administered by the National Park Service as part of Gateway National Recreation Area. Carry in/carry out trash policy and parking by seasonal permit. 718-318-4300 nps.gov/gate <u>Getting there</u>: 2 to Flatbush (last stop) to Q35 Bus; or A to Rockaway Park to Q22 Bus.

**Jacob Riis Park** Atlantic Ocean. Beach 169 St. A one-mile long beach and boardwalk built by Robert Moses in the 1930s and named for the muckraking journalist. The bathhouse and clock tower are on the National Register of Historic Places and NYC Landmarks. Nude sunbathing is tolerated near the west end of the beach. 718-318-4300 nps.gov/gate Getting there: 2 to Flatbush Ave., transfer to Q35 Bus.

**Rockaway Beach** Atlantic Ocean. Beach 9 St to Beach 149 St. 96 acres of barrier coast stretching 7.5 miles with 5 miles of boardwalk. Action centers at Beach 116 Street. Surf-only area is Beach 87 to 92 Sts. and Beach 67-69 Sts. Barbecue at Beach 17, 88 and 98 Sts. Very limited street parking during the summer season. 718-318-4000 nycgovparks.org Getting there: A to Beach 116 St.

## Staten Island

**Great Kills Beach** Atlantic Ocean & Great Kills Harbor. Hylan Blvd. Sand beach, dunes, and nature trails in a 1,200-acre National Park, offering swimming, fishing, marina, bike trails, and kayak launch facilities. 718-987-6790 nps.gov/gate Getting there: SIRT to Great Kills; S78 bus.

**South Beach** Lower Bay. Father Capodanno Blvd. A stretch of orange sand along the south coast bound by the 2.5 mile long WPA-built FDR Boardwalk. 718-987-0709 nycgovparks.org Getting there: SIRT to South Beach; Bus S78.

**Midland Beaches** Lower New York Bay. Father Capodanno Blvd. Fishing piers, playgrounds, and athletic and recreation facilities. 718-987-0709 nycgovparks.org Getting there: SIRT to South Beach; Bus S78.

**Wolfe's Pond Beach** Prince's Bay Hylan Blvd. A rocky shore with low-lying dunes offering freshwater and saltwater fishing, rowboating in the pond, and sunbathing. 718-984-8266 nycgovparks.org Getting there: SIRT to South Beach; Bus S78

## Water Taxi Beaches

Serving tons of sand for sunning, beach volleyball, and picnicking at a few Water Taxi stops on the East River, including Hunter's Point in Queens, South Street Seaport's Pier 17 and the newest location on the shore of Governors Island. The faux beaches have Tiki bar cafes and music, but no swimming or water access. The beaches feature native plantings of beach plums, which can be harvested. harborexperience.com

### COASTAL CLEAN UP

Thousands of volunteers clean and document close to a ton of debris at over 300 sites across New York State in coastal cleanups coordinated by the American Littoral Society. (alsnyc.org)

Most of the debris comes from street litter that washes down storm drains and catch basins during rain showers, eventually ending up on beaches. The NYC Department of Environmental Protection operates a fleet of skimmer boats and maintains booms around major sewer outflows in the city to capture floating debris in the harbor. It is still one of the biggest problems facing urban beaches.

Top trash found on city shores:

- Cigarette butts
- Plastic
- Styrofoam

# BIRDING

New York City is an avian crossroads providing habitat to more than 330 species. Each spring, millions of migrating birds pass through the city on their way to breeding grounds. The scene reverses in the fall when the birds head south to winter nest sites. The transients rest and feed in freshwater ponds, salt marshes and other natural areas along the city's coast. Birds navigate mostly at night using the moon and the stars to guide them. They follow a 10,000 mile route along the Eastern Seaboard called the Atlantic Flyway, one of four ancient avian routes in North America. The peak migration seasons are in late April and early September.

Wading birds are urban dwellers roosting on uninhabited island sanctuaries in the Harbor Heron Complex within the New York Harbor Estuary. Egrets populate Goose Island, adjacent to Co-op City in the Bronx. North Brother Island at the mid-section of the East River is home to a large colony of Black-crowned Night Heron, while a few Great Blue Heron have been seen foraging on nearby South Brother Island. Great-backed Gulls and Herring Gulls nest on Mill Rock offshore of Gracie Mansion. Double-Crested Cormorants spread and flap their wings to dry on U Thant Island in the shadow of the United Nations. Just below the Verrazano-Narrows Bridge, Hoffman Island has a large colony of Heron. Osprey and Ibis are regularly spotted on the mudflats of Jamaica Bay.

The over 9,000 acre Jamaica Bay Wildlife Refuge, part of Gateway National Recreation Area, is winter home to large numbers of snow geese and other water fowl. Rare Piping Plover nest in the dunes of Arverne and Breezy Point. At JoCo Marsh, where JFK Airport Runway 22 bisects the marshy home of the only Laughing Gull colony in New York State, the gulls pose a threat to aircraft from bird strikes; a bird sucked into the engine can bring down a jet. The Port Authority has engaged falcons, natural gull predators, to fly over the field in an attempt to coax the colony to relocate.

Birders don't necessarily need a field guide to see exotic birds in the city. Eye the famed Red-tail Hawk, Pale Male through a telescopic lens near Conservatory Waters in Central Park. Visit penguins in the Ice Zone at the park's zoo or see the Sea Bird Colony at the Bronx Zoo. The aviary at the Queens Zoo is a geodesic dome designed by Buckminster Fuller for the 1964 World's Fair. *The Birds of America* folio at The New York Historical Society is the largest repository of John James Audubon plates including 435 watercolors.

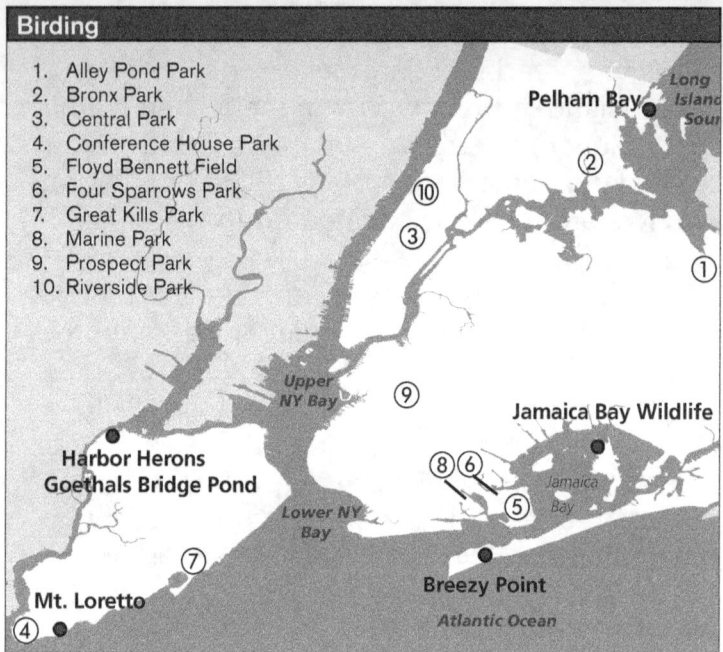

## Birding

1. Alley Pond Park
2. Bronx Park
3. Central Park
4. Conference House Park
5. Floyd Bennett Field
6. Four Sparrows Park
7. Great Kills Park
8. Marine Park
9. Prospect Park
10. Riverside Park

## Top Birding Sites

**Jamaica Bay Wildlife Refuge**
One of the prime birding spots in North America with over 300 species recorded, from migrating shorebirds, raptors, gulls, terns, and water fowl to more unusual sightings. Osprey platforms sit on stilts above the grassy marshes; trails circumnavigate two brackish ponds where water fowl winter and monarch butterflies and dragonflies pass through each fall. Obtain a permit and map at the Visitor's Center, open daily 8:30am to 5pm. 718-318-4340 nps.gov/gate

**Breezy Point/Fort Tilden** Miles of Atlantic beachfront on the western tip of Rockaway Peninsula is vital habitat for migrating shorebirds and nesting colonies of endangered piping plovers, terns and skimmers. Marked trails keep humans from disturbing the birds and nesting areas are closed in the spring when about a dozen monogamous pairs of plovers lay eggs and rear their young. Birding passes can be obtained at Fort Tilden Ranger Station, Beach 169 St. 718-318-4300 nps.gov/gate

**Pelham Bay Park** A wide range of habitat supports populations of wading birds, wren, rail, and owls. Over 200 species have been recorded along the many nature trails. Heron and egret colonies nesting on Goose Island are visible from park trails. The park is also a well-known winter owl and fall hawk watch site.

**Harbor Herons Complex**
A network of 14 uninhabited, protected nesting islands for colonial wading birds, especially herons, egrets, and ibis. The complex encompasses 111 acres in Staten Island, including Hoffman and Swinburne islands, Isle

**Roger Tory Peterson,** Painter & Naturalist (1908-1996). Peterson moved to New York City to pursue a career as a commercial artist and attended the Art Students' League and the National Academy of Design. He was a founding member of the Bronx County Bird Club. In 1934, Peterson combined his painting skills and love of birds to create *A Field Guide to the Birds*. The book, initially rejected by four publishers, presented a simple system for identifying birds that revolutionized bird-watching. The Peterson Identification System was so successful that it has been applied to all manner of flora and fauna, and was employed in WWII to identify enemy aircraft.

of Meadows, Prall's Island, Shooters Island, and wetlands surrounding Goethals Bridge Pond and Old Place Creek adjoining wetlands. There is parking and viewing area at Goethals Bridge Pond. North Brother and South Brother Islands in the East River are also part of the large preserve.

**Mount Loretto** Follow the trails through grasslands, marsh and shore habitat to see nesting warblers, eastern meadowlark, waterfowl and a large variety of seasonal migrants.

## Birding Clubs

In the 1920s, ornithologist Joseph Hickey, naturalist Allan Cruickshank, and artist, Roger Tory Peterson, and other bird enthusiasts formed the Bronx County Bird Club to pursue their interest in the birds of New York City. Birdwatching is the second most popular outdoor activity in the country today. Membership in city birding clubs exceeds 10,000.

**Audubon Society** Brooklyn-born George Bird Grinnell founded the first Audubon Society in 1886. The NYC Chapter is one of the nation's largest with 8,000 members and offers a wide range of field trips and programs, for all levels of experience, from beginners to consummate bird watchers. nycaudubon.org

**Brooklyn Bird Club** Founded in 1909, Prospect Park is homebase to the club's 150 members, enjoying field trips and educational programs. brooklynbirdclub.org

**Linnaean Society of New York** Founded in 1878 by 10 amateur birders, including John Burroughs, the club is named for the inventor of the system for classifying plants and animals. Programs range from field research to free lectures. Meets monthly at the American Museum of Natural History, Lindnur Theater. linnaeannewyork.org

**Manhattan Bird Club** Bird advocacy group offering nature and bird walks. manhattanbirdclub.com

**Queens County Bird Club** Group meets monthly at Alley Pond Environmental Center and offers a full calendar of local and regional field trips. qcbc.all.at

### Project Safe Flight

During migration seasons, NYC Audubon enlists owners of tall buildings in Project Safe Flight, a program to help save avian lives by turning off lights during bad weather when birds drawn by the light are in danger of flying into the buildings. Bird-Safe Building Guidelines available online at nycaudubon.org.

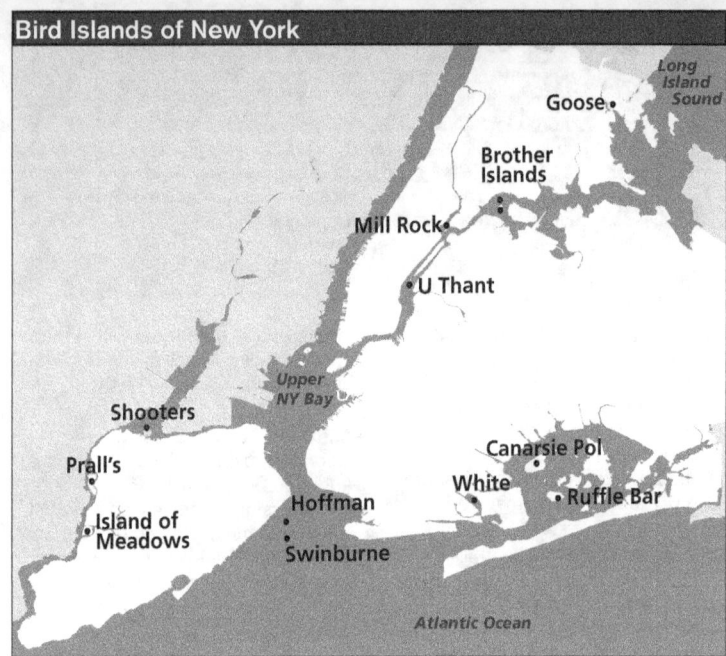

*To report a rare bird sighting, call 212-979-3070. To find out the birds currently seen in the NYC area, visit at ebird.org and nycbirdreport.com.

## Birdwatching Programs

**Gateway National Recreation Area** Year-round ranger guided bird walks and educational programs at the Jamaica Bay and Staten Island units. nps.gov/gate

**Prospect Park Audubon Center** The first urban Audubon Center in the country offers birding programs for beginners and youth. 718-287-3400 prospectpark.org

**Urban Park Rangers** Bird walks and programs for children and adults at nature centers in various city parks. nycgovparks.org

## Birding Cruises

**NY Water Taxi's Audubon Eco Cruises** The scheduled 90-minute cruise departs South Street Seaport, Pier 17. 212-742-1969, nywatertaxi.com

**Jamaica Bay Sunset Cruise** See nesting Peregrine falcons, osprey, egrets, shorebirds and waterfowl on a narrated three-hour cruise hosted by the American Littoral Society. alsnyc.org

**Riis Landing Eco Cruises** National Park Service Ranger led tour of Jamaica Bay casts off from Riis Landing on Rockaway Peninsula.

# BOATBUILDING

In the early 1990s Floating the Apple began building Whitehall Gigs in a midtown Manhattan storefront. They wheeled the finished rowboats across 42 Street to launch in the Hudson River. The wooden boats are modeled on the Brooklyn-built Whitehall *American Star*, which in 1824 beat a British boat in a race in New York Harbor. The boats are built by community boathouses from blueprints of the original craft and in the process preserve traditional boatbuilding techniques such as lofting, pattern-making, steam bending, and assembling traditional wooden Whitehall's, skiffs, dories, dinghies, and other rowing craft from scratch. The learning programs teach school and youth groups lessons in water ecology, maritime trades, woodworking, and seamanship.

There were no line drawings in early yacht design. Vessel features first had to be worked out on scale models known as builder's models. After the boat was constructed a presentation model was crafted for the owner. The Navy also used models to aid in ship identification. H. E. Boucher Company started as a naval modeling firm, later developing into one of the premier modelers in the world and chief modeler for the NY Yacht Club.

## Boatbuilding Workshops

**Floating the Apple (FTA)** The originator of public boatbuilding and rowing of Whitehall gigs in NYC. Open to all ages at Pier 84 in Hudson River Park. floatingtheapple.org

**Lang on the Hudson** The New School. Students construct and row 26-foot Whitehall gigs. newschool.edu

**New York Harbor School** Public High School offering maritime curriculum and boatbuilding program on board South Street Seaport's *Wavertree* administered by Rocking the Boat. The school has plans to move to Governors Island in 2010. newyorkharborschool.org

**Rocking the Boat** Local high school students build full size traditional wooden boats from scratch in Bronx-based after school programs. rockingtheboat.org

**South Street Seaport Museum** Volunteer shipwrights help restore the old ships berthed at Pier 16 and learn maritime trades. Skilled docents share expertise on the museum fleet of schooners, tall ships and work boats. 212-748-8690 southstreetseaportmuseum.org

## Boat Modeling

**Conservatory Waters** Central Park near E 72 St. at 5 Ave. One of the earliest ponds designed with model sailing in mind. On a lazy summer afternoon, spectators view a fleet of handsome radio-controlled yachts and wind-powered schooners navigating the large pond. Regattas are held every Saturday morning. Sailors can bring their own boat or rent one from a nearby concession cart. **Wolfe Pond Park** Model boat pond in the active seaside park on Staten Islands southern shore.

## Model Boat Collections

**Forbes Magazine Gallery** 52 5 Ave. Over 500 antique tin and cast iron toy boats, representing the great makers from 1870s to the 1950s. Free. 212-206-5548 forbesgalleries.com

**India House** One Hanover Square, Founded by captains of industry in 1914, the exclusive club holds a rare collection of merchant vessel models and ship's portraits. 212-269-2323 indiahouseclub.org

**Maritime Industry Museum** SUNY Maritime College, Bronx. Scale models of famous passenger ships and a scale model of the 1942 Brooklyn Navy Yard with a full fleet of related military models. 718-409-7218 maritimeindustrymuseum.org

**Museum of the City of New York** 1220 5 Ave. Models of ships that plied the waters of New York Harbor. Not all are on display. 212-534-1672 mcny.org

**New York Historical Society** 170 Central Park West. More than two dozen ship models, from Henry Hudson's *Half Moon* to the builder's half-model for the *USS Monitor*. 212-873-3400 nyhistory.org

**New York Yacht Club** 37 W 44 St. World renowned collection of yacht models, including George Steers builder's model of schooner *America* built in 1/2" scale. 212-382-1000 nyyc.org

**Noble Maritime Collection** 1000 Richmond Terr., Staten Island. A vast collection of model ships, only a fraction is on display. 718-447-6490 noblemaritime.org

**Seamen's Church Institute** 241 Water St. Ship models and artifacts. 212-349-9090 seamenschurch.org

**Gibbs & Cox**, Naval Architecture and Marine Engineering. Since its founding in 1929, 6000 naval and commercial ships have been built to Gibbs & Cox, Inc. designs, including the WWII Liberty ship, New York's famous *Fireboat* and the celebrated passenger liner *United States* (1952). The firm was founded by design genius William Francis Gibbs, his brother Frederick H. Gibbs and Daniel Cox, a noted yacht designer. The company continues to be an international leader in the advancement of naval architecture and technology. (gibbscox.com)

**South Street Seaport Museum**
207 Front St. The miniature fleet of over 2000 scale models and ships-in-bottles, including Cunard's *Queen Mary* and Seaman's Bank for Savings' 2,000 models, which came to the museum during the banking crises of the 1980s. 212-748-8600 southstreetseaportmuseum.org

## Model Boat Clubs

**Brooklyn Battery Naval Brigade**
The club builds and contests scale models of actual warships dating from the dreadnought era, 1906 to 1946. pittelli.com/warship/bbnb

**Central Park Model Yacht Club**
Conservatory Water, Central Park E 72 St. Founded in 1916, members meet each Saturday from April to November beginning at 10 am, racing several classes of sailing yacht. cpmyc.org

**Empire State Model Mariners**
Scale model club established 1988, which holds sailing regattas on Sundays at Bowne Lake Park, Flushing or Hall's Pond in West Hempstead. empirestatemodelmariners.com

**The Kerbs Boathouse** Adjacent to Conservatory Waters, the miniature boathouse provides storage of models no more than 72 inches in length for an annual permit issued by NYC Department of Parks & Recreation.

**Maritime Craft Center** South Street Seaport Museum. Model ship building, restoration and repair by volunteer craftsmen, who demonstrate their skills daily. southstreetseaport.org

**Shipcraft Guild of New York**
Group of ship modelers formed in 1954 meets the third Tuesday of each month, 7pm at South Street Seaport Museum. shipcraftguild.org

# BOATING

New York State ranks seventh nationally in the number of registered pleasure boats, close to 500,000, that generate $1.8 billion and account for about 20,000 jobs. Over 30,000 recreational power and motor boats are registered in the five boroughs. Queens has the most.

The Good Samaritan Law requires every maritime vessel to render assistance to any other vessel that may be in distress at sea. The Mayday distress call comes from the French phrase m'aider, which translates as "help me."

Boat slips and winter storage space are in high demand citywide. There is a wait of four years for slips at the 79 Street Boat Basin and up to 15 years at other marinas. The city's largest full-service facility with 600 slips is Gateway Marina, a concession of the National Park Service.

There are numerous transient docks, even some places to dock and dine. Very few marinas accommodate year-round live aboards, as does the Boat Basin on Manhattan's westside. Houseboat rentals are available at Venice Marina.

Paved launch ramps can be found at most marinas for a fee of about $15 to launch and park. Free public ramps, rare in New York City, are operated by NYC Parks at Clason's Point in the Bronx, near Bayside Marina and at World's Fair Marina in Queens, and at Lemon Creek on Staten Island, as well as a National Park Service launch in Great Kills Park.

| | |
|---|---|
| Recreational Vessel Speed: | 5 mph within 100 ft of shore or float |
| Currents: | 1-2 knots at flood tide; max 6 knots |
| Knot: | 1.06 mph or 1.852 km/hr. |
| Nautical Mile: | 1.1508 statute miles or 1852 meters |
| League: | 3 Nautical Miles |
| Fathom: | 6 Feet |

## Boating Resources

**NYC Department of Environmental Protection (DEP)** regulates sewage treatment, storm water management and recreational access within New York City's upstate watershed system. nyc.gov/dep

**NYC Department of Parks & Recreation Marine Division** operates the Boat Basin and World's Fair Marina and oversees numerous park concession marinas and boat clubs. 718-478-0480 nycgovparks.org

**NY Marine Trades Association** represents over 150 marine businesses in NYC and Long Island. 631-691-7050 nymta.com

**NY Police Department Harbor Unit** was founded in 1858 to combat piracy aboard merchant vessels anchoring in New York Harbor. Today the unit patrols 146 square miles of navigable waters and 576 miles of waterfront. 718-765-4100 or VHF Channel 17

**NYS Department of Motor Vehicles** All motor driven boats, including sailboats, operated on public waters for more than 90 days must be registered. Registration is valid for three years, cost is determined by the size of the vessel. 518-473-5595 dmv.org

**NYS Office of Parks, Recreation & Historic Preservation** has jurisdiction over floating objects in navigable waters of the state. The Bureau of Marine & Recreational Vehicles publishes *The NYS Boater's Guide* about registration, rules of the road, operations, and safety. 518-474-0445 nysparks.state.ny.us/boating/

**NYS Department of Environmental Conservation (DEC) Region 2** provides enforcement of environmental regulations and resources on boat launches, pumpouts, public fishing and boating access maps. Spill hotline: 518-457-7362 dec.state.ny.us

**Notice to Mariners First Coast Guard District** Special notice of security zones and other water activities. navcen.uscg.gov/lnm

**USCG Sector New York** Management of waterways covering everything from security to events. 24 hour hotline: 718-354-4120 homeport.uscg.mil

### No Wake Zones

Excessive speed causes wakes that endanger boaters, kayakers and rowers, and can do damage to shore habitat, marinas, and piers. Vessel Regulation Zones where all boats must operate at idle speed of 4 mph are enforced in Orchard Beach Lagoons, Great Kills Harbor, and Harlem River, from University Heights Bridge to High Bridge and from Spuyten Duyvil Trestle to the Broadway Bridge.

# Boater Safety

**Kingsborough Community College** Captain's License and marine management training. kingsborough.edu

**New York Boating Safety** Safe boating and jet ski certificate. nyboatingsafety.com

**New York School of Seamanship** Captain's license training for pleasure and working mariners. 718-720-6977 newyorksos.com

**NYPD Auxiliary Harbor Unit** Safe boating certification for personal watercraft licensing is held at Brooklyn Army Terminal. 718-520-9243

**SUNY Maritime College** Boater safety and hands-on powerboat handling courses, as well as all levels of commercial maritime education. 718-409-7200 sunymaritime.edu/waterfront

**USCG Auxiliary** Boating safety courses and free vessel safety inspections. 212-668-7990 nws.cgaux.org

**US Power Squadron** The world's largest boating group offers safe boating courses in each borough. usps.org

**Vessel Safety Check** (VSC) USCG Auxiliary and US Power Squadrons perform free inspections of pleasure craft, covering all federal and state requirements.

## Personal Watercraft

Since first introduced by Kawasaki in 1974, wave runners are responsible for more boating accidents than other vessels. As a result, more restrictions are placed on personal watercraft. New York State has a mandatory boater education law that applies to all operators of personal watercraft (PWC), regardless of age. Reckless operation, such as wake jumping is a misdemeanor. Jet skis are banned in all waters of Gateway National Recreation Area encompassing most of Jamaica Bay, and the area along the eastern coast of Staten Island.

## Harbor Charts

| | |
|---|---|
| 12327 | New York Harbor |
| 12334 | Upper Bay & Narrows |
| 12335 | Hudson & East Rivers |
| 12339 | East River: Tallman Island to Queensboro Bridge |
| 12363 | Western Long Island Sound |
| 12341 | Hudson River-Days Point to George Washington Bridge |
| 12350 | Jamaica Bay/Rockaway Inlet |

---

**Robert Fulton**, Inventor (1765-1815). Fulton aspired to be an artist and moved to Europe to pursue painting but soon abandoned art for engineering. After 20 years overseas, Fulton returned to America in 1806 with numerous patents, including a machine for spinning flax and an amphibious craft. He received funding from statesman Robert Livingston Jr. to construct what became the first commercially successful power boat, the steamship *Clermont*. For years, Fulton and Livingston had a monopoly on ferry service on the Hudson River. Fulton was also responsible for significant improvements in submarine and torpedo design.

| | MARINAS | Fuel | Dining | Boat Launch | Pumpout | Repair | Fishing | Parking | Restrooms | Storage |
|---|---|---|---|---|---|---|---|---|---|---|
| **MANHATTAN** | 79th St. Boat Basin (DPR)<br>W 79 St., Hudson River | | • | | • | | | • | • | |
| | Dyckman Marina (✵ 2010)<br>Dyckman Rd., Hudson River | | | • | • | • | • | • | • | • |
| | Hudson River Park Moorings<br>Pier 40, Hudson River | | • | | | | • | • | • | |
| | North Cove<br>Battery Park City, Hudson River | | • | | | | | • | • | |
| | Surfside 3<br>Chelsea Piers, Hudson River | | • | | | | • | • | • | |
| | Skyport Marina<br>E 23 St, East River | • | | | | | • | • | • | |
| **BRONX** | City Island Gas Dock<br>City Island Ave., Eastchester Bay | • | | | | • | | | • | |
| | Evers Marina<br>Outlook Ave., Eastchester Bay | | | • | | • | • | • | • | • |
| | Hammond Cove Marina<br>Reynold Ave., Long Island Sound | | • | • | • | • | • | • | • | |
| | Metro Marine Sales<br>Commerce Ave., Westchester Creek | | | | | | | | | |
| | Sailmaker Marina<br>Schofield St., Long Island Sound | | | | | • | | • | • | |
| **BROOKLYN** | All Seasons Marina<br>Kings Plaza, Rockaway Inlet | • | • | • | | • | • | • | • | • |
| | Gateway Marina (NPS)<br>Flatbush Ave., Jamaica Bay | | | • | • | | • | • | • | |
| | Marine Basin Marina<br>Shore Pkwy., Gravesend Bay | • | | • | | • | • | • | • | • |
| | Mill Basin Marina<br>Ave. Y & E 69 St., Mill Basin | | | • | | • | • | • | • | • |
| | Sheepshead Bay Moorings (DPR)<br>Emmons Ave., Sheepshead Bay | | • | | | | • | | | |
| | Tamaqua Marina<br>Ebony Ct., Shellbank Creek | • | • | • | | | • | • | • | • |
| | Venice Marina<br>Emmons Ave., Plumb Beach Chan. | • | • | • | • | • | • | • | • | • |

| MARINAS | | Fuel | Dining | Boat Launch | Pumpout | Repair | Fishing | Transients | Restrooms | Storage |
|---|---|---|---|---|---|---|---|---|---|---|
| QUEENS | Bayside Marina<br>Cross Island Pkwy., Little Neck Bay | • | • | • | • |  | • | • | • |  |
| QUEENS | Beach Channel Marina<br>Beach Channel Dr., Jamaica Bay |  |  | • |  |  | • | • | • |  |
| QUEENS | World's Fair Marina (DPR)<br>Northern Blvd., Flushing Bay | • | • | • | • |  | • | • | • | • |
| STATEN ISLAND | Atlantis Marina<br>180 Mansion Ave., Great Kills |  | • | • | * | • | • | • | • | • |
| STATEN ISLAND | Mansion Marina<br>112 Mansion Ave., Great Kills | • | • |  |  | • | • | • | • | • |
| STATEN ISLAND | Nichols Great Kills Marina (NPS)<br>Great Kills Park, Lower Bay |  |  | • |  |  | • | • | • | • |
| STATEN ISLAND | Port Atlantic Marina<br>225 Ellis St., Arthur Kill |  |  | • |  | • | • | • | • | • |
| STATEN ISLAND | Staten Island Yacht Sales<br>222 Mansion Ave., Great Kills | • | • | • |  | • | • | • | • | • |
| STATEN ISLAND | Tottenville Marina<br>201 Ellis St., Arthur Kill |  |  | • |  | • | • | • | • | • |

\* Visit goingcoastal.org for a complete list of marinas & yacht clubs.

**Charles F. "Chap" Chapman**, Editor (1881-1976). Chapman authored *Piloting, Seamanship & Small Boat Handling* - the bible of recreational boating. It was originally written as a training manual for the Naval Reserve in WWI. He was a founding father of the U.S. Power Squadron, formed the New York Power Squadron, and was a prime mover in establishing motor boat racing as a major sport. Chap reached legendary status as editor of *Motor Boating & Sailing* from 1912 to 1958 and he served as chairman of the American Power Boat Association (APBA) for 25 years.

## Clean Boating

- Plastics are deadly to marine life. It is illegal to dispose of plastic trash in ocean waters under U.S. control.
- Dumping garbage within three miles of shore is a felony punishable by imprisonment of up to six years and fines up to $250,000.
- Prevent the spread of invasive species by removing all mud and plants from boats before departing from your boating location.
- Donate, don't abandon, your boat. Disposal must comply with U.S. EPA regulations. Call 212-637-3797 or visit epa.gov/region02/water/oceans/wrecks.htm. For boat donation pick up, call 800-237-5714.
- Free dockside pumpout facilities are available throughout New York Harbor and a pumpout boat operates in Jamaica Bay. For a complete list, visit goingcoastal.org.

### Marine Sanitation

It is legal to discharge raw sewage three miles offshore, in the ocean. The discharge of any boat sewage, even treated waste, is prohibited in EPA designated No Discharge Zones (NDZ), including the Hudson River, from the Battery to Troy Dam, and all Inland Waters of New York State. Efforts are underway to designate Jamaica Bay and all of Long Island Sound NDZ.

Any boat with a marine head must be equipped with a marine sanitation device (MSD). Type I & Type II MSDs are onboard mini sewage treatment plants that purify boat sewage to EPA standards for discharge into the water. Type III, a boat holding tanks doesn't treat waste, but uses pumpouts to remove sewage out of tanks for treatment.

# BRIDGES

The bridges of New York City set the standard for bridges built all over the world. They are feats of daring and visionary engineering that unite the five boroughs and tie the city to the land. Their elegant and grand designs and the geniuses who built them are an integral part of the city's culture.

King's Bridge was the first, constructed in 1693 across Spuyten Duyvil Creek between Manhattan and the Bronx. It was demolished in 1917. Highbridge is the oldest standing bridge. Brooklyn Bridge is the oldest open to vehicles. The Verrazano-Narrows is the newest, longest and highest of the big bridges. George Washington is the busiest, with over 100 million crossings a year. The world record for the longest single span was set and later broken in turn by the Brooklyn, Manhattan, George Washington and Verrazano-Narrows bridges.

Brooklyn Bridge attracts the most jumpers. Robert Odlum was the first person to jump to his death in 1885. A year later on July 23, barkeep Steve Brodie achieved fame when he claimed to have survived the 135 foot plunge. From professional jumpers to would-be suicides, 235 people applied to be the first to jump from the Queensboro Bridge.

There are over 30 bridges linking the five boroughs of New York. A sail under or a walk over any of the them affords a unique perspective to admire the graceful structure while enjoying breathtaking water views.

## Bridges of New York

Six bridges cross the East River. All have walkways and thousands of cyclists pedal across the bridges to work each day. The Harlem River has the most bridges, with 15 fixed and moveable bridges. There are 25 moveable bridges in all in the city, which must open for tall ships. Some are drawbridges, also called bascule bridges, others are swing spans or vertical lifts.

The Carroll Street Bridge is a landmark retractile wooden bridge over Brooklyn's Gowanus Canal. Opened in 1889, it slides back horizontally on wheels set on steel rails to open. The connections between New York and New Jersey are operated by the Port Authority (PA). Interborough links are controlled by the MTA or Triborough Bridge & Tunnel Authority. NYC Dept. of Transportation (DOT) oversees the toll-free East River crossings and most small moveable bridges.

The procedures for opening the movable bridges are stipulated by US Coast Guard regulations. Advance notice of from two to six hours directly to the bridge by marine radio or call 212-371-7836 is required for most moveable bridges. Boaters signal for opening with one long, followed by one short blast of the horn.

After years of neglect, many of the great bridges are getting facelifts. Visit nycroads.com for detailed descriptions of local bridges.

Submerged over 90 feet below water, the tunnels of New York also set engineering standards. The 1927 Holland Tunnel was the world's first ventilated underwater tunnel, where giant fans blow air in and out to dispel carbon monoxide. The chief engineer, 41-year-old Clifford Milburn Holland died during a tonsillectomy just as "sandhogs" holed through to the midway point between Manhattan and New Jersey. The Lincoln is the world's only 3-tubed underwater tunnel and the Brooklyn Battery Tunnel is the longest underwater vehicular tunnel in North America. The twin tubes of the Queens-Midtown Tunnel, a New Deal project designed by noted tunnel engineer Ole Singstad, dug under the East River in 1940 are one and a half feet wider than that of the older Holland to accommodate larger cars.

### Bayonne Bridge

Opened: November 15, 1931

Type: Arch

Engineer: Othmar Ammann

Total Length: 8,275 feet

Water Clearance: 150 feet midspan

Water Crossing: Kill Van Kull

The second-longest steel-arch span in the world, the Bayonne Bridge is slightly askew, not built on a right angle to the water but at a 58 foot angle. There are plans to raise the bridge connecting Staten Island and Bayonne, NJ, so that the Post-Panamax vessels can fit under the bridge. Bike riders must walk bikes, enter Morningside Rd. at Hooker Place, Staten Island. There are stairs on the New Jersey side.

## Bridges of New York

1. Bayonne
2. Bronx-Whitestone
3. Brooklyn
4. Hell Gate
5. High Bridge
6. George Washington
7. Manhattan
8. Marine Parkway
9. RFK/Triboro
10. Queensboro
11. Throgs Neck
12. Verrazano Narrows
13. Williamsburg

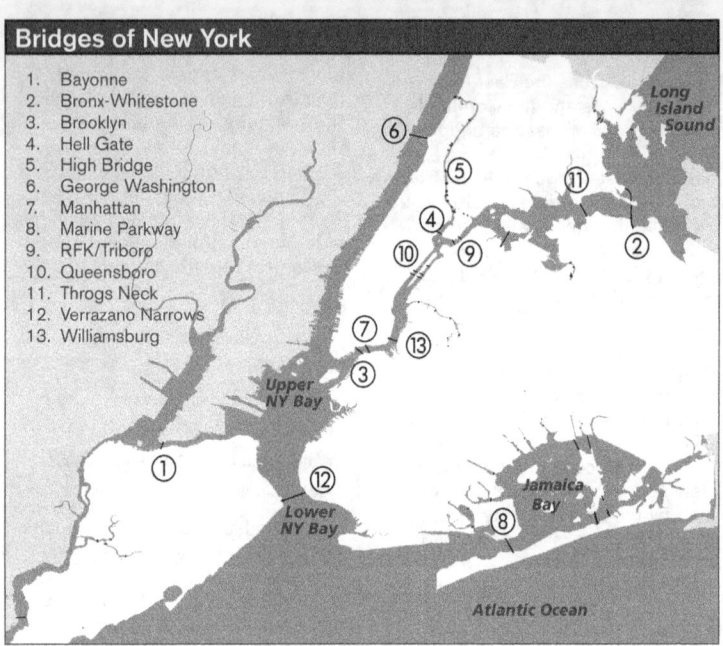

Opened: April 29, 1939
Type: Suspension
Engineer: Othmar Ammann
Total Length: 7,140 feet
Water Clearance: 150 feet
Water Crossing: East River

Built for the 1939 World's Fair, the span is anchored in the Bronx and Queens. Ammann streamlined design was refitted with stayed cables in the 1940s, which took out the original walkways. Heavy trucks are banned due to concerns over structural integrity. The QBx1 bike-on-bus runs during the summer.

### Brooklyn Bridge

Opened: May 24, 1883
Type: Suspension
Engineer: John Roebling
Water Clearance: 135 feet
Water Crossing: East River

It cost $15 million and 30 lives and took 13 years to build the world's first steel cable suspension bridge poised between two 276-feet granite towers featuring twin neo-Gothic arches. The wide promenade is entered at Centre St., NY and Adams St., Brooklyn.

### Hell Gate Arch

Opened: September 30, 1916
Type: Arch
Engineer: Gustav Lindenthal
Total Length: 17,000 feet
Water Clearance: 135 feet
Water Crossing: East River

The red railroad bridge spanning the Hell Gate to connect Astoria and Randall's Island was the heaviest and longest steel-arch bridge in the world

**Othmar Ammann,** Bridge Engineer (1879-1965) Swiss born, Ammann perfected the art of the long span suspension bridge in New York. He is responsible for six of the most significant and beautiful bridges spanning the city's waterways, including: George Washington, Throgs Neck, Bayonne, Whitestone, Triborough and Verrazano-Narrows bridges. Arriving in New York in 1904, Ammann worked for Gustav Lindenthal and served as bridge engineer to the Port Authority from 1925 to 1939. The 70-story high Verrazano-Narrows was his last great bridge completed when he was 85 years old.

at the time of its completion, and is still the world's strongest. It took more steel than the Manhattan and Queensboro bridges combined. The bridge is used by Amtrak, CSX, and freight lines and painted "hell gate" red. No access to the bridge. Toy train maker Lionel offers the bridge in miniature.

### High Bridge

Opened: July 4, 1848
Engineer: John Jervis
Total Length: 1,450 feet
Water Clearance: 114 feet
Water Crossing: Harlem River

Like a Roman aqueduct in design, High Bridge carried water as part of the Croton Aqueduct System until it shut down in 1917 because of WWI security concerns. Five of the bridges eight arches were removed in 1927 to provide better boat clearance. The picturesque landmark pedestrian bridge is in a state of disrepair since the walkway closed in 1970, after a rock thrown from the bridge injured a Circle Line passenger. It is part to be part of the Old Croton Aqueduct Greenway.

### George Washington Bridge

Opened: October 25, 1931
Type: Suspension
Engineer: Othmar Ammann
Total Length: 4,760 feet
Tower Height: 604 feet

**John A. Roebling,** Engineer (1806-1869) The inventor of steel wire suspension cables who designed the Brooklyn Bridge. He died of Lockjaw from an injury incurred at the Brooklyn Fulton Ferry slip the same year President Grant approved plans for the bridge. John's son, **Washington Roebling,** Engineer (1837-1926) completed his father's bridge. He spent substantial time in the caissons 80 feet below the surface of the East River and developed decompression sickness, or "the bends." Although the disease left him partially paralyzed and unable to speak by 1872, Washington continued to direct construction from his Brooklyn townhouse until completion of the bridge, relying on his wife. **Emily Warren Roebling** (1843-1903) learned mathematics and other points of bridge engineering while supervising the construction site daily. She kept all her husband's records and represented him in business. She was the first woman to address the American Society of Civil Engineers and the first of 150,000 people to cross the Brooklyn Bridge on opening day May 24, 1883.

Water Clearance: 213 feet
Water Crossing: Hudson River

The world's busiest and heaviest bridge is suspended on four giant cables of Roebling wire between exposed framework towers at the narrowest part of the Hudson River between W 178 St. to Fort Lee, NJ. The lower deck was added in 1962, allowing for 14-lanes of traffic. There are walkways on both sides and a bike path on south side.

### Manhattan Bridge
Opened: December 31, 1909
Type: Suspension
Engineer: Gustav Lindenthal
Total Length: 6,855 feet
Water Clearance: 135 feet
Water Crossing: East River

The span supported by 322-foot-tall light blue towers carries seven vehicle lanes and four subway tracks from Canal Street to Flatbush Avenue in Brooklyn. It is the first suspension bridge using deflection theory, which uses the bridges weight to stabilize the structure. The south side footpath and dedicated bike path on north side offer excellent views of the Brooklyn Bridge.

### Marine Parkway Gil Hodges Bridge
Opened: July 3, 1937
Engineer: David Steinman
Total Length: 4,022
Water Clearance: 55 feet; 150' lifted
Water Crossing: Rockaway Inlet

A steel truss span, named for the star first baseman for the Brooklyn Dodgers, carrying traffic from Flatbush Avenue to Jacob Riis Park. The bridge walkway linking the Shore Greenway to the Rockaway Greenway is popular with anglers.

### Robert F. Kennedy/Triborough Bridge
Opened: July 11, 1936
Engineer: Othmar Ammann
Total Length: 13,820 feet
Water Clearance: 143 ft. East River
Water Crossing: East/Harlem Rivers

Actually three bridges, which all meet on Randalls Island, connecting Manhattan, Queens, and the Bronx – the East River suspension span between Randalls Island and Astoria, the Bronx Kill truss bridge with 55-foot clearance to Port Morris, and the Harlem River lift bridge. The Triborough was the first project of President Roosevelt's Public Works Administration. A narrow 2-mile

path cyclists are required to walk. Manhattan: 124-126 Sts. Queens: Hoyt Ave. has steep stairs. Bronx: 134 St. & Cypress Ave.

### Queensboro Bridge

Opened: March 30, 1909

Type: Cantilever

Engineer: Gustav Lindenthal

Total Length: 7,449 feet

Tower Height: 350 feet

Water Clearance: 130 feet

Water Crossing: East River

The National Historic Landmark twin cantilever-truss "59 Street Bridge" is a work of art and the East River's busiest crossing. Bridgemarket, the Gustavino vaults under the bridge, were a busy open-air market until 1930 and after restoration now house merchants and a public plaza. The Bridge travels from E 60 Street to Plaza/Crescent Street in Long Island City. The North outer road has a bike path.

### Throgs Neck Bridge

Opened: January 11, 1961

Type: Suspension

Engineer: Othmar Ammann

Total Length: 1,800 feet

Water Clearance: 142 feet

Water Crossing: East River

Built two-miles east of the Whitestone Bridge astride the confluence of the East River and Long Island Sound to help ease traffic flow, the bridge has an inherent design flaw in its approach and heavy trucks cause fatigue cracks.

### Verrazano-Narrows Bridge

Opened: November 21, 1964

Type: Suspension

Engineer: Othmar Ammann

Total Length: 13,700 feet

Tower Height: 693 feet

Water Clearance: 228 feet

Water Crossing: The Narrows

At the time it was built, the Bridge was the longest and costliest suspension bridge in the world. It spans the gateway to Upper New York Bay straddling the Narrows from Fort Hamilton in Bay Ridge to Fort Wadsworth on Staten Island. The towers are farther apart at the top than at the base to compensate for the curvature of the earth, and the roadway is 12-feet lower in summer than in winter due to seasonal contraction and expansion.

### Williamsburg Bridge

Opened: December 19, 1903

Type: Suspension

Engineer: Leffert L. Buck

Total Length: 7.308 feet

Tower Height: 310 feet

Water Clearance: 135 feet

Water Crossing: East River

The utilitarian design, inspired by architect Alexander Gustave Eiffel, has been called an "engineer's bridge." It is the largest of the East River suspension spans carrying 8 traffic lanes and two subway tracks. There is an asphalt path with steep a ascent and stairs linking Delancey St. in Manhattan to Roebling & Broadway in Brooklyn.

# CRUISELINERS

Close to a million passengers sail out of New York City each year making it one of the country's busiest cruise ports. New York has welcomed the world's great luxury liners since 1840, when Sir Samuel Cunard inaugurated regularly scheduled transatlantic voyages and Royal Mail service from Liverpool. Memories of the celebrated international lines, including Cunard, Collins, White Star, North German Lloyd, the Italian Line, the French Line, and the United States Lines, evoke the romance and elegance of a bygone era of travel. The legacy of Atlantic crossings continues with Cunard's *Queen Mary 2*, the highest, widest, and longest ocean liner ever built, until Royal Caribbean's *Freedom of the Seas* took its maiden voyage from Southampton, UK to New York in 2006. Even bigger ships capable of carrying over 6,000 people are currently under construction.

New York Cruise Terminal handles about 250 vessel calls per year at piers 88, 90 and 92 on the Hudson River. Former cargo docks on Atlantic Basin in Brooklyn have been transformed to accommodate the world's most luxurious ships, including the *Queen Mary 2*. Royal Caribbean opened passenger docks at Cape Liberty Cruise Port in Bayonne, New Jersey. The cruise port of New York is the fourth largest in the nation, generating over $1 billion in direct spending in 2007 and responsible for over 13,000 jobs. During peak season, May through October, ships depart from the Port of New York-New Jersey to Bermuda, New England, Canada and the Caribbean.

Cruise ship arrivals and departures were once prominently announced in major city newspapers. Today, a dedicated few still observe and photograph the comings and goings of cruise ships in New York Harbor. Fort Wadsworth on Staten Island offers one of the best spots for capturing ships passing through the Narrows. Large crowds turned out on January 13, 2008, when New York saw the first and only call of Cunard's three Queens – *Queen Elizabeth 2, Queen Mary 2*, and the new *Queen Victoria*. Cunard's oldest ship, the 40 year old *QE2*, left Manhattan for its 26th and final voyage, officially retiring as a floating hotel in Dubai.

## Cruise Terminals

**Cape Liberty Cruise Port**
430-acre man-made peninsula at Bayonne, NJ, formerly known as the Military Ocean Terminal Bayonne, is homeport to Royal Caribbean and Celebrity Cruises. cruiseliberty.com

**Brooklyn Cruise Terminal**
The East Coast's newest port and official first stop for transatlantic ocean liners, the terminal accommodates ships that have outgrown the Manhattan terminal. The 180,000 sq. ft. Red Hook's dock is port of call to Cunard's *Queen Mary 2* and Princess Cruises. nycruise.com

**Manhattan Cruise Terminal**
711 12 Ave. (46 to 54 St). Built in the 1930s, and last renovated in the early 1970s, it is capable of docking five cruise ships in 1000-foot-long berths. Owned by the City of New York, the terminal has recently been upgraded with three modern berths. nycruise.com

## Ocean Liner Enthusiasts

**Ocean Liner Council** South Street Seaport Museum is one of the world's largest centers for ocean liner study, with an extensive collection of memorabilia and models. southstreetseaportmuseum.org

**Steamship Historical Society of America** A group of amateur and professional historians preserving the heritage of engine-powered vessels. sshsa.org

**World Ship Society** Port of NY Chapter (PONY) Founded in 1965, the chapter has over 300 members sharing their enthusiasm for cruise ships. worldshipny.com

## Ship-Spotting Web Cams

You can watch the Cruise Ship Terminal from atop the empire State Building (esbnyc.com), view live images of the luxury cruiseships on the Pied Piper webcam during daylight hours (http://home.att.net/~PIED-PIPER-TRAVEL/Webcam.html) or see from the webcam mounted high atop the Intrepid (earthcam.com/usa/newyork/intrepid).

## Clean Cruising

Cruise Liners are like floating cities. A typical ship can produce up to 30,000 gallons of sewage a day and generate tons of solid waste, oily bilge water, wastewater from showers and galleys, and hazardous waste from onboard dry cleaning.

Cruise ships can throw garbage overboard, just 12 miles from the coast and dump sewage into the sea as near as three miles from shore.

The air pollution emitted from ship diesel engines is equivalent to the pollution created by thousands of automobiles.

International law prohibits disposal of plastic items at sea. Passengers on ships, who observe dumping of plastic, should report it to the USCG National Response Center by calling 800-424-8802.

**Dorothy Marckwald**, (1898-1986) Maritime Interior Designer. A native New Yorker and graduate of Packer Collegiate Institute of Brooklyn, Dorothy's ground breaking designs set the standard for 20th century seagoing luxury. She joined the Madison Avenue design firm of Elsie Cobb Wilson in the early 1920s and was soon celebrated for her art deco styling and uniquely American fashion for the express steamer America. Dorothy designed interiors for many vessels of naval architect Gibbs and Cox, Grace Lines' South American Santa liners, Farrell Lines, and American Export Line's *Constitution* and *Independence*. Marckwald ultimately fashioned the austere interior for the greatest ocean liner of the day, the 14,000 passenger *United States*, which was launched by United States Lines in 1951.

## Home Port New York

| | | |
|---|---|---|
| Carnival Cruise Lines | 888-CARNIVAL | carnival.com |
| Crystal Cruises | 866-446-6625 | crystalcruises.com |
| Cunard Line | 800-7CUNARD | cunard.com |
| Holland America | 877-932-4259 | hollandamerica.com |
| Norwegian Cruise Line | 800-327-7030 | ncl.com |
| Princess Cruises | 800-PRINCESS | princess.com |

## New York Port of Call

| | |
|---|---|
| Aida Cruises | aida.de |
| Costa Cruises | costacruise.com |
| Fred Olsen Cruise Line | fredolsencruises.com |
| Hapag-Lloyd Cruises | hl-cruises.com |
| Hurtigruten | hurtigruten.us |
| Japan Grace Ltd | peaceboat.org/english |
| MSC Italian Cruises | msccruisesusa.com |
| Norwegian Costal Voyage | norwegiancoastalcruises.com |
| NYK Cruises | nyk.com |
| P & O Cruises | pocruises.com |
| Phoenix Reisen Cruises | phoenixreisen.com |
| Regent Seven Seas Cruises | rssc.com |
| Residencesea | residensea.com |
| Saga Cruises | saga.co.uk |
| Silversea Cruises | silversea.com |

# DINING WITH A VIEW

Sweeping views of New York Harbor set the stage for amazing on the water dining experiences in the world's largest restaurant market. So much water, yet there are few waterside dining opportunities. The River Café, a barge under the Brooklyn Bridge, was one of the first to take advantage of the Manhattan skyline and river vistas. On the water dining can be had aboard the permanently moored barges of Manhattan's Water Club and Water's Edge on the East River in Queens, which even offers direct ferry service from E 34 Street. New York Water Taxi has stops at several waterside eateries in Manhattan and Brooklyn. In all five boroughs there are restaurants that offer boat slips to dock and dine.

New York is a seafood town. Fulton Fish Market, the country's oldest and largest wholesale fish market, set sail in 2005 after more than 170 years on the East River shore to new quarters on the banks of the Bronx River in Hunts Point. It is one of the largest seafood markets in the world with more than 175 million pounds of fish passing through each year. Local oysters where once a delicacy. Today, the city's most historic raw bar is below sea level at Grand Central Station, serving bluepoints since 1913. For a taste of local striper, sea bass, fluke and more, take a trip to Sheepshead Bay at around 4pm when the fishing fleet sells the day's catch right from the dock.

# Manhattan

**Antica Venezia** 396 West St. View of the Hudson River, plus a waterfall and fireplace. 212-229-0606 avnyc.com

**Battery Gardens** 17 State St. Views of the Upper Bay from Manhattan's southern tip, inside Battery Park. 212-809-5508 batterygardens.com

**Bayard's** One Hanover Square. Landlocked, but seaworthy fine dining surrounded by the maritime collection of India House, such as the nautical paintings of Buttersworth and ship models. 212-514-9454 bayards.com

**Boat Basin Cafe** W 79 St. Riverside Park. Seasonal outdoor patio offering breathtaking sunset views above the houseboats and yachts at the Hudson River marina. 212-496-5542 boatbasincafe.com

**Carmine's Italian Seafood Restaurant** 140 Beekman Street, South Street Seaport area 1930s fish house with partial water views across from the old Fulton Fish Market. 212-962-8606

**Chelsea Brewery Co.** Chelsea Piers, Pier 59. A microbrew pub with al fresco dining facing powerboat slips on the Hudson River. 212-336-6440 chelseabrewingco.com

**Filli.Ponte** 39 Desbrosses St. Old-style Italian eatery in Tribeca features rooms of exposed brick with beautiful Hudson River views. 212-226-4621 filliponte.com

**Gigino** 20 Battery Pl. Italian fare and gelato on the green lawn of Wagner Park, offering spectacular views of New York Harbor and Lady Liberty. 212-528-2228 gigino-wagnerpark.com

**Harbour Lights** 89 South St. Pier 17. A sophisticated setting with a view of the Brooklyn Bridge. 212-227-2800 harbourlightsrestaurant.com

**Heartland Brewery** 93 South St. Chain brew pub on the site of the old Sloppy Louie's, immortalized in Joseph Mitchell's *Up in the Old Hotel*. 646-572-BEER heartlandbrewery.com

**Hudson Beach Café** Riverside Park at 105 St. Seasonal outdoor spot near the jogging path and gardens. 917-370-3448 pdohurleys.com

**Hudson Terrace** 621 46 St. A salon made of beams reclaimed from wooden ships wit a rooftop terrace offering river views. 212-315-9400 hudsonterracenyc.com

**Indian Road Cafe** 600 W 218 St. at Indian Rd. Sweeping water views from Inwood Hill; tables and chairs from the Sopranos set. 212-942-7451 indianroadcafe.com

**Jason's Riverside Grill** Pier 60 Chelsea Piers. South Beach-style restaurant serving Hudson River views. 212-989-8400 chelseapiers.com

**Loeb Boathouse** Central Park, E. 74 St. Feast from the seasonal outdoor patio beside the scenic freshwater pond. 212-517-2233 thecentralparkboathouse.com

**Brass Monkey** 55 Little West 12 St. Sip a Guinness while watching river traffic cruise by from the roof deck of this meatpacking district Irish Pub. 212-675-6686 brassmonkeynyc.com

**Paris Tavern** 119 South St. Peer a narrow East River view from the landmark bar built in 1873 that served as Thomas Edison's office. 212-240-9797 theparistavern.com

**P.D. O'Hurley's** Pier 84 12 Ave. at W 44 St. Al fresco pub offering scenic river views, sandwiched between

> ### Rooftop Bars with Riverviews
>
> - Cabanas at Maritime Hotel
> - Sky Terrace at Hudson Hotel
> - Pen-Top at Peninsula Hotel
> - Plunge at Hotel Gansevoort
> - Pooldeck at Empire Hotel
> - Ravel Hotel Rooftop
> - Rise Bar at Ritz-Carlton
> - Rooftop at Hotel Bentley
> - The Terrace at Sutton Place
> - Terrace in the Sky
> - Top of the Tower Beekman

the busy Hudson River Park piers of the Circle Line and Intrepid Museum. 212-873-1900 pdohurleys.com

**Pier i Cafe** Riverside Park South, W 70 St. Casual menu and coffee served from a seasonal kiosk on the Hudson River pier. 212-362-4450 piericafe.com

**Pier 66 Maritime** Terrific riverside seating at tiki hut bar and grill aboard a Lackawanna Railroad Barge that serves as anchorage to historic ships. 212-989-6363 pier66maritime.com

**PJ Clarke's on the Hudson** 4 WFC. Ice cold oysters, legendary burgers and Guinness on tap sidling North Cove Marina overlooking the Statue of Liberty. 212-285-1500 pjclarkes.com

**Rise Bar** Ritz-Carlton 2 West St. 14 Fl. Al fresco lounge eying harbor panorama. 212-344-0800

**River Room** Riverbank State Park, Riverside Dr. at 145 St. A terrace atop a water pollution plant serving Latin-Caribbean cuisine overlooking the Hudson River. 212-491-1500 theriverroomofharlem.com

**The Rusty Knot** 425 West St. Nautically decorated dive bar serving razor clams, peel-and-eat shrimp and tiki drinks with Hudson River views. 212-645-5668

**Seaport Café** 89 South Street Pier 17. Touristy outdoor café. 212-964-1120

**Sequoia** South Street Seaport Pier 17. Restaurant with views of the harbor and city skyline. 212-732-9090 arkrestaurants.com

**Skipper's Pierside Café** 89 South St. Pier 16. Outdoor seating on the historic ship pier. 212-349-1000

**SouthWestNY** 225 Liberty St. World Financial Center. Indoor and outdoor seating overlooking luxury yachts berthed at North Cove marina. 212-945-0528 southwestny.com

**Steamers Landing** 375 South End Ave. Garden terrace on the Battery Park City esplanade. 212-432-1451 steamerslanding.com

**The Grill Room** 225 Liberty Street. Hudson River views from the World Financial Center. 212-945-9400 arkrestaurants.com

**U.N. Delegates Dining Room** 1 Ave. at 46 St. Views of the East River from where world leaders tread. Security screening. 212-963-7626 aramark-un.com

**The Water Club** 500 E 30 St at FDR Dr. A floating barge on the East River decked out like a high-end yacht with a classic American kitchen and Crow's Nest bar. 212-683-3333 thewaterclub.com

**Water Taxi Beach** South Street Seaport and Governors Island. Summer fun on a large sand playground with full bar serving burgers and fish tacos. harborexperience.com

# Bronx

**City Island Lobster House** 691 Bridge St. Just over the City Island Bridge, arrive by land or sea to dine on the outdoor terrace that overlooks a marina on the Eastchester Bay. 718-885-1459 cilobsterhouse.com

**Johnny's Reef** 2 City Island Ave. Popular seasonal fish shack serving fried fare cafeteria-style on the southern tip of City Island overlooking Long Island Sound and Stepping Stone Lighthouse. 718-885-2086

**The Harbor Restaurant** 565 City Island Ave. Enjoy seafood and steak along with a scenic view of Eastchester Bay. Call ahead for dock and dine. 718-885-1373 theharborrestaurant.com

**Harbour Inn** 50 Pennyfield Ave. Throgs Neck neighborhood pub serving German fare on the Long Island Sound. 718-892-9148

**Ice House Cafe** 140 Reynolds Ave. Comfortable sandwich place on Locust Point beside the docks of Hammond Cove Marina. 718-892-3012 hammondcovemarina.com

**The Lobster Box** 34 City Island Ave. Surf and turf in an elegant dining room that looks out at Long Island Sound. 718-885-3232 lobsterbox.com

**Portofino's** 555 City Island Ave. Italian seafood and views of sailboats bobbing on Eastchester Bay and the New York City skyline beyond. 718-885-1220 portofinocityisland.com

**Seafood City** 459 City Island Ave. Fresh seafood and Eastchester Bay views from the outdoor deck. 718-885-3600 seafoodcityci.com

**Sea Shore Restaurant** 591 City Island Ave. Serving seafood and water views on Eastchester Bay since the

1920s, plus a full marina with dock and dine berths available. 212-885-0300 seashorerestaurant.com

**Tony's Pier** 1 City Island Ave. Fish fry with patio on the Long Island Sound. 718-885-1424

**Wave Hill Cafe** 675 W 252 St. A light menu and pot of tea on the terrace in the beautiful garden, with sweeping views of the Hudson River and Palisades. 718-796-8538 wavehill.org

# Brooklyn

**Alma** 187 Columbia St. 3-story Mexican restaurant has a roof deck overlooking Brooklyn's working waterfront with views of the Upper Bay and Manhattan skyline beyond. 718-643-5400 almarestaurant.com

**Brooklyn Ice Cream Factory** One Water St. Fulton Ferry Landing Pier. Old-fashioned ice cream parlor in 1920s fireboat house under the Brooklyn Bridge. 718-246-3963

**Bubby's Pier Co.** 1 Main St. Comfort food and views of Lower Manhattan and Brooklyn Bridge from DUMBO. 718-222-0666 bubbys.com

**Clemente's Maryland Crabhouse** 3939 Emmons Ave. Maryland sweet crab and cold beer at Venice Marina

**Nathan Handwerker**, Restaurateur (1892-1974) He did not invent the hot dog that credit goes to Charles Feltman in 1874, but Handwerker did open America's first hot dog stand in Coney Island in 1916. Nathan was a Polish immigrant who came to New York in 1912 at the age of 20. Eddie Cantor and Jimmy Durante put up a $300 loan to open the original Nathan's, where it cost a nickel for his garlic-spiced sausage on a roll. Signs were erected declaring the ultimate beach food "world famous" from opening day. The first hot dog eating contest took place July 4, 1916 when James Mullen ate 13 Nathan's in 12 minutes to settle a disagreement. Takeru "Tsunami" Kobayashi won the coveted Mustard Yellow Champion belt five years in a row, 2001 to 2005, with world record feats of eating as many as 53 Nathan's hot dogs and buns in 12 minutes. Joey Chestnut beat Kobayashi in 2007, 66-63 Nathan's hot dogs, and held the title in 2008.

on Shellbank Creek. 718-646-7373 clementescrabhouse.com

**Fairway Cafe** 500 Van Brunt St. A patio behind the Red Hook supermarket with superb views of the Upper Bay and Statue of Liberty, and a water taxi stop. 718-694-6868 fairwaymarket.com

**Fusion** 2007 Emmons Ave. South Beach-style restaurant and dance club on the Sheepshead Bay waterfront. 718-616-0400

**Giando On the Water** East River 400 Kent Ave. *Soprano*'s-style Italian on the banks of the East River under the Williamsburg Bridge. 718-387-7000 giandoonthewater.com

**Ikea Restaurant** One Beard St. Red Hook. Instore restaurant serving Swedish meatballs and harbor views at the former shipbuilding docks. Free ferry from Pier 11/Wall St. 718-246-4532

**Il Fornetto** 2902 Emmons Ave. Sheepshead Bay waterfront dining. 718-332-8494 ilfornettorestaurant.com

**Jordan's Lobster Dock** 3165 Harkness Ave. Lobster pound and cafe that looks on Shell Bank Creek. 718-934-6300 jordanslobsterdock.com

**Lai Yuen** 10033 Fourth Ave. Chinese food under the Verrazano-Narrows Bridge. 718-567-2300

**Moscow Café** Brighton 6 St. Low cost Ukrainian food on the boardwalk. 718-368-4445

**Nathan's Famous** 1310 Stillwell. Hot dogs are served from the original location and a stand on the boardwalk. . 718-946-2202 nathansfamous.com

**Nick's Lobster** 2777 Flatbush Ave. Lobster pound with views of the big pleasure boats at the private docks on Mill Basin. 718-253-7117

**Paradise Garden** 2814 Emmons Ave. One of the few dining places directly on the Sheepshead Bay waterfront. 718-891-2020 paradisegardenny.com

**Pete's Downtown** 2 Water St. Hearty Italian fare and river views from below the Brooklyn Bridge. 718-858-3510 petesdowntown.com

**Randazzo's Clam Bar** 2017 Emmons Ave. The Italian clam shack is a Sheepshead Bay classic since 1920. 718-615-0010 randazzosclambar.com

**River Café** One Water St. One of the city's most enchanting restaurants is on a barge moored under the Brooklyn Bridge offering breathtaking views of the Harbor and Lower Manhattan skyline. 718-522-5200 rivercafe.com

**Tamaqua Bar** 84 Ebony Ct. Fishermen's bar at the marina on Shell Bank Creek. 718-646-9212 tamaquamarina.com

**Tatiana Grill** 3145 Brighton 4 St. Russian fare and seaside seating on the boardwalk at this "Little Odessa" favorite. 718-646-7630 tatianagrill.com

**Tatiana Cafe/Night Club** 3152 Brighton 6 St. Russian supper club with cafe seating on the boardwalk. 718-891-5151 tatianarestaurant.com

**TGI Fridays** 3181 Harkness Ave. National chain offers patio dining on Shell Bank Creek. 718-934-5700 brooklyn.myfridays.com

**Volna** 3145 Brighton 4 St. Blinis and vodka on the Brighton Beach boardwalk. 718-332-0341

**Winter Garden Club** 3152 Brighton 6 St. Ocean views by day, Russian supper club by night, serving caviar and vodka. 718-934-6666

**Yiasou Estiatorio** 2003 Emmons Ave. Greek seafood restaurant in view of Sheepshead Bay. 718-332-6064

## Queens

**The Bayhouse** 500 Bayside Dr., Breezy Point. Serving casual waterfront dining on American cuisine. 718-318-9660 bayhouse.retro69.net

**Bayview Restaurant** 25 Van Brunt Rd., Broad Channel. Overlooks the grass islands of Jamaica Bay. 718-634-4555 bcbayview.com

**Caffé on the Green** 201-10 Cross Bay Blvd., Bayside The cafe overlooks the Throgs Neck Bridge from the grounds of Clearview Golf Course, the former resort home built in 1919 by silent film star Rudolph Valentino, which was later owned by Mayor Fiorello LaGuardia. 718-423-7272

**FrenAsia** 163-35 Cross Bay Blvd. Asian fusion on the banks of Shellbank Basin. 718-322-7690

**Kennedy's On the Bay** 406 Bayside Walk. Italian seafood house in Breezy Point with dramatic views of Jamaica Bay and Manhattan skyline. 718-945-0202 kennedysbreezypoint.com

**Lenny's Clam Bar** 161-03 Cross Bay Blvd. Clam shack with a seasonal outdoor tent on Shellbank Basin in Howard Beach. 718-845-5100 lennysclambar.com

**Riverview Lounge** 20-01 50 St. Long Island City. Outdoor seating adjacent to Gantry State Park on the East River shore of Queens West. 718-392-5000 riverviewny.com

**Rockaway Lobster House** 375 Beach 92 St., Rockaway Beach. Lobster restaurant and bait shop set atop wooden pilings on Jamaica Bay. 718-634-2500 rockawaylobsterhouse.com

**Sand Bar** 120 Beach 116 St. Rockaway. Oceanside clam bar at the boardwalk and beach.

**Sugar Bowl** Bedford Ave. & Oceanside. Seasonal beach bar in Breezy Point.

**Starbucks** 157-41 Cross Bay Blvd. Frappuccinos served on the roof sun deck on Shellbank Basin in Howard Beach. 718-641-9332

**Tennisport Restaurant** 51-24 2 St. at Borden Ave. Tennis club with spectacular Manhattan skyline views serving lunch and dinner. 718-392-1880 tennisport.com

**Pier 92** 377 Beach 92 St., Rockaway Park. Dockside dining on Jamaica Bay, offers dock and dine. 718-945-2100

**Water's Edge** 44 Dr. Panoramic views of the city skyline from aboard a stylish barge moored on the East River shore. Free ferry at E 34 St. Pier, Manhattan. 718-482-0033 watersedgenyc.com

**Water Taxi Beach** 2 St. & Borden Ave. Riverside sandbox with snack bar and skyline views at the Hunter's Point stop. harborexperience.com

**The Wharf** 416 Beach 116 St. Rockaway Beach. Beach pub on Jamaica Bay. 718-474-8807

**World's Fair Marina Restaurant** World's Fair Marina. Watch planes take off over Flushing Bay from the glitsy Indian palace. 718-898-1200 worldsfairmarina.com

# Staten Island

**Angelina's on the Water** 399 Ellis Rd. Tottenville Italian eatery on the Arthur Kill near the Outerbridge Crossing. 718-227-3329 angelinasristorante.com

**Carmen's** 750 Barclay Ave. Platters of paella, music and flamenco dancing served oceanside. 718-356-2725 carmensrestaurant.com

**Cole's Dockside** 369 Cleveland Ave. Watch the sailboats on Great Kills Harbor while enjoying fresh seafood. 718-948-5588 colesdockside.com

**Coral Bay Café** 722 Rockaway St. Seaside oyster bar with a view of Conference Park beach and Raritan Bay. 718-356-3531

**Fiore di Mare** 227 Mansion Ave. Serving northern Italian fare on Great Kills Harbor. 718-227-9771 fioredimaresi.com

**Fresca's on the Bay** 225 Ellis St. Nightclub and clam bar overlooking Port Atlantic Marina on the Arthur Kill. 718-305-1129 frescasonthebayny.com

**Joe & John Toto's Restaurant** 809 Father Capodanno Blvd. Italian cafe serving pizza and panini looking out on Midland Beach. 718-979-1888

## WATERSIDE GRILLS

- Alley Pond Park
- East River Park
- Inwood Hill Park
- Kaiser Park
- Flushing Meadows
- Manhattan Beach Park
- Orchard Beach,
- Rockaway Beach 17, 88, 98
- Randalls Island

## Seafood Lover's Guide

The Seafood Lover's Guide is a consumer guide to eating seafood responsibly by ranking popular seafood choices on a Fish Scale from green (abundant, healthy) to red (problematic species). The program is designed to enable consumers to select fish that are both healthy and likely to ensure sustainable fish populations.
- Audubon's Living Oceans wallet card for handy reference. 888-397-6649 seafood.audubon.org
- Wildlife Conservation Society 718-220-5155 wcs.org/gofish

**Marina Cafe'** 154 Mansion Ave. Glass enclosed dining room serving seafood and views of Great Kills Harbor. 718-967-3077 marinacafegrand.com

**R. H. Tugs** 1115 Richmond Terrace. Pub and outside patio that overlooks tugboats, barges and supertankers plying the waters of the Kill Van Kull. 718-447-6369 rhtugs.com

**Ruddy & Dean North Shore Steak Co.** 44 Richmond Ter. An outdoor patio on offering breathtaking views. 718-816-4400 ruddyanddean.com

**South Fin Grill** 300 Fr. Capodanno Blvd. Fine dining and south coast views. 718-447-7679 southfingrill.com

## Seaworthy Dive Bars

**The Boat Livery** 663 City Island Ave., Bronx. Budweiser and boat rentals at this dive bar/bait & tackle combo on Eastchester Bay. 718-885-1843

**Cha Cha's** On the Coney Island Boardwalk, live music & a bucket of ice cold beer. 718-946-1305 chachasofconeyisland.com

**Ear Inn** 326 Spring St. The landmark former home of African-American tobacconist James Brown, it was at the water's edge when it opened in 1817, before landfilling. 212-226-9060 earinn.com

**Montero's Bar** 73 Atlantic Ave. Curb-side view of the Brooklyn docks at this former longshoremen's dive with maritime bric-a-brac and photos. 718-624-9799

**Ruby's Old Time Bar & Grill** W 12 St. Coney Island boardwalk dive bar since 1922. 718-372-9079

**Sunny's** 253 Conover St. A vintage Red Hook watering hole pouring since 1890. 718-625-8211 sunnysredhook.com

**Waterfront Crabhouse** Borden Ave. at 2 St. Long Island City. A bathtub full of peanuts, boxing memorabilia and seafood. 718-729-4862

# EXCURSION BOATS

Sightseeing vessels of all shapes and sizes ply the waters of New York, past the skyscrapers of Manhattan, under the Brooklyn Bridge and around the Statue of Liberty. From Harbor Tours, Sunset Sails, Eco-Cruises, Historic Ship Sails, Hidden Harbor Tours, Manhattan Island Circumnavigation Voyages, and Private Charters, the opportunities for enjoying New York City by water abound. Take pleasure in wine and cheese aboard a historic sailing ship, dinner on a luxury yacht or a high speed wake spewing blast in the harbor. Many of the main sightseeing operators offer specialty cruises including jazz and blue cruises.

# Public Sail & Excursions

**Bateaux** Chelsea Piers, Pier 62. A glass covered French riverboat, the Celestial, offers lunch, dinner and private charters accommodating 300 passengers aboard one of the most elegant New York Cruise boats. Formal dinner attire suggested. 212-727-7735 bateauxnewyork.com

**Circle Line** Pier 83, W 42 St. 212-563-3200 circleline42.com
- *The Beast* Prepare to get wet on 30-minute cruise around the Harbor at speeds of 45 mph. aboard a power racing boat.
- *Full-Island Cruise* Circle Line has been sailing around Manhattan Island on the red, white, and green boats since 1945, the three-hour cruise is the most popular way to explore city waterways, covering 3 rivers, 7 major bridges, and 5 boroughs. Also offering harbor lights, semi-circle and Liberty sightseeing cruises.
- *Harbor Lights Cruise* Two-hour sunset cruise of the harbor as the city light up. Sails down the Hudson, around the Battery, up the East River, and under the Brooklyn Bridge.

**Circleline Downtown** Pier 16, South St. Seaport. 866-925-4631 circlelinedowntown.com
- *Shark* Speedboat ride.
- *Zephyr* Seaport Liberty Cruise One-hour narrated harbor cruise aboard yacht. 866-925-4631

**Classic Harbor Line** Chelsea Piers, Pier 62. 212-209-3370 sail-nyc.com
- *Adirondack* Regularly scheduled public day sails and sunset cruises aboard 80 foot classic schooner, sailing daily from Chelsea Piers, May through October. Sailings are about 2 hours and travel to the Statue of Liberty, also special jaunts such as the Monday "sushi & sake" sail and Tuesday "beer & cheese" sail.
- *Imagine* Chelsea Piers, Sail the harbor aboard an 80-foot, 1890's style pilot schooner featuring teak decks with mahogany trim built by Scarano Boat Building in Albany, NY.
- *Manhattan* Circle Manhattan Island while dining aboard a classic 1920s-style motor yacht.

**Duck Tour** W 34 St. The only tour aboard an amphibious vehicle covering both land and sea. Trip starts with a ride through Times Square and splash down for a cruise on the Hudson River. Tour starts on Broadway at 47 Street, purchase tickets at any Gray Line office. 212-768-1888 coachusa.com/nycducks

**Hidden Harbor Tours** South Street Seaport, Pier 17. Tour the backwaters of New York's working port on these scheduled boat tours narrated by harbor pilots, tugboat captains and maritime historians. workingharbor.com

**Manhattan by Sail** 212-619-0885 manhattanbysail.com
- *Clipper City* Pier 17, South Street Seaport. Scheduled sailings aboard a replica 1854 square top schooner, the largest USCG certified sailing vessel in the U.S.
- *Shearwater* North Cove Marina, Battery Park City. Scheduled public sunset, happy hour and brunch sailings on a 82-foot double-mast 1929 Newport schooner. shearwatersailing.com

**NY Water Taxi Excursions** South Street Seaport, Pier 17. 212-742-1969 harborexperience.com
- *Gateway to America Cruise* One-hour water taxi tour of the Harbor Parks of New York operated by the National Park Service, including the Statue of Liberty, Governor's Island and Fort Wadsworth. Weekends only, year-round.
- *Hop On/Hop Off Sightseeing* at Hudson and East River landings.

**New York Waterway** Pier 78, W 38 St. 800-533-3779 nywaterway.com
- Harbor Tour 90-minute skyline cruises and city lights sunset cruises.
- History Cruise conducted by the New York Historical Society.
- AIA Architecture Cruise browsing the city's waterfront buildings.

**South Street Seaport Excursions** Pier 16, South St. Seaport. Historic vessels and floating museum ships. 212-748-8590 southstreetseaport.org
- *Pioneer.* Bring your own wine and cheese for sunset sails aboard the historic sailing schooner.
- *W.O. Decker* See the working waterfront aboard a historic wooden tug, limit of 6 passengers.

**Seastreak** Sightseeing cruise sails past the Sandy Hook Lighthouse, under the Verrazano-Narrows Bridge and around New York Harbor, departs Atlantic Highlands, NJ, Pier 11 & E 35 St. 800-262-8743 seastreak.com

**Skyline Princess Cruises** World's Fair Marina, Pier 1, Flushing. Luxury dinner and sightseeing cruises. 718-446-1100 skylinecruises.com

**Spirit of New York** Chelsea Piers, Pier 62. Dinner and dancing cruises. 212-727-7735 spiritofnewyork.com

**Statue of Liberty Ferry** Service to Liberty and Ellis Islands departs from both Battery Park and Liberty State Park, year-round. Reserve tickets available, includes a Monument Pass that allows you to go inside the pedestal. 877-523-9849 statuecruises.com

**Ventura** North Cove Marina, Battery Park City. Landmark yacht offers public sails on Friday sunsets and Sunday brunch. 212-786-1204 sailnewyork.com

**World Yacht** Pier 81, W 41 St. New York's premier dinner cruise features live band, dancing, and dramatic skyline views daily, serving up to 500 passengers aboard three vessels. Also offers Sunday brunch and happy hours cruises. Dress code: no jeans, shorts or sneakers. Jackets required on dinner cruise. 212-630-8100 worldyacht.com

## Beach Excursions

**Sandy Hook Express** South Street Seaport, Pier 16. circlelinedowntown.com

**Riis Landing** Seasonal trip aboard the American Princess to Rockaway beaches from Pier 11, Wall St. and Brooklyn Army Terminal. 718-474-0555 nywatertaxi.com

## Eco-Cruises

**Audubon Eco-Cruise** Guided birding cruise explores heron habitats on the lesser-known islands like Swinburne Island, where you might even see a 250 pound Harbor Seal.

**Jamaica Bay Eco-Cruise** American Littoral Society's seasonal three-hour sunset tours depart Sheepshead Bay piers on scheduled dates. 718-318-9344 alsnyc.org

**Riis Landing Eco-Cruise** National Park Service led tours of Jamaica Bay. nywatertaxi.com

## Fall Foliage Tours

**Circle Line Bear Mountain Cruise** Pier 83. 212-563-3200 circleline42.com

**NY Waterway Shades of Autumn** Pier 78. 800-533-3779 nywaterway.com

**Seastreak Fall Foliage Cruise** Atlantic Highlands, NJ, Pier 11 & E 35 St. 800-262-8743 seastreak.com

## Party Cruises

| | | |
|---|---|---|
| Affairs Afloat, Inc. | 212- 734-0605 | affairsafloat.com |
| City Lights Cruises | 212-822-8573 | citylightscruises.com |
| Party Cruises | 212-288-1975 | paddlewheelqueen.com |

## Yacht Charters

| | | |
|---|---|---|
| Amberjack V Yacht | 212-679-3970 | amberjackv.com |
| Atlantic Sail & Charter | 212-786-1204 | sailnewyork.com |
| Bacon Yacht Charters | 212-873-7558 | abaconyachtcharter.com |
| CharterPro Yachts | 212-695-4849 | charterproyachts.com |
| Cloud Nine Charters | 212-248-3800 | cloud9charters.com |
| Dove Yacht Charters | 212-594-1561 | doveyacht.com |
| Eastern Star Yacht Charters | 800-445-5942 | easternstarcruises.com |
| Lots of Yachts | 212-505-2214 | lotsofyachts.com |
| Manhattan Yacht Charters | 212-995-5470 | manhattanyachtcharters.com |
| Marco Polo Cruises | 212-691-6693 | marcopolocruises.com |
| NY Yacht & Boat Charters | 212-496-8625 | nyyachtcharter.com |
| New York Boat Charter | 212-496-8625 | newyorkboatcharter.com |
| Paddlewheel Queen | 212-213-2002 | paddlewheelqueen.com |
| Prada Yachts | 212-489-9216 | pradayachts.com |
| Prestige Yacht Charters | 212-717-0300 | boatsnyc.com |
| The River Rose | 845-222- 5648 | theriverrose.com |
| Symbiosis Sailing | 908-461-5890 | sailnyharbor.com |
| Skyline Cruises | 718-446-1100 | skylinecruises.com |
| Urban Desire Charters | 212-734-0605 | urbandesirecruises.com |
| VIP Yacht Cruises | 212-385-9400 | vipyachtcruises.com |
| Windridge Yacht Charters | 212-247-3333 | windridgeyachts.com |
| Yacht Charter NY | 212-691-6693 | yachtcharterny.com |
| Yachts for All Seasons | 212-534-6380 | y4as.com |

# FISHING

The city offers world-class saltwater fishing for more than 200 species. Anglers will find pier, surf, bank, bay, fly casting, and party boat opportunities in all five boroughs. There are restrictions on fishing season, by species, minimum size, and daily catch limits on the number of fish caught. The new saltwater license requirements may take effect in October 2009 for fishing in all marine waters of the state.

The Atlantic's second largest striped bass spawning run passes through New York Harbor and up the Hudson River at the end of March. Stripers can exceed 30 pounds. By the time the bass return from spawning in late spring, bluefish begin to come in. Mid-April to early June is the time to fish for American shad on the Hudson. The adult spawning fish are only in the river and lower estuary for six to eight weeks. The warm waters of Jamaica Bay are a magnet for fluke, stripers, weakfish, bluefish, bonito, Spanish mackerel, tautog, false albacore, sea bass, and skipjack tuna. By fall, bunker schools arrive with big bass and bluefish following close behind. The best times to drop a line are either dawn or dusk. Shore casting is allowed from beaches only and off limits from rocky areas, jetties and historic structures. It is prohibited to fish from guarded city beaches from May 15 to September 15 between 8am and 8pm.

Urban anglers and fishing clubs are active conservationists, helping to monitor fish populations on New York State artificial reefs, while members of the American Littoral Society (alsnyc.org) participate in the world's largest tag and release program monitoring striped bass, summer flounder and bluefish. Anyone catching a tagged fish is asked to return the tag.

There is excellent close to home freshwater game and pan fishing in city parks. From late spring to late fall, one can cast for bass, brown trout, pickerel, carp, bluegills, perch, black crappie, and catfish. Everyone over the age of 16 must have a fishing license in their possession while fishing. A license is required on all freshwater bodies and on all Hudson River tributaries from Troy Dam to the Tappan Zee Bridge. Fishing licenses are administered by the Bureau of Fisheries and can be purchased online or at county clerk offices and sporting goods stores.

Freshwater ponds and streams throughout the city are teeming with fish. Central Park's Harlem Meer is stocked with white bass. Trout Unlimited has restored trout habitat at Alley Creek Lake in Queens stocking the city's first trout stream. And river herring are thriving after being reintroduced in the Bronx River.

At the New York Aquarium there is an exhibit called Native Sea Life. In it, local fisherman can see the fish that nibble their lines and sometimes are pulled in for sport or the family dinner table. It's just a glimpse of what inhabits the coastline of New York City.

# Fish of New York Harbor

**Black fish – tautog** *(Tautoga onitis)*
Blackfish are a popular fish with anglers along a jetty or from a party boat. They are easy to catch and are good eating (what could be better?). A member of the wrasse family, this fish has the buck-toothed incisors that are characteristic of that family. Blackfish feed primarily on mussels, but will eat almost any mollusk (shellfish) or crustacean (shrimp and lobsters). Therefore any scrap of food on a hook will make tempting bait. Blackfish can be almost as long as 36 in. and over 24 pounds, but that would be a monster in New York waters. It does have a minimum size limit of 14" in NY.

**Bluefish** *(Pomatomus saltatrix)*
To imagine a more ferocious predator than the bluefish, one might envision sharks or piranha. But probably only man can be compared, for the bluefish wantonly cuts into schools of prey and kills in excess of what it needs to consume. Bluefish are common to New York waters throughout the summer. They are excellent sport fish, although one needs a steel leader to prevent their sharp teeth from cutting the line. They also are good to eat, especially if brought right to the grill and cooked fresh. "Snappers" are small bluefish and are often a child's first fishing experience since they bite any line and can be caught almost on every cast. Bluefish can weigh over 30 pounds. The maximum length is 51.18 inches. In Florida some reported "shark attacks" may have actually been when swimmers happened into a school of feeding bluefish. A toe could easily be taken by an adult bluefish.

**Fluke-Summer flounder** *(Paralichthys dentatus)* Fluke is another favorite of New York fishers. It is a flatfish that lives its adult life on its side. As a newly hatched larval fish, it swims upright and looks like any "normal" fish. As it develops, it turns to its side; in this case, to its left side. One eye migrates to the side, so that both eyes are on the left side. Other flounders turn the opposite way to become members of the "right-handed" family. The juvenile fish then goes to the bottom where it lives its life completely sideways. The side facing up develops coloration that matches the surroundings, and the downward side is white. Hold a fluke perpendicular, and you will see a normal fish; dorsal fin up, pectoral fins on the sides, tail fin vertical, vent on the bottom, normal in every way except that both eyes are on one side and the sides are different colors. Fluke are excellent eating, with firm white flesh.

**Menhaden** *(Brevoortia tyrannus)*
Schools of menhaden mass like clouds in the surface waters of New York throughout the summer and young menhaden can fill the inlets around the harbor. Like the herds of African plains these "grazers" are massed in great hordes. They are the prey for the predators like stripers and blues. Smaller fish are taken by birds when the predators drive them to the surface. Menhaden feed by straining plankton from the rich waters around New York. On the inner side or their gills are protrusions called "gill rakers". As the fish swim with open mouths, the gill rakers filter the plankton (mostly algae) from the water. They therefore will not take a hook, and are caught only by net or "jigging" where they are so close together that a plain hook or "jig" is likely to catch into the body of one or another. They are excellent bait for stripers. Menhaden are poor quality for human food and are harvested usually for bait or, by the ton, for oil, fishmeal, or fertilizer.

**Sand Tiger Shark** (Carcharias Taurus) The sand tiger shark is one of the common sharks off NYC. Most people would rather not know about the shark populations around the beaches of NYC, but they are out there. Fortunately, most, like the sand tiger are not dangerous to humans. The sand tiger is a popular shark in aquariums because it has a mouthful of sharp teeth and excites the public viewer. These teeth are designed to catch fish. They are thin and sharply pointed. Dangerous sharks usually have flat teeth that are good for biting pieces out of large prey. These sharks rarely come near the beaches of NYC. Other sharks in New York waters are the sand bar shark, is also a fish eater, and since it probably patrols the sand bars just off the beaches of Coney Island, bathers will never be aware that a grey, six foot, sharky-looking, shark, swims so near. The Aquarium has also noted small thresher sharks that fishermen have caught in their nets. These young animals must have been born in the area, for the adults are off-shore sharks. They are known for the extraordinarily long tail that they use to herd fish into tight balls when they feed. Local fishermen often land the smooth dogfish that is also called "sand shark". This is a totally harmless shark that feeds on small fish, crustaceans, and mollusks.

**Shad** (*Alosa sapidissima*) The shad is another member of the herring family, like the menhaden. It is "anadromous", meaning it runs from the ocean upriver to spawn. Shad have thinner gill rakers than the menhaden, and consume slightly larger plankton, mostly copepods and small shrimp. They are caught in the Hudson as they go upriver to spawn every spring. Shad have a large mouth compared to other herring and will actually take a hook. They provide a good fight if they can be tempted to bite. Shad are flavorful smoked, and are a favorite "planked" around fires at shad festivals along the Hudson. Adults can average 20 to 23 inches in length and five to six pounds in weight.

## Fish Consumption

To protect against eating fish that may contain contaminants, the NYC Dept. of Health issues advisories for eating locally caught fish. Anglers are advised to eat no more than one meal (one half pound) per week of fish and shellfish taken from state's fresh waters and marine waters in New York Harbor. Women of childbearing age, and infants and children under the age of 15 should not eat any locally caught fish. It is also advised to eat no more than six blue crabs per week. It is preferable to eat migratory fish such as striped bass and shad, which spend most of their time in ocean waters with less exposure to pollutants than resident fish populations. 800-458-1158 health.state.ny.us/nysdoh/fish/fish.

**Striped bass** (*Morone saxatilis*) The striped bass is the premiere sport fish in New York waters. It also makes a wonderful meal. This popular fish has been raised in aquaculture and introduced to lakes and into the Pacific along the west coast. Stripers can be huge, although the chance of catching a giant is an unfulfilled dream for most New York anglers. The maximum-recorded length is 78.7 inches. (Bigger than most fishermen) and over 125 pounds! Stripers run along the sandy beaches all along the east coast. They stay close to shore so that they are within range of surf casters or pier fishermen. The State of New York imposes a minimum size limit on striped bass. Only fish over 28 inches can be kept. Smaller fish must be released, but are still fun to catch.

*Paul L. Sieswerda, Curator NY Aquarium & author of* Sharks

## Learn to Fish

**Big City Fishing** Hudson River Park, Pier 40 & Pier 84. Catch and release fishing with rod, reel and bait provided each weekend from Memorial Day to Labor Day. Participants learn how to fish and about the Hudson River environment. 212-627-2020 hudsonriverpark.org

**Battery Park City Conservancy** Wagner Park. Free catch and release fishing for school groups and the public on select days, all gear provided. Master Angler programs are conducted for adult volunteers. 212-267-9700 bcparks.org

**Dana Discovery Center** Central Park 110 St. Bamboo poles are available for free catch-and-release fishing. nycgovparks.org

**Fishmobile at LES Ecology Center** E 10 St. & East River. Catch-and-release fishing clinics for kids under 15, Fridays from 5-7pm during the summer months. 212-477-4022 lesecologycenter.org

**I Fish New York** The NYS Department of Environmental Conservation conducts (DEC) free hands-on fishing clinics with loaner poles at public sites and waterfront festivals in all five boroughs. The program also offers classroom visits. 718-482-4022 dec.state.nyc.ny.us

**Trout in the Classroom** Students learn about fish and the environment by incubating trout eggs in an aquarium in the classroom for later release in the wild. troutintheclassroom.org

**Urban Park Rangers** Both saltwater and freshwater fishing basics, open to all ages, offered on weekends at various DPR Nature Centers. nycgovparks.org

## Permits & Licenses

**Gateway National Recreation Area** National Park Service. Permits are required for vehicle parking ($50), which allows fishing access to parking areas after dark. To obtain a permit present driver's license, car registration and at least a 7-foot-long fishing rod at the Ranger Station. Monofilament fishing line recycle bins are located at all Gateway units. nps.gov/gate

**NYS Department of Environmental Conservation, Region II** 1 Hunters Pt. Plaza, 4740 21 St., Long Island City. Check for marine recreational size and catch limits and freshwater fishing license fees. 718-482-4022 dec.ny.gov

**NYSDEC Fish Wildlife Marine Resources** Sets marine recreational fishing catch and size limits. 518-402-8924 dec.ny.gov

**NYC Dept. of Environmental Protection** A public access permit allows for fishing on NYC Water Supply land and reservoirs. nyc.gov/html/dep/html/watershed_protection/home.html

**NYC Dept. of Parks & Recreation** (DPR) Catch and release fishing only. Use barbless hooks, lead weights are not allowed. nycgovparks.org

**NYS Office of Parks, Recreation and Historic Preservation** There are seven state parks in the five boroughs, some do not permit fishing. 212-866-3100 nysparks.state.ny.us/parks

**Saltwater Fishing License** New fees $19 residents, $40 nonresidents due to take effect October 1, 2009.

**SUNY Maritime College** Seasonal permit ($50) for fishing access to the campus, apply at the security gate. 718-409-7200 sunymaritime.com

# Fishing Clubs

## Manhattan

**The Anglers Club of NY** 101 Broad St. Century-old gentlemen's social club "active in all matters related to fly fishing." Lunch and dinner served. 212-425-7333

**Capital Fishing Tackle Company** 132 W 36 St. Opened in 1867 as a cutlery store, they have been equipping freshwater and saltwater anglers since the 1960s. 212-929-6123 capitolfishing.com

**Coastal Conservation Association** National association of recreational saltwater anglers working to preserve and restore local marine resources. 917-256-1805 ccany.org

**Juliana's Anglers** Women's fly fishing club for both beginners and advanced anglers offering clinics, lessons and trips. julianasanglers.com

**NYC Trout Unlimited** Local chapter of nation's leading freshwater conservation group with over 1000 members, which offers skills clinics and local conservation activities. nysctu.org

**Orvis** 522 5 Ave. America's oldest mail order company has been supplying fly fishing gear since 1856. The local retail outlet offers fly clinics, casting school and tackle. 212-827-0698 orvis.com

**Theodore Gordon Flyfishers** Fly only, no kill rule at club formed in 1964, and now one of the leading fly fishing organizations in the country named for the creator of the American fly fishing tradition. In addition to many recreational and conservation programs, the organization works to help handicapped anglers gain better access to fishing sites. tgf.org

**Urban Angler** 206 5 Ave., third floor. Fly fishing outfitter offering custom rods, classes, travel and guides. 212- 689-6400 urban-angler.com

**World Fly Fishing of Japan**
A membership organization offering clinics, conservation, trips, and support of Team Japan to attend the world championships. wffj.org

## Bronx

**Ampere Fishing & Yacht Club**
1610 Bayshore Ave. Local club features outings and competition on Long Island Sound. 718-822-8707

## Brooklyn

**Bay Ridge Rod & Gun Club**
Sport's club founded in 1954 offers fishing outings and youth programs. 718-745-1067 gunsports.com

**Gateway Striper Club** Surf club out of Breezy Point that offers fishing outings, clinics and youth programs. gatewaystriper.com

**Helen Keller Fishing Club** Boat fishing since 1948, it is the only deep sea fishing club for persons who are blind or visually impaired. Volunteers help bait hooks and set lines. 718-522-2122 x-347

**Metropolitan Rod & Gun Club**
162 Pacific St. The club, founded in 1934, began fishing instruction for kids under 16 in 1947 at Prospect Park Lake. Members have use of 800 acres of fishing land in Delaware County. 718-625-8019 metrorgc.org

## Queens

**Bayside Anglers** Saltwater fishing club conducts free fishing clinics and conservation activties around Queens, from Little Neck Bay to Gantry State Park. baysideanglers.com

**Rockaway Surf Anglers Association.**
Fishing in and around Rockaway Peninsula and on Jamaica Bay rockawaysurfanglers.com

**Salty Flyrodders** Saltwater fly fishing club with about 200 local members offering fly-casting skills clinics and trips. saltyflyrodders.org

**Striper Surf Club** Formed 1951 by members of the Coney Island Rod & Gun Club, members have fish nights and tournaments. stripersurfclub.com

## Staten Island

**Andrew E. Zimmer Fish & Game Protective Assiation** 4411 Arthur Kill Rd. Sportsmen's club engaged in local conservation, recreational fishing and youth fishing programs. 718-949-9599 aezclub.com

**Beachcomber Surf & Gun Club** 505 Watchogue Rd. Established in 1947 by freshwater and saltwater anglers on Staten Island. 718-372-7287 beachcombersurfandgunclub.com

**Staten Island Tuna Club** Boat anglers with a focus on wreck fishing and offshore ocean waters off New York. situnaclub.com

### Migratory Species

Excessive commercial fishing has wiped out 90% of the worlds large fish populations. Species in danger include cod, halibut, flounder, marlin, shark swordfish, and tuna. Vessel owners who recreational fish for Highly Migratory Species (HMS), such as Atlantic tuna, swordfish, sharks or billfish in Atlantic waters must obtain a federal fishing permit. 888-872-8862 nmfspermits.com

# Marine Waters Season & Catch Limits

| SPECIES | SEASON | SIZE (INCHES)/ BAG LIMIT (#) |
|---|---|---|
| American Eel | All year | 6"/50# |
| American Lobster | All year, permit required | 3-5/16" carapace/6 |
| American Sturgeon | Moratorium | Moratorium |
| Atlantic Cod | All year | 22"/no limit |
| Blackfish (Tautog) | Oct 1-Dec 20/Jan 17-Apr 30 | 14"/4# |
| Black Sea Bass | All year | 12.5"/25# |
| Blue Crab | All year | 4.5"/50# |
| Bluefish | All year | no size limit/first 10 12"/next 5 |
| Flounder | March -June/Sept-Nov | 12"/10# |
| Fluke (Summer Flounder) | May 15-June 15/July 3-Aug 17 | 21"/ 2# |
| Haddock | All year | 19"/no limit |
| Horseshoe Crab | All year | no size limit/5# |
| Monkfish | All year | 17"/no limit |
| Oyster Toad Fish | July 16 - May 14 | 10"/3 |
| Pollock | All year | 19"/no limit |
| Scup (Porgy) | All year | 10.5"/10# |
| Shad | All year | no size limit/5# |
| Spanish Mackerel | All year | 14"/15# |
| Striped Bass | Apr 15 - Dec 15 (S GW Bridge) | 28" - 40"/1# + 40"/1 |
| Striped Bass | Mar 16 - Nov 30 (N GW) | 18"/1# |
| Weakfish | All year | 16"/6# |

* Regulations effective April 28, 2009 for Marine Waters South of George Washington Bridge. For information about catching and landing sharks visit NYS-DEC dec.ny.gov or call National Marine Fisheries at 978-281-9278

## Party Boats

Brooklyn's Sheepshead Bay is the hub of city fishing. A fishing fleet of charters and party boats are moored at ten concrete piers on Emmons Avenue. Party boats cruise from the Rockaway inlet, past Breezy Point on the western tip of the Rockaway Peninsula and into the Atlantic. There are also day fishing trips from City Island in the Bronx on Long Island Sound. Boats out of Howard Beach, Queens fish Jamaica Bay. On Staten Island, boats from Great Kills Harbor cruise Raritan Bay.

    Vessels come in all sizes from small inshore pilot boats to large offshore cabin cruisers. Rods, reels, tackle, and bait are furnished. Half day, full day and night fishing trips are offered. Open boat fees start at $40 per passenger. Headboats fish for specific species depending on the season. Boats feature offshore, wreck and Hudson Canyon fishing overnight trips for sportfish, including tuna, shark, and billfish.

    Charters (*) handle one to six anglers for all inshore species and sightseeing, rates start at $300 for half day. Another option is to rent a small skiff for half and full day in Jamaica Bay at Smitty's Fishing Station on Broad Channel or The Boat Livery on City Island to fish the Long Island Sound.

## Party & Charter Boats

### Bronx

| | |
|---|---|
| Daybreak III | 718-409-9765 |
| Island Current islandcurrent.com | 917-417-7557 |
| North Star II northstar2.net | 718-885-9182 |
| Riptide III riptide3.com | 718-885-0236 |
| SkipJack* | 347-341-5767 |

### Brooklyn

| | |
|---|---|
| Big M Express* | 917-822-6770 |
| Blue Sea V blueseavfishing.com | 718-769-2927 |
| Brooklyn VI brooklynvifishing.com | 718-743-8464 |
| The Bullet* | 718-265-6915 |
| The Capt. Dave | 917-251-2628 |
| Dorothy B VIII dorothyb.com | 347-582-1716 |
| Explorer explorerfishing.com | 917-733-5993 |
| Flamingo III flamingo3.com | 718-763-8745 |
| Golden Sunshine newgoldensunshine.com | 718-945-6931 |
| Karen Ann* | 718-634-4669 |
| Lady L* ladylcharters.com | 917-838-3726 |
| Marilyn Jean* marilynjeancharters.com | 917-650-3212 |
| Ocean Eagle V | 718-258-4126 |
| Pilot II | 516-599-0700 |
| Sea Queen VII seaqueenvii.com | 917-642-0265 |
| Sea Wolf | 718-356-7556 |

### Queens

| | |
|---|---|
| Capt. Mike captmike.org | 917-747-4789 |
| The Rocket* rocketcharters.com | 718-423-6007 |

### Staten Island

| | |
|---|---|
| Angler* | 718-965-3718 |
| Atlantis Princess atlantisprincess.com | 718-966-2845 |
| Capt. Paul* | 718-966-6990 |
| Capt. Scotti* | 718-356-0553 |
| Lady Kim* | 718-698-6582 |

## Fly Fishing Charters

Harbor Sportfishing 201-725-6755
nyharborfishing.com

Manhattan Fly 917-531-4783
manhattanfly.com

Urban Fly Guides 917-847-9576
urbanflyguides.com

One More Cast 718-757-7339
NYCFlyFishing.com

Fin Chaser 718-317-1481
finchaser.com

On The Bight 718-967-9095
flyfishnyc.com

## Where to Fish NYC

The New York State Department of Environmental Conservation's I FISH NY program has published a guide to saltwater fishing in the New York City area, which includes complete fishing access details, maps and tips on how to get started fishing local waters. The guide can be downloaded at dec.ny/outdoor/8377.html. NY Sea Grant provides a complete list of fishing fact sheets at seagrant.sunsb.edu/fishny.

**Lee Wulff**, Father of Catch and Release Fishing (1905-1991) One of the best known fly fisherman in the world, Wulff was a prolific outdoor writer, photographer, fly-tier and advocate for "no kill" fishing. His family moved from Alaska to Brooklyn in 1913. After obtaining an engineering degree from Stanford, he studied art in Paris, and ultimately left a career in advertising to pursue his passion for fishing. Wulff was among the founders of Theodore Gordon Flyfishers, a group that has cast a long shadow over American fly fishing. Called the "Boys of Manny Wolfe's" after the landmark steakhouse where they held their meetings (now Smith and Wollenskys), the group included Ted Rogowski, Arnold Gingrich, Donal O'Brien, and Ed Zern. Lee Wulff was an inventor and innovator best known for creating the Royal Wulff series of fly patterns. He and his wife a Joan Salvato started a fly fishing and casting school on the banks of the Beaverkill that survives today.

# Shellfish & Crustaceans

Shellfish are filter feeding mollusks that pump large amounts of water to capture food and in the process purify the water. One oyster can filter up to 50 gallons of water per day. Shellfish cluster into reef structures that provide marine habitat for hundreds of species.

New York Harbor was one of the most productive shellfish grounds in the world in the 19th century. Oysters, mussels, scallops, and clams were plentiful and vital to the local economy. From briny Gowanus oysters to sweet Little Neck clams, shellfish were once the city's biggest export. Overharvesting, pollution, and disease led to the closure of shellfish beds in Raritan Bay, Jamaica Bay and areas around New York City. There is an effort today to restore wild shellfish populations in the New York Bight. Community based oyster gardening is carried out by coastal stewards throughout the five boroughs, such as The River Project and Baykeeper.

New York State certifies the safety of local shellfish growing waters. The Federal government monitors water quality standards and performs monthly inspections of licensed dealers to make sure shellfish have the proper tags which indicate the harvester, water body and bed where they were grown. The Atlantic Coast from Fort Tilden to East Rockaway, within the three-mile limit is deemed Certified Water. A permit is not required for recreational shellfish harvesting from state lands. The limit is one bushel per day.

## Shellfish of New York

**American oyster** (*Crassostrea virginica*) populations are being restored around the Estuary through aquaculture and oyster gardening. Restoration begins with volunteers growing seed oysters at private docks and piers. Once mature, the oysters are planted on piles of discarded shells where they will attach themselves to the hard surface and remain for life. There is a restored oyster reef near Liberty Island.

**Bay scallops** (*Aequipecten irradians*), NYS's official shell, were wiped out by an exotic algae, called brown tide in the 1980s. Restoration efforts begin with planting eelgrass which scallop need to reproduce. Once spat have matured, it swims by using its siphon to propel around the sea floor.

**Blue Crab** (*Callinectes sapidus*) live in brackish waters of the Estuary year-round. Recreational and commercial harvesting occurs seasonally. It is illegal to take an egg-bearing female.

**Hard clams** (*Mercenaria mercenaria*) or quahogs live in sandy bottom areas. From 1987 to 2002, they were commercially harvested under special permit in Raritan Bay where clams taken from the Bay were transplanted to Certified Waters off Long Island for 21 days to clean out before sale to the public. Raritan Bay transplants accounted for more than 45% of the state's harvest by 2002, when beds were closed due to a fatal parasite in the harvest area. The beds remained closed until 2008.

**Ribbed mussels** (*Geukensia demissa*) attach themselves to the cordgrass of salt marshes in Jamaica Bay and Marine Park. Large beds of blue mussels (Mytilus edulis) cling to the rocky shores of Pelham Bay.

## Artificial Reefs

The flat and sandy bottom of New York Harbor provides little natural habitat. Artificial reefs enhance underwater habitat and create new opportunities for anglers and divers.

The NYS DEC has exclusive authority to obtain permits from the Army Corps of Engineers for construction of artificial reefs in state waters. Over 300 patch reefs have been built, made up of everything from M1 Army tanks and old ships to construction rubble and harbor dredge. The only patch reef within city limits is the Rockaway Reef, which is made up of 6,000 rubber tires. It covers 413 acres in 40 feet of water, just 1.6 nautical miles south of Rockaway Beach.

Thousands of decommissioned "Red Bird" subway cars, in-service since the 1964 World's Fair, have been donated to reefs all along the Atlantic seaboard, from the New Jersey Highlands to the Georgia Coast. New York State opted not to take any of the stripped down cars, out of environmental concerns.

### Recycle Fishing Line

Whenever possible recover fishing line. Monofilament fishing line is by design strong and invisible underwater. It is non-biodegradable and can last over 600 years. Improperly discarded line can injure swimmers and divers, entangle and poison wildlife, and damage boat motors. Recycle line at bait and tackle shops or PVC line collection bins posted at fishing sites in Gateway National Recreation Area, at local marinas and some city parks. To find out how to start a fishing line recycling program at your favorite fishing spot, visit goingcoastal.org.

# Bait & Tackle

## Manhattan

Capitol Fishing Tackle Co.
218 W 23 St. 212-929-6132

Ideal Pet
116 & 1 Ave. 212-876-5093

Pacific Aquarium
46 Delancey St. 212-995-5895

## Bronx

Al's Tackle Shop 86 Lincoln Ave,
Pelham. 914-738-4589

City Island B & T 632 City Island Ave.
718-885-2153

Franks Sport Shop 430 E Tremont Ave.
718-299-9628

Interboro B & T 3561 E Tremont Ave.
718-863-8085

Jack's B & T 551 City Island Ave.
718-885-2042

The Boat Livery 663 City Island Ave.
718-885-1843

## Brooklyn

Bernie's B & T 3128 Emmons Ave.
718-646-7600

Dream Fishing Tackle 673 Manhattan
Ave. 718-389-9670

JV B & T 2702 Emmons Ave.
718-646-9754

Name-It B & T 2157 Bath Ave.
718-373-6233

Parkway Fishing Center 3 Plumb 3 St.
718-763-9265

Stella Maris Fishing Station 2702
Emmons Ave. 718-646-9754

Shoreway Marine Knapp St.
718-648-0046

Tastee Bait Co. 3035 Emmons Ave.
718-769-1816

## Queens

Crossbay B & T 164-26 Crossbay Blvd.
718-835-1018

Crossbay Fishing Station
158-35 Crossbay Blvd. 718-843-3800

First Fishing Supplies 150-46 Northern
Blvd. 718-886-7322

Pro-Fishing & Tackle 134-22 Northern
Blvd. 718-461-9612

Seaman's Wholesale Bait 25 First St.
718-525-6430

Seoul Fishing & Tackle 5319 Roosevelt
Ave. 718-565-2376

Smitty's Fishing Station 224 9 St, Broad
Channel. 718-945-2642

## Staten Island

Biggie's B & T 65 Page Ave.
718-966-9206

Great Kills B & T 4044 Hylan Blvd.
718-356-0055

Michaels' B & T 187 Mansion Ave.
718-984-9733

Scag's B & T 114 Victory Blvd
718-727-7373

# Harbor Forts

The remains of dozens of military forts stand sentry at the portals of New York Harbor. Begun in 1794, the harbor defense program was the first in a series of fortification construction that continued for more than a century. Built to defend the city from naval assault, the seacoast fortifications were vital strategic defenses from the time of the Revolution to the Cold War era. The surviving structures represent every sort of technological advance in defense engineering. Advances in weaponry after 1940 made coastal artillery nearly obsolete and the ascendancy of the airplane as a military weapon lead to the conversion of coastal armaments into anti-aircraft artillery units.

# Harbor Defenses

## Castle Clinton

Battery Park, Manhattan

Built: 1808

Current Use: National Monument, Museum, Concert Venue

Contact: 212-344-7220 nps.gov/cacl

A circular fort made of red sandstone was called the Southwest Battery when originally built on an outcropping of rocks 200 feet off the southern tip of Manhattan. It was built to defend the city in the War of 1812, but the fort never had occasion to fire on the enemy. Land filling joined the structure to the Battery and the fort was later renamed for Mayor DeWitt Clinton. It was ceded to the city in 1823 and has since housed a restaurant, opera house, immigration depot, and the first home of the NY Aquarium. Now the centerpiece of Battery Park, Castle Clinton offers historic exhibits and tours, while also serving as a performance venue. Restoration of the roof and the addition of a second level are planned for the structure. Getting there: 1 to South Ferry.

## Castle Williams

Governors Island, Manhattan

Built: 1807-1811

Current Use: National Monument

Contact: 212-514-8271 nps.gov/gois

The first casement fort built in North America and the sister fort of Castle Clinton, Castle Williams looks out on the harbor channel. It is named for its designer, Lt. Colonel Jonathan Williams, the first superintendent of West Point. The structure has 40-foot high, 8-foot thick sandstone walls, still guarded by some of the original canons. Originally, twenty-seven French 35-pound cannons lined the lower tier, and thirty-nine 20-pounders lined the second tier. Castle William served as a prison camp for confederate soldiers during the Civil War and, decades later, as jail to U.S. WWII recruits attempting to go AWOL, including Walt Disney and boxer Rocky Graziano. The fort is listed on the National Register of Historic Places. Getting there: Governors Island Ferry from Battery Maritime.

## Fort Gibson

Ellis Island, Manhattan

Built: 1808

Current Use: Nat'l Monument/Museum

Contact: 212-363-3200 nps.gov

Fort Gibson served as a battery and munitions arsenal for the Union Army during the Civil War on Oyster Island., now Ellis Island. The archeological remains of Fort Gibson are located at the southeast end of the island. Getting there: Statue of Liberty Ferry.

## Fort Hamilton

The Narrows, Brooklyn

Built: 1825-1831

Current Use: Active Army Post, Museum

Contact: 718-630-4349

Fort Hamilton is one of the oldest Army garrisons in the country and the oldest granite fort in the harbor. A small Battery was first established here on July 4, 1776, when General Knox fired on the *HMS Asia* as it approached the Narrows. Capt. Robert E. Lee, "Stonewall" Jackson and Capt. Abner Doubleday served at Fort Hamilton. Army Recruiting Battalion, Reserve, the Army Corps of Engineers, and National Guard units are active at the fort today. The old part of the fort is open to the public as part of the Harbor Defense Museum. Getting there: R to 95 St., Bay Ridge.

## Forts of New York Harbor

1. Castle Clinton
2. Castle William
3. Fort Jay
4. Fort Wood
5. Fort Gibson
6. Fort Wadsworth
7. Fort Hamilton
8. Fort Schuyler
9. Fort Totten
10. Fort Tryon
11. Fort Tilden
12. Miller Field

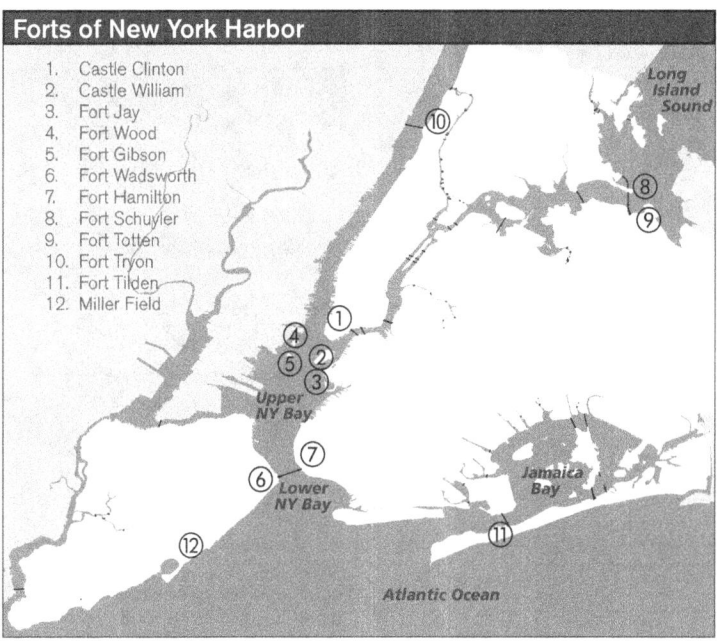

### Fort Jay

Governors Island, Manhattan
Built: 1798/rebuilt 1806-1809
Current Use: National Monument
Contact: 212-514-8271 nps.gov/gois

The fort is located on the highest point of the island, surrounded by earthen covered walls and a star-shaped dry moat. Originally named for statesman John Jay, the first Chief Justice of the Supreme Court, the fort was rebuilt as Fort Columbus in 1803, and restored to Fort Jay in 1904. Three Rodman cannons with one-mile range are still in place from the Civil War. It served as headquarters of the First U.S. Army (first on beaches of Normandy) after WWII until 1966. It is now operated by the National Park Service and open to the public. Getting there: Governors Island Ferry from Battery Maritime.

### Fort Schuyler

Throgs Neck, Bronx
Built: 1826-1845
Current Use: Maritime College, Museum
Contact: 212-409-7218

A granite fort built to protect the East River approach to New York Harbor, Fort Schuyler has an irregular pentagon shape, based on French forts. During the Spanish-American War mines were planted in the water between the fort and its counterpoint across the East River Narrows, Fort Totten on the Queens shore. Decommissioned in 1934, the fort occupies the grounds of SUNY Maritime College where it is home to the Maritime Industry Museum. It is listed on the National Register of Historic Places. Open to the public. Getting there: 6 to Westchester Sq. transfer Bx40 Bus, last stop.

### Fort Tilden

Rockaway Peninsula, Queens

Built: 1917

Current Use: National Park

Contact: 718-318-4300

The fort is a former military post and naval air station on 317 acres named for former Governor Samuel J. Tilden. Battery Harris worked together with a battery six miles across the harbor at Fort Hancock in Sandy Hook, New Jersey. A Nike missile site for much of the cold war, Fort Tilden was active until 1974 and is now part of Gateway National Recreation Area, administered by the National Park Service. Hiking trails pass the buried remains of gun platforms and old batteries are used as raptor and bird-watching platforms. Open to the public. Getting there: A to Rockaway/Beach 116 St., transfer to Q35 Green bus.

### Fort Totten

Willet's Point, Queens

Built: 1858

Current Use: Park

Contact: 718-352-4793 nycgovparks.org

Originally called the Fort at Willet's Point, Totten guards the "back door" to NY Harbor with Fort Schuyler across the river in the Bronx. The Nike missile defense system was developed here. The Fort served as a school for the Army Corps of Engineers and the landmark 1870 Officers' Club building is still the insignia of the ACE. The site has been a staging facility for various commands up until the Gulf War. Getting there: LIRR to Bayside.

### Fort Tryon

Hudson River, Manhattan

Built: 1776

Current Use: NYC Park

Contact: nycgovparks.org

Originally part of Fort Washington, the fortification was the last stronghold against British forces on Manhattan Island during the Revolutionary War. In the battle, Margaret Corbin took up her fallen husband's post and became the first American woman wounded on the battlefield. In 1779, "Capt. Molly" was compensated by Congress for her distinguished bravery. The park was renamed for the British governor of colonial New York. Getting there: A to W 190 St.

### Fort Wadsworth (1900)
### Fort Tompkins (1807)
### Battery Weed (1860)

The Narrows, Staten Island

Current Use: National Park

Contact: 718-354-4500 nps.gov/gate

Fort Wadsworth is the oldest continuously manned military installation in the country, first fortified by the Dutch in 1636, active during the Revolutionary War and enlarged for the War of 1812. The site is actually a complex of numerous forts and batteries located under the Verrazano Bridge. The navy was the last military tenant departing in 1995. Now inactive, the fort is open to the public and offers exhibits, tours, and family programming, administered by the National Park Service as part of Gateway National Recreation Area. Getting there: Ferry to Bus S51

### Fort Wood
Liberty (Bedloe) Island, NY Harbor
Built: 1808-1811
Current Use: National Monument
Contact: 212-363-3200 nps.gov/stli

Originally known as Star Fort because of its 11 point star-shaped battery, the Fort was named for Eleazor Wood, a hero of the War of 1812. Some of the old ramparts can still be seen near the entrance to the Statue of Liberty, which is through the old Fort's 20-foot thick walls and sally port door. The promenade was originally a gun platform along the wall of the fort.
Getting there: Statue of Liberty Ferry.

### Miller Field
Atlantic Ocean, Staten Island
Built: 1919
Current Use: National Park
Contact: 718-351-6970 nps.gov/gate

An Air Service Coast Defense Station, which has served as a Coast Guard Artillery gun site, a Nike Missile repair depot, and a base for US Army Special Forces. Miller Field is now parkland with a large complex of athletic fields, picnic areas and fishing beach in the Staten Island Unit of Gateway National Recreation Area.
Getting there: Staten Island Ferry to Bus S76.

# HISTORIC SHIPS

The historic ships of New York Harbor are unique cultural resources that provide insight into the maritime heritage of the city and the nation. They present an intimate view of life at sea, chart the growth of the port, and trace innovation in naval technology. Historically significant ships are costly and difficult to restore and maintain, so rely on skilled and amateur volunteers to assist in the restoration and operation, in the process preserving maritime trades. Most of the harbor's historic vessels are afloat and open for public tours, with South Street Seaport Museum berthing the country's largest fleet of privately maintained historic ships. The collection highlights the range of craft that sailed New York Harbor in the 19th and early 20th centuries.

## Historic Ship Clubs

**North River Historic Ship Society**
Group promotes historic ships and the working waterfront. The Working Harbor Committee organizes annual Hidden Harbor Tours. nrhss.org

**Ocean Liner Council** of South Street Seaport Museum hosts sympoisums and lectures and presents its Silver Riband award to renowned maritime historians. southstreetseaportmuseum.org

**Save Our Ships** A New York State chartered museum to hold historic vessels, wharves, floats, and artifacts. SOS is the owner of the John J. Harvey. sosny.org

**Working Harbor Committee**
A group of maritime enthusiasts and boat operators that educate people about the city's working waterfront through pubic Hidden Harbor Tours and programs featuring a behind the scenes look at the historic industrial waterfront and present-day port.

**World Ship Society** The Port of New York Branch of this global organization, are enthusiasts of passenger shipping past and present. worldshipny.com

## Historic Ships of New York

**Clearwater**
79 Street Boat Basin (seasonally)
Length: 106  Beam: 25
Mast Height: 108 Gross Tons: 70
Hull: WOOD
Original Use: Replica sloop
Current Use: Enviro Education
Contact: 845-454-7673
Website: clearwater.org

Offering 3-hour public sailings aboard the single mast sloop, "the flagship of America's environmental movement" designed after traditional 18th century sailing sloops by Pete Seeger in 1969 to bring attention to the natural beauty and ecology of the Hudson River.

**Clipper City**
Pier 17, South Street Seaport
Length: 160  Mast Height: 135
Gross Tons: 200
Hull: WOOD
Original Use: Replica barquentine
Current Use: Excursion
Contact: 212-619-0907
Website: clippercityny.com

Offering public sailings aboard a huge sailing ship replicated from an 1854 topsail schooner from plans held at the National Archive.

**Fire Fighter**
FDNY Marine #9, Pier 14 Staten Island
Built: 1938 United Shipyards, NY
Length: 134, Beam 32, Draft-9
Hull: STEEL
Current Use: Active fireboat
Designation: National Historic Landmark

*Fire Fighter* cost $983,000, can do 15 knots and has water guns with output of 20,000 gallons per minute.

Designed by William F. Gibbs, she was New York's first diesel electric boat and received the "Gallant Ship Award" for rescuing 30 seamen from fire aboard the *Esso Brussels* and *Sea Witch* collision in the harbor in 1972. *Fire Fighter* answered the call at Marine Fire Co. 9 until her retirement in 2009.

### Growler

Pier 86, North River

Built: 1958 Portsmouth Naval Shipyard, NH

Length: 317.7, Beam: 27.2

Draft: 19, Displacement: 2768

Hull: STEEL

Original Use: Combatant

Current Use: Floating Exhibit

Contact: 212-245-0072

Website: intrepidmuseum.org

The only guided missile submarine open to the public, *Growler* was one of three subs designed to carry Regulus cruise missiles. She was dispatched on nuclear deterrent patrol from 1958 to 1964. The vessel was saved from becoming a torpedo target by the Intrepid Sea-Air-Space Museum in 1988.

### Intrepid

Pier 86, North River

Built: 1943 Newport News Shipbldg., VA

Length: 856, Beam: 93, Draft: 30/54.6

Displacement: 33292

Hull: STEEL

Original Use: Combatant

Current Use: Dockside museum

Designation: National Historic Landmark, Nat'l Register of Historic Places

Contact: 212-245-0072

Website: intrepidmuseum.org

One of 24 *Essex* Class carriers, Intrepid weighs 42,000 tons and is as tall as a 16-story building. She could reach speeds of 30 knots. *Intrepid* has had an active career beginning in WWII, where she joined the fleet at Leyte Gulf, the largest naval engagement in history. She has survived kamikaze hits, seven bomb attacks and a torpedo strike. The vessel served in Korea and Vietnam, and was the prime recovery ship for NASA, finally retiring in 1974, to become the centerpiece of the Intrepid Sea-Air-Space Museum and host to annual Fleet Week events each May.

### John J. Harvey

Pier 66, North River

Built: 1931 Todd Shipyards, Brooklyn

Length: 130, Beam: 28

Draft: 9.0, Gross tons: 268

Hull: STEEL

Original Use: FDNY Fireboat

Current Use: Floating museum

Designation: National Register

Website: fireboat.org

The *John J. Harvey* is the fastest large fireboat in the world, clocking over 17 knots, and once the most powerful with eight water canons that can pump 18,000 GPM. She answered the call for the *Normandie* fire in 1942 and aided in World Trade Center relief efforts on 9/11. Named

for a downed fireboat captain, the *Harvey* was the longest serving NYC Fire Dept. fireboat when it retired in 1995. It was purchased at auction in 1999 and today preservationists and volunteers maintain the boat and share its classic water display at harbors celebrations.

**Lehigh Valley RR Barge No. 79**

Pier 44, Conover St. Red Hook

Built: 1914 Perth Amboy Dry Dock Co.

Length: 86, Beam: 30

Draft: 2 Tons: 454, Displacement: 150

Hull: WOOD

Original Use: Cargo

Current Use: Museum/Event Space

Designation: National Register

Contact: 718-624-4719

Website: waterfrontmuseum.org

The only surviving wooden-covered barge of the Lighterage Era (1860-1960) afloat today, it once carried up to 450 tons of cargo between rail lines and the waterfront. Rescued and restored in 1986 by performer and professional clown David Sharps, the barge now offers educational programs and live performances at the Red Hook Garden Pier.

**Lettie G. Howard**

Pier 16, South Street Seaport Museum

Built: 1893 Arthur D. Story Essex, MA

Length: 125.4, Beam: 21, Draft: 10.6

Displacement: 102 Hull: WOOD

Original Use: Fishing

Current Use: Educational vessel

Designation: Nat'l Historic Landmark, National Register

Contact: 212-748-8786

Website: southstreetseaportmuseum.org

One of the last surviving examples of the two-masted *Fredonia* schooners, Lettie worked the inshore fishing and oystering trades out of Gloucester, MA, the Yucatan Peninsula, and Gulf of Mexico until the 1960s. She is similar to ships that carried their catch to the Fulton Fish Market. Adults have the opportunity to join adventure education sails learning traditional seamanship on trips aboard the landmark schooner.

**Lightship Ambrose LV-87**

Pier 16, South Street Seaport Museum

Built: 1907 NY Shipbldg. Co. Camden, NJ

Length: 135.9, Beam: 29

Depth of Hold: 13

Gross/Net Tons: 683/488

Hull: STEEL

Original Use: Aid to Navigation

Current Use: Floating Exhibit

Designation: National Historic Landmark, National Register

Contact: 212-748-8786

Website: southstreetseaportmuseum.org

From 1907 until 1932, the lightship marked the entrance to New York Harbor as the Ambrose station, eight miles east of Rockaway Point. The first radio beacon in the U.S. was installed on the ship in 1922. She served various stations, finally as the *Scotland* near Sandy Hook until decommissioned in 1962.

**Lightship Frying Pan LV-115**

Pier 66 Maritime, North River

Built: 1929 Charleston Drydock, SC

Length: 133.3, Beam: 30

Draft: 13.8, Gross tonnage: 630

Hull: STEEL

Original Use: Aid to Navigation

Current Use: Attraction/Event Space

Designation: National Register of Historic Places

Contact: 212-989-6363

Website: fryingpan.com

One of only 13 lightships surviving from more than 100 built, she served from 1930 to 1965 as the floating lighthouse at Frying Pan Shoals, which is located at the entrance to Cape Fear River in North Carolina. Employed as an examination vessel and net tender during WWII, the ship retired in 1965. It was recovered from the bottom of Chesapeake Bay in 1989 and today enjoys a full life in Hudson River Park's Pier 66 Maritime.

### Lilac

Pier 40, North River
Built: 1933
Length: 173
Original Use: Lighthouse Tender
Current Use: Under restoration
Contact: lilacpreservationproject.org

Originally built for the U.S. Lighthouse Service, *Lilac* is an 800-ton vessel powered by two-triple expansion steam engines. She was later employed as a training vessel for merchant marines and decommissioned in 1973. A nonprofit group of historic ship and steam power enthusiasts own the ship and have begun restoration.

## Shipworms

Cleaner water quality in New York Harbor has resulted in a resurgence in all forms of marine life, including the reappearance of wood boring organisms. Shipworms (really a type of clam) and microscopic wood-eating gribbles, an underwater termite, destroy wooden ships, barges and pilings that support piers. The pests threaten many of the historic wooden vessels in the port. Preventive measures include use of toxic-free anti-fouling treatments and paints.

### Marion M

Pier 16 South Street Seaport Museum
Built: 1932 Virginia
Length: 60.6, Breadth: 22.5,
Depth of Hold: 5.4. Gross Tonnage: 41
Hull: WOOD
Original Use: Chandlery lighter; freight
Current Use: Floating exhibit/work boat
Contact: 212-748-8786
Website: southstreetseaportmuseum.org

A former oyster shell hauler, motor freighter, then finally a chandlery lighter of the Standard Boat Company on Staten Island, she now is a support vessel for the museum's floating exhibit of historic ships.

### Mary A. Whalen

Atlantic Basin Red Hook, Brooklyn
Built: 1938
Length: 172, Gross tonnage: 613
Hull: STEEL
Original Use: Coastal tanker
Current Use: Event, Exhibit Space
Website: portsidenewyork.org

The work boat's eight cargo tanks carried gas, diesel and kerosene for delivery along the New England and Mid-Atlantic coast until 1994, when it was cleaned up for an office in Brooklyn's Erie Basin. Work continues as the vessel is readapted once again.

### Noble Houseboat Studio

Noble Maritime Museum, Staten Island
Original Use: Floating Artist Studio
Current Use: Gallery exhibit
Contact: 718-447-6490
Website: noblemaritime.org

The studio barge was built by noted maritime artist John Noble, who constructed it from salvaged boats, including a 100-year-old teakwood salon from an abandoned yacht. The furnished artist's studio boat was

**Bard Brothers,** Maritime Artists, James (1815-1897) and John (1815-1856). Born in Chelsea in 1815, twin brothers James and John Bard collaborated on their first ship portrait painted for Cornelius Vanderbilt at the age of twelve. It became the first of many for the brothers, who worked together to create over 350 ship portraits between 1831 and 1849. Masterfully combining elements of both folk and fine art, the self-taught artists were particularly lauded for the detail with which they depicted the steamboats, schooners and sloops navigating the Hudson River and New York Harbor. After John Bard's death in 1856, James continued to work alone until 1890, and at the time of his retirement had reportedly completed over 4,000 paintings.

dismantled and stored for years before being reassembled at the museum, where it is on permanent display.

### Peking

Pier 16 South Street Seaport Museum
Built: 1911 Blohn & Voss, Hamburg
Length: 321, Beam: 47
Gross/Net Tons: 3080/2850
Hull: STEEL.
Original Use: Cargo windjammer
Current Use: Floating Exhibit
Contact: 212-748-8786
Website: southstreetseaportmuseum.org

A four-masted barque built to carry freight on long distance sailing voyages. She is one of the largest and last of the generation of windjammers ever built. After retirement she served as a training vessel in England and now recalls the "Age of Sail" to museum visitors, who can view a screening of "Peking at Sea" a film of the vessel's sailing trip around Cape Horn.

### Pioneer

Pier 16 South Street Seaport Museum
Built: 1885 Pioneer Ironworks, PA
Length: 102, Beam: 22, Draft: 4.5/12
Hull: STEEL, originally iron
Original Use: Cargo sloop
Current Use: Excursion Boat
Contact: 212-748-8786
Website: southstreetseaportmuseum.org

The two masted schooner is the only iron-hulled American sailing schooner still in existence. She was the delivery vehicle of her day, originally used to carry sand mined near the mouth of the Delaware, re-rigged as a schooner in 1895. Public sails are offered daily and volunteer docents learn how to sail.

### Tug Helen McAllister

Pier 16 South Street Seaport Museum
Built: 1900 Burlee Drydock, Port Richmond
Length: 112.12, Breadth: 29
Depth: 15.4 Tonnage: 488 Hull: STEEL
Original Use: Towing coal barges
Current Use: Under restoration
Contact: 212-748-8786
Website: southstreetseaportmuseum.org

Donated to the museum by McAllister Towing, the tug was originally launched as *Admiral Dewey* and worked the Carolina Coast.

### Tug Pegasus

Built: 1907 Skinner Baltimore, MD
Length: 103, Breadth 24, Depth: 12
Gross tonnage: 186 Hull: STEEL
Original Use: Oil tug
Current Use: Educational Vessel
Designation: National Register
Contact: 212-406-2225
Website: tugpegasus.org

One of only four "Battleship Tugs" —named for their size and 650 horsepower steam engines. *Pegasus* was converted to diesel in 1954. She worked for 90 years, for Standard Oil Co. out of Bayonne, NJ, and as part of the McAllister fleet for 35 years. In 1987, the tug was acquired by Hepburn Marine and retired after a decade to offer public education programs.

### Tug W. O. Decker

Pier 16, South Street Seaport Museum
Built: 1930 Russell Yard, Long Island City
Length: 52, Breadth: 15, Depth: 5.6
Draft: 6, Gross Tonnage: 27
Hull: WOOD
Original Use: Newtown Creek Towing Co.
Current Use: Excursion Boat
Designation: National Register
Contact: 212-748-8786
Website: southstreetseaportmuseum.org

One of the last steam-powered docking tugs built in the harbor, now re-powered with diesel. The museum operates tours of the working waterfront onboard the little tug.

### Ventura Cutter

North Cove, Battery Park City
Built: 1922 Herreshoff Co., RI
Length: 62.5, Beam: 14.3, Draft 5
Gross/Net Tons: 26/21 Hull: WOOD
Original Use: Private Yacht
Current Use: Excursion/Charter
Designation: National Historic Landmark
Contact: Atlantic Sail 212-786-1204
Website: sailnewyork.com

A graceful wooden sailing ship with a hull made of solid mahogany and decks of Indian teak originally launched as a duck hunting yacht by the founder of Citibank.

### Wavertree

Pier 16 South Street Seaport Museum
Built: 1885 Southampton, UK
Length: 279, Breadth: 40.2
Depth: 24.4, Gross Tonnage: 2170
Hull: IRON
Original Use: Cargo
Designation: National Register
Current Use: Floating Exhibit
Contact: 212-748-8786
Website: southstreetseaportmuseum.org

The full rigged ship is the largest sailing ship afloat and one of the last built of wrought iron. A tramp ship for hire from India to South America, she was sold in 1910 and used as a warehouse in Chile, later converted to a sand barge then acquired by the Seaport in 1968.

# LIGHTHOUSES

New York City, known for its brightly lit streets and skyscrapers, dazzles residents and tourists alike with its luminous skyline. In the background of this busy city, a different kind of light shines out of sight of most busy New Yorkers – the lighthouses of New York Harbor. The need for permanent aids to navigation to protect cargo and people coming into port was realized by New York businessmen who solicited the New York State Assembly to sponsor a lottery for the building of the Sandy Hook Lighthouse (formerly called the New York Lighthouse) in 1764. As New York Harbor grew in importance the need for additional lighthouses grew over the years to accommodate the increased traffic into the harbor.

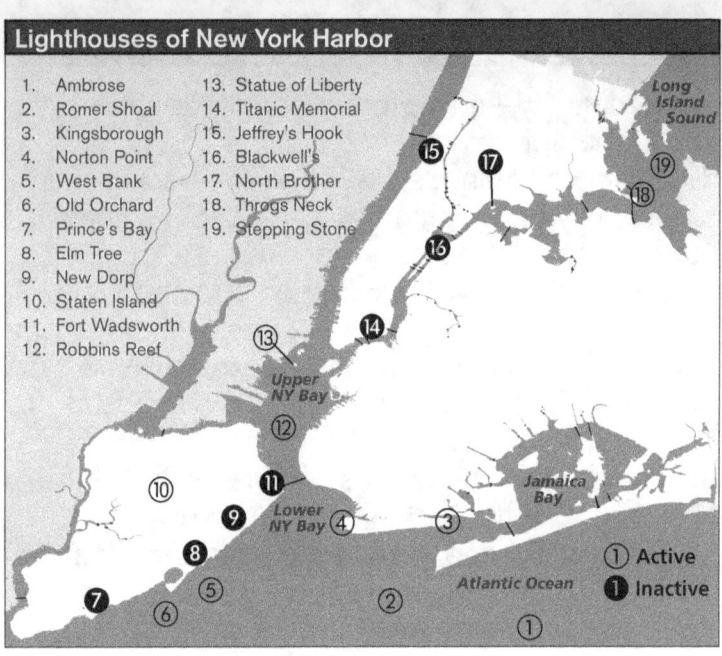

## Lighthouses of New York Harbor

1. Ambrose
2. Romer Shoal
3. Kingsborough
4. Norton Point
5. West Bank
6. Old Orchard
7. Prince's Bay
8. Elm Tree
9. New Dorp
10. Staten Island
11. Fort Wadsworth
12. Robbins Reef
13. Statue of Liberty
14. Titanic Memorial
15. Jeffrey's Hook
16. Blackwell's
17. North Brother
18. Throgs Neck
19. Stepping Stone

① Active
● Inactive

## Lighthouses of NYC

### Ambrose Light Tower

Ambrose Channel, New York Harbor

Current Use: Active

Established: 1967

Owner: USCG

From 1908 to 1967, three lightships served the Ambrose Channel entrance to New York Harbor; one is on exhibit at South Street Seaport. Lightships were used where the water was too deep for a standard lighthouse. In 1967, the lightship was replaced by a Texas-style tower, which was later damaged in a collision with an oil tanker. In 1999, a solar powered tower with fog signal, radio and radar beacons marked the harbor entrance. That tower was also damaged in a collision and was dismantled in 2008 and replaced by flashing buoys.

### Blackwell Island Lighthouse

East River, Roosevelt Island

Current Use: Historic site

Established: 1903

Designation, NYC Landmark, National Register of Historic Places

Owner: NYC DPR nycgovparks.org

The octagon-shaped Gothic-style tower stands 50 feet tall at the northern tip of Roosevelt Island in Lighthouse Park. Designed by James Renwick Jr., designer of St. Patrick's Cathedral, the tower was built by convict labor in 1872 of locally quarried gray gneiss stone. It takes its name from the Blackwell family that owned the island from 1685 to 1823 and served as a private navigational aid for over 70 years. An esplanade on the island's westside leads to the tower, which is still lit at night. Visit the light up close or view from FDR Drive or Hallet's Cove in Queens.

**Coney Island Lighthouse**

Beach 47 St. Norton's Point, Brooklyn
Current Use: Active
Established: 1890
Owner: USCG, lease-Sea Gate Assn.

Situated on a spit of land in the gated community of Sea Gate, the skeletal light covering the Main Channel stands 75 feet tall and its red flashing beacon can be seen for 14 miles. The keeper's cottage was home to the last civilian lightkeeper, Frank Schubert, who joined the Lighthouse Service in 1937 and administered Coney Island light from 1960 until he passed away in 2003. He is credited with saving the lives of 12 sailors. The original Fresnel lens is now on display at South Street Seaport Museum. The light and grounds are closed, but can be viewed from Sea Gate Beach or the Shore Parkway Greenway. Occasional public tours are offered.

**Elm Tree Light**

Miller Field, Staten Island
Current Use: Inactive
Established: 1852
Owner: National Park Service
Contact: nps.gov/gate

The Swash Channel light also served as Front Range Light for the New Dorp Lighthouse, replaced by a concrete aviation warning beacon in 1939, which had a green light for aviators and white light for mariners. First came the light, Miller Field was built adjacent to it 1919.

**Fort Wadsworth Lighthouse**

The Narrows, Staten Island
Current Use: Historic site
Established: 1903
Owner: National Park Service
Contact: 718-354-4500 nps.gov/gate

The light atop Battery Weed, visible for 14 miles at sea, helped guide ships through the Narrows until 1965, when it was rendered obsolete by the Verrazano Bridge. It has been restored with a solar-powered light by volunteer Joe Esposito. The park grounds are open to the public and the light can be seen from above at Fort Tompkins.

### Jeffrey's Hook Lighthouse

Hudson River, Fort Washington Park
Current Use: Private navigation aid
Established: 1921
Owner: NYC Parks
Contact: nycgovparks.org

Situated on an outcropping of rocks called Jeffrey's Hook under the George Washington Bridge, the Light was deactivated in 1947 and slated for demolition. The children's book, *The Little Red Lighthouse and the Great Grey Bridge* by Hildegarde H. Swift, which is about being small in a big world, inspired preservation of the lighthouse. Relit in 2002, Urban Rangers conduct tours and the light is celebrated with a festival each fall.

### Kingsborough Community College

Rockaway Inlet
Current Use: Private aid to navigation
Established: 1990
Owner: City University of New York
Contact: 718-368-5000

A skeletal tower on top of the round Marine Academic Center, the light rises 114 feet above sea level, has a range of 11 miles and flashes a white light every four seconds.

### New Dorp Light

Lower NY Bay, Staten Island
Current Use: Private residence
Established: 1856
National Register of Historic Places
Owner: Private

An inland light, 40 feet high and 192 feet above sea level, active from 1856 to 1964. It served as a rear range light for the Swash Channel in concert with Elm Tree Lighthouse. The lighthouse has been privately owned since 1974, the current owner has maintained the exterior appearance in it original form at Beacon Avenue.

### North Brother Light

Bay of Brothers, East River
Current Use: Abandoned
Established: 1869
Owner: NYC Parks

The light served as a guide across the Hell Gate and on the Bay of Brothers from 1869 to 1953. The tower has since been razed. North Brother Island, now a wading bird rookery, was once home to Typhoid Mary at Riverside Hospital. Brother Island was also the site of the greatest maritime disaster in New York City history, when on June 15, 1904 the excursion boat

## Lighthouse Museum

The former U.S. Lighthouse Service Depot on Staten Island, which beginning in 1862 assembled, tested, and repaired lighthouses for close to a century, was to transition to the National Lighthouse Museum. It is considered one of the most significant maritime heritage sites in the nation selected for the museum project by the U.S. Lighthouse Society in 1998.

The 10 acre property contains six designated historic buildings and an 850 foot pier, in addition to underground vaults once used to store fuels. It is administered by the NYC Economic Development Corporation, which has neglected museum plans in favor of development.

> **Katherine Walker**, Lightkeeper (1848-1931) 4'10" Kate Walker began tending Robbins Reef Lighthouse, located on a tiny reef two miles southwest of the Statue of Liberty, upon the death of her husband John in 1886. His last words were "Mind the light, Kate." Officially given the title of lightkeeper in 1894, Kate was paid $600 a year and is credited with saving as many as 50 people and at least one dog from drowning in the nearby waters. In addition to maintaining the light for 35 years, she raised two children, Jake and Mamie, on Robbins Reef, rowing them one mile each way to Staten Island to attend school. She retired in 1919 at the age of 71, and she moved to the Staten Island shore where she could see the light, now called Kate's Light.

*General Slocum* was consumed by fire and lost 1000 lives on its shore.

### Old Orchard Shoals Light

Gedney Channel, Lower New York Bay

Current Use: Active

Established: 1893

Owner: USCG

The white beacon is about three miles off the south shore in Raritan Bay. The brown and white tower stands 50.5 feet tall and sits on a caisson foundation. It is a spark plug or "bug light," which is a prefab cast-iron cylinder about 20-feet across that were assembled on-site. Sold in 2009 into private ownership for $235,000 by online auction.

### Prince's Bay Light

Mount Loretto Preserve, Staten Island

Current Use: Inactive, parkland

Established: 1828

Owner: NYS DEC

Contact: 718-482-4953 dec.ny.gov

A brownstone keeper's house and attached tower, the lighthouse was active from 1828 to 1922, serving the oystermen of Prince's Bay. For many years, Mt. Loretto orphanage owned the property and a statue of the Virgin Mary stood in the tower, in place of a light. The land is now a New York State-owned nature preserve, open to the public.

### Robbins Reef "Kate's" Light

Upper New York Bay

Current Use: Active

Established: 1883 stone; 1933 iron

Owner: USCG

The 45-foot high spark plug lighthouse sits on a small islet in the middle of the Upper Bay. Before the light was constructed, this hidden ledge of rocks had caused many wrecks. It is passed by the Staten Island Ferry and is best known for its keeper, Kate Walker.

### Romer Shoal Light

Swash Channel, Lower New York Bay

Current Use: Active

Established: 1898

Owner: USCG

A red band marks the 54-foot tall spark plug lighthouse fixed with a fourth order Fresnel lens showing a white flashing light. The lighthouse was originally located at the Lighthouse Service Depot, where it was used to test new oils and lenses.

### Sandy Hook Lighthouse

New York Lower Bay, NJ

Current Use: Active

Established: 1764

The nation's oldest operating lighthouse marks the southern entrance to New York Harbor from the shores of Sandy Hook, New Jersey. New York merchants conducted a lottery to raise funds to build the 85' tall rubblestone New York Lighthouse, later renamed Sandy Hook Light. It is part of the Gateway National Recreation Area.

### Staten Island Light

Ambrose Channel, Staten Island

Current Use: Active

Established: 1912

NYC Landmark

Owner: USCG

Located on a hilltop in a residential neighborhood, the beacon is visible for a range of 18 miles at sea. The rear channel light works in tandem with the West Bank Lighthouse. The structure has an octagonal tower and was one of the last brick lighthouses built. The keeper's house on Edinboro Road is now a private residence.

### Statue of Liberty

Liberty (Bedloe) Island

Current Use: National monument

Established: 1886

Owner: National Park Service

An aid to navigation from 1886 to 1902, Liberty Enlightening the World was the first lighthouse to use electricity. An onsite electric plant generates power to the electric torch, which was visible for 24 miles at sea.

### Stepping Stone Light

Long Island Sound

Current Use: Active

Established: 1878

Owner: USCG

The red brick lighthouse on a granite foundation, just off City Island. Its green flashing light warns mariners of the mussel encrusted reefs to the south. The keeper's house is no longer in use and the light has been put up for auction. Seen from the Bronx, but resides in Nassau County waters.

### Titanic Memorial Lighthouse

South Street Seaport, Manhattan

Current Use: Memorial

Established: 1915

Owner: South Street Seaport Museum

Marking the entrance to the Seaport district at the corner of Fulton and Pearl Street, the light is a tribute to those lost in the *SS Titanic* disaster on April 15, 1912. The 60-foot tall light was originally located on top of the old Seaman's Church Institute at South Street and Coenties Slip. A time ball attached to its pole would drop at noon each day, alerting ships in the port to set their watches.

### Throgs Neck Light

East River at Long Island Sound

Current Use: Active

Established: 1827; current tower 1934

At Fort Schuyler on the campus of SUNY Maritime College, the skeletal tower topped by an automated fixed red light with a range of 11 miles sits under the Throgs Neck Bridge. The first keepers, Samuel Young and Jeth Bayles, operated a bar for boaters and anglers at the site.

### West Bank Light

Ambrose Channel, Lower New York Bay

Current Use: Active

Established: 1901

Owner: USCG

The brown conical tower is the tallest of the offshore lights at 70 feet and shows a fixed white light. It is located five miles south of the Verrazano-Narrows Bridge, at the juncture of Ambrose Channel and visible from the beaches of Coney Island. The light was sold at auction for $245,000 to private owners who will maintain the structure while the US Coast Guard keeps the lights.

# MARITIME MUSEUMS

The high quality maritime collections of local institutions, historical societies and special libraries tell the story of the great seaport and preserve our maritime heritage through the artifacts on display and their archives. The repositories interpret this history through exhibits and educational services. They depict New York's maritime past and the vital role the harbor played in the economic life and growth of the metropolis.

The Morgan Library holds one of the most significant documents pertaining to the city's maritime heritage–the Cellere Codex. This report of Giovanni da Verrazano's voyage of 1524 for Francis I, King of France about the discovery of New York Harbor is the earliest first hand account of European exploration of North America.

# Maritime Collections

**City Island Nautical Museum**
190 Fordham St. Bronx. The museum, recently reopened after a fire, depicts the rich nautical history of this small island community. The collection includes paintings, photographs and memorabilia on famous yacht-builders and the role of City Island in the yachting industry, America's Cup challenges and Hell Gate Pilots. The museum is situated on one of the island's highest points in old Public School 17, originally built in 1897. Hours: Saturday and Sunday from 1 to 5pm or by appointment. Admission is free. 718-885-0008 cityislandmuseum.org Getting there: 6 to Pelham Bay Park, transfer to Bx29 Bus.

**Coney Island Museum** 1208 Surf Ave. at W 12 St. Artifacts of the amusement town's heyday, including a Steeplechase Horse, paired with a visitor and research center. Hours: Saturday and Sunday, 12-5pm. 718-372-5159 coneyislandusa.com Getting there: D, F, N, Q to Stillwell Ave.

**Ellis Island Immigration Museum**
National Park Service. Three floors of exhibits chronicle the history of the immigration processing station, where 12 million steerage and third class passengers entered the country between 1892 and 1954. The Main Building, an ornate French Renaissance Revival structure, houses the museum, a family history research center containing ship manifests and passenger lists, and library with a comprehensive oral history collection. Hours: Daily 9:30am-5pm. Admission is free, pay for ferry only. 212-363-3206 nps.gov/elis Getting there: Statue of Liberty Ferry from Battery Park.

**Fraunces Tavern Museum** 54 Pearl St. The site of Washington's farewell address to his troops and the founding

of the New York Yacht Club. The 1719 Georgian-style yellow brick house was purchased by Samuel Fraunces in 1762 and turned into a tavern. Sons of the Revolution, a genealogical organization preserving the memory of the struggle for liberty, purchased the property in 1904 for a museum. Hours: Tuesday to Saturday 12-5pm. 212-425-1778 fraincestavernmuseum.org Getting there: N to Whitehall St.; 1 to South Ferry; J, M, Z to Broad St.

**Governors Island National Monument**
The historic island, returned to the public after 200 years of restricted military use, is the site of the pivotal summit between President Reagan and Mikhail Gorbachev. The historic district, administered by the National Park Service, contains landmark Castle William, Fort Jay, and many significant buildings. Seasonal free access, guided tours, exhibits, and events. 212-825-3045 nps.gov/gois Getting there: Governors Island Ferry at Battery Maritime Building or Fulton Ferry Landing.

**Harbor Defense Museum** 230 Sheridan Loop, Fort Hamilton, Brooklyn. The museum occupies Fort Hamilton's caponier, a freestanding bastion located within the fort's dry moat. It features a collection of military artifacts dating from the Revolutionary War to WWII as well as a library and archive for public use. Hours: Monday to Friday 10am-4pm, Saturday to 2pm.

Admission is free. 718-630-4349 harbordefensemuseum.com Getting there: R to 95 St.

**India House** One Hanover Square. Originally founded as a private lunch club by merchant ship owners in 1914, India House preserves a collection of maritime art, which traces the history and expansion of American maritime commerce and includes the charter for the 1770 Marine Society of the City of New York. Tours by appointment. 212-269-2323 indiahouseclub.org Getting there: 4, 5 to Wall St.; A, C to Broadway-Nassau.

**Intrepid Sea-Air-Space Museum** Pier 86, W 46 St. A rare look at a grand military vessel, the 900-foot long aircraft carrier *USS Intrepid* together with the guided missile sub *Growler*, 25 military aircraft on the ships deck and a 204-foot long Concorde supersonic jet. Hours: Vary by season. April to September open daily 10am-5pm. 212-245-0072 intrepidmuseum.com Getting there: A, C, E to 42 St./Port Authority; M42 Bus to 12 Ave.

**Maritime Industry Museum** SUNY Maritime College at Fort Schuyler, Bronx. One of the largest collections of maritime industry artifacts in the nation, from the Evolution of Seafaring exhibit and a scale model of the 1942 Brooklyn Navy Yard to models of famous passenger liners and underwater artifacts recovered from ships sunk in and around New York harbor. Hours: Monday to Saturday, 9am-4pm. Admission is free. 212-409-7218 sunymaritime.edu Getting there: 6 to Westchester Sq. transfer to Bx40 Bus; Express Bus: Manhattan-Throgs Neck, call 718-994-5500 for schedule.

**Monitor Museum** Charted by the State in 1996 to establish a home near the original homeport of the *USS Monitor* on Bushwick Inlet. 718-383-2637 greenpointmonitormuseum.org

**Museum of the City of New York** 1220 5 Ave. Maritime artifacts, carved figureheads, nautical instruments and prints, as well as a hundred ship's models and paintings by local marine artists. Hours: Tuesday to Sunday 10am-5pm. 212-534-1672 mcny.org Getting there: 6 to E 103 St.

**National Museum of the American Indian** One Bowling Green. Located in the former Alexander Hamilton U.S. Custom House, a Beaux Arts building designed by Cass Gilbert and ornamented in shells, marine creatures, and sea signs decorating the interior. In the rotunda dome, maritime murals by New York painter Reginald Marsh (1898–1954) trace the course of a ship entering New York Harbor. The museum is part of the Smithsonian Institution. Hours: Daily 10am-5pm, Thursdays to 8pm. Admission is free. 212-514-3700 nmai.si.edu Getting there: N, R to Whitehall St., 4, 5 to Bowling Green, 1 to South Ferry.

**New York Historical Society** 2 W 77 St. The collection includes ship logs, Hudson River School landscapes, John James Audubon's watercolors for "The Birds of America," and millions of manuscripts, maps, books, and artifacts. 212-873-3400 nyhistory.org Getting there: B, C to W 79 St.

**Noble Maritime Collection** Snug Harbor, 1000 Richmond Ter. The collection features maritime paintings, drawings and lithographs by artist John A. Noble and other maritime artists. Noble's restored houseboat studio is on exhibit along with a maritime library and over 6,000 historical photographs. Hours: Thursday–Sunday 1-5pm. 718-441-6490 noblemaritime.org Getting there: Staten Island Ferry to Bus S40.

**New York Unearthed** 17 State St. An urban archeological center, a project of South Street Seaport Museum, features dioramas and artifacts from

> **John A. Noble**, Maritime Artist (1913-1983) Born in Paris, John Noble came to America in 1919. Although he studied to be an artist, Noble made his living as a seaman on schooners and marine salvage vessels beginning in 1928. In 1941, Noble began to build a houseboat art studio out of salvaged parts from the yards on the Kill van Kull. He retired from seafaring in 1946 to become a full-time artist. Inspired both by the ships that surrounded him and the men that worked on them, Noble chronicled New York maritime life at a time when sailing ships were being replaced by newer vessels. He led the fight against developers to preserve the 83-acre seamen's retirement compound, Snug Harbor, which is now a cultural center housing a collection of Noble's work and the restored houseboat studio.

the city's archeological digs spanning 6,000 years of history. The museum lost hundreds of thousands of artifacts in an underground lab at the Twin Towers on September 11, 2001. Open by appointment only. 212-748-8786 southstreetseaportmuseum.org Getting there: 1 to South Ferry; 4, 5 to Bowling Green; N, R to Whitehall St.

**Rockaway Museum** 88-08 Rockaway Beach Blvd., Queens. A permanent exhibit featuring 350 years of memorabilia and archival materials of Rockaway's halcyon days. Contact for hours or operation. 718- 634-4000 Getting there: A to Rockaway Park.

**Seamen's Church Institute** 241 Water St. A public gallery displays visiting maritime exhibits and a permanent collection of ships models, paintings and artifacts at one of the city's oldest maritime institutions, founded in 1834 to minister to merchant seafarers. 212-349-9090 seamenschurch.org Getting there: J, M, Z, 2, 3, 4, 5 to Fulton St.

**South Street Seaport Museum** 12 Fulton St. The museum encompasses an 11-square-block historic district of 19th century buildings and a fleet of century old vessels docked at Pier 16. The landmark Schermerhorn Row (12 Fulton St.) counting houses, built on landfill in 1812 by ship owner Peter Schermerhorn, are the architectural centerpiece of the Seaport District. The upper floors of the block-long "Row" and the adjoining A.A. Low Building contain 24 galleries that house the museum's exhibits which chronicles the seaports history dating to the Dutch colonial era. The floors above 92-93 South Street were formerly occupied by the Fulton Ferry Hotel, which inspired writer Joseph Mitchell in his classic story *Up in the Old Hotel*. Additional exhibits are on view at the Water Street galleries. Hours vary by season. 212-748-8786 southstreetseaportmuseum.org Getting there: A, C to Broadway-Nassau; J, M, Z, 2, 3, 4, 5 to Fulton St.

**Snug Harbor Cultural Center** 1000 Richmond Terrace, Staten Island. Established in 1833, Snug Harbor was the nation's first seamen's retirement home and hospital. The sanctuary was created at the bequest of Captain Robert Randall, who left his fortune to create a home for "aged, decrepit and worn-out sailors." A cultural center since 1976, the 83 acre site is a National Historic Landmark District containing 26 historic buildings. Hours: Tuesday to Sunday 10am-5pm. 718-448-2500 snug-harbor.org Getting there: Ferry to S40 Bus.

**Staten Island Museum** 75 Stuyvesant Place, Staten Island. Founded in 1881, the collection features maritime art, shells, specimens, history archives and a library. Hours: Monday to Sunday 12-5pm. 718-727-1135 statenislandmuseum.org Getting there: Staten Island Ferry, just two blocks from the St. George Terminal.

**Statue of Liberty Museum**
In the pedestal of Lady Liberty, the museum displays the original torch and history of the statue. Hours: Daily 9:30am-5pm. 212-363-3206 nps.gov/stli Getting there: Statue of Liberty Ferry.

Waterfront Museum 290 Conover St. Red Hook, Brooklyn. A floating museum housed in a restored 1914 railroad barge founded in 1986, it has a permanent exhibit of artifacts and serves as a classroom to bring maritime history to life for students and visitors. 718-624-4719 waterfrontmuseum.org Getting there: F, G to Smith/9 St. transfer B77 bus to Conover St.

## Libraries & Historical Societies

**American Family Immigration History Center** 292 Madison Ave., Ellis Island. The Ellis Island Archives include arrival records of more than 22 million immigrants. 212-561-4588 ellisisland.org

**Bayside Historical Society Maritime Gallery**, Bldg. 208, Fort Totten. The Society is based in the historic 1870 Officer's Club, a landmark Gothic Revival structure built by the Army Corp of Engineers, on the National Register of Historic Places. The space exhibits the collection of the old Bayside Yacht Club. 718-352-1548 baysidehistorical.org

**Broad Channel Historical Society** Broad Channel Library 16-26 Cross Bay Blvd. The society documents the history of this unique island community. broadchannelhistoricalsociety.org

**Bronx County Historical Society** 3309 Bainbridge Ave., Bronx. Research library and historical archives. 718-881-8900 bronxhistoricalsociety.org

**Brooklyn Historical Society** 128 Pierrepont St. Exhibits highlight the borough's working waterfront. 718-222-4111 brooklynhistory.org

**Gotham Center of NYC History** CUNY Graduate Center 265 5 Ave. Established by *Gotham* author Mike Wallace to promote the historical assets of the city. 212-817-8460 gothamcenter.org

**Greater Astoria Historical Society** 35-20 Broadway, 4 Flr, Long Island City. Preserves the past of the Queen's waterfront community. 718-278-0700 astorialic.org

**John Ericsson Society of New York** 250 E 63 St. Organization dedicated to research concerning the life and work of Capt. John Ericsson, the Swedish engineer who designed the ground breaking USS Monitor. johnericsson.org

**Melville Library** 213 Water St. The library of South Street Seaport Museum shelving 20,000 books and publications related to the history of the Port. It is currently open by appointment. 212-748-8786 southstreetseaportmuseum.org

**Queens Historical Society**
143-135 37 Ave. In the historic 1785 Kingsland Homestead farmhouse, the space holds a museum, research library and archives. 718-939-0647 queenshistoricalsociety.org

**National Archives** NE Division
201 Varick St. The records of the 1904 *Slocum* disaster are among the archives, which offers exhibits and genealogy workshops. 212-401-1620 archives.gov/northeast/nyc

**NYC Department of Parks & Recreation Library** 830 5 Ave. The Arsenal, Central Park. A public library and photo archive of more than 200,000 images devoted to the history of city parks. Open by appointment. 212-360-8240 nycgovparks.org

**New York City Municipal Archives**
31 Chambers St. Founded in 1950, the archives maintain over 90,000 cubic feet of records, including the papers of Robert Moses, manuscript records of the Works Progress Administration (WPA) NYC unit, and the original plans for the Brooklyn Bridge. Hours: Monday to Thursday, 9am-4:30pm, Friday to 1pm. 212-788-8580 nyc.gov

**New York Correction History Society**
Chronicles the history of the city's prisons at places like Hart, Welfare and Rikers islands. correctionhistory.org

**New York Public Library** 5 Ave at 42 St. The local history division and map collection provide a wealth of maritime historical information, including early charts of the harbor. nypl.org

**Old York Library** CUNY Graduate Center, Seymour B. Durst Reading Room. The unique collection of late real estate developer Seymour Durst consists of books, maps, postcards and memorabilia. By appointment only. oldyorklibrary.org

**Roebling Chapter of the Society of Industrial Archeology** Promotes the study of the City's industrial past. sia-web.org

**Roosevelt Island Historical Society**
Maintains a complete archive of Roosevelt Island's unique history. rihs.us

**Sandy Ground Historical Society**
1538 Woodrow Rd. Staten Island. Museum and library chronicling the oldest community of freed slaves in North America, who made their living as oystermen in Raritan Bay. Hours: Tuesday to Sunday 1 to 4pm. 718-317-5796

**Staten Island Historical Society & Historic Richmond Town** 441 Clarke Ave. A living museum village containing 15 buildings and archival records in the former county seat of Richmond County. Hours vary with season. 718-351-1611 historicrichmondtown.org

**Stephen B. Luce Library** SUNY Maritime College, Bronx. Archives document maritime history since 1700's, including 80,000 volumes in marine engineering and transportation, naval architecture and oceanography. 718-409-7236 sunymaritime.edu/stephenblucelibrary

# PADDLING

Paddling New York City's busy waters offers great adventure to explore nearly 578 miles of coastline from a completely new perspective, sea level. The New York City Water Trail, inaugurated in 2008, connects miles of rivers, bays, creeks, canals and inlets where experienced and novice paddlers alike can drift past the amazingly scenic canyon of skyscrapers in Lower Manhattan or enjoy Jamaica Bay's quiet salt marshes and natural beauty. Human-powered craft share the water with commercial vessels, excursion boats, ferries and pleasure boats, all of which have right of way in some of the most heavily trafficked waterways in the country. Visibility on the water and knowledge of local currents and tides are critical. Boats must be carried to the water. The water is cold, there is chop and the currents are swift, reaching four knots.

Canoes are great for exploring the shallow creeks that meander through the saltwater wetlands of city parks or, take it up a notch, and paddle an outrigger canoe. Unlike traditional canoes, 45-foot-long, six-person Hawaiian-style outriggers are seafaring boats with a built-in stabilizer - ama. The Liberty World Outrigger race is one of the largest competitive sporting events on local waters. Nearly 100 international teams participate in the race around the Harbor.

To get your feet wet, community boathouses offer free public kayaking during warm weather months. Once you learn the basics, join guided paddles around the harbor. In addition to the free programs, local outfitters provide instruction and guided tours.

Seasonal canoeing activities are offered by Urban Park Rangers and National Park Service at Gateway National Recreation Area. Tours are offered of the Bronx River with Bronx River Alliance and the Gowanus Dredgers schedule paddles on the Gowanus Canal. Experienced paddlers can try a circumnavigation paddle around Manhattan Island. The 28.5-mile trip takes seven to ten hours timed to take full advantage of tides. The season starts April 1 to October 31. Chart your course on the city's blueways with a NYC Water Trail Map and Guide, available at city parks and community boathouses.

# Kayak & Canoe Programs

**Appalachian Mt. Club NY/NJ** 5 Tudor City Place. Canoe & kayak lessons, boats for rent, training and trips. amc-ny.org

**Bronx River Alliance** Guides lead canoe tours of the upper and lower stretches of the Bronx River, and organize full river paddles and the Bronx River Flotilla each spring. bronxriver.org

**Columbia University Kayak Club** Whitewater club open to Columbia students, alumni, faculty, and staff. columbia.edu/cu/kayak

**Downtown Boathouse** The boathouse that started the city's kayak craze, runs free public walk-up kayaking at locations on the Hudson River at Pier 40, Pier 96, and Riverside Park South (their home at Pier 26 is being rebuilt) on summer weekends and holidays from 10am-5pm. Also offers free harbor trips, storage, training sessions and winter pool program. downtownboathouse.org

**Gowanus Dredgers Canoe Club** Free Discovery Tours of the Gowanus Canal are scheduled monthly. Membership is not necessary to participate in programs. The Container-boathouse and launch are at 2 St., Brooklyn. gowanuscanal.org

**Hudson River Paddlers Guild** Nonprofit that promotes kayak safety programs, such as its Captains & Paddlers Day where commercial operators meet with human-powered boaters to share safety concerns. hrpg.net

**Hudson River Water Trail Association.** The trail stretches from Albany to Manhattan, featuring launches and campsites every seven miles. Membership includes a trail guide. hrwa.org

**Inwood Canoe Club** The city's oldest canoe and kayak club, founded in 1902 offers open house paddles on Sundays during summer. Paddling trips, competition and boat storage from the red boathouse on the Hudson River at the foot of Dyckman St. about 100 yards south on the service road. inwoodcanoeclub.org

**Kayak Staten Island** Free walk-up kayaking for all ages on weekends at both South Beach and Midland Beach, where they have a shipping container-boathouse. kayakstatenisland.org

**Long Island City Community Boathouse** Free walk-up kayaking and scheduled paddles on the East River from Hallet's Cove and the group's boathouse at Hunters Point. licboathouse.org

**National Park Service (GATE)** Free beginner kayaking at Canarsie Pier, plus guided canoe trips from Floyd Bennett Field by park rangers of the Jamaica Bay Unit of Gateway National Recreation Area, home to the annual kayak fishing tournament. 718-338-3799 nps.gov/gate

**New York City Water Trail Association** Representing more than 20 local paddling, rowing and waterfront advocacy organizations, the group was formed to promote water access and expand the New York City Water Trail. nycwatertrail.org

**NY Kayak Polo** Hudson River Park, Pier 66. Play is weekly on the Hudson. Also offers introductory sessions and tournament play. nykayakpolo.org

**NY Outrigger Club** Hudson River Park, Pier 66. Hawaiian-style canoe paddling, instruction and racing. Host of the annual Liberty World Challenge. Free early morning introductory paddles. newyorkoutrigger.org

## TIDES

| | |
|---|---|
| Tide | Vertical rise and fall of sea level caused by the gravitational pull of the moon and sun on the Earth |
| Tidal Current | Horizontal movement of a body of water |
| Tidal Day | Interval between 2 high tides - 24h:51 min (Lunar Day) |
| Tidal Cycles | New York Harbor has semidurnal tides, 2 high and 2 low changing each 6h:12.5m |
| Tidal Range | Tides in NY Harbor are 4 - 6 ft (The difference in height between high and low water) |
| Ebb Tide | Retiring tide, outflowing water |
| Eddy | Current moving counter to the main flow |
| Flood Tide | Incoming, rising tide |
| Neap Tide | Less than average tide, occurs two times a month, during first and thrid quarters of the moon |
| Slack Tide | Still water at the turn of low tide |
| Spring Tide | Greater than average tide occurring at new and full moon |

Plan your route with the currents. A current chart shows direction and speed of each tidal current cycle by hour. Use the *Eldridge Tide And Pilot Book* to determine currents and the timing of high and low tides.

**NY River Sports** Pier 66 boathouse is home to a variety of human-powered boating groups, including Manhattan Kayak, NY Kayak Polo, Outrigger, and Hudson River Community Sailing. pier66nyc.org

**Red Hook Boaters** Free paddling scheduled monthly at Valentino Pier Park at the end of Coffey St. in Red Hook, Brooklyn. redhookboaters.org

**Sebago Canoe Club** Paerdegat Basin. Human-powered boating club offering Olympic flatwater sprint racing, clinics, boat storage, club fleet, instruction, canoe/kayak fly fishing, trips, and youth programs. 718-241-3683 sebagocanoeclub.org

**Touring Kayak Club of New York** 205 Beach St. Established in 1927, located on the City Island waterfront with access to Long Island Sound. 718-885-3193 touringkayakclub.org

**Urban Park Rangers** Free guided trips, moonlight paddles and clinics at city parks in all five boroughs. nyc.gov/parks/rangers

### Outfitters

**Manhattan Kayak Company** Hudson River Park, Pier 66. All levels of instruction and tours, including full moon paddles, paddle & pub and a popular sushi tour. manhattankayak.com

**NY Kayak Company** Hudson River Park, Pier 40. Full service outfitter and folding kayak specialist, with storage. nykayak.com

## Launch Policy & Permits

**Hudson River Park (HRP)** There are several boathouses each operated by various community boating clubs and offering free public programs. A permit is not necessary. Contact boathouses directly for launching or landing. hudsonriverpark.org

**Governors Island** A floating dock is for landing only, open for group events by special permit. Contact GIPEC 212-440-2202 govisland.com

**Jamaica Bay Hand Vessel Permit (NPS)** The National Park Service requires a vessel permit tag be displayed at all times for paddlers using the launches on the Jamaica Bay Water Trail. The annual fee is $50 for a permit obtainable at the Floyd Bennett Field Ranger Station. 718-338-5094 nps.gov/gate

**NYC Department of Parks & Recreation Launch Permit (NYC)** Most of the public launches are on city parkland. The annual launch sites permit is $15, purchased at NYC DPR offices in each borough. Launch facilities open from dawn to dusk, April 1 to December 1. 212-360-8133 nycgovparks.org

**NYS Office of Parks, Recreation, & Historic Preservation** Operates Roberto Clemente Park launch used by college crews. 212-866-3100 nysparks.state.ny.us

**US Coast Guard Event Permit** Required for large in-water events, such as large group paddle trips. 718-354-4197 uscg.mil/d1/units/actny

### Places to Canoe

- Alley Pond Park
- Bronx River
- Fresh Creek/Richmond Creek
- Gowanus Canal
- Inwood Hill Park
- Jamaica Bay
- Orchard Beach Lagoons
- Marine Park
- Davis Wildlife Refuge
- Wolfe's Pond Park

## NYC Water Trail Launches

| | Launch | Permits | Beach | Floating Dock | Ramp | Drinking Water | Fishing | Parking | Restrooms | Storage |
|---|---|---|---|---|---|---|---|---|---|---|
| **MANHATTAN** | **1** Pier 40, W Houston St. Hudson River | HRP | | • | | • | • | • | • | • |
| | **2** Pier 66, W 26 St. Hudson River | HRP | | • | | • | | | • | • |
| | **3** Pier 84, W 42 St. Hudson River | HRP | | • | | • | • | • | • | |
| | **4** Pier 96, W 56 St. Hudson River | HRP | | • | | • | • | • | • | • |
| | **5** Riverside South, W 72 St. Hudson River | NYC | | • | | • | • | | • | |
| | **6** 79th St Boat Basin, W 79 St. Hudson River | NYC | | • | | • | • | • | • | • |
| | **7** West Harlem Piers, W 125 St. Hudson River | NYC | | • | | • | • | • | • | |
| | **8** Inwood Hill Park, Dyckman Rd. Hudson River | NYC | • | | | • | • | | | |
| | **9** Sherman Creek, W 202 St. Harlem River | NYC | • | | | • | • | • | | |
| **BRONX** | **10** Barretto Point Park, Tiffany St. East River | NYC | • | | • | • | • | • | • | |
| | **11** Hunts Point Riverside Park, Lafayette Ave. Harlem River | NYC | | • | | | • | | | |
| | **12** Shoelace Park, 219 St. Bronx River | NYC | • | • | • | • | • | • | • | |
| | **13** Clason Point Park, Sound View Ave. Pugsley Cr | NYC | | | • | | • | | | |
| | **14** Pelham Bay Park, Lagoons, Long Island Sound | NYC | • | | | • | • | • | • | |

250 Get Wet

| | NYC Water Trail Launches | Permits | Beach | Floating Dock | Ramp | Drinking Water | Fishing | Parking | Restrooms | Storage |
|---|---|---|---|---|---|---|---|---|---|---|
| BROOKLYN | **15** Newtown Creek<br>Provost St. Newtown Creek | DEP | | | • | • | | • | • | |
| BROOKLYN | **16** Valentino Pier & Park<br>Buttermilk Channel | NYC | • | | | • | • | • | | |
| BROOKLYN | **17** Gowanus Canal<br>2 St. Gowanus Canal | | | • | | | | | | |
| BROOKLYN | **18** Plumb Beach<br>Belt Pkwy, Rockaway Inlet | NPS | • | | | • | • | • | • | |
| BROOKLYN | **19** Salt Marsh Nature Center<br>Ave U & E 33 St. Gerritsen | NYC | | | • | • | | • | • | |
| BROOKLYN | **20** Floyd Bennett Field<br>Flatbush Ave. Dead Horse Bay | NPS | | | • | • | • | • | • | |
| BROOKLYN | **21** Mill Basin Outlet<br>Floyd Bennett Field | NPS | • | | | • | • | • | • | |
| BROOKLYN | **22** Mill Basin Marina<br>Ave. Y & 69 St. Mill Basin | NYC | | • | | • | • | • | • | • |
| BROOKLYN | **23** Paerdegat Basin<br>Jamaica Bay | NYC | | • | | • | • | • | • | • |
| BROOKLYN | **24** Canarsie Pier<br>Belt Pkwy. Jamaica Bay | NPS | • | | | • | • | • | • | |
| QUEENS SOUTH | **25** North Channel Bridge<br>Cross Bay Blvd. Jamaica Bay | NPS | • | | | | • | • | • | |
| QUEENS SOUTH | **26** Idlewild Park Preserve<br>Huxley & Craft Ave. | NYC | | | • | | | | | |
| QUEENS SOUTH | **27** Bayswater Park<br>Beach 35 St. Jamaica Bay | NYC | • | | | • | • | | • | |

| | NYC Water Trail Launches | Permits | Beach | Floating Dock | Ramp | Drinking Water | Fishing | Parking | Restrooms | Storage |
|---|---|---|---|---|---|---|---|---|---|---|
| **QUEENS NORTH** | **28** Bayside Marina<br>Cross Island Pkwy. | NYC | | • | • | • | • | • | • | • |
| | **29** Little Bay Park<br>Totten Ave. Little Neck Bay | NYC | • | | | • | • | • | • | |
| | **30** Francis Lewis Park<br>3 Ave. East River | NYC | • | | | • | • | | • | |
| | **31** World's Fair Marina, Pier 1<br>Northern Blvd. Flushing Bay | NYC | | | • | • | • | • | | • |
| | **32** Hallets Cove<br>Vernon Blvd. East River | NYC | • | | | | | | • | |
| **STATEN ISLAND** | **33** Buono Beach/Austen House<br>Hylan Blvd. Lower Bay | NYC | • | | | | • | • | • | |
| | **34** South Beach<br>Fr. Capadanno Blvd. | NYC | • | | | • | | • | • | |
| | **35** Midland Beach<br>Fr. Capadanno Blvd. | NYS | • | | | • | | • | • | |
| | **36** Great Kills Park<br>Hylan Blvd. Atlantic Ocean | NPS | • | | • | • | • | • | • | |
| | **37** Lemon Creek Park<br>Seguine or Sharrot Ave. | NYC | • | | | • | • | • | • | • |
| | **38** Conference House Park<br>Hylan Blvd. Arthur Kill | NYC | • | | | | • | • | • | |

## Free Community Boating

Free walk-up kayaking, canoe trips, and community rowing opportunities are offered in all five boroughs by the following clubs and organizations:

- Bronx River Alliance
- Downtown Boathouse
- Floating the Apple
- Gowanus Dredgers
- Inwood Hill Canoe Club
- LIC Community Boathouse
- Kayak Staten Island
- Red Hook Boaters
- Rocking the Boat
- Sebago Canoe Club
- Urban Divers
- Village Community Boathouse

## NYC Water Trail

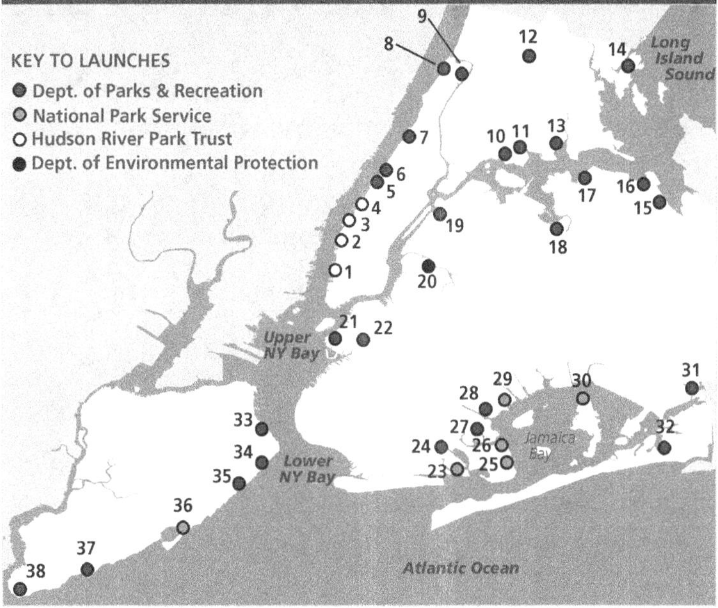
KEY TO LAUNCHES
Dept. of Parks & Recreation
National Park Service
Hudson River Park Trust
Dept. of Environmental Protection
Long Island Sound
Upper NY Bay
Lower NY Bay
Jamaica Bay
Atlantic Ocean
1
2
3
4
5
6
7
8
9
10
11
12
13
14
15
16
17
18
19
20
21
22
23
24
25
26
27
28
29
30
31
32
33
34
35
36
37
38

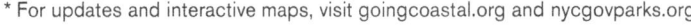

* For updates and interactive maps, visit goingcoastal.org and nycgovparks.org

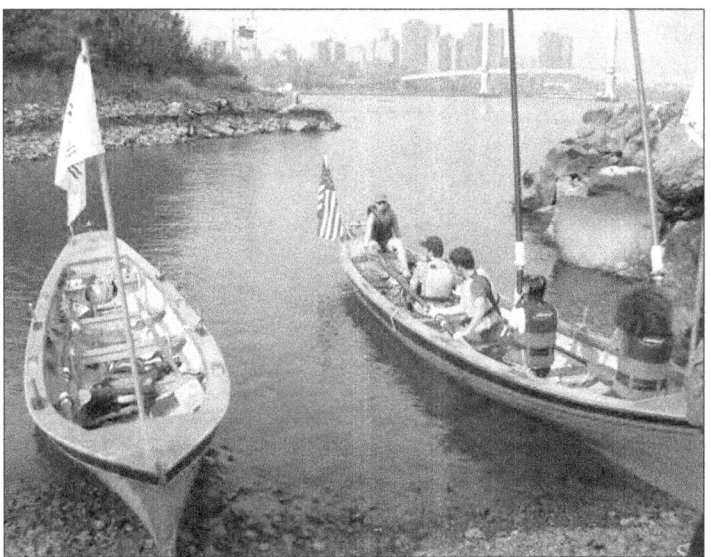

# ROWING

On December 9, 1824, the first rowing competition in the United States took place in New York Harbor. The Whitehall gig *American Star* rowed to victory against a British rowing team before a crowd of 50,000 spectators to win $1000 in prize money. John Magnus was the 14-year-old coxswain who steered the U.S. team to victory, and a year later presented the sleek Brooklyn-built *American Star* as a gift from the city to the Marquis de Lafayette. The boat, still on display in La Grange, France, is the oldest Whitehall in existence. Whitehalls, believed to be named for the busy landing at the foot of Whitehall Street, were the water taxis of the harbor in the 1800s. Today, classic 25-foot-long, four-oared Whitehall gigs have been revived in boat building and rowing programs throughout the city. The annual American Star Race commemorates the city's first rowing event and celebrates the sturdy Whitehall gigs of the Harbor.

New York is the birthplace of both the indoor rowing machine and the sliding seat, invented by John Babcock in 1870. The early history of American sculling was born on the Hudson and Harlem rivers. So many boathouses lined the riverbanks that it was called "Sculler's Row." Atalanta at Christopher Street was one of the earliest, and the first boating club to row around Manhattan Island, which they did in 1848. The country's first women's crew launched on the Harlem River in 1932.

Columbia University's team drills on the 2000 meter, three-lane Harlem River Course. During the spring race season, shuttles transport spectators from starting line at Class of 1929 Boathouse to the regatta finish at Sherman Creek. Races can be viewed from High Bridge Park. College crews also pull oars on the Orchard Beach Lagoons, which were first dredged in 1964 for Olympic flatwater trials. Sculls are the long oars used to propel the shell (boat) through the water. A racing shell is 60-feet-long, 22-inches wide and accommodates eight-oarsmen. In recent years, rowing has been re-eintroduced on the Harlem. New York Restoration Project built one of the first new boathouses on the Harlem River in close to a hundred years, the $10 million Peter Jay Sharp floating boathouse.

## Rowing Programs

**East River C.R.E.W.** Community Recreation & Education on the Water offers youth rowing programs with Whitehalls on the East River out of E 90 Street. eastrivercrew.org

**Floating the Apple Team Rowing** Pier 84, Hudson River Park. Public rowing for adults and youth, and boat building, coxwain training, team rowing and racing. floatingtheapple.org

**Rocking the Boat** Youth rowing and open rowing in Whitehalls out of the Bronx. rockingtheboat.org

**Village Community Boathouse** Rowing Whitehall gigs out of Pier 40 in Hudson Rive Park. villagecommunityboathouse.org

## Sculling Programs

**Harlem River Community Rowing** Operating out of a "mobile boathouse" with boats, and modular dock. harlemrivercommunityrowing.org

**New York Athletic Club Rowing** Founded in 1868, one of the oldest teams in the country rowing from a boathouse on Travers Island on the Lagoons. nyacrowingclub.com

**New York Rowing Association** (NYRA) Community rowing and learn to row programs at Peter Jay Sharp boathouse. nyrowing.org

**Row New York** Free rowing program for high school girls that combines rowing skills, academic tutoring and self-esteem building. rownewyork.org

---

**Harbo & Samuelson**, Rowers. On June 6, 1896 at 5:00 p.m., two Norwegian immigrant fishermen, George Harbo (1869-1908) and Frank Samuelson (1865-1946) launched from the Battery and rowed across the Atlantic Ocean to Isles of Scilly, UK in an 18-foot-long boat with a 5-foot beam, they crafted themselves and named *Fox*. The perilous 3,000 mile voyage took 55 days and set a world record that still stands today. They rowed an average distance of 56 miles a day and survived being capsized by a huge wave. The trip was in response to a newspaper challenge offering the winner $10,000 and the rowers hope the feat would bring fame and fortune. Unfortunately, both men had to return to fishing shortly after their success.

# SAILING

The waters surrounding New York City offer a great variety of sailing conditions for sailors of all stripes – from luxury yachtsmen and ocean racers to day sailors and gunkholers. New York is a city of skyscrapers in a very nautical sense; the term was originally used to describe the tall masts of sailing ships. Today, forests of masts still reach for the sky at sheltered anchorages throughout the harbor. Navigational demands include strong currents, dense commercial traffic, shoals, and boats at anchor. Prevailing winds are generally from the southwest, but can come from anywhere. Tall buildings can cause a wind tunnel effect. Summer winds tend to blow in from the Atlantic Ocean. Whether cruising, bareboating, taking a sunset sail, or learning to tack, there are many sailing options in New York Harbor.

Basic Keelboat is the course that introduces beginners to the sport of sailing. After learning the basics, club membership is the best way to hone skills and gain access to sailboats. Clubs generally offer two categories of membership, Skipper or Crew, depending upon experience. Sailboats are available for rent at the New York Sailing Center on City Island.

Floyd Bennett Field provides some of the best land sailing around. The same winds that make Rockaway Inlet such a great place to sail a boat make the old airport runways ideal for sailing three wheeled carts.

## Sailing Clubs & Programs

### Manhattan

**Appalachian Mountain Club NY-NJ** Sail instruction aboard day sailers and cruisers on the Long Island Sound. 212-986-1430 amc-ny.org

**Atlantic Yachting** Basic Sailing and Youth Sailing Camp on the Hudson River from 79 Street Boat Basin. atlanticyachting.com

**Gotham City Sailing Association** Sailing enthusiasts meetup for crew opportunities. sailing.meetup.com/4/

**Hudson River Community Sailing** Youth sail program and adult lessons from Hudson River Park's Pier 66a. hudsonsailing.org

**Knickerbocker Sailing Association** Gay and lesbian sailing club offering basic learn to sail, cruising, racing, club fleet, and social activities. ksa-nyc.org

**Manhattan Sailing School** Upper New York Bay. A program of the Manhattan Yacht Club, sailing from North Cove in Battery Park City. The club offers a fleet of J/24 sailboats, clubhouse, cruising, regattas, and social and teen sailing programs. The clubhouse and spectator platform, designed by world-renowned Sparkman & Stephens, is anchored

**Morris "Rosie" Rosenfeld**, Maritime Photographer (1884-1968) One of America's foremost photographers of sailing yachts, Rosenfeld began taking photographs in grammar school. In 1910 he opened a studio near South Street, at first specializing in industrial and advertising photography. He began covering the America's Cup in the 1890s, served as Commodore of the Regatta Circuit Riders and helped found the Press Photographers Association in 1946. Mystic Seaport Museum holds a collection of his prints.

in the Harbor near Ellis Island. 212-786-0400 sailmanhattan.com

**New York Yacht Club** 37 W 44 St. The landmark 1901 clubhouse, a gift from J.P. Morgan, has eight bedrooms, the famed model room and a large collection of fine art. Members enjoy access to club fleet and clubhouse, one in Manhattan and another in Newport, cruising, regattas, and social activities. 212-382-1000 nyyc.org

**NYC Community Sailing Association** Offers basic sailing certification, use of club boats and frostbite winter series from facilities at Lincoln Harbor, Weehawken. sailny.org

**New York Harbor Sailing Foundation** Organizes sailing regattas and annual Sailor's Ball. "Operation Optimist" is a junior sailing program serving kids from 8 to 13 years of age. 212-786-1743 nyharborsailing.com

**New York Sailing Club** Members enjoy sailing New York Harbor and Long Island Sound. Members include boat owners and "Corinthians" – novices who learn by crewing on other member boats. nysailingclub.com

**Offshore Sailing School** National sailing school offers operating at Chelsea Piers. offshore-sailing.com

**SailTime NY** Long Island Sound. Fractional sailing provides group ownership in a sailboat and guaranteed sailing time, available in Manhattan and City Island. Also offering ASA certified sail training. 646-283-0452 sailtime.com

**South Street Seaport** Pier 16, East River. Free sailing lessons aboard the historic sailing ships are provided to docents helping to maintain the fleet. Volunteers crew the sloop *Pioneer* during public, school, and group sailing charters. The schooner *Lettie G. Howard* is certified as a Sailing School Vessel. 212-748-8786 southstreetseaportmuseum.org

## Bronx

**City Island Yacht Club** 63 Pilot St. Racing on the Long Island Sound since 1904, the club hold regattas, races and cruising, has a clubhouse, restaurant and offers non-boater memberships. cityislandyc.org

**Harlem Yacht Club** 417 Hunter Ave. City Island. In 1855, HYC started as a model yacht club at the foot of 125 St. Today, its clubhouse overlooks Eastchester Bay. 718-885-3078 hyc.org

**Eastchester Bay Yacht Racing Assn.** Consortium of City Island yacht clubs organizing inter-club races. ebyra.com

**Morris Yacht & Beach Club** 25 City Island Ave. The 150-year old clubhouse was devastated by fire in 2006, but is being rebuilt on the club's three park-like acres on the tip of City Island. morrisybc.com

**Olin Stephens**, Yacht Designer (1908-2008) Ranked number one on the New York Yacht Club's seniority list at the time of his death, Olin Stephens is considered the greatest yacht designer of the 20th century. Stephens produced a record eight America's Cup winners between 1937 and 1980, including: *Ranger* (1937), *Columbia* (1958), *Constellation* (1964), *Intrepid* (1967), Ted Turner's *Courageous* (1974), and *Freedom* (1980). Born in the Bronx and largely self-taught, Stephens partnered with yacht broker Drake Sparkman in 1929 to design some of the century's ground-breaking yachts and left an indelible stamp on sailing. The firm won acclaim when their boat *Dorade* was victorious in the 1931 Trans-Atlantic Race. In 1938, the Stephens brothers designed the Lightning class sailboat. The drafting boards of Sparkman & Stephens carry on in New York today. (sparkmanstephens.com)

**NY Sailing Center & Yacht Club** 560 Minneford Ave. The school has been in operation for over 35 years, offering sail instruction and member benefits, as well as sailboat rentals. 718-885-0335 startsailing.com

**Offshore Sailing School** Learn to sail from SUNY Maritime College campus at Fort Schuyler on Colgate 26 sailboats and Hunter cruising boats. 800-221-4326 offshore-sailing.com/fortschuyler.asp

**Project Sail, Inc.** Community-based youth sailing program aboard the *Green Lantern* sloop based on City Island. projectsail.net

**Stuyvesant Yacht Club** Eastchester Bay. 10 Centre St. The club takes its name from an East River ferryboat, the *Gerard Stuyvesant* that served as its first clubhouse in 1890. Benefits include waterfront clubhouse, club fleet, sail instruction, junior sailing programs, marine facilities, restaurant, and social activities. 718-885-1023 stuyvesantyc.org

## Brooklyn

**Deep Creek Yacht Club** Jamaica Bay. Started in 1959, the club was reactivated in 1999 at Gateway Marina, where members have regattas and social activities, as well as land sailing at Floyd Bennett Field. deepcreekyachtclub.com

**Miramar Yacht Club** 3050 Emmons Ave. Learn to sail programs at clubhouse on the coast of Sheepshead Bay, that includes a fleet of Ensigns, marina facilities, outdoor barbecue area, social events and swimming pool. 718-769-3548 miramaryc.com

**National Park Service (GATE)** The rangers at Floyd Bennett Field offer low cost sailing lessons for adults and youth groups in July and August. Reservations are required. 718-338-3799 nps.gov/gate

**Sebago Canoe Club** Jamaica Bay. 1400 Paedergat Ave. N. Human-powered boating club offers weekly Thursday evening races, cruises and canoe sailing, along with skills clinics. Club facilities include a mixed fleet of Sunfish and Lasers. 718-241-3683 sebagocanoeclub.org

**Sheepshead Bay Yacht Club** 3076 Emmons Ave. Bayfront clubhouse and bar, which offers members cruising, racing, a small boat fleet, transient moorings, social activities, and swimming pool. 718-891-0991 sheepsheadbayyc.com

**New York Yacht Club** The clubs's 132 year hold on the America's Cup is the longest winning streak in sporting history. The Cup is the oldest trophy in sports and the most coveted award in yachting. The elite yachting fraternity, founded in 1844 by John Cox Stevens and eight friends aboard Stevens' yacht *Gimcrack* while sailing in New York Harbor, has successfully defended 25 challenges. On August 22, 1851, the schooner *America* won the 100 Guinea Cup (renamed America's Cup) from the Royal Yacht Squadron by defeating 14 British yachts in a 53-mile race around the Isle of Wight. The syndicate that captured the trophy later assigned the Winner's Cup to the New York Yacht Club with a Deed of Gift, under condition that it be preserved as a perpetual Challenge Cup for friendly competition between foreign nations. The first challenge race took place in Upper New York Bay off the coast of Staten Island on August 8, 1870. In 1893, the series was moved to open seas off the New York coast and in 1930 the race was transferred to Newport, Rhode Island. The landmark Manhattan clubhouse of NYYC displays the carved eagle escutcheon of the yacht *America*.

## Queens

**TASCA - The American Small Craft Assn.** Meadow Lake, Flushing Meadows Corona Park. Affordable sailing programs with free advanced classes and use of club boats. sailtasca.org

**Rockaway Point Yacht Club** Jamaica Bay. The 1909 club affords easy access to some of the best city sailing at Rockaway Inlet from the clubhouse overlooking Jamaica Bay. There is a wait list for membership 718-474-9001 rockawaypointyachtclub.com

## Staten Island

**Richmond County Yacht Club** 142 Mansion Ave. The club established in 1923 is situated at the head of the club's pier and deep water facilities on Great Kills Harbor. The club offers a frostbite race series and youth sail training. 718-356-4120 rcyachtclub.org

**SailTime State Island** Fractional sailing from Staten Island and New Jersey sites: Jersey City, and Sandy Hook. 210-445-3020 sailtime.com

# SCUBA DIVING

There are more wrecks per square mile in the waters of New York Harbor than any place else on Earth. About 100 wrecks are explored regularly by divers. Most sent to the bottom by storms, sandbars, and collisions, they form accidental reefs that create fascinating underwater scenes and are great places to catch lobster, called "bugs" by divers, and spearfish. Wreck sites are also popular fishing grounds, so divers must be cautious not to get entangled in fishing line.

New York waters offer 10 to 15 feet of visibility inshore, 20 to 50 feet offshore, and up to 80 feet visibility when the Gulf Stream visits each year. Bottom temperatures reach 50° F in summer. Open Water Certification is the entry level course that prepares the beginner for dives of up to 60 feet. The next level takes the diver to depths of 130 feet. Certification starts with classroom and pool sessions then progresses to open water; it lasts a lifetime and is recognized worldwide. Further skills require other types of certification, such as wreck, nitrox, rescue, master, and commercial.

### Wreck Dives in New York Harbor

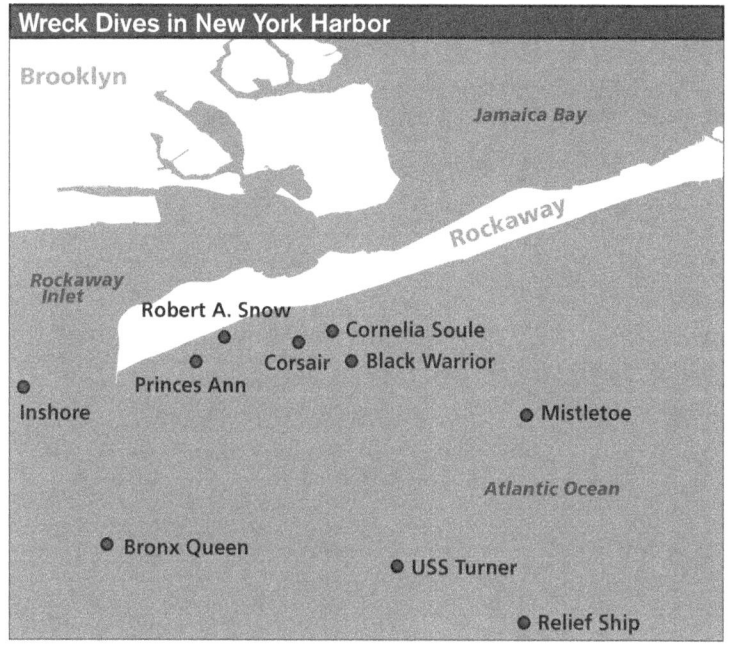

# Wreck Dives

### Black Warrior

Built: 1852
Sank: February 20, 1857
Loran: 26951.8 43755.3

The 225 foot long wooden side wheel steamer rigged with sails ran aground on the Rockaway shoals in dense fog and sits in 35 feet of water off Jacob Riis Park.

### Bronx Queen

Built: 1942
Sank: December 2, 1989
Loran: 26968.8 43735.1

A wooden hulled 110 foot long fishing party boat, converted from a WWII sub chaser built by Mantic Yacht of Camden, NJ, that sank off Breezy Point where she rests at a depth of 35 feet.

### Cornelia Soule

Built: unknown
Sank: April 26, 1902
Loran: 26954.7 43759.1

A three masted wooden hulled schooner, also known as the *Granite Wreck* so named for her cargo of granite jetty stones when she wrecked one mile off Rockaway Point and now lies in 25 feet of water.

### Inshore Schooner

Built: unknown
Sank: circa 1860
Loran: 27030.1 43774.5

An unidentified wooden schooner sits in 30 feet of water southwest of the Verrazano-Narrows Bridge, where divers have salvaged coconut shells and bottles.

### Mistletoe

Built: 1872
Sank: October 5, 1924
Loran: 26933.3 43747.6

Wooden paddle wheel lighthouse tender converted to a fishing charter that burned to the waterline and sank. She rests in 42 feet of water four miles southwest of East Rockaway Inlet.

### Princess Ann

Built: 1897
Sank: February 6, 1920
Loran: 26968.3 43758.1

Three decked passenger liner that ran aground on the Rockaway shoals and now sits at a depth of 20 feet east of Rockaway Point.

### Relief Ship

Built: 1904
Sank: 1960
Loran: 26903.5 43695.9

Lightship struck by a freighter while on station at the entrance to New York Harbor, she lies intact in about 100 feet of water near Ambrose buoy.

### Robert A. Snow

Built: 1886
Sank: February 8, 1899

A cargo schooner, also called *Derrick Barge*, sank carrying a load of fertilizer and lies two miles east of Rockaway Point in 23 feet of water.

### USS Turner

Built: 1942
Sank: January 3, 1944
Loran: 26936.4 43725.6

A destroyer sunk in Ambrose Channel in an explosion resulting in 136 fatalities. It was dragged from shipping lanes and is scattered in 50 feet of water five miles off Debs Inlet.

## Submerged Cultural Heritage Resources

Some ship remains have been found during construction in Lower Manhattan, where ship hulls were often used for fill to extend the shoreline. In 1916, a worker digging the new subway line beneath Greenwich and Dey Streets hit on the charred remains of mariner Adriaen Block's *Tyger*. The ship, loaded with a cargo of furs, burned to the waterline in 1613 at the mouth of the Hudson. Today, the remnant is part of the collection at the Museum of the City of New York.

In 1982, during construction of a high rise at 175 Water Street, the hull of an 18th century merchant ship was discovered in colonial era landfill. It was nicknamed the Ronson Ship after the developer who held up construction while archeologists excavated the wreck. The ship, a British merchant frigate, was too costly to remove and conserve. Only the bow was preserved and is now on display at the Mariners Museum in Newport News, Virginia.

All abandoned shipwrecks and archeological resources located under New York's navigable waterways, within three nautical miles of shore, become the property of the people of New York State and are protected from scuba looters by law: "no collecting or excavating may occur on underwater sites without a permit." Five state agencies have jurisdiction over submerged cultural resources. Preserves protect artifacts for historians and provide public access for recreational divers.

### Submerged Heritage Permits
New York State Museum in Albany issues permits for underwater research and applications for underwater preserves. nysm.nysed.gov

### NPS Submerged Resource Center
Surveys the submerged resources in National Parks, such as the waters surrounding Ellis Island, Liberty Island

and Gateway National Park Area sites including Miller Field and Sandy Hook. They have mapped the remains of the steam ferryboat *Ellis Island*, which carried millions of immigrants from the Immigration Station to Manhattan between 1904 and 1954 and lies at the head of the ferry slip where it sank after the station closed. nps.gov/applications/submerged

**National Marine Sanctuaries** Established by NOAA in 1972 to protect shipwrecks and underwater sites, and designate sites marine sanctuaries. sanctuaries.noaa.gov

**National Ocean Services** Maintains a database of all wrecks and obstructions in U.S. waters, available online at noaa.gov.

**Navy Historical Center** Cultural Resource Section regulates preservation of sunken Navy ships and aircraft, issuing permits for archeological research. history.navy.mil

**Sea Grant's Underwater Cultural Resources** Coordinates a system of diving sites along the Seaway Trail. seagrant.sunysb.edu

# Dive Clubs & Shop

## Manhattan

**Adventure Scuba** 1737 York Ave. Dive center offers the National Geographic Diver Program to broaden diver awareness of underwater realms, in addition to gear, tank fills, certification courses, and scuba travel. 212-876-3483 adventurescubany.com

**Aqua-Lung School of New York** 436 W 20 St. School founded by diving legend Frances "Fran" Garr, PADI's first female master instructor, performer at the NY Worlds Fair "Sea Hunt" and a inaugural member of the Women Divers Hall of Fame. School offers training, travel and underwater photography. 212-582-2800

**Empire Divers** 303 E 81 St. PADI Dive Center offering scuba certification, travel, and equipment. 212-249-4534 empiredivers.com

**Leisure Pro** 42 W 18 St., 3 Floor. Dive gear and equipment showroom. 212-645-1234 leisurepro.com

**Mad Dog Expeditions International** Adventure and technical diving in remote regions of the world. 212-744-6763 maddogexpeditions.com

**Pan Aqua Diving** 460 W 43 St. Dive shop offering gear rentals, tank fills, local trips, travel and certification classes. 212-736-3483 panaqua.com

**Scuba Network** 655 6 Ave. & 669 Lexington Ave. Two locations offering gear rental, certification, and local dive trips. scubanetwork.com

**Sea Gypsies** Scuba club with over 100 members, meetings held on the second Wednesday of the month feature presentations on scuba-related topics. Club offerings include local dive trips, day and weekend charters, and dive travel. seagypsies.org

**Village Divers** 125 E 4 St. Full service dive shop providing gear rental, tank fills, certification, technical training, and local dives in New York Harbor. 212-780-0879. villagedivers.com

**Village Dive Club** Gay/lesbian diving club offers certification, local dive trips and dive vacations. villagediveclub.org

**YMCA Scuba** The "Y" began the first national scuba certification course in 1959. Select branches offer scuba training. ymcascuba.org

## Bronx

**Captain Mike's Diving Center**
530 City Island Ave. An International Training Center and PADI facility offering certification, equipment, gear rental, tank fills, night dives, local dive trips, wreck and salvage dives, and technical and rebreather training. 718-885-1588 captainmikesdiving.com

## Brooklyn

**Cultural Research Divers** A groups of commercial divers educate the public about underwater realms through programs like "Classroom on the Pier" live underwater tours and exhibits of items recovered from local wrecks. researchdivers.org

**Kings County Divers** 2417 Ave. U. No dues. Affordable introductory scuba course, no dues, club activities, tank fills, nitrox training, and dive trips. 718-648-4232 kcdivers.com

**NYPD Scuba Team** A part of the New York Police Department Harbor Unit, headquartered at Brooklyn Army Terminal, the team numbers about 30 officers performing water search and rescue, evidence recovery, and anti-terrorism. Scuba officers have a dual designation as U.S. Customs Agents for inspection of ships below the waterline for drugs and contraband. 718-765-4100 VHF Ch17

**Ocean Horizons Scuba**
861 71 St. Scuba instruction conducted at Prospect Park YMCA and Fort Hamilton HS. Retail shop and dive vacations. 718-833-3207 oceanhorizonscuba.com

**SCUBA New York** 2672 Gerritsen Ave. Dive shop with heated pool offering certification, gear rental, nitrox, and rescue training and local dive trips. 718-769-0099 scubanewyork.com

**Stingray Divers** 762 Grand St. Full service shop and scuba instruction. 718-384-1280 stingraydivers.com

**Urban Divers Estuary Conservancy (UDEC)** Educational programs at their Harlem River Ecology Center and Brooklyn Marine Field Station raise awareness of the harbor estuary through underwater video exploration, on water activities such as water monitoring, canoeing and eco-cruises. urbandivers.org

## Queens

**Aquatic Voyagers Scuba Club (AVSC)** Local chapter of the National Association of Black Scuba Divers offering members certification classes, dive trips, and youth instruction. avscdivers.org

**New York Scuba Diver** 35-44 Union St. Flushing. Scuba shop offering certification and local trips. 718-888-0245 nyscubadiver.com

## Staten Island

**Outdoor Adventures** 88 Guyon Ave. Retail outfitter and dive training center. 718-980-7547 sioutdooradventures.com

**Staten Island Sport Divers Meetup** Meet others who share a passion for scuba diving. meetup.com/sisdny

### Underwater Docents

The New York Aquarium invites dive volunteers to help maintain exhibit tanks and teach the public about the aquatic environment. Volunteers must be over 18 years old, certified, and have logged more than 25 dives. 718-265-4738 nyaquarium.org

*HMS Hussar* New York City's most famous and sought after wreck, the British frigate has been the object of search, salvage and speculation since 1780 when the 114-foot-long 26 gun vessel swept onto Pot Rock in Hell Gate and sank off the Bronx shore purportedly carrying the Redcoat payroll of $1 billion in gold and 50 American prisoners of war. The British made several attempts to locate the vessel. Thomas Jefferson even financed an early search and submarine inventor Simon Lake surveyed the site in the 1930s. Amateur archeologist Robert Apuzzo covers the century-old speculations in the book *The Endless Search for the HMS Hussar*.

## Dive Boats

Dive boats offer regularly scheduled wreck diving packages that can include full wet suit and tank rentals, air fills, instruction, wreck tours and live aboard trips. Day charters start at about $85 for two dives while overnight packages, including two days' diving plus onboard stay, are about $150.

**Eastern Dive Boat Association**
A local organization of dive boat owners and operators that promotes ocean conservation and historical preservation. edba.com

**Jeanne II** Sheepshead Bay, Pier 5. Shipwreck diving trips with Capt. Bill Redden aboard his 47 foot boat, offers two dives, plus a barbecue. 718-332-9574 jeanne-ii.com

**John Jack** Mansion Marina, Staten Island. Inshore and offshore ocean wreck diving, plus gear rental, tank fills, instruction and guided tours. 732-681-0806 captainzero.com

**Karen** Tamaqua Marina, Brooklyn. Captain Bob Hayes former commander of NYPD SCUBA team offers scheduled dive trips. 718-421-5547 diveboatkaren.com

**Sea Hawk** Little Neck. Capt. Frank Persico offers dive charters, instruction and light salvage. 718-279-1345 seahawkdive.com

**Wreck Valley** East Rockaway Inlet. Join Capt. Dan Berg for wreck diving, spear fishing, treasure hunting and more as you explore wrecks in New York waters. aquaexploreres.com

# SURFING

The beach the Ramones immortalized in their 1977 hit song, *Rock, Rockaway Beach* has attracted urban surfers since 1912, when the world's most famous surfer, Duke Paoa Kahanamoku, demonstrated surf boarding on Beach 38. Ever since, surfing has been a year-round tradition in Rockaway Beach. It is the only surfable break within city limits and is accessible by subway. The waves, currents, rocks, and riptides make the jetties very dangerous for inexperienced boarders.

The most consistent surf arrives in fall and winter. Average wave size is three to five feet with longshore drift traveling east to west, parallel to the shore. During hurricane season, distant storms send swells exceeding ten feet. Water temperature ranges from 35° F in the winter to 78° F by late summer, and wet suits are worn most of the year. The best time to surf is at high tide. The take off zone is the long rock jetty, where surfers sit on their boards waiting their turn at the waves. The jetty creates a hollow take off with left beach break over wood pilings. The shallow water causes plunging waves, called dumpers because the waves turn over on themselves. There are hundreds of regulars who surf Rockaway Beach, including a few national competitors. The line up includes short boarders, long boarders, knee boarders, and belly boarders. On good days, areas of ridable surf are crowded. The first surfer on the wave has right of way.

Beyond the Rockaways, New York City has plenty of devoted kiteboarders, wave surfers, standup paddleboarders, and windsurfers. Windsurfers rig and launch at Plumb Beach on Dead Horse Bay and Rockaway Inlet. The shallow water is flat to moderately choppy, making it a great place for beginners. Kite-surfers also fly there. In six to eight knot winds, a kite surfer can travel 20 mph piloted by a 20 meter foil kite, making up to 30 foot lifts on a 6 foot surfboard. Winds are best in spring and fall, and wind strength better in late afternoon. When the wind direction is offshore, sailboarders launch from the bay side of Breezy Point. A group of international surfers raises funds for charity with a standup paddle around Manhattan Island each summer. Standup paddleboards are classified as boats in the eyes of the Coast Guard, boarders must wear a lifejacket, carry a whistle, and follow boating safety.

# WAVES

| | |
|---|---|
| Wave | A disturbance, like wind, that transfers energy from one place to another |
| Crest | The highest point of a wave |
| Trough | Lowest point of a wave |
| Wave Height | Vertical distance between trough & crest |
| Wave Length | Horizontal distance between two crests |
| Wave Period | Time for two wave crests to pass the same point |
| Fetch Length | Length of sea over which a wind has blown; fetch + wind speed determines wave size |
| Swell | Waves that have moved past the wind that generated them |

## Surfing Sites

**Breezy Point Surf Beach (GATE)** 219 St. Dunes and wide beach at the western tip of the Rockaway Peninsula provide uncrowded surf but no facilities. nps.gov/gate

**Plum(b) Beach (GATE)** This is the place for kite boarding and windsurfing with convenient beachside parking and port-o-sans. nps.gov/gate.

**Rockaway Beach** The city's two surf-only beaches are between Beach 67-69 Streets and between jetties from Beach 87 to 92 Streets. DPR posts surf beach rules on their website. nycgovparks.org

## Learn to Surf

**Irie Brothers Surf Lessons** Sharing their experience and passion for surfing, packages include 3-hours of lessons, wet suit, board, snacks, and best wave photo. 646-932-9228 surflessonsnyc.com

**New York Kiteboard** 333 E 119 St. Kitesurfing lessons in all levels, single or multiple day clinics, with all gear. 646-752-4980 ny-kiteboard.com

**New York Surf School** Board rentals and surf lessons. 718-496-3371 surflessonsnewyork101.com

## Surf Clubs & Shops

**Billabong** 1515 Broadway. National outlet for surf wear. 212-840-0550 billabong.com

**Boarders** 192 Beach 92 St. Rent a board or locker and buy surf gear. 718-318-7997 boarderssurfshop.com

**Gotham Surf Club** 139 Beach 97 St. Club competition and surf events. 917-596-5011 gotham-surf-club.com

**Eastern Surfing Association** Amateur surf group for all skill levels. surfesa.org

**FTW Beach** 116 St. Rockaway. West coast transplanted gangsta surf shop.

**Kitesurf NYC** Charts, wind check and real-time and historical weather information for Rockaway Inlet. kitesurfnyc.com

> SURF REPORTS
> Iwindsurf.com
> magicseaweed.com
> Newyorksurf.com
> Surfline.com

**Mollusk** 210 Kent Ave. San Francisco board shop with outlet in Williamsburg, Brooklyn. 718-218-7456 mollusksurfshopnyc.com

**New York Bodyboarding** Shop, photo gallery, and forums for bodyboarders. nybodyboarding.com

**New York City Spongers** Urban bodyboarding club. nycspongers.com

**New York Pipe Dreams** 1623 York Ave. Surf board and wet suit sales, along with board repair. 212-535-7473 newyorkpipedreams.com

**Quiksilver Boardriders Club** 587 5 Ave. & 3 Times Square. National retailer of surf wear, boards and accessories. quiksilver.com

**Rockaway Beach Surf Shop** 177 Beach 116 St. The oldest surf retailer on the peninsula sells surf board, New York surf wear, and other beach stuff. 718-474-9345

**SEA Paddle NYC** World class surfers stand-up paddle for charity 28 miles around Manhattan Island in this project of Surfers Environmental Alliance to raise awareness of autism seapaddlenyc.org

**Surfers Environmental Alliance** An environmental organization committed to surfing, public beach access, and the coastal environment. seasurfers.org

**Surfrider NYC Chapter** The national surfing advocacy and conservation group with over 700 local members offering programs that include youth education, beach cleanups, water monitoring, and events, such as the Surf Film Festival. Chapter meetings are held on the 2nd Wednesday of the month at PostWorks located at 227 E 45 Street, summer meetings in Rockaway. surfrider.org/nyc

# SWIMMING

New York City hosts the world's longest swim race—the Manhattan Island Marathon. The demanding event attracts close to 100 swimmers, from world class marathoners to local relay teams. First organized in 1982, it is among the top marathons in the world and a qualifier for the English Channel swim. Swimmers have nine hours to complete the 28.5 mile counterclockwise, tide-assisted circuit around Manhattan Island. The race record 5 hours, 45 minutes, and 25 seconds, set in 1995 by Australian Shelly Taylor-Smith, who retired in 1998 following a record fifth victory in the marathon swim.

A growing number of competitive open water events allow people to legally swim in harbor waters. Otherwise, swimming is permitted only at approved beaches. There is a shortage of lifeguards which limits beach openings. The Department of Parks and Recreation hires more than 1000 lifeguards each summer and offers free training and a guaranteed job.

Coney Island is home to the famous Polar Bear Club, the country's oldest fraternity of cold water swimmers, founded in 1903. The club's New Year's Day plunge into the frigid Atlantic Ocean is a century old tradition. The Polar Bears host weekly swims during winter months and the club is the official registrar of winter swimming nationwide. The average dip lasts about five minutes in water temperatures 40° F and below.

## Learn to Swim

**Asphalt Green** Swim training for all ages and skill levels. 212-369-8890 asphaltgreen.org

**Learn-to-Swim** Free swim lessons for ages 3 to 14 at city park pools. 718-760-6969 nycgovparks.org

**NY Red Cross** Water safety instruction for lifeguards offered at Y's and heath clubs in all boroughs. nyredcross.org

**NYC Dept. of Parks & Recreation** Free lifeguard training and certification for eligible candidates. 212-397-3157 nycgovparks.org

**Swim Jim** 3 W 102 St. Aquatic education for all ages. swimjim.com

**Swim to Safety** A drowning prevention program for kids with little or no swimming ability. swimtosafety.org

**YMCA-NY** Swimming instruction at branches citywide. ymcanyc.org

## Open Water Swimming

Swim only at beaches with lifeguards. Undertows or rips are strong on the beaches of Rockaway, but can occur on any beach where waves are breaking. Rip currents are narrow, powerful channels of water pulling away from the shore. To swim out of the rip stay calm and swim parallel to the shore.

**Coney Island Brighton Beach Open Water Swimmers** Free open water swim training, races and weekly scheduled group swims April through November. cibbows.org

**Coney Island Polar Bear Club** The first in winterbathing clubs, the famed New Year's plungers swim every Sunday at 1:00 pm October through April, meets on Boardwalk at Stillwell Ave. polarbearclub.org

**Manhattan Island Foundation** Host of competitive open water swims, like the Manhattan Island Marathon. 212-873-8311 nycswim.org

**Gertrude Ederle**, swimmer (1906-2003). Known as "Trudy, Queen of the Seas," Gertrude Ederle grew up on the Upper West Side of Manhattan and gained international fame in 1926 by being the first woman to swim across the English Channel. Only 19 years old, Ederle swam 35 miles in 14 hours, 39 minutes, bettering the men's record by nearly two hours. Upon her return to New York, Trudy was greeted with a ticker tape parade attended by two million people. Gertrude Ederle's swimming career began at age 14 when she swam past 51 international athletes to win a 3.5 mile race from Manhattan to Brighton Beach. From 1921 to 1925, Ederle set 29 U.S. and world records for swimming. In 1924, she won three Olympic medals and a year later, swam from the Battery to Sandy Hook, NJ in 7 hours 11 minutes, breaking the men's record – a record that stood until 2006. Ederle in later life became deaf from her channel swim and devoted herself to teaching aquatics to hearing-impaired children. Today, the Manhattan Island Foundation hosts the annual 17.5 mile Ederle Swim between the Battery and Sandy Hook.

## Public Pools

The city's first public swimming pools were floating bathhouses stationed in the East and Hudson rivers. Launched in the late 1870 to about 1915, as many as 15 pools were moored off Manhattan's shores. The pools were large pontoon frames with netting in the center where people swam in the river. They were closed because of water pollution. Today, there is renewed interest in floating pools.

City Park's has 54 outdoor swimming pools and 10 indoor pools located in parks and recreation centers. Outdoor city pools are free, open June through Labor Day. Indoor city pools charge an annual fee. Here's a few with water views:

**Astoria Pool** 19 St. & 23 Dr. Queens. The city's largest and oldest public pool offers breathtaking views of the East River from the hilltop in Astoria Park.

**Faber Pool** 2175 Richmond Ter. Staten Island. Built of colored limestone, the pool overlooks the Bayonne Bridge and the tugs and tankers on the Kill Van Kull.

**Floating Pool Lady** A pool built on a steel deck barge, now at Barretto Point Park in the Bronx. floatingpool.org

**John Jay Park Pool** E 77 St. & cherokee Pl., Manhattan. A 145 foot pool, plus a diving pool overlooking the East River since 1940.

**Roberto Clemente State Park** Olympic pool on the Bronx banks of the Harlem River.

**Sunset Park Pool** 7 Ave. at 41 St. Brooklyn. Outdoor pool with water views of the Brooklyn Army Terminal.

### CSO

Wait 12 hours before swimming after heavy storms because of combined sewer overflow (CSO), when rainfall overwhelms water treatment plants resulting in raw sewage entering the water from New York City's 460 discharge pipes, plus New Jersey's 250 outfalls located throughout the harbor.

# WATER RESOURCES

The waterways and coast are a public commons. Everyone has the right to walk on the beach, fish from the shore and navigate the waters. The entitlement to coastal access is known as the Public Trust Doctrine. It has its roots in Roman civil law codified by Emperor Justinian in 530 AD, which states that flowing water, the sea, and the shores of the sea are common to all mankind. This concept that no individual can own the waters and submerged lands came to be recognized as property held by the State in trust for the people. The doctrine applies to all water influenced by the ocean's tide and includes the beaches up to the mean high water mark. Historically, the waterfront benefits held in trust were those crucial for commerce and navigation.

### Time Required for Waste to Dissolve at Sea

Paper: 4 week
Cotton Cloth: 1-5 month
Painted Wood: 13 years
Tin Can: 100 years
Aluminium Can: 200-500 years
Plastic Bottle: 450 years
Monofiliment Fishing Line: 600 years

## City

**FDNY Marine Division** Fireboats have protected the city's waterfront since 1840. Units: Marine Company 1 Manhattan, Marine Company 6 Brooklyn, Marine Company 9 Staten Island. nyfd.com/marine/marine.html.

**Dept. of City Planning (DCP)** 22 Reade St. Oversees land use regulation and zoning, and supervises coastal management. nyc.gov/dcp
• **Waterfront Revitalization Program (WRP)** Citywide coastal zoning framework for waterfront development, water dependent industries, public access, water quality, historical and cultural resources and restoration.

**Dept. of Environmental Protection (DEP)** 59-17 Junction Blvd. Flushing. Delivery of drinking water and wastewater treatment, administration of pumpouts and enforcement of air, noise, and hazardous material rules. Public access permits to fish State reservoirs and hike watershed lands. nyc.gov/dep

**Dept. of Health (DOH)** Conducts beach water sampling, issues beach swimming advisories, beach closings, and fish consumption advisories. 212-442-9666 nyc.gov/doh

**Dept. of Parks & Recreation (DPR)** 830 5 Ave. Responsible for 28,000 acres of parkland, 14 miles of beach, pools, rec centers, historic house museums, all city trees, natural preserves and "Forever Wild" sites, and marinas on park property. Water trail launch permits. nycgovparks.org

**Dept. of Transportation (DOT)** Oversight of greenways, bike maps and bike rack placement, heliports, Staten Island ferry and free bridges. nyc.gov/dot

**Economic Development Corp.** Port and waterfront redevelopment. 212-312-3600 nycedc.com

**Soil & Water Conservation District** 290 Broadway, 24th Flr. Water and soil resources preservation and promotes watershed and water monitoring and environmental education. nycswcd.net

**NYPD Harbor Unit** Pier One, 140 58 St. Brooklyn. VHF Channel 17. Founded in 18585 to combat piracy, the unit patrols city waterways and the waterfront. nyc.gov/nypd
• **Scuba Unit** Formed in 1967 to perform search, rescue and recovery.
• **Harbor Unit Auxiliary** Volunteer group that assists with harbor patrol. Launch No. 5 is a restored police boat manned on patrol by the auxiliary. bentwheelclub.org

# State

**Dept. of Environmental Conservation**
Region 2 (DEC) 47-40 21 St. Long Island City. Stormwater discharge and wetland construction permits. Manages Mount Loretto Preserve. 718-482-4900 dec.ny.gov
• **Bureau of Marine Resources** Management of finfish, crustaceans and shellfish, as well as marine habitat protection.
• **Natural Heritage Program** Documents and protects the State's rare animals, plants, and significant natural communities—forests, fresh and saltwater wetlands and grasslands.

**Dept. of Motor Vehicles** (DMV) Boat registration with form MV-82B, valid for 3 years. nydmv.state.ny.us

**Dept. of State** (DOS), Division of Coastal Resources helps communities revitalize the waterfront and improve access. 212-417-5801 dos.state.ny.us
• **Coastal Management Program** Establishes state policy for coastal natural resources, public access and coastal revitalization.

**Dept. of Transportation** (NYS DOT) 1 Hunters Point Plz, Long Island City. Responsible for ports, waterways, and transportation. nysdot.gov

**Office of General Services** (OGS) Land management division issues permits to build on land under water. ogs.state.ny.us

**Office of NYS Parks, Recreation & Historic Preservation** (OPRHP) 163 W 125 St. Manages 7 state parks within city limits, conducts boat safety courses, and recommends properties for State and National Register of Historic Places. 212-866-2740 nysparks.com
• **Bureau of Marine and Recreational Vehicles** Licenses commercial vessels in state waters and issues permits for in water regattas. Publishes NYS Boater's Guide. nysparks.com/boating/docs/boaters_guide.pdf

# Regional

**Clean Ocean & Shore Trust** (COAST) Bi-state legislative committee that provides for the enhancement, enjoyment and conservation of marine resources of the Hudson-Raritan Estuary and the New York Bight. nynjcoast.org

**Cornell Cooperative Extension** 16 E 34 St. Established in 1948, NYC programs cover aquaculture, hydrophonic gardening and fishing along with other agricultural, environmental, and related topics. 212-340-2900 cce.cornell.edu

**Interstate Environmental Commission** Regulates, enforces and monitors effluent water quality standards in the interstate marine waters of New York, New Jersey and Connecticut. iec-nynjct.org

**NY-NJ Harbor Estuary Program** (HEP) 290 Broadway. Created by the EPA to preserve, protect and restore the estuary. One of 28 such programs established for estuaries nationwide. 212-637-3816 harborestuary.org

**NY Sea Grant** (NOAA) SUNY and Cornell University program, part of nationwide network that promotes better understanding, conservation, and use of America's coastal resources. seagrant.sunysb.edu

**Port Authority of New York New Jersey** 225 Park Ave. South. Founded in 1921, to handle bi-state conflicts, PANYNJ oversees all aspects of harbor use and port facilities, including interstate tunnels, bridges, marine terminals and major airports. 212-435-7000 panynj.gov

**Robert Moses**, Urban Planner (1888-1981) Public works inaugurated by Moses transformed the urban landscape and waterfront of New York City. A graduate of Yale, Oxford and Columbia universities, Moses launched his career in public service in 1919 and retired in 1968, at age 80. At one time he held 12 different city and state jobs, in both state and city parks departments simultaneously, he was chairman of the Triborough Bridge Authority. He drafted the laws that created most of the jobs he held. Under Moses's leadership two million acres of parkland, a dozen bridges, miles of scenic parkways, and long stretches of public beach were built. Moses's portfolio of city projects includes: Harlem River Drive, East River Drive, Randall's Island Park, Orchard Beach, Shore Parkway Greenway, and Jacob Riis Park. He established Jamaica Bay as a protected wildlife refuge, redeveloped the dump at Flushing Meadow into the World's Fair grounds, and had a hand in building Shea Stadium, the United Nations, Lincoln Center and the New York Coliseum.

# Federal

**Army Corps of Engineers NY** 26 Federal Plaza, Javits Federal Building. Since 1890, the Corps has regulated activities in U.S. waters, including navigation channels, dredging projects, beach nourishment, flood control and issues permits for wetlands development. It is one of the largest users of contract commercial diving services in the world and a leading provider of waterbased recreation nationwide. 917-790-8411 nan.usace.army.mil

**Coastal America** Partnership of federal agencies working to preserve, protect, and restore America's coastal heritage. coastalamerica.gov

**National Park Service** Administers Gateway National Recreation Area (GATE) and the National Parks of New York Harbor. nps.gov/npnh

**National Oceanic & Atmospheric Agency** (NOAA) Surveys coastline, navigable waters, monitors climate activity, fisheries, oceans and marine sanctuaries, and creates marine navigation charts. noaa.gov

**Coast Guard Sector NY, First District.** 212 Coast Guard Dr., Staten Island. Operates Vessel Traffic Control, regulates ships and shipping, licenses masters and pilots, posts local notice to mariners, and is responsible for port security, marine safety, search & rescue, Marine event permits, lighthouses and moveable bridges over navigable waters. 718-354-4037 homeport.uscg.mil/newyork

**U.S. Dept. of the Interior** Manages one out of every five acres of land in the country.
• **Fish & Wildlife Service** Conservation of habitat for birds, fish, wildlife, plant species, and endangered species. National fish hatcheries, Wildlife Refuges, reviews permits for filling in wetlands, and construction in navigable waters, dredging and beach fill. fws.gov
• **U.S. Geological Survey** Water resources and coastal and marine geology programs. usgs.gov

**U.S. Environmental Protection Agency** (EPA) Region 2. Safeguards public health and the environment, administers Superfund monies, and federal laws protecting water resources. 212-637-3000 epa.gov

# Photo Credits

COVER PHOTOS Top right (clockwise): Outrigger's in NY Harbor by Bernard Ente; Salt Marshes of Jamaica Bay by Don Riepe (alsnyc.org); Red Whitehall by Robert Buchanan (newyorkharborbeaches.org); Windsurfer by Paul Margolis (paulmargolis.com); Back Cover by Bernard Ente. Special thanks to the NYC Department of Parks and Recreation (DPR) and to photographer, photo editor and friend Hans Carlo Michael Basso.

| | |
|---|---|
| v | Author photo by Geri Cimbala |
| viii | Henry Hudson Statue by Mario Burger |
| 2 | A Train to Rockaway by Mario Burger |
| 3 | Biking Marine Park by Mario Burger |
| 4 | Midtown Ferry Terminal by Mario Burger |
| 7 | Water Taxis Homeport Red Hook by Zhennya Slootskin |
| 11 | Statue of Liberty by Don Riepe, courtesy of American Littoral Society (alsnyc.org) |
| 13 | Battery Marine Terminal by Zhennya Slootskin |
| 14 | Battery Park by Malcolm Pinckney, property of NYC DPR |
| 15 | Pier A by Christina Sun (bowsprite.wordpress.com) |
| 16 | Battery Park City by Zhennya Slootskin |
| 17 | Battery Park City by Zhennya Slootskin |
| 20 | West Village Waterfront by Mario Burger |
| 22 | Hudson River Park, Pier 66 Maritime by Zhennya Slootskin |
| 23 | Hudson River Park Pier 66a by Zhennya Slootskin |
| 25 | Manhattan Cruise Terminal by Mario Burger |
| 27 | Riverside South by Daniel Avila, property of NYC DPR |
| 28 | Riverside Park by Daniel Avila, property of DPR |
| 30 | Little Red Lighthouse by Malcolm Pinckney, property of NYC DPR |
| 32 | Spuyten Duvil Railroad Bridge by Christina Sun (bowsprite.wordpress.com) |
| 35 | High Bridge by Spencer Tucker, property of DPR |
| 39 | United Nations by Bernard Ente |
| 40 | Roosevelt Island Aerial Tramway by Mario Burger |
| 43 | Skyline Marina with rowers at Waterside Plaza by Bernard Ente |
| 44 | East River Piers 35-42 by Mario Burger |
| 48 | Titanic Memorial Lighthouse by Zhennya Slootskin |
| 52 | Riverdale Station by Zhennya Slootskin |
| 54 | C-Rock by Mario Burger |
| 55 | Yankee Stadium by Mario Burger |
| 55 | Bronx Kill by Rob Buchanan (newyorkharborbeaches.org) |
| 60 | Bronx River Waterfall by Maro Burger |
| 61 | Hunts Point Riverside Park by Jay Gorman |
| 66 | Orchard Beach by Malcolm Pinckney, property of NYC DPR |
| 67 | City Island by Zhennya Slootskin |
| 69 | High Island by Mario Burger |
| 72 | Newtown Creek by Bernard Ente |
| 73 | Newtown Nature Walk by Zhennya Slootskin |
| 75 | Domino Sugar by Mario Burger |
| 75 | Brooklyn Navy Yard by Zhennya Slootskin |
| 77 | Brooklyn Bridge Park by Mario Burger |

| Page | Description |
|---|---|
| 78 | Tobacco Warehouse by Etienne Frossard (etiennemf@verizon.net) |
| 81 | Ikea Esplanade by Zhennya Slootskin |
| 82 | Grain Elevator by Norman Brouwer |
| 83 | Gowanus Canal by Zhennya Slootskin |
| 86 | 69 St. Pier 9/11 Memorial by Mario Burger |
| 89 | Yellow Submarine on Coney Island Creek by Mario Burger |
| 91 | Coney Island by Zhennya Slootskin |
| 94 | Sheepshead Bay Cottages by Lisanne Anderson |
| 94 | Sea Wolf by Lisanne Anderson |
| 96 | Plumb Beach by Lisanne Anderson |
| 96 | Plumb Beach by Mario Burger |
| 97 | Salt Marsh by Mario Burger |
| 98 | Ryan Visitor's Center at Floyd Bennett Field by Mario Burger |
| 104 | Seining in Jamaica Bay by Mario Burger |
| 105 | Airplane over Jamaica Bay by Mario Burger |
| 106 | Idlewild Kayak/Canoe Launch by Velma Segars, property of NPR |
| 107 | Broad Channel by Don Riepe, courtesy of the American Littoral Society (alsnyc.org) |
| 111 | 9/11 Memorial *Heavens over Rockaway* by Mario Burger |
| 113 | Jacob Riis Beach, Rockaway by Mario Burger |
| 114 | Rockaway Beach Boardwalk by Mario Burger |
| 118 | Bayside Marina by Zhennya Slootskin |
| 118 | Fort Totten by Daniel Avila, property of DPR |
| 119 | Officers Club, Bayside Historical Society at Fort Totten by Mario Burger |
| 121 | World's Fair Marina with Citi Field/Shea Stadium by Mario Burger |
| 125 | Big Allis by Mario Burger |
| 127 | Long Island City at 44 Drive by Zhennya Slootskin |
| 130 | Newtown Creek by Bernard Ente |
| 133 | Staten Island Ferry by Mario Burger |
| 135 | Fort Wadsworth by Mario Burger |
| 136 | Swinburne Island by Mario Burger |
| 138 | Midland Beach by Mario Burger |
| 140 | Prince's Bay by Robert Catalano |
| 143 | Purple Martin Birdhouse by Robert Catalano |
| 144 | Conference Park Overlook by Daniel Avila, property of DPR |
| 147 | Graveyard of Ships by Mario Burger |
| 150 | Richmond Creek by Mario Burger |
| 150 | Staten Island Lighthouse by Mario Burger |
| 153 | New York Containerport by Mario Burger |
| 155 | Snug Harbor courtesy of the Noble Maritime Collection (noblemaritime.org) |
| 160 | Cyclone Roller Coaster by Mario Burger |
| 160 | Parachute Jump by Zhennya Slootskin |
| 161 | Horseshoe Crab by Don Riepe, courtesy of the American Littoral Society (alsnyc.org) |
| 164 | Tiger Sharks at New York Aquarium courtesy of Gary Burke |
| 166 | Marine Park Nature Center by Mario Burger |
| 167 | Paragliding at Riis Park by Mario Burger |
| 168 | Rockaway Beach by Malcolm Pinkney, property of NYC DPR |
| 172 | Sandpipers by Don Riepe, courtesy of the American Littoral Society (alsnyc.org) |
| 177 | Whitehalls by Kam Truhn |
| 182 | Jet Ski by Don Riepe, courtesy of the American Littoral Society (alsnyc.org) |

| | | |
|---|---|---|
| 184 | Venice Marina by Zhennya Slootskin | |
| 185 | Cigarette Boat docked on Mill Basin by Mario Burger | |
| 187 | George Washington Bridge by Dave Frieder (davefrieder.com) | |
| 189 | Marine Parkway Bridge by Don Riepe, courtesy of the American Littoral Society (alsnyc.org) | |
| 191 | Verrazano-Narrows Bridge by Dave Frieder (davefrieder.com) | |
| 193 | Cruiseship by Bernard Ente | |
| 194 | Brooklyn Cruise Terminal by Mario Burger | |
| 199 | City Island Lobster House by Mario Burger | |
| 201 | Nick's Lobster House by Mario Burger | |
| 202 | Rockaway Lobster House by Mario Burger | |
| 204 | Excursion Sail by Mario Burger | |
| 213 | I Fish NY on Governors Island by Zhennya Slootskin | |
| 217 | *Sea Queen* Party Boat by Mario Burger | |
| 220 | Stella Maris Fishing Station by Zhennya Slootskin | |
| 221 | Castle William, Governors Island by Mario Burger | |
| 224 | Fort Wood, Liberty Island by Mario Burger | |
| 225 | Fort Schuyler, SUNY Maritime by Mario Burger | |
| 226 | *John J, Harvey* Fireboat by Nernard Ente | |
| 227 | *Ambrose* Lightship by Zhennya Slootskin | |
| 228 | *Tug Pegasus & Waterfront Museum Barge* Courtesy of Tug Pegasus Preservation Project & Waterfront Museum (tugpegasus.org/waterfrontmuseum.org) | 281 Photo Credits |
| 233 | Robbins Reef Lighthouse by Jim Crowley | |
| 235 | Coney Island Lighthouse by Mario Burger | |
| 239 | South Street Seaport Museum by Christina Sun (bowsprite.wordpress.com) | |
| 240 | Ellis Island by Mario Burger | |
| 243 | City Island Museum by Mario Burger | |
| 246 | Kayakers in the Upper Bay by Bernard Ente | |
| 249 | Canoers on the Bronx River by Daniel Avila, property of NYC DPR | |
| 253 | Whitehalls at Mill Rock Island by Rob Buchanan (newyorkharborbeaches.org) | |
| 255 | Outrigger Canoe by Bridget Gorman (newyorkoutrigger.org) | |
| 256 | Sculling on Orchard Beach Lagoons by Mario Burger | |
| 258 | Sailing by the Colgate Clock by Bernard Ente | |
| 259 | Sailing at Rockaway Inlet by Mario Burger | |
| 262 | Scuba Diver by Austin Tolling | |
| 269 | Surfers *The Other Lineup* courtesy of Casey Mergen (nycwahine.com) | |
| 273 | *The Floating Lady* Pool by Daniel Avila, property of DPR | |
| 275 | *The Fireboat* by Mario Burger | |

www.ingramcontent.com/pod-product-compliance
Lightning Source LLC
Chambersburg PA
CBHW071858290426
44110CB00013B/1197